D1450284

Diseases
of
Ornamental
Plants

Revised Edition

Junius L. Forsberg

UNIVERSITY OF ILLINOIS PRESS
Urbana Chicago London

CONTENTS

Causes of Plant Diseases.............................. 1

Control of Plant Diseases........................... 5

Fungicides... 6

Soil Sterilization 10

Diseases of Specific Plants......................... 16

Bibliography 181

Glossary.. 208

Index... 211

Metric Conversions 220

FOREWORD

Ornamental plants are plants that are grown for beautification purposes. Flowers, shrubs, and trees that adorn homes, parks, and city streets are included in this classification. Ornamental plants, like all other kinds of plants, are affected by many different kinds of disease. The purpose of this publication is to make available to home owners, amateur and professional gardeners, and commercial florists the information they need for the identification and control of ornamental-plant diseases.

Since there are several thousand known species of ornamental plants, no attempt has been made to include all of them in this publication. Trees have been omitted, and only a few of the common flowering shrubs have been included. Neither has it been feasible to discuss all of the diseases that occur on the plants mentioned in this book. An attempt has been made, however, to give the symptoms and control measures for the most commonly encountered diseases of ornamentals.

Diseases of Ornamental Plants was first published in 1946 by the Colorado Agricultural and Mechanical College (now Colorado State University). The 1946 edition was extensively revised by the author and republished by the University of Illinois. For the present edition the author has revised and updated the material of the 1963 edition, particularly the sections on controls. Seven plants have been added and 48 additional diseases have been included. About 160 new entries were added to the extensive bibliography, from which much of the information was obtained.

Scientific names of causal fungi are used as given in U.S. Department of Agriculture Agricultural Handbook No. 165, *Index of Plant Diseases in the United States,* unless more recent research has shown another name to be preferable. Names of bacteria are used as given in the seventh edition of *Bergey's Manual of Determinative Bacteriology* published by The Williams and Wilkins Company in 1957.

Unless specifically credited to another institution, photographs are either from the author's collection or by the Illinois Natural History Survey.

CAUSES OF PLANT DISEASES

The causes of plant diseases are many but they fall into two main groups, the parasitic and the nonparasitic. In the parasitic group are the diseases caused by fungi, bacteria, viruses, and nematodes. These parasitic organisms attack plants and live at the expense of their hosts, disturbing the normal functioning of the attacked plants. The result is a disease. In the nonparasitic group are the diseases caused by unfavorable growing conditions. Deficiencies, excesses, or improper balance of the elements essential to plant growth fall in this category. Other factors are excessive moisture, drought, improper light conditions, extremes in temperature, spray injuries, and gas injuries.

Fungi. Fungi are lower forms of plant life. They lack the green coloring matter, chlorophyll, that is used by the higher plants in the manufacture of food from water, carbon dioxide, and minerals. Hence, fungi must obtain nourishment either from dead organic matter or from other living organisms. Those that feed on other living organisms are known as parasites, and the organisms attacked are called hosts. Such an attack causes a disturbance that we recognize as a disease.

The typical fungus body is a delicate, branched, filamentous structure known as the mycelium. Individual threads of the mycelium are known as hyphae and form an interlacing tangle, or a loose, woolly mass, or sometimes even a compact, solid body. A parasitic mycelium may grow on the surface of its host, appearing as delicate, whitish, cobweblike threads or as sooty-brown or black threads; or it may be completely within the host and not evident on the surface.

Most fungi reproduce by spores which vary greatly in size, shape, color, and method of production. Some kinds of spores are produced on the ends of specialized branches of the hyphae, while others are produced in complex fruiting bodies. Many fungi produce more than one kind of spore.

Millions of spores may be produced by a single fungus, and a single spore, under favorable conditions, is capable of germinating and developing into a new fungus. Spores are spread by air currents, water, insects, and other agencies. If they happen to land on a susceptible plant when environmental conditions are favorable, infection is likely to occur and the plant will become diseased.

Many fungi form resting bodies known

A culture of the fungus *Rhizoctonia solani* growing in a petri dish. The four colonies developed from bits of diseased plant tissue.

A portion of the vegetative body (mycelium) of a fungus as it appears when seen through a microscope.

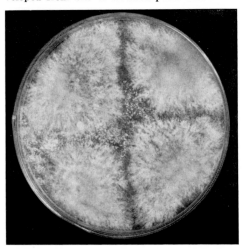

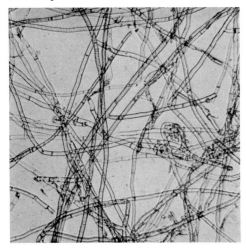

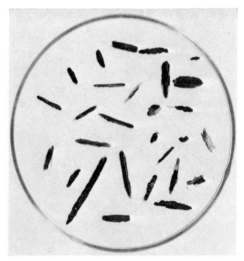

Sclerotia of the peony stem rot fungus are hard, black bodies. These bodies serve to carry the fungus through unfavorable conditions.

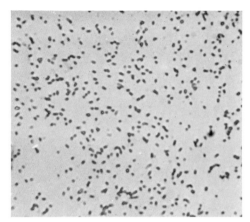

Bacteria as they appear under the microscope. Nearly all the bacteria that cause plant disease are short rods such as these.

as sclerotia. These are compacted masses of hyphae and stored food materials in the form of oil and other compounds. Sclerotia can endure extreme desiccation, long periods of high temperature, or the extreme cold of winter.

Bacteria. Bacteria are microscopic, single-celled organisms. Under favorable conditions bacteria reproduce rapidly by fission, a single individual dividing to form two. Bacteria obtain their food in much the same way as fungi. Many kinds of bacteria are beneficial, but some forms are parasitic on living plants and animals and cause serious diseases.

Viruses. Viruses are ultramicroscopic entities, visible only through the electron microscope, that can produce diseases in plants and animals. Although it is not known whether viruses are living, they have many properties of living things. The most thoroughly investigated viruses have been found to be complex proteins. In some unknown way they are able to reproduce and perpetuate themselves only in the body of a living host. Many of the viruses are carried from diseased to healthy plants by insects. Many viruses are carried over in cuttings and dormant plant parts such as tubers, corms, and bulbs. A few viruses are seedborne.

Mycoplasmas. Mycoplasmas are highly pleomorphic, plastic organisms without cell walls. Some diseases formerly thought to be caused by viruses are now known to be caused by mycoplasmalike organisms.

Nematodes. Nematodes are tiny, round worms that attack various plants. The best known nematode is the root-knot nematode, which causes swelling and distortion of the attacked tissues.

Nematodes as seen under the microscope. Several stages of development are shown.

At right, powdery mildew conidiophores and conidia. These fungi are so named because these reproductive structures appear as white powder on the surface of their host plants.

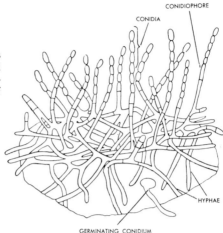

Line drawings by Karol Thomas

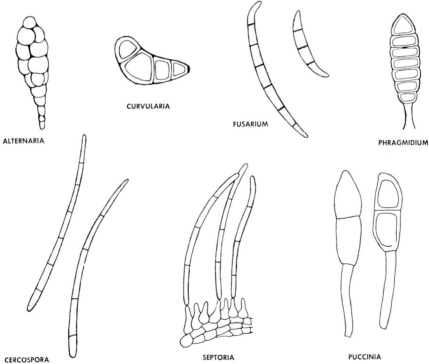

Fungus spores vary greatly in form. Presence of a particular kind of spore on diseased plant tissue aids in determining the cause of the disease. Spores of the types shown above are associated with the following diseases: *Curvularia* — Curvularia corm rot and leaf spot of gladiolus; *Alternaria* — Alternaria blight of carnation; *Fusarium* — Fusarium rot of gladiolus; *Phragmidium* — rose rust; *Cercospora* — hollyhock leaf spot; *Septoria* — Septoria leaf spot of chrysanthemum; *Puccinia* — hollyhock rust.

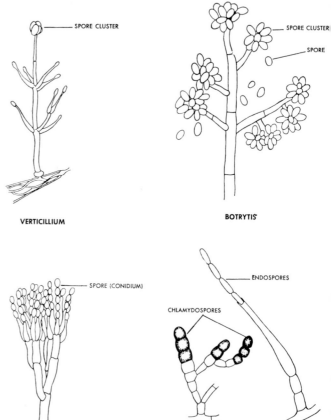

VERTICILLIUM

BOTRYTIS

Below, three types of asexual fungus spore fruits commonly found in diseased plant tissue. Presence of these structures, usually barely large enough to be seen as tiny dots by the naked eye, aids in identifying the cause of a plant disease.

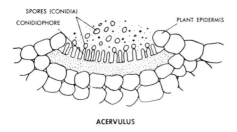

ACERVULUS

PENICILLIUM

THIELAVIOPSIS

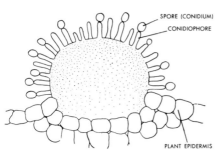

SPORODOCHIUM

Fungus spores are produced on special branches of the mycelium known as conidiophores. Four of the more complex types are shown above. Diseases caused by fungi belonging to these groups are: *Verticillium* — lilac wilt; *Botrytis* — Botrytis blight of geranium; *Penicillium* — Penicillium rot of gladiolus; *Thielaviopsis* — sweet pea root rot.

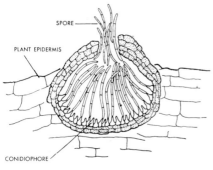

PYCNIDIUM

CONTROL OF PLANT DISEASES

Control of plant diseases is based primarily on prevention. With few exceptions, diseased plants cannot be cured in the sense that affected parts can be restored to normal functioning. Infection by a parasitic organism usually results in injury or destruction of the whole or a portion of the plant. A parasite cannot be reached by chemical dusts and sprays after it has entered the plant. Any treatment drastic enough to destroy a parasite within the plant usually destroys the plant itself. Thus control measures must be based upon the application of one or more of six fundamental principles: sanitation, exclusion, eradication, protection, development of resistance, and cultural practices.

Sanitation. The practice of strict sanitary measures is of utmost importance in preventing the spread of fungus and bacterial diseases. Sometimes diseased plants should be removed from a planting because they are sources of infection that may spread to healthy plants. This applies to greenhouse conditions as well as to outdoor plantings. Since many disease-producing organisms overwinter in plant debris, all old plant parts should be raked up and burned late in the fall, or in the spring before new growth begins.

Exclusion. It is often easier to exclude diseases from plantings than it is to control them after they appear, and individual growers can do much to prevent the introduction of diseases into their plantings. Federal and state quarantine regulations have been established to prevent the spread of certain dangerous insects and diseases. Extreme caution should be exercised in accepting plants that are not known to be disease-free. If field inspection of plants cannot be made prior to purchase, it is well to establish and maintain segregation plots at some distance from the main planting. Mother blocks of healthy plants for propagation purposes should be established for plants that are propagated by cuttings, for example, carnations, chrysanthemums, and geraniums. The subject of mother blocks is more fully discussed in connection with diseases of carnation (see page 43).

Eradication. Eradication involves getting rid of the parasites after they have become established in a planting. In many instances diseased plants should be removed from the planting and destroyed as soon as they are noticed. Sometimes only a portion of the plant need be removed. When the causal agent of a disease is soilborne, sterilization of the soil is necessary. Certain parasites that occur almost entirely on the surface of the host, such as powdery mildews, can be eradicated by spraying or dusting the plant with appropriate fungicides.

Protection. Certain diseases may be prevented by using fungicides to protect the plants from infection. Sprays or dusts must be applied before the disease appears, or at least before it has become well established. Sprays and dusts are most effective when applied before rains, heavy dews, fogs, or application of water because infection occurs only when moisture is present. It is essential to obtain complete coverage and it is usually necessary to make repeated applications.

Development of resistance. Varieties of plants that are resistant to certain diseases have been developed. Other factors being equal, resistant varieties should be used whenever possible. Many nursery and seed catalogs designate varieties that are resistant to certain diseases.

Cultural practices. Proper cultural practices can do much to prevent certain diseases. Vigorous, well-kept plants usually have a better chance of escaping disease than do poorly-cared-for plants. Over-fertilization, especially with nitrogen fertilizers, should be avoided. Adjusting the temperature and humidity helps to control mildews and leaf molds in greenhouses. Avoidance of overwatering does much to prevent damping-off.

FUNGICIDES

Fungicides are chemicals that are toxic to fungi. They are usually applied to the aerial or above-ground parts of plants in the form of sprays or dusts, although in some cases they are used to treat seeds, corms, and bulbs, before planting. Some fungicides are applied to the soil to destroy certain soil-inhabiting organisms. No single compound is suitable for all purposes or effective against all fungi. Some fungicides will burn tender foliage if they are used improperly; others are undesirable because they discolor the plants. Growers should follow recommendations closely when using fungicides on a large scale.

Thoroughness is essential when applying fungicides. A good sprayer covers all surfaces of the plants with a uniform film that cannot be washed off easily after drying. High-pressure equipment produces a finer mist that results in more perfect coverage, less danger of spray burn, and less loss from dripping or run-off than when low pressure is used. Selection of equipment, of course, depends on the kind of crop and the area to be covered. Suitable sprayers and dusters, ranging from small hand-operated equipment to large power outfits, are available.

In general the purpose of fungicides is to protect plants from infection. To be effective, fungicides must be used before a disease becomes well established. The timing and number of applications can be better regulated if one knows the life history of the parasite. An organism can be combated most effectively during certain periods in its life cycle. Such periods may vary in length with different parasites.

Some progress has been made in development of systemic fungicides. These are chemicals that, when absorbed by the plant, act against a fungus already within the plant or prevent the fungus from infecting the plant. The use of systemic chemicals, or plant chemotherapy, holds promise but is not fully developed.

The decision whether to dust or spray plants depends on a number of factors. Dusting can be done more quickly than spraying, but sprays usually have a more lasting effect. Dusting equipment is usually lighter and easier to handle than spray equipment. Dusts are less likely to burn and they do not discolor the foliage as do some sprays. Dusts are usually more expensive than sprays. Spray coatings adhere to most plants more readily than dusts, especially if a good spreader or sticker is used in the spray mixture.

Most of the older fungicides contained copper, sulfur, or mercury as the toxic principle. Most of the newer materials are complex organic chemicals. Since many fungicides of similar composition are sold under different trade names, growers may become confused when selecting a fungicide. Federal regulations require that the percentage composition of fungicides be printed on the containers. Before using any fungicide a grower should read the label to make certain the material contains the ingredients recommended for use on the plant and against the disease to be controlled.

Copper-containing fungicides. Bordeaux mixture is the best known and most widely used copper-containing fungicide. Although it has been largely replaced by newer fungicides, bordeaux mixture is still used by many growers. Bordeaux mixture is composed of copper sulfate, lime, and water. The formula 2-4-50 indicates that 2 pounds of copper sulfate and 4 pounds of lime are mixed with 50 gallons of water. The amounts of copper sulfate and lime may be varied according to the intended use. A 2-2-50 formula has given satisfactory control of many diseases.

Homemade bordeaux is prepared by dissolving the copper sulfate in 25 gallons of water. The lime is slaked in just enough water to slake it well, then mixed with 25 gallons of water. The solutions are then poured simultaneously into a third container to ensure thorough mixing and an excellent suspension of the small lime particles. Hydrated lime may be substituted for the quicklime used in the standard formula, in which case the slaking step may be omitted.

If only a small amount of this spray is required it may be made up by dissolving 2 ounces of copper sulfate in 1 gallon of water, and 2 ounces of hydrated lime in 2 gallons of water, then pouring the copper sulfate solution into the lime water. This makes 3 gallons of 2-2-50 bordeaux mixture.

Various commercial companies offer ready-prepared bordeaux powders that may be used immediately when the material is mixed with water, following directions found on the containers. These preparations are convenient when only a small amount of spray is needed.

A solution of burgundy mixture may be used instead of bordeaux to avoid spotting the foliage. It is composed of 2 pounds of copper sulfate and 3 pounds of sodium carbonate (sal soda) in 100 gallons of water. The copper sulfate and sodium carbonate should be dissolved separately, each in one-half the quantity of water, then poured together as in mixing bordeaux. Five gallons of this spray can be made by using 2 ounces of copper sulfate, 3 ounces of sodium carbonate, and 5 gallons of water. The two chemicals should be dissolved separately, then mixed before using.

Copper-lime dusts have been used as substitutes for copper-containing sprays. The usual mixture contains 80 percent of hydrated lime and 20 percent mono-hydrated copper sulfate by weight. The dust can be mixed at home. It should be applied when the plants are wet.

Yellow cuprous oxide may be mixed with water and used as a spray instead of bordeaux mixture.

Sulfur fungicides. Sulfur is one of the oldest fungicides, and still one of the best for certain purposes. Dusting sulfurs are specially prepared dry forms of sulfur, powdered fine enough to pass through a 325-mesh screen. The ordinary flowers of sulfur is too coarse for dusting purposes. A green-colored sulfur, which leaves no unsightly stain on the foliage, is available.

Wettable sulfurs are combinations of one of the powdered sulfurs with a wetting agent that enables the sulfur to mix readily with water to form a spray mixture. These preparations adhere well and do not burn the foliage unless they are used when the temperature is extremely high.

Vaporized sulfur is the best material available for control of powdery mildew in greenhouses. A slurry made by mixing 1 pound of wettable sulfur in 1 pint of water may be painted on heating pipes in the greenhouse. The heat vaporizes the sulfur into the air, where it condenses and settles in fine particles on the plants. Flowers of sulfur may be vaporized in special sulfur vaporizers.

Lime-sulfur can be purchased in powder form or as concentrated lime-sulfur solution. As a summer spray it is used at the rate of 1 gallon of liquid or 4 pounds of dry lime-sulfur to 50 gallons of water (⅗ pint or 10 ounces to 3 gallons). As a dormant spray the strength used is one part liquid to nine parts water, or 2 pounds of dry lime-sulfur in 5 gallons of water. Lime-sulfur is injurious to some plants and therefore should be used with caution if its effect on the plants is not known.

Synthetic organic fungicides. Many organic fungicides have been developed and some have replaced the older fungicides in disease control programs.

The fungicides recommended for use in this publication have been found to be effective in control of the diseases for which they are recommended. However, some fungicides are becoming unobtainable. If a recommended fungicide cannot be obtained, information regarding a suitable substitute should be requested from the Illinois Natural History Survey or an agricultural experiment station.

Organic fungicides recommended for control of diseases in this publication are listed below. No criticism is implied of similar products that are not listed.

Chemical names of the active ingredients in commercial fungicides were obtained from the following sources: *Pesticide Index* by D. E. H. Frear (College Science Publishers, 1961); "Chemical Names for Active Ingredients of Fungicides" by S. E. A. McCallan, Lawrence P. Miller, and Mary A. Magill (*Phytopathology* 45:295–302, June 1955); "Identities and Structures of DuPont Pesticides," *DuPont Agricultural News Letter* 30:6–7, 1962; *Dictionary of Pesticides* (Farm Chemicals, 1972).

Actidione — cycloheximide; an antibiotic fungicide used to control powdery mildews.

Agrimycin — see streptomycin sulfate.

Arasan — see thiram.

Bacticin — 2, 4-xylenol and *m*-cresol in an emulsified formulation of hydrocarbons and water; a horticultural bactericide for eradication of crown gall tumors.

Benlate — see benomyl.

Benomyl — methyl 1-(butylcarbamoyl)-2-benzimidazole-carbamate; a systemic fungicide used for the control of many plant diseases.

Botran — 2, 6 dichloro-4-nitroaniline; a dust or wettable powder used to control Stromatinia rot of gladiolus and Botrytis blights.

Bravo — see chlorothalonil.

Busan 72 — 60 percent 2-(thiocyanomethylthio) benzothiazole; a liquid used for treating seeds and gladiolus corms.

Captan — N-trichloromethylthio tetrahydrophthalimide; a dust or wettable powder used as a foliage fungicide and a seed treatment.

Carboxin — 5, 6-dihydro-2-methyl-1, 4-oxathiin-3-carboxanilide; a wettable powder systemic fungicide and seed treatment.

Chloranil — tetrachloro-*p*-benzoquinone; a yellow powder used for treating seeds and bulbs. Sold as Spergon.

Chloropicrin — trichloronitromethane; or nitrochloroform; a fumigant used as a soil insecticide, fungicide, and nematocide.

Chlorothalonil — tetrachloroisophthalonitrile; a fungicide used to control diseases caused by Botrytis.

Daconil 2787 — see chlorothalonil.

Dexon — *p*-(dimethylamino) benzenedi-azo sodium sulfonate; a soil fungicide and seed treatment used to control diseases caused by *Pythium* spp.

Dichlone — 2, 3-dichloro-1, 4-naphthoquinone; a yellow powder used as a spray, dust, or in seed treatment. Sold under the name Phygon.

Dithane Z-78 — see zineb.

Dowicide B — 85 percent sodium 2, 4, 5-trichlorophenate; a water-soluble crystalline material used for treating gladiolus corms.

Dyrene — 50 percent 2,4-dichloro-6-(*o*-chloroanilino)-*s*-triazine; a wettable powder used as a foliage fungicide.

Ferbam — ferric dimethyldithiocarbamate; a black powder used as a foliage spray and soil drench.

Fermate — see ferbam.

Folpet — see phaltan.

Fore — a special formulation of a coordination product of zinc ion and manganese ethylene bisdithiocarbamate, and is related to both maneb and zineb; a broad spectrum fungicide used in the control of a variety of diseases of flowers, ornamental trees, and shrubs.

Karathane — 22.5 percent dinitro (1-methylheptyl) phenyl crotonate, 2.5 percent dinitro (1-methylheptyl) phenol; a yellow powder used as a spray for the control of powdery mildew.

Lysol — a liquid mixture of crude cresols used for treating gladiolus corms.

Maneb — manganese ethylenebisdithiocarbamate; a grayish-yellow wettable powder used as a foliage spray.

Manzate — see maneb.

Mildex — see Karathane.

Mylone — tetrahydro-3, 5-dimethyl-2H-thiadiazine-2-thione; when applied in the soil it releases methyl isothiocyanate which acts as a soil fumigant to control soil fungi, nematodes, weeds, and soil insects.

Nabam — disodium ethylenebisdithiocarbamate; a liquid used with zinc sulfate as a foliage spray.

Parzate — see zineb.

Parzate Liquid — see nabam.

PCNB — pentachloronitrobenzene; a powder or liquid soil fungicide used for the control of diseases caused by *Rhizoctonia*.

Phaltan — N-trichloromethylthiophthalimide; a wettable powder used as a foliage fungicide.

Phygon — see dichlone.

Plantvax — 5, 6-dihydro-2-methyl-1, 4-oxathion-3-carbox-anilide-4, 4-dioxide; a systemic fungicide highly effective in controlling carnation rust.

Spergon — see chloranil.

Streptomycin sulfate — an antibiotic used to control certain bacterial diseases of plants. Available as wettable powder.

Termil — tetrachloroisophthalonitrile as a tablet; when it is heated to 600° to 800°F it vaporizes to form a gas which condenses to form ultrafine particles that are deposited on all plant surfaces, resulting in an almost invisible layer of protection against *Botrytis*.

Terraclor — see PCNB.

Tersan — see thiram.

Thiram — tetramethylthiuram disulfide; a powder used as a seed, bulb, and corm treatment, spray, and soil drench.

Truban — 5-ethoxy-3-trichloromethyl-1, 2, 4-thiadiazole; a wettable powder or emulsifiable concentrate used as a soil treatment to control seedling diseases and certain other soilborne diseases.

Vapam — sodium methyldithiocarbamate; a liquid soil fumigant.

Vitavax — see carboxin.

Vorlex — a mixture of methyl isothiocyanate and chlorinated hydrocarbons; a soil fumigant applied as a preplant treatment to control weeds, fungi, insects, and nematodes.

Zineb — zinc ethylene bisdithiocarbamate; a wettable powder or dust used as a foliage fungicide.

Ziram — zinc dimethyldithiocarbamate; a wettable powder or dust used as a foliage fungicide.

Directions for mixing fungicide spray materials often provide for a larger quantity of the spray mix than is needed for home garden or greenhouse use. A measuring cup, a set of measuring spoons, and a medicine dropper may be used for accurate measurement of small amounts of spray material. Liquid measure equivalents are as follows:

    1 gallon = 4 quarts
    1 quart = 2 pints
    1 pint = 2 cups
    1 cup = 8 fluid ounces
    1 fluid ounce = 2 tablespoonfuls
    1 tablespoonful = 3 teaspoonfuls
    1 teaspoonful = 80 drops

The table at the bottom of the page may be used to determine the correct amount of liquid concentrate to use for small quantities when the directions are based on mixing 100 gallons of spray.

See page 220 for conversion tables for translating weight, volume, and temperature into metric equivalents.

Wettable powders should be weighed because they vary in weight per unit of volume. Also, powdered materials may be compacted or fluffed up to make smaller or larger volumes without changing the weight. If scales are unavailable for weighing small amounts of dry concentrates, use light, fluffy materials at the rate of 2 tablespoonfuls per gallon of water, and heavier, compacted materials at 1 tablespoonful per gallon when the recommended rate is 1 pound per 100 gallons.

Amount of Liquid Concentrate to Use in Making Spray Mixtures

For 100 gallons	For small quantities			
	5 gallons	3 gallons	1 gallon	1 quart
1 pt.	5 tsps.	1 Tbsp.	1 tsp.	20 drops
1 qt.	10 tsps.	2 Tbsps.	2 tsps.	½ tsp.
1 gal.	¾ cup + 4 tsps.	½ cup	8 tsps.	2 tsps.

SOIL STERILIZATION

The purpose of soil sterilization is to destroy plant pathogens or disease-producing organisms in the soil. Heat is the most common, as well as the most effective, agent used in soil sterilization. Certain chemicals, when properly introduced into soil, are effective in destroying some plant pathogens.

Regardless of the method used, certain requirements must be observed if soil sterilization is to produce the desired effect. First, for best results the soil should be loose and moist but not wet at the time of sterilizing. Second, the operation must be done thoroughly. If heat is employed, the soil must be heated throughout. A temperature of 160°F maintained for 2 hours is sufficient to destroy all disease-producing organisms. If chemicals are used they must be applied so that all parts of the soil will be reached by the action of the chemical.

The third requirement of effective soil sterilization is to guard against recontamination after the soil has been sterilized. If plants are rooted in sand and transplanted to temporary benches before being planted in permanent locations it is equally important to sterilize the sand and soil in the propagating benches, and the soil for the permanent plantings. Benches should be disinfected to prevent the transfer of disease organisms into the soil from unsterilized boards. Harmful parasites are also introduced into sterilized soils by the use of contaminated tools.

Steam. Steam is the most effective and most practical soil-sterilizing agent for the greenhouse. (A pressure cooker may be used for steam sterilization of small amounts of soil in the home.) It is best to steam the soil in the benches where the plants are to be grown because this destroys any disease-producing organisms that might be harbored in the benches as well as in the soil. However, in some instances it may be desirable to steam the soil in a special sterilizer and then transfer the steamed soil to the benches. If this method is used, the benches should first be cleaned thoroughly and washed with a disinfectant such as formaldehyde.

The length of time required for thorough sterilization depends on the method of introducing the steam, the amount of pressure, and the type of soil.

A small soil sterilizer built at one end of a greenhouse. Steam is admitted by means of a pipe at the bottom.

Tiles laid on the bottom of ground beds are used to carry steam for sterilizing soil in the bed. The tiles are covered with soil and steam is run through the tiles until the soil is thoroughly heated. After steaming is completed, tiles may be left in the beds or removed.

Various methods are used to introduce steam into the soil. In ground beds, steam can be forced through 3-inch tiles or perforated pipes laid in lines 15 to 20 inches apart and buried 12 to 15 inches deep. In benches, the pipes may be laid on the bottom of the bench and covered with soil. The surface of the soil should be covered with canvas while steaming is in progress.

Another means of introducing steam is the inverted-pan method. A shallow pan of convenient size to fit a portion of the bench is made of metal, and a short pipe is inserted through the wall of the pan, preferably near the center. The pipe is fitted with hose connections so that steam can be turned in under pressure. The pan is placed over a section of the bed or bench and soil is banked around the sides to prevent excessive escape of steam.

The Thomas method of steam sterilization is effective and efficient. Strips of canvas hose are connected to a steam outlet and laid about 18 inches apart on top of the soil. The hose may run the full length of the bench. Perforated downspouting or agricultural tile may be used instead of hose. The bench is then covered with a specially treated steamproof canvas that will hang about 1 foot over each side of the bench. The canvas may be battened to the sides of the bench if necessary. Steam is turned in under pressure to fill the full

The inverted-pan sterilizer in use on a greenhouse bench.

length of hose and is allowed to penetrate into the soil.

Temperatures should be taken at various locations in the bench to make sure that all areas become thoroughly heated. If a thermometer is unavailable, a convenient method of determining when the soil has been heated sufficiently is to bury a medium-sized potato in the soil. When the potato is baked through, the steaming has been sufficient to kill all plant parasites in the soil.

Steamed soils have varying effects on plants set in them. In some soils no ill effects are evident if plants are set as soon as the soil has cooled. In other soils the plants fail to grow vigorously and may even be seriously stunted. This is usually caused by the release of harmful soluble salts and organic acids during the steaming process. These substances usually can be leached out by heavy watering. Aerating the soil is also helpful. Soils that are high in organic matter or that were heavily fertilized prior to steaming are most likely to give this kind of trouble.

Hot water. Hot water has been used for sterilization but is less effective than steam. It is difficult to apply enough hot water to thoroughly heat all of the soil, and some soils puddle badly when this treatment is used.

Fumigants. A number of soil fumigants are available and may be used under certain conditions. Chloropicrin is such a material. It destroys many soilborne fungi and is also efficient against nematodes. Chloropicrin is a heavy, colorless, noninflammable, nonexplosive liquid that readily vaporizes into a pungent tear gas. When chloropicrin is injected into the soil the gas that is formed diffuses in all directions.

Chloropicrin gives best results when used on light, sandy soil, medium in moisture content and maintained at a temperature above 65°F during treatment. When treating small amounts of soil, 7 to 10 milliliters of the liquid is placed in each cubic foot of soil. After treatment, the soil should be watered lightly or covered with a wet canvas or paper. For treating large amounts of soil, the liquid is injected 3 to

A bench, ready for the Thomas method of steam sterilization. A portion of the cover has been rolled back to show how the hose is laid.

4 inches deep, staggered at points 10 to 12 inches apart. Usually 2½ to 3 milliliters of liquid is sufficient for each point of injection. Applicators that automatically measure the desired amount of liquid are available. The soil should be firmed over each injection. After all injections have been made the soil should be watered so that it is wet to a depth of about one-half inch. It should be covered with wet canvas

The MacLean Fumigun is used to apply liquid fumigants to soil.

or paper to seal the gas in the soil. This cover should be maintained for 3 days. Occasional sprinklings to keep the cover moist may be necessary during this time. The soil then may be uncovered and allowed to dry. Usually the gas will leave the soil in 7 to 10 days, although it may take longer. Stirring the soil hastens the escape of the gas. All tools should be sterilized before they are used in treated soil.

Certain precautions must be observed when using chloropicrin. Because the fumes are toxic to plants, soil treatments or aerations following treatments cannot be made indoors where plants are growing. Planting cannot be done until all traces of the gas have disappeared from the soil. The gas causes extreme discomfort to human beings; therefore a gas mask should be worn by anyone who handles large quantities of chloropicrin. The conditions of soil temperature, moisture, and after-covering must be regulated carefully. Unsatisfactory results are likely in heavy, tight, nonporous clay soils, or in cold or extremely wet soils.

A solution of 1 gallon of commercial formalin diluted in 50 gallons of water and applied at the rate of ½ to 1 gallon of solution to each square foot of soil is effective in destroying many harmful soil fungi. The soil should be spaded before the solution is applied. The treated soil should be covered with canvas or wet paper for 24 hours, then allowed to dry out. It is not safe to plant until all formaldehyde odor has disappeared from the soil.

Vapam, for example, is a fumigant that is used in much the same way as chloropicrin and formaldehyde. Detailed instructions on specific uses of Vapam are supplied by the manufacturer.

At right, diagram of a plant showing parts that may be affected by disease. Note that the vascular system extends from the roots, through the stems and into the leaves. Certain systemic diseases, such as Fusarium wilt, may involve all of these parts.

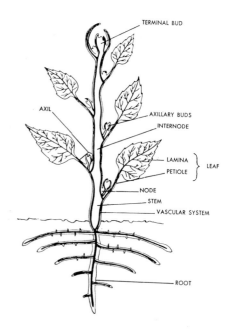

At left, diagram of a complete flower showing the arrangement of the component parts. Some flowers lack one or more of these parts and are known as incomplete flowers.

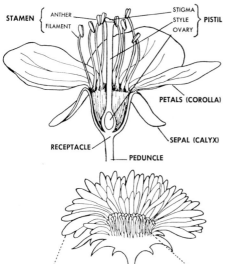

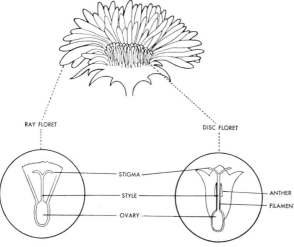

Section of a composite flower. Composite flowers, such as chrysanthemums, are made up of clusters of florets. Some florets have both stamens and pistils and are known as disc florets. Some have only pistils; they are called ray florets. Typical composite flowers are zinnias, chrysanthemums, asters, and marigolds.

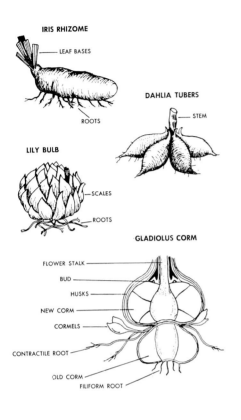

IRIS RHIZOME
— LEAF BASES
ROOTS

DAHLIA TUBERS
— STEM

LILY BULB
— SCALES
— ROOTS

GLADIOLUS CORM
FLOWER STALK
BUD
HUSKS
NEW CORM
CORMELS
CONTRACTILE ROOT
OLD CORM
FILIFORM ROOT

Modified stems (left). Many plants produce modified stems which serve to reproduce the plant vegetatively. Certain diseases are often carried over into the next season in these reproductive parts.

Below, diagram of the cross section of a stem showing the location of the various tissues mentioned in the descriptions of symptoms of diseases on certain plants.

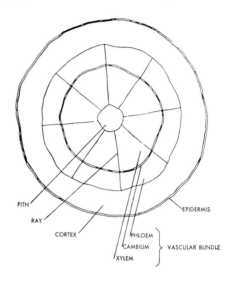

PITH
RAY
CORTEX
PHLOEM
CAMBIUM
XYLEM
EPIDERMIS
VASCULAR BUNDLE

Many plants produce flowers in a cluster known as an inflorescence. Two types of inflorescence are the cyme and the spike, shown below. The arrangement of the florets determines the type of inflorescence.

Below, types of dry fruits. A capsule develops from a compound pistil consisting of two or more united carpels. A follicle originates from a single, simple pistil and opens along a single suture.

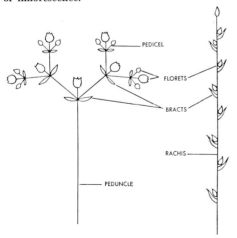

PEDICEL
FLORETS
BRACTS
RACHIS
PEDUNCLE

CYME   SPIKE

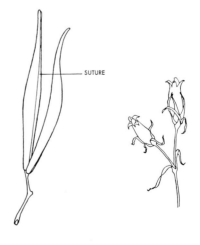

SUTURE

OXYPETALUM FOLLICLES   CARNATION CAPSULES

Diseases Of Specific Plants

AFRICAN VIOLET (SAINTPAULIA)

Although African violets (*Saintpaulia ionantha*) are not affected by a large number of parasites, they are subject to a few diseases that occasionally become troublesome.

BOTRYTIS BLIGHT

Symptoms. The first symptom of Botrytis blight usually appears on the underside of the leaf petioles near the pot rim. The disease starts with a small, water-soaked lesion that may enlarge rapidly until it involves the leaf blade. The necrotic area becomes brown to black with age. Flowers appear water-soaked and fade prematurely. Under conditions of high humidity, poor air circulation, and low light intensity, the causal fungus, *Botrytis cinerea,* may form large numbers of spores on the infected tissue. Leaves may become infected when diseased corollas drop on them. The disease will spread from one leaf to another when leaves are in direct contact.

Control. Sanitation and adequate spacing of the plants are most important. Spacing allows good air circulation and prevents the plants from touching one another. All diseased and dead tissue should be removed from the plants to prevent an accumulation of the causal fungus. Mites should be controlled, because they injure the plants directly, and because mite injury frequently is followed by invasion of *Botrytis.* Spraying with Bravo is helpful.

PETIOLE ROT

Symptoms. Petiole rot starts with an orange-brown or rust-colored lesion at the point where the petiole comes in contact with the pot rim or at the base of the petiole where it is in contact with the soil. Suddenly the petiole and leaf shrivel and collapse.

Control. Petiole rot is a result of chemical injury brought on by accumulated soil salts on the rim of the pot or on the soil surface. The trouble may be prevented by avoiding the use of excess fertilizer or by flushing the soil occasionally with heavy watering. A collar, made of metal foil or of cardboard dipped in paraffin, placed on the rim of the pot will prevent contact of the plant with any salts that may accumulate there.

POWDERY MILDEW

Symptoms. Grayish, fuzzy or powdery areas appear on petioles, leaves, petals, and flower stems.

Control. Dust the plants with dusting sulfur, or spray with wettable sulfur, 1 tablespoonful to 1 gallon of water.

RING SPOT

Symptoms. White, yellow, or brown rings appear on the leaves. Leaves most severely affected may die.

Control. Ring spot is caused by cold water getting on the foliage or by the sun shining on wet leaves. The trouble can be avoided by watering the plants from below or by applying the water carefully so as to keep it off the leaves. Use of water a few degrees warmer than air temperature is helpful.

Ring spots that resulted from cold water touching Saintpaulia leaves during watering.

ROOT AND CROWN ROT

Symptoms. A sudden permanent wilting may be the only symptom visible in the above-ground parts of an African violet plant affected with root and crown rot, caused by the fungus *Pythium ultimum*. In other instances, the lowermost leaves and petioles in contact with the soil may decay and dry up. Occasionally, after wilting, the entire above-ground portion of the plant may become completely decayed and brown. In some plants the above-ground parts show no symptoms, but the plants can easily be lifted from the surface of the soil. In such plants the crown has rotted off just below the soil level, but sufficient water is absorbed through the remaining sound tissues to retain the turgidity of the leaves. Roots on permanently wilted plants are brown and decayed. Occasionally only the roots are decayed, but more frequently the crown is also involved and usually is rotted up to the soil surface. In other plants the entire crown is decayed and this usually is accompanied by the decay of the petioles and leaves. Plants of all ages may be affected.

Control. Root and crown rot will not be a problem if the rooting medium and potting soil are sterilized. Young plants developed from cuttings rooted in a non-nutritive medium, such as water, sand, or vermiculite, should be planted in soil as soon as the root system is sufficiently developed. If they must be left for an extended period of time in such a medium they should be fed occasionally with a dilute fertilizer solution until they can be potted. Overwatering should be avoided.

Although it is not a good practice to propagate from diseased plants, specially prized plants may sometimes be saved if root and crown rot in a plant is discovered before the disease reaches the terminal phase — that is, while part of the crown is still sound. Remove the affected portion of the crown, cutting it off well above the line of decay. The remainder of the plant may be rerooted in water or in a sterile medium such as vermiculite.

ROOT-KNOT NEMATODES

Symptoms. Root-knot nematodes may infect not only roots, but also crowns, petioles, and leaves of African violets. Infection usually occurs along the vascular tissues. The crowns and petioles exhibit slight swellings to heavy thickenings, even to distortions in heavily infected crowns.

The leaves are thickened in spots and often have blisterlike galls.

Control. All infected plants should be destroyed as soon as detected. Only plants that are free of nematodes should be used for propagation by crown separations. If leaves are used for propagation they should be taken only from plants that are free of infection.

AMARYLLIS

Amaryllis (*Amaryllis* spp.) is subject to only a few diseases, the most serious being red blotch.

RED BLOTCH

Symptoms. Flower stalks are severely stunted and distorted. Affected stalks do not make a normal upright growth but grow at an angle, some almost at a right angle to the main axis of the plant. This type of growth is associated with cankers that have developed on only one side.

Young cankers are bright red or vermillion, but as they enlarge and elongate the

Large and small lesions produced by *Stagonospora curtisii* on amaryllis flower stalks.

center of the lesion becomes soft, brown, and sunken. In still later stages a mat of the white or brownish-gray mycelium of the causal fungus, *Stagonospora curtisii,* develops in the center, while the border of the canker retains the pronounced red color. Cankers are ¼ to ½ inch wide and may be several inches long. Elongated red spots on the leaves, and red streaks on the scapes, also appear. The flower buds borne on cankered stalks may open normally and remain in good condition for as long a time as those of healthy plants, but on severely infected plants the flower stalks may dry up without producing flowers. Since any bruise on the tissues of an amaryllis plant usually turns red, all red spots on these plants are not necessarily associated with the red blotch disease.

Control. The fungus may be present in dormant bulbs. Badly infected bulbs should be discarded, and those kept for planting should be soaked for 2 hours in formaldehyde solution, 1 pint to 12 gallons of water. Plants should be sprayed with ferbam, zineb, or copper oxychloride, beginning at the small-leaf stage and repeating at 10-

to 14-day intervals until blooming. Sufficient spreader-sticker must be added to obtain coverage. The spray should be allowed to run down into the base of the bulbs. Because the disease is favored by warm, humid conditions, the air in the greenhouse should be kept as dry as possible, and an even temperature of about 65°F should be maintained from the time bulbs are planted until the plants bloom.

BULB ROTS

Symptoms. Amaryllis bulbs may be rotted from attacks of certain kinds of fungi such as *Botrytis cinerea, Rhizopus stolonifer,* and *Sclerotium rolfsii.*

Control. Discard all bulbs showing symptoms of rot. Plant clean bulbs in sterilized soil.

MOSAIC

Symptoms. A light-green to yellow mottling appears on the leaves. Plants, flowers, and bulbs become smaller each year.

Control. Destroy all affected plants.

Amaryllis bulb rot. The external view shown at right shows how the rot has developed on one side of the bulb. The sectioned bulb shows the progression of the rot through the scales.

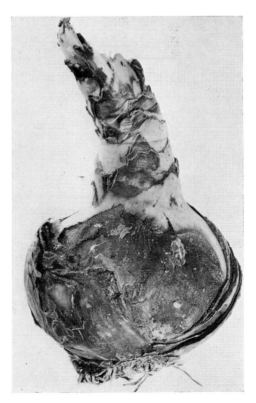

ASTER (CHINA-ASTER)

At least 23 different diseases have been reported on China-aster (*Callistephus chinensis*) in the United States. The most common diseases on this host are wilt and yellows.

FOOT ROT

Symptoms. Foot rot, caused by the fungus *Phytophthora cryptogea*, resembles Fusarium wilt, but foot rot usually destroys the plants more rapidly than does wilt. Rapid, permanent wilting of the leaves occurs and a blackish-brown discoloration develops on the lower part of the stem. The stems rot, shrivel, and collapse at or near the ground line, causing the plants to fall over. A soft, water-soaked, blackish-brown, odorless decay appears on invaded roots and stems. At first this decay is localized in the cortex but later involves all tissues. Adventitious roots may develop at the upper edge of the diseased part of the root. Diseased plants are easily pulled, but invariably the outer portions of the tap root and lateral roots slough off and remain in the soil.

Control. Foot rot is favored by excessive soil moisture, inadequate drainage, and cool weather. The disease may be held in check by using well-drained soils and by applying only enough water to satisfy growth requirements. Infested soil should be treated with steam, chloropicrin, or formaldehyde if asters are to be replanted.

FUSARIUM WILT

Symptoms. Fusarium wilt is caused by the fungus *Fusarium oxysporum* f. *callistephi*. If very young seedlings are attacked, the plants topple over suddenly, then wither and die. Plants attacked at a somewhat older stage may show two common types of symptoms. The plants are stunted and show a one-sided development. There is a decided yellowing of leaves or parts of leaves. When the stem of such a plant is cut, the vascular ring is found to be brown, especially on the side most affected. Such plants finally wither. In the other type of symptom the lower leaves are first to show signs of wilting. This is followed by the collapse of the entire plant which then withers and dies. The stems in these plants usually are externally blackened at the base and for some distance above. This condition is sometimes called stem rot. A general browning of the vascular tissues is evident in cross sections of the stem. In some cases wilt may not become apparent until the plants are coming into full bloom, when they suddenly collapse and wither.

Control. The use of wilt-resistant strains of asters is the most effective method of avoiding the disease. Wilt-resistant strains are available at most seed houses. Asters grown in the greenhouse should be planted in steam-sterilized soil. Asters grown out-

Aster plant with withered leaves on one side as a result of Fusarium wilt.

A black, elongated lesion often develops on one side of an aster stem when the plant has Fusarium wilt. Branches on the same side of the stem usually die suddenly.

side should not be planted where the disease has occurred unless the soil is replaced or disinfected with chloropicrin, or formaldehyde.

LEAF BLIGHT, ROOT ROT, AND STEM ROT

Symptoms. The fungus *Rhizoctonia solani* causes a leaf blight, root rot, and stem rot of China-asters. Symptoms of leaf blight first appear on the lowermost leaves that have come in contact with the soil. Affected tissues are characterized by a clearly defined, water-soaked area that progresses rapidly over the leaf. Within a short time the infected area usually collapses and becomes flabby, turning from a deep green to a dead brown. More or less concentric rings of alternating light and dark brown spreading from an infection center may be seen. After collapse of the leaf blade, the infection spreads down the petioles to the stem and a stem rot develops. In other instances the stem and

roots may be attacked directly. During warm, cloudy weather, plants may be killed within a few days.

Control. Control measures should be directed entirely toward eliminating *R. solani* from the soil before asters are planted. This is best accomplished by steam sterilization. If steam is not available the soil may be treated with Terraclor.

LEAF SPOTS

Symptoms. The fungi *Septoria callistephi, Ascochyta asteris,* and *Stemphylium botryosum* produce brown spots on aster leaves. Calyxes, petals, and stems also are attacked sometimes. The foliage may gradually wither and die from the lower part of the plant upward. Leaf spots usually produce little injury except in isolated cases. They may become troublesome in locations watered by overhead sprinklers.

Control. Spraying with ferbam or copper oxychloride will afford protection during the growing season. Ditch irrigation should be used instead of overhead sprinkling. Planting in low, humid areas should be avoided.

RUST

Symptoms. Orange-red pustules develop on the underside of the leaves. In severe

Aster leaf showing clusters of rust pustules on the lower surface.

cases the leaves turn yellow and die. The alternate stage of this rust fungus, *Coleosporium solidaginis,* occurs on several species of pines, where it produces a blister rust on the needles.

Control. This disease seldom becomes so serious as to require special control measures. Spraying several times with wettable sulfur, ferbam, or copper oxychloride usually will give effective control. Several rust-resistant varieties of asters have been reported.

YELLOWS

Symptoms. Aster yellows disease is caused by a mycoplasmalike organism that attacks many kinds of plants. The first symptom of the disease on aster is a slight yellowing along the veins of a young leaf. This symptom is known as veinclearing. Leaves become more chlorotic as they develop, until eventually they are chlorotic throughout. The chlorosis may affect leaves on only one side, and sectors of a plant may show symptoms while the remainder appears healthy. Affected plants do not wilt or die but show a peculiar spindling growth that prevents their proper development. The growing tips of affected plants are a light greenish yellow instead of the normal dark green. Leaves that are mature

A spindly type of growth, with branches forming acute angles with the main stem, is typical of aster yellows, as shown above.

Aster flower from a plant affected by yellows. The normal color of the petals was purple; the light-colored petals in the photograph had turned a yellowish green. Affected flowers are usually dwarfed, deformed, or lopsided.

when the symptoms appear on the plant do not change color, but the yellow color develops in the stem and leaves above the point where the trouble begins.

One of the most striking symptoms is the abnormal production of secondary shoots. Such shoots frequently arise in the axils of leaves that are a normal green and that were mature before the plant became affected. The secondary shoots are always thin and etiolated or yellowed.

Plants that become diseased before maturity are always stunted. The internodes of the main stem are greatly shortened but the internodes on the secondary shoots are lower than normal. Flower heads are always somewhat dwarfed.

If infection occurs early, plants usually do not bloom. If infection is late, the flowers are deformed, and are a sickly, yellowish green regardless of the normal color of the variety. The root systems of diseased plants appear normal but are smaller than those of healthy plants. Diseased leaves stand upright instead of lying flat, and frequently are somewhat deformed. The petioles are longer than healthy ones of the same age, and the blades are narrower and shorter than normal.

Control. The causal agent is spread by leafhoppers. The insects are incapable of transmitting the disease until 10 days after feeding on infected plants, but they are known to remain infectious for 100 days or longer.

The yellows disease is so widespread and severe on China-aster in some areas that commercial and home-garden culture of this plant has been largely abandoned. Commercial florists have controlled the disease successfully by growing asters under frames completely covered with shade cloth. The shade afforded by such cloth houses also promotes flowers of higher quality. All infected plants should be pulled and destroyed or removed from the premises as soon as the first symptoms of aster yellows are noticed.

The causal agent is known to overwinter in certain biennial and perennial plants such as sowthistle, daisy, and chrysanthemum. It is carried from these plants to young asters in early summer by leafhoppers. If possible, asters should not be planted closer than 200 feet from weed borders.

AZALEA AND RHODODENDRON

Although azaleas and rhododendrons (*Rhododendron* spp.) are usually classified separately by growers, there are no technical characters that warrant such separation. Several of the diseases that attack this genus of plants are found on both groups within the genus.

ANTHRACNOSE

Symptoms. Anthracnose, caused by the fungus *Glomerella cingulata*, is characterized by numerous small, round spots on both leaf surfaces. The spots have definite margins and are olive brown to rusty brown in color. With light infection the lesions are distinct, whereas with heavy infection the lesions coalesce and form large, irregular spots. Young lesions have a smooth surface; older lesions are somewhat swollen and rough and are dark brown. Heavily infected leaves fall prematurely, resulting in more or less severe defoliation. In extreme cases defoliated shoots fail to produce new growth the next growing season. Symptoms and development of the disease are in general the same on both the Indica and Kurume azaleas.

Control. Spraying with bordeaux mixture 4-4-50, Tribasic copper sulfate, C-O-C-S, or ferbam will effectively check progress of this disease.

BUD BLAST

Symptoms. When the fungus *Briosia azaleae* attacks the buds they "blast" or rot, turn dark brown, and fail to open. The external bracts become silvery and are covered with fine, black, bristling fruiting structures of the causal fungus.

Control. Pick and burn infected buds and destroy the seed pods after blooming is completed. Spray with bordeaux mixture once a month after the blooms fade.

CHLOROSIS

Symptoms. The leaves lose their green color, turn yellow, and sometimes fall off.

Control. Chlorosis is a physiological condition caused by iron deficiency or defective drainage. It is most common in neutral or alkaline soils. Chlorosis can be overcome by determining the cause of the trouble and correcting it. This may involve adjusting the soil pH, improving drainage, or supplying iron to the plants.

CROWN ROT

Symptoms. When azalea and rhododendron plants have crown rot, caused by the fungus *Phytophthora cryptogea*, the affected branches wilt and die. A brown discoloration of the wood may be seen in the basal portions of the stems and in the main roots.

Control. Prune out infected branches. Remove and destroy badly infected plants and replace the surrounding soil.

CYLINDROCARPON WILT AND BLIGHT

Symptoms. Symptoms of wilt appear about the time flower buds begin to show color. Few of the buds develop to full bloom; most of them wither and dry on the stem. The foliage wilts; some of the leaves fall but the majority remain on the plant, imparting a generally unhealthy appearance. A red-brown canker may appear on the main stem at soil level. When the bark is peeled away from this canker the woody tissue beneath is brown. The wood of smaller branches and twigs also may show browning. Wilting may occur only on one side of the plant or the entire plant may be affected.

Control. Infected branches should be pruned out. Severely infected plants should be removed and destroyed.

CYLINDROCLADIUM BLIGHT AND WILT

Symptoms. When azaleas are attacked by the fungus *Cylindrocladium scoparium* two kinds of symptoms may appear — blight and wilt. With blight the infected leaves turn brown to black, the petiole bases are softened, and the leaves usually drop in 3 or 4 days. In advanced stages the leaves and stems may be covered with a sparse to luxuriant mass of brownish mycelial strands. Powdery white masses of conidia may develop on the stems of cuttings in the greenhouse.

The wilt phase of the disease is usually confined to cuttings and consists of leaf wilt followed by leaf drop without the production of visible leaf spots or stem cankers. The bark and wood at the base of wilted cuttings are discolored and often water-soaked. In advanced stages, vascular discoloration may extend to the cutting tip.

Control. Benomyl 50W at 1 pound in 100 gallons of water has given complete control of this disease of azalea cuttings being rooted under intermittent mist.

DIEBACK

Symptoms. In dieback, caused by the fungus *Phytophthora cactorum,* large, water-soaked areas form on the foliage. The infected areas become brown and zoned, silvery white in spots on the upper surface, and light chocolate brown below. Dark-brown, sunken cankers and a general dieback of the branches occur on tender new growth. Older stems may be girdled, killing all the terminal portions of the infected branch. In many cases the entire plant is killed. This disease also occurs on lilacs.

Another dieback of azalea caused by the fungus *Phomopsis* sp. is often wrongly attributed to cold or insect damage. The primary symptoms are discoloration of the wood in diseased stems and permanent wilting and death of leaves, which usually turn reddish brown and remain attached to the dead stems. The disease usually appears on larger branches of old, established plants of the Indica type and is not apparent from the stem surface. The causal fungus is chiefly a wound parasite.

Control. Cut out and burn all diseased branches. After the plant has bloomed, make two applications of bordeaux mixture 2-2-50, 10 to 14 days apart. Reduce the amount of shade if possible.

FLOWER SPOT OR PETAL BLIGHT

Symptoms. Flower spot, caused by the fungus *Ovulinia azaleae,* occurs on cultivated azaleas. It attacks chiefly the Indian and Kurume types but all others are susceptible and occasionally infected.

The spots are first apparent when about the size of a pinhead. They are pale or whitish on colored flowers and rust-colored on white flowers. The spots are at first circular but enlarge readily into irregular blotches with the affected tissue becoming soft and disorganized. Eventually the entire corolla collapses. Affected petals are somewhat slimy and fall apart if rubbed gently between the fingers. In this manner the diseased flowers can be distinguished from those injured by weather, insects, or other causes. Diseased flowers dry and cling to the plants for some time, presenting an unsightly appearance, whereas normal flowers of Indian azaleas fall from the plants while still displaying color and normal shape. Under favorable conditions the disease may spread so rapidly as to destroy in a few days practically all the flowers of an extensive planting.

Control. Control of this disease is difficult. In the blighted flowers the fungus produces hard, black objects, known as sclerotia, which overwinter in the soil. From these sclerotia, fruiting bodies develop in the spring, bearing spores that may infect relatively few flowers, but secondary spores are produced in large numbers on the initial infections. The secondary spores are responsible for widespread, destructive outbreaks of flower spot.

Ovulinia flower spot occurs primarily on azaleas grown out-of-doors in the warm southern states, but it has been introduced into the North in shipments of plants from the South. It is conceivable that survival of sclerotia might be limited by unfavorable conditions out-of-doors in the North, but there is no question that the greenhouse environment provides both an abundance of inoculum (the causal organism) and favorable conditions for its growth. Ample inoculum is provided by sclerotia in old flower tissue and by free sclerotia that drop to the ground and remain undetected. Unsold plants, forced one year and held over for forcing again the following year, also are sources of inoculum.

Picking and destroying affected flowers, and replacing the surface litter around infected plants with uncontaminated material, are means of reducing the sources of primary infection.

Ground sprays of ferbam at the rate of 6 pounds per 1,000 square feet of area have helped to prevent the formation of the shooting spore stage. Applications should be made just before flowering time.

Spraying once a week with benomyl at the rate of one-half pound of the 50 percent wettable powder in 100 gallons of water has given excellent control of this disease. Spraying two or three times a week with zineb (Parzate or Dithane Z-78), 1 pound in 100 gallons of water, has also been effective. Spraying with thiram (Thylate), 1 pound in 100 gallons of water, has given excellent control of petal blight. It provides long protection and leaves little visible residue on the blossoms. Spraying should be started when the first signs of disease appear and it should be continued throughout the blooming period. Sprays should be applied as a fine mist or fog and should thoroughly cover all the flowers.

The most important control in the greenhouse is to reduce the humidity. The spores responsible for the secondary spread are extremely susceptible to dryness, and merely lowering the humidity to 80 or 85 percent is enough to control the disease.

GALLS

Symptoms. The fungus *Exobasidium vaccinni* causes white galls to form on the leaves and stems.

Control. Pick off the galls, and spray the leaves with bordeaux mixture 2-2-50, zineb, or captan, 1½ pounds to 100 gallons of water (2½ to 3 tablespoonfuls to 1 gallon).

LEAF SPOTS

Symptoms. Several different leaf-spot diseases are caused by different species of fungi. *Pestalotia macrotricha* and *P. rhododendri* cause spots that are silvery gray on the upper leaf surface and light brown below. Black spore-producing bodies of the causal fungus are conspicuous on the lower surface. These fungi enter the plant through weakened or injured tissues.

Lophodermium rhododendri produces large, silvery-white spots with red, raised margins. Prominent black, oval fruiting bodies appear on the upper side of the leaf. The lower surface of an infected area is a light chocolate brown.

Cercospora rhododendri produces angular, dark-brown spots on the upper leaf surface. A grayish down appears in the center of the spots.

Guignardia rhodorae produces spots that are either near the edges or the tips of the leaves. The dark-brown, ringed,

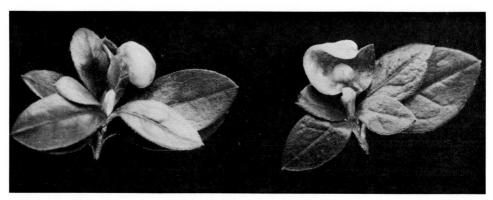

Azalea leaf galls caused by *Exobasidium vaccinii*. Similar galls are produced on stems and flower parts. A whitish "bloom" develops on the surface of the galls.

dead areas commonly cover half the leaf.

Exobasidium burtii affects seedlings, producing distinct yellow spots on the foliage. At first these spots are minute and circular; then they enlarge, and develop irregular or scalloped margins and brown centers. In some instances the margins are tinged with red. Spores of the causal fungus appear as a fine white meal on the lower surface of these spots.

Phomopsis sp. produces a leaf spot and a twig blight. Rather large spots with broad, definite, reddish-brown borders are formed on the leaves. These spots are silvery white in the center and have definite borders. Numerous minute black fruiting bodies of the causal organism are arranged in rings around the spots on the upper leaf surface. This fungus also causes cankers on the older stems, resulting in death of the infected branches.

Irregular, angular, brown lesions occur on leaves attacked by the fungus *Septoria azaleae*. This disease is known as angular leaf spot or scorch. In late stages of the disease, yellow zones surrounding the lesions are common. Usually the lower leaves are affected first, but occasionally lesions will be scattered through the foliage. Infected leaves tend to fall off, and severely infected plants may be defoliated except for a few whorls of new leaves at the tops. Plant growth is retarded when leaf drop is severe.

Control. Several applications of bordeaux mixture, ferbam, or zineb, 10 to 14 days apart, starting immediately after blooming, should keep leaf spots under control. Mulching, use of windbreaks, and control of insects — practices that keep the foliage in sound condition and prevent the entrance of many leaf-spotting fungi — will aid in controlling leaf spots.

RHIZOCTONIA LEAF BLIGHT

Symptoms. The first symptoms of leaf blight caused by the fungus *Rhizoctonia solani* are small necrotic water-soaked areas. At first the spots are tan and regular in outline. They enlarge rapidly and become dark brown, almost black, irregular lesions. Usually the enlarging lesions advance along the leaf margin and inward toward the midrib, frequently extending over half of the leaf surface. By the time of abscission, which occurs when the petiole is affected, the lesions may encompass the entire leaf surface. Leaves in all stages of development are susceptible, but the disease predominates on the older ones near the peat surface where water of condensation persists until midmorning or later. Under conditions of supersaturation, diseased leaves may become matted through the intertwining effect of superficial mycelium of the causal fungus, and hang suspended in clusters from branches of the plant. Defoliation may reach 100 percent, accompanied by a superficial browning of the stem. Death normally does not occur, but may follow, particularly on smaller plants. When conditions are less favorable for disease development, growth is resumed, and eventually results in a plant free of leaf symptoms. Until full vigor is regained, the new leaves are smaller than usual.

Control. Spray with thiram (Thylate) 2 pounds in 100 gallons of water twice weekly at first, then once a week. After the disease has been brought under control, use a preventive spray once every 2 to 4 weeks.

STEM CANKER AND DIEBACK

Symptoms. The fungus *Botryosphaeria ribis* causes a perennial dieback and canker disease on rhododendron. The fungus enters the stems through wounds. Reddish-brown to black sunken cankers develop, girdle the stems, and cause subsequent dieback. Discoloration is confined to the bark during early stages of disease development; later reddish-brown discoloration appears in wood and pith. Leaves on affected branches droop and roll downward along the midvein.

Control. Dieback and canker has become a serious nursery problem because the disease is difficult to eliminate through the use of sanitation and chemical sprays. Sanitation may reduce, but will not eliminate, sources of inoculum because both the host and the disease are perennial. The fungus can be spread from diseased to healthy plants by use of contaminated pruning tools. Therefore, pruning tools should be disinfected frequently during pruning operations.

WILT AND ROOT ROT

Symptoms. Wilt and root rot are caused by *Phytophthora cinnamomi* and *P. citricola* and occasionally by three other species of *Phytophthora*. The foliage of an affected plant first becomes a dull yellowish green, followed soon by permanent wilting. The roots are more or less decayed, and the base of the stem is brownish at the soil level and below. Removing the outer tissues of the stem shows reddish-brown streaks extending for varying distances up the stem. When the infection has reached the current season's growth, brown sunken

cankers may be connected with these discolorations. These streaks frequently extend to the tip of the growing point, where the young terminal leaves are invaded and a dieback occurs. This disease primarily affects young stock and is particularly severe on *Rhododendron ponticum* and hybrid seedlings. It occurs frequently on grafted plants 2 and 3 years old, but seldom affects older plants.

Control. The most important step in the control of diseases of woody plants, in general, is the production of healthy rooted cuttings. Canadian or German sphagnum peat is an excellent rooting medium, which provides excellent drainage and has a pH of 3.5 to 4.1 which checks the development of several pathogens. Aeration may be improved by the addition of perlite and coarse sand. Cuttings should be free of soil, insects, and disease before they are taken. Cutting dips or soakings should be avoided. Before starting the propagation program all unpainted wooden flats, baskets, and greenhouse benches should be treated with 2 percent copper naphthenate. When all the plants are out of the greenhouse the interior should be treated with formaldehyde (1 part of 37 percent formaldehyde solution in 50 parts of water). After the entire propagating area has been sprayed the greenhouse should be kept closed for 24 hours, then aerated until all odor of formaldehyde is gone. All propagating tools should be disinfected before each use. A new or sterilized medium should be used in the propagating beds. After the cuttings have been stuck into the rooting medium they should be watered with a combination wetting agent and Dexon 35 percent wettable powder at the rate of 10 ounces in 100 gallons of water. All wilted or diseased plants and cuttings should be removed from the propagating and growing area.

One of the most critical factors for successful production of rhododendrons that are free of root rot is adequate drainage of the soil mix. Air volume of container media should be at least 20 percent. It is important that the air volume does not decrease in containers during the growing season because of breakdown of organic constituents. Containers should be placed on gravel, not on plastic, because plastic allows rapid spread of zoospores from infected containers to surrounding healthy plants.

WITCHES'-BROOM

Symptoms. The fungus *Exobasidium vaccinii-uliginosae* causes an excessive number of twigs to form on infected branches, producing a witches'-broom effect. The leaves are yellowish white and covered on the lower surface with a dense, mealy felt of fungus growth.

Control. Entire infected plants should be removed and burned.

BALSAM

The garden balsam (*Impatiens balsamina*) is affected by a few diseases which may become quite troublesome.

LEAF SPOTS

Symptoms. The fungus *Stemphylium botryosum* causes dark-brown circular lesions of various sizes on infected leaves. Light-tan circular areas develop in the center of older lesions. Coalescing of lesions is common.

This disease is favored by high humidity and is encouraged when plants are grown in crowded conditions in greenhouses. Because the fungus can infect more than one species of bedding plants, the opportunity for inoculum build-up is increased.

The fungi *Cercospora fukushiana, Phyllosticta* sp., and *Septoria noli-tangeris* cause small, more or less circular brown spots on leaves of this host.

Control. Inasmuch as infection is increased with high humidity, proper spacing of plants and taking measures to lower the humidity will reduce the occurrence of leaf spots. In mild cases infected leaves can be picked off and destroyed. Weekly applications of maneb at the rate of 1½ pounds to 100 gallons of water have given good control in some instances.

BEGONIA

Begonias (*Begonia* spp.) are affected by a few troublesome diseases, the most common being bacterial leaf spot, Botrytis blight, powdery mildew, and Pythium crown and stem rot.

BACTERIAL LEAF SPOT

Symptoms. Bacterial leaf spot, caused by *Xanthomonas begoniae,* first appears as small, circular, blisterlike spots on the leaves. These spots later become more conspicuous and appear translucent when a leaf is held up to the light. The spots gradually enlarge and coalesce to form large, blisterlike areas of dead tissue. These lesions usually appear water-soaked, but occasionally a yellow, dry ooze may be observed on dry specimens. The leaves often fall prematurely. In severe cases the main stem may be invaded by the bacteria, resulting in a gradual softening of all tissues and sometimes in collapse of the entire plant.

Control. Dip leaf cuttings for 5 minutes in a 4-4-50 bordeaux mixture just before sticking them in the sand. When rooted begonia leaves are placed in 2¼-inch pots the upper surface of the leaves should be sprayed immediately with bordeaux mixture. It is not necessary to spray the underside of the leaves. Should the disease develop later, spotted leaves should be re-

Bacterial leaf spot on Lady Mac begonia. The translucent halo is easily seen when the leaf is held up to the light.

moved and destroyed. Warm, moist, poorly
ventilated, crowded conditions favor development of the disease. Adequate spacing, with regulated temperature and
moisture, is usually effective in preventing
or arresting development of the disease.

BOTRYTIS BLIGHT AND STEM ROT

Symptoms. Dead areas occur on leaves,
flowers, and stems of plants attacked by
Botrytis cinerea. The diseased leaf areas
enlarge rapidly under favorable conditions,
and eventually entire leaves may turn
black. Usually the affected flowers and
leaves become covered with a brownish-
gray mold.

Stem lesions are irregular in shape, dark
brown, water-soaked, and occasionally
sunken. They usually occur at or near the
base of the stem, but may also develop
at some distance above the soil surface.
Stem lesions may first develop at the nodes
or on internodes, later spreading to involve both areas. Sometimes the lesions
coalesce to form larger lesions that may encircle the stem. The stem may shrivel and
mummify. In advanced stages of the disease, all internal stem tissues are invaded
and the stem so weakens that it breaks at
or above the ground line, depending upon
the location of the lesion or lesions.

Control. All old leaves, broken branches,
old flowers, and diseased parts should
be removed from the plants periodically,
and the plants should be inspected for stem
lesions. Decayed areas should be carefully
cut out with a flamed scalpel and then
covered with a thick paste of ziram. All
wounds, leaf scars, and growth cracks
should be painted with ziram paste. The
ziram paste can be prepared by mixing
water with commercially prepared ziram
dust. Plants should be spaced to improve
air circulation. Heat and ventilation should
be used to reduce the humidity in the
greenhouse. Spraying with benomyl, zineb,
or captan is helpful.

POWDERY MILDEW

Symptoms. A white, powdery coating
forms spots up to one-half inch in diameter

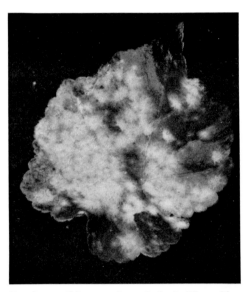

Powdery mildew on begonia leaf. The white,
powdery growth is more abundant on the upper
surface of the leaf.

on the surface of leaves, stems, and flowers.
In severe infections reddish margins of
dead tissue may surround the white spots.

Control. The disease develops most
readily under humid conditions. Proper
ventilation will do much to prevent the
disease in the greenhouse. Spraying with
benomyl, wettable sulfur, Mildex, or Acti-
dione PM may be used to clean up established infections. Sulfur, vaporized from
the steam pipes or from sulfur vaporizers,
is effective.

PYTHIUM CROWN AND STEM ROT

Symptoms. In crown and stem rot,
caused by species of *Pythium,* the crown
and lower portion of the stem become
somewhat discolored, water-soaked, and
soft. Infection may progress up the stem
2 or 3 inches, causing the stem to collapse.
Petioles on infected leaves become limp
and dark, and the leaf blades are water-
soaked and flaccid. Infected leaves may
fall off.

Control. Use sterilized soil for planting.
Avoid excessive watering, and keep the
plants well spaced to allow good air
circulation.

Leaf spot on Boston ivy, caused by **Guignardia bidwellii**. The spots may become so numerous that the leaf dies and falls from the plant.

BOSTON IVY

Several fungi cause leaf spots on Boston ivy (*Parthenocissus tricuspidata*) and Virginia creeper (*P. quinquefolia*), especially during rainy seasons. The most common disease on these hosts in Illinois is caused by the fungus *Guignardia bidwellii*.

LEAF SPOTS

Symptoms. *G. bidwellii* produces brown, more or less angular spots, which are delimited by the veins. Black pinpoint pycnidia or fruiting bodies of the causal fungus appear on the upper surfaces of the spots.

Cercospora ampelopsidis produces small, reddish-brown, circular to angular spots that sometimes are bulging on the upper surface.

Control. Pick off and burn infected leaves as soon as they are noticed. Spray the plants with a copper or a carbamate fungicide.

BUTTERCUP

The Persian buttercup (*Ranunculus asiaticus*) is subject to a root rot caused by the fungus *Pythium debaryanum* when grown under excessively wet conditions.

Root rot of **Ranunculus**, caused by **Pythium** sp. A healthy plant is shown on the right. (Photograph courtesy of Division of Plant Pathology, University of California, Berkeley.)

ROOT ROT

Symptoms. The most striking symptoms of buttercup root rot consist of general wilting followed by rapid collapse and death of the plant. The roots, tubers, stems, and petioles may be invaded by the fungus. The roots and tubers of infected plants are dark brown, water-soaked, and flaccid.

Control. The disease is favored by excessive rainfall or irrigation, poor drainage, cool weather, and crowding of the plants. Control is dependent upon the selection of well-drained sites, and placing the plants so they will not be crowded.

CALLA LILY

Calla lily (*Zantedeschia* spp.) is subject to several diseases, the most common being root rot and soft rot.

LEAF BLIGHT

Symptoms. Pink calla is subject to a leaf blight caused by the fungus *Phytophthora erythroseptica*. In the early stages of the disease the green leaves (of plants grown either from seed or corms) suddenly show a general chlorosis or yellowing and are less turgid than healthy leaves. Infected leaves soon become yellow and distorted, and the edges tend to curl upward. At the same time, for some distance above and below the soil surface, a wet, odorless, brownish-black discoloration of the petioles is noticeable. At first this area is firm but soon turns soft and becomes mushy. With the rapid destruction of the supporting tissues in the petioles, the leaves collapse, singly or in groups, until all in the cluster are prostrate. This occurs within a few hours, and the foliage dies within a day or two. No infection of the roots or corms occurs.

Control. Always use sterilized soil for growing pink callas. Avoid high humidity and keep the foliage dry.

LEAF SPOT

Symptoms. Leaf spot, caused by the fungus *Coniothecium richardiae,* is characterized by roughly circular or elliptical spots that coalesce to produce irregular, blighted areas on the leaves. Leaf stalks also may be affected, and the flowers occasionally are spotted.

Control. Leaf and stem debris should be destroyed. Ventilate properly to avoid high humidity, and keep the foliage dry.

PYTHIUM ROT

Symptoms. The first evidence of Pythium rot, caused by the fungus *Pythium ultimum,* on pink and yellow calla corms, after harvest, consists of small to large, irregular-shaped, shallow, water-soaked lesions that quickly destroy the thin skin. One or more lesions may occur on the same corm, and often they coalesce to form larger lesions. Infection may rapidly involve most of the skin of both the flowering-sized corms and the attached small corms or offsets. Destruction of the skin causes the creamy-white flesh of the corm to turn pink on exposure to air.

Within a few days infection may spread deeply into the flesh of the corm from the watery surface lesions, producing small to large, irregular-shaped, light-gray lesions that are sharply delimited — sometimes by a narrow, marginal, black line — from the adjoining healthy tissue. Internal lesions are irregular in shape, soft to firm, rubbery, water-soaked to dry, and odorless. On the surface of the corms, older lesions become dry, dark brown to black in color, and may be slightly sunken, in marked contrast to the light-tan skin of healthy corms. Infected corms may be partially to completely destroyed.

Control. The disease is favored in its development and spread by a humid atmosphere and by moisture contained in the soil particles adhering to the corms. Air temperatures below 50°F will retard the disease.

The causal fungus is a wound parasite and does not invade sound, healthy corms. By avoiding injury to the corms at harvest time a minimum amount of infection may be expected. All corms should be cleaned soon after they are dug. Decayed areas should be cut away with a sharp knife. The cut surface should then be covered with a thin layer of a mixture (equal parts by volume) of Spergon and Celite 505. Corms should be stored in well-ventilated trays at an air temperature of 50°F or less.

RHIZOME ROT

Symptoms. A rhizome rot of white calla is produced by a different strain of the same fungus, *Phytophthora erythroseptica,* that causes leaf blight in pink callas. External symptoms of the disease on the rhizomes consist of small to large lesions that are irregular in shape, dark brown, and water-soaked. With age these lesions become dry, shriveled, and slightly sunken. When the rhizomes are cut in cross or lengthwise sections, the internal diseased tissues appear light gray, and are firm but rubbery in texture, and separated from healthy tissues by a definite line of demarcation. The decay is odorless. Internal lesions may involve small to large areas of tissue and are in marked contrast to healthy tissue.

Control. The measures outlined for the control of root rot should control this disease also.

ROOT ROT

Symptoms. The first symptoms of root rot, caused by the fungus *Phytophthora cryptogea* var. *richardiae,* is a yellowing along the margins of the outer leaves. Gradually the entire leaf yellows and droops. Other leaves are affected progressively inward. If the plants flower at all, the tip of the blossom turns brown and does not open properly. The feeder roots start rotting at the tips and the rot progresses backward to the rhizomes. The diseased roots have a water-soaked appearance and all that finally remains of them is the epidermis, which appears as a hollow tube. New roots are sent out from the rhizome and these, in turn, rot. Rhizomes may be attacked but usually not extensively. The rot in the rhizome is more or less dry and spongy, never wet and slimy.

Control. Clean old rhizomes thoroughly. Cut out the rotted spots and allow the rhizomes to dry. Then treat them, using one of the following methods:

1. Soak the rhizomes 1 hour in a 2-percent formaldehyde solution. Drain and plant immediately.

2. Soak the rhizomes 10 minutes in a 1-percent peracetic acid solution. Drain and plant immediately.

Since treated rhizomes start growth more slowly than those that are untreated, it is advisable to plant them 2 weeks earlier. Soaking rhizomes for 1 hour in water at 122°F will kill the fungus in dormant rhizomes and does not delay blooming.

It is better to grow callas in pots rather than in benches if root rot is present. When the disease starts in a bench, the fungus spreads through the soil and infects other plants. Sterilize used pots before planting rhizomes in them. Steam or formaldehyde may be used for this purpose. Soil should be sterilized with steam before callas are planted in it.

SOFT ROT

Symptoms. Plants affected by soft rot, caused by the bacterium *Erwinia aroideae,* rot off at the soil surface. The rot may progress upward, causing blighting of the leaves, and downward, producing a soft rot of the rhizome. The roots also may soften and become slimy. The entire plant may

Healthy calla plants (left) were grown from treated rhizomes; the two rows at right were not treated. Rhizomes in both lots had been severely affected by root rot the preceding season.

Upper photo shows distorted, streaked, and spotted flowers from a calla plant affected by spotted wilt. The lower photo shows calla leaves that are distorted, spotted, and savoyed as a result of the same disease.

wilt suddenly and die. The leaf edges of infected plants become flaccid and slimy without losing their green color. Later the leaf droops, yellows, shrivels, and dies. Flower stalks may be attacked; the flower turns brown and the flower stalk eventually falls over.

Control. The methods suggested for control of root rot will also control soft rot. Do not plant calla rhizomes more than 2 inches deep and do not overwater them. Outbreaks of the disease may be checked by soaking the soil with a solution of streptomycin sulfate.

SPOTTED WILT

Symptoms. Spotted wilt, caused by a virus, is characterized by whitish or yellowish spots, streaks, or less frequently, concentric rings that occur along or near the leaf veins. Brown necrotic spots develop, and large portions of leaf blades or entire leaves may be killed.

Numerous white or yellowish streaks also occur on leaf petioles and flower stalks. Pale, blotchy spots and streaks appear on the green flower buds, and, as the buds open, pale, greenish spots and blotches appear on the flowers. The leaves are "savoyed" or abnormally crinkled and twisted, and the flowers are deformed.

Control. Spotted wilt is transmitted from diseased to healthy plants by thrips. It is carried from one generation to the next in infected rhizomes. Destroy all diseased plants as soon as they are noticed. Select healthy planting stock and keep thrips under control at all times.

CAMELLIA

Although camellias (*Camellia japonica* and *C. sasanqua*) are principally a crop of the warm southern states, they are also grown to some extent in greenhouses in the North. The diseases that occur in outdoor-grown camellias in the South also occur to some extent on northern greenhouse-grown camellias.

DIEBACK AND CANKER

Symptoms. This disease, caused by the fungus *Glomerella cingulata,* is characterized by the formation of cankers and the dying back of twigs and branches. The symptoms vary considerably with age and size of the organ affected.

Dieback of young growth occurs during the first flush of new growth. Young, succulent shoots suddenly wilt and die. The dead leaves turn dark brown to black and usually remain attached to the wilted shoot for some time. At the junction of the dead and living portions of the shoot there is an area about an inch long where the bark, as well as the woody tissue, is dark brown. Infection that causes this type of injury often occurs at the base of the new shoot but occasionally is found some distance above the base. A similar type of dieback occurs in grafted plants, apparently originating at the graft union.

Dieback of twigs and small branches is similar to that in young growth but the wilting occurs at any time during the season and is not restricted to the early growth. Cankers almost invariably accompany this type of dieback. The cankers are sometimes inconspicuous, slightly depressed areas in the bark at the base of the necrotic portion of the twig or branch, or sometimes sunken and well defined. Usually the cankers are localized either at the base of the dead twigs, where infection occurred through leaf scars, or on the branches, developing around the necrotic remnants of twigs that were killed earlier.

Dieback of larger branches and of entire plants is the most destructive of the dieback infections, causing loss of large branches or of the entire plant when the main stem is girdled. Definite cankers are present. Death occurs only when the branch or stem has been girdled. The foliage on partially girdled branches may be sparse and chlorotic, and dieback of small twigs may occur.

Control. Remove dead or dying twigs and discolored wood around cankers on the large branches. Paint the wounds with an asphaltum-fungicide paint. Spraying with bordeaux mixture 4-4-50 or captan, 3 pounds to 100 gallons of water, has effectively reduced infection through the scars left by fallen leaves. Ferbam or captan, 3 pounds to 100 gallons, should be

Camellia canker that developed around the base of a dead twig.

Blossom blight of camellia. Diseased flower below, healthy one above. (Photograph courtesy of Division of Plant Pathology, University of California, Berkeley.)

used as dips for scions and grafting tools to prevent establishing the causal fungus in the graft wounds.

FLOWER BLIGHT

Symptoms. Infection of the individual flower by the blight organism *Sclerotinia camelliae* may take place soon after the tips of petals are visible in the opening bud or at any time thereafter. Few to many, small, irregular, brownish specks appear on the petals of expanding flowers. Under favorable conditions of temperature and moisture these specks enlarge and unite to form large spots that soon involve an entire petal. Eventually the whole flower becomes uniformly dull brown and drops

A canna leaf that was attacked by the bud-rot bacterium while the leaf was still rolled in the bud.

from the plant. When infection begins near the base of the petals the entire center of the flower may be killed, while the tips of the petals retain their normal form and color.

There is no rapid disintegration of invaded tissues and infected flowers retain their shape and firmness for many days after they turn completely brown and fall to the ground. While the flowers are resting on the wet earth, shiny black streaks or masses of spores often are produced on the petals, giving the appearance of a wet rot. After the flower is completely blighted the causal fungus continues to develop within the basal parts of the petals, but soon grows beyond the petal limits to form hard, dark-brown to black sclerotia.

A similar disease is caused by *Sclerotinia sclerotiorum*.

Control. Gather and destroy all fallen flowers. This may have to be done for at least two consecutive seasons because the sclerotia remain alive in the soil for at least 2 years and probably longer. Drenching the soil with Terraclor is effective in suppressing germination of the sclerotia.

CANNA

Cannas (*Canna* spp.) seldom are troubled by diseases, but occasionally bud rot, mosaic, and aster yellows may occur.

BUD ROT

Symptoms. Bud rot infection by the bacterium *Xanthomonas cannae* usually takes place while the leaves are still rolled in the bud. When there are numerous points of infection and the disease has not progressed far, the leaf appears covered with tiny white spots when it opens. When the infection is far advanced, the leaf is wholly or partly blackened when it unfolds. The entire stalk may be killed. The lesions do not enlarge in the older leaves but these leaves show the effects of the earlier attack in the form of brown spots, streaks, and a distorted condition. Flowers are often ruined by infection of the young buds or decay of the stem.

Control. Select root stalks from healthy plants. Surface sterilization of the dormant corms is advisable. Plants started in a greenhouse should be watered carefully to keep the young growth dry. Ventilate properly to keep the humidity down, and allow plenty of space. Set only disease-free plants out-of-doors and space them well apart.

MOSAIC

Symptoms. Early leaf symptoms are fine, chlorotic lines connecting to branch veins. Later, spindle-shaped chlorotic areas may appear. In advanced stages, continuous or broken chlorotic stripes extend from the midrib to the leaf margin parallel with the veins, and the leaf may become wrinkled or curled. Such stripes may become brown and necrotic in late stages. Streaking of the petal color may occur.

Control. The canna mosaic virus is transmitted from diseased to healthy plants by certain species of aphids. Diseased plants should be removed and destroyed as soon as mosaic symptoms are noticed. Aphids should be kept under control at all times.

ASTER YELLOWS

Symptoms. When young, actively growing canna plants are attacked by the aster-yellows organism, yellowing appears first in the youngest leaves, which later become flaccid and wither. These effects may progress until the shoots die back to the soil line. Lateral shoots that may develop later are weak, yellowed, and dwarfed. When plants are infected late in the growing season, the plants developing from these root stalks the following year are much dwarfed and yellowed, and virescent or greenish flowers may develop.

Control. The disease is usually not a serious menace to cannas, but may occur where the incidence of aster yellows on other hosts is high. Weed hosts should be kept down, and leafhoppers, which carry the causal agent, should be kept under control as well as possible.

CARNATION

The carnation (*Dianthus caryophyllus*) is one of the most widely grown of all flower crops. It is subject to a number of diseases, several of which can become so serious that crops cannot be grown profitably without rigid disease control.

ALTERNARIA BLIGHT

Symptoms. Symptoms of blight, caused by the fungus *Alternaria dianthi*, occur on the leaves and stems, and occasionally on the flowers. Infections may develop on either surface of the leaf and are first evident as tiny purple spots. These spots soon develop a broad yellow-green border; later, as the more or less circular spots enlarge, a small, light-brown to grayish, dead, sunken place appears in the center of each. With further enlargement the dead center becomes proportionately much larger and is surrounded by a narrow, yellow-green border, and, in some varieties, by a broader, purple inner ring. Frequently, several expanding lesions coalesce, resulting in large, irregular dead areas. Finally the healthy tissue between spots turns yellow and withers, and the entire leaf is

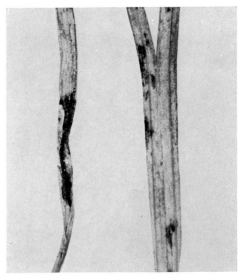

Carnation leaves showing Alternaria blight lesions. The larger spots were formed when two or more spots coalesced.

killed. The discolored, diseased areas become covered with a black layer of spores, especially under moist atmospheric conditions.

Branches are infected most frequently at the nodes. Stem lesions are at first confined to the outer tissues and to one side of the stem, but later they usually involve the inner tissues and girdle the stem. The affected stem tissue is sharply defined from the adjacent healthy tissue and has the appearance of a dry, brown rot. Black crusts of spores form on the dead areas, and some of the black deposit remains long after the branch has died. The branches and leaves finally become completely dry and straw colored.

Another characteristic of Alternaria blight is the mottled appearance of the terminal leaves on stems that have lesions or cankers below. First the center terminal, followed shortly by the outer terminal leaves, becomes light green and then develops the peculiar mottled appearance. This symptom should not be confused with the mottling that accompanies the virus diseases. Gradually these and the remaining leaves of the shoot turn yellow. Wilting and death follow.

Control. Control of Alternaria blight involves, first of all, the prevention of primary infections in the cutting bench. The selection of clean cuttings from healthy plants is thus of utmost importance. Plants kept in a greenhouse during the summer remain practically free of infection without requiring spraying, and may produce more than twice as many flowers as plants grown in the field, especially in a wet season that favors field infection.

If field culture cannot be avoided a thorough spray program should be practiced. Spray applications should be made at weekly or 10-day intervals, starting soon

An Alternaria lesion girdling a carnation stem, causing death of the upper portion. Black spore masses show on the surface of the lesion.

Yellowish mottling and ring-spot patterns produced in upper young leaves of a carnation with an Alternaria lesion or canker on its stem.

after transplanting in the field and continuing until just prior to benching. Any of the fungicides Bravo, zineb, captan, ferbam, and ziram can be used, at the rate of 1½ to 2 pounds in 100 gallons of water. Because of the waxy leaves, a good spreader is necessary to obtain a good coverage.

ANTHER SMUT

Symptoms. Carnation plants attacked by anther smut, *Ustilago violacea,* are stunted in growth, with excessive axillary or side-shoot development that gives the plants a grassy appearance. Shoot growth on infected plants is generally weakened; internodes are short and leaves are smaller. Flower bud production is increased on the main stems. Buds are short and squat, and there is a marked tendency of the calyx tubes to split when the flowers open. Flowers on infected plants are made unsightly by the production of large masses of purplish-black spores which replace the pollen normally produced in the anther sacs. The spores shed abundantly over the flower petals, giving them a sooty appearance and making the blossom quite messy.

Control. Remove and burn all infected plants as soon as they are detected. Propagate only from stock that is known to be entirely free of the disease.

BACTERIAL LEAF SPOT

Symptoms. Dead, sunken, oval-shaped spots appear on leaves affected by bacterial leaf spot, caused by *Pseudomonas woodsii.* When viewed by reflected light, the centers of these spots are pale brown surrounded by purplish concentric rings. If viewed by transmitted light the outer zones of the spots appear water-soaked and yellow. With high humidity the bacteria may ooze out in small drops on the surface of the lesions. The spots are about one-half inch long and may cover the entire width of the leaf. With numerous infections, the spots tend to coalesce. Several spots usually cause death of the leaf. This killing begins with a yellowing that occurs in advance of the water-soaked margin around the older lesions. The leaf gradually turns straw yellow, withers, and dies, while the spots remain a rusty brown. The disease progresses from the lower leaves upward. Symptoms always have been observed first on the lower leaves, under both field and greenhouse conditions.

While bacterial spot is primarily a foliage disease, infections sometimes occur on the stems and flower buds. In cases of severe infection the plants may be killed. When infection is less severe, flower production may be reduced for some time.

Control. Mild infections can be cleaned up by picking off and burning diseased leaves. Keep the foliage as dry as possible. Water the plants early in the day, preferably on bright days, so that there will not be too much dampness about them at night. Keep water off the foliage as much as possible. Application of sulfur dust has given satisfactory control in some cases.

BACTERIAL SLOW WILT OR STUNT

Symptoms. Plants infected with the carnation strain of *Erwinia chrysanthemi*

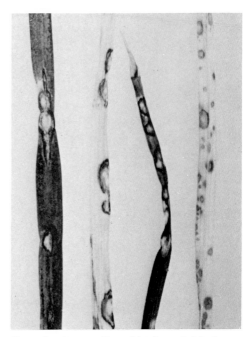

Carnation leaves affected by bacterial leaf spot. The tissue between the spots turns yellow while the spots remain a rusty brown.

may exhibit a wide range of symptoms, giving rise to some confusion regarding the name of the disease and field diagnosis of infected plants. Soon after the plants have been set in their permanent location infected plants often can be detected by their unthrifty appearance, lighter color, flaccidity, and loss of bloom of the leaves. A slow, progressive wilt develops and plants become gray-green. These symptoms usually develop over many months before the plant is finally killed. Progressive wilting does not always occur but plants may be stunted and make little growth. A root rot accompanies the aerial symptoms but basal stem rotting does not occur. The stems of infected plants often are extensively cracked. Twisting, curling, stunting, and wilting of lower leaves and side shoots may occur.

The inner wood of the infected stem is usually brown at the base. The discoloration trails off into streaks that become lighter, dry, and frayed towards the top

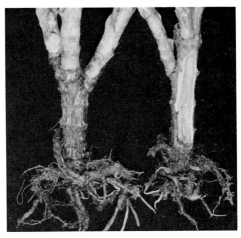

Carnation plants with the rotted roots associated with bacterial wilt. The bark has been sliced from the plant on the right to show the brown, discolored wood.

of the stem. Sometimes, particularly in young plants, the wood is discolored only in streaks at the stem base. Where the stem is cracked the underlying wood is often disorganized, leaving a dry, necrotic pocket.

Control. The control measures suggested for control of Fusarium wilt and bacterial wilt will also control bacterial slow wilt.

BACTERIAL WILT

Symptoms. Sudden wilting of the tops or some of the branches is the characteristic symptom of bacterial wilt, caused by *Pseudomonas caryophylli*. In some plants wilting occurs first in one or more branches on one side of the plant. In other cases the entire plant wilts suddenly. Wilted branches dry, turn gray-green and finally tan or brown. Distortion, caused by the tendency of the plant to curl to one side as described for Fusarium wilt (page 42), is not characteristic of bacterial wilt.

Internally the stems of wilting plants are yellowish to brown. When the wilting is confined to one side of the plant, the discoloration in the basal part of the stem is usually restricted to the side on which wilting appears. The bark on the lower parts of the stems of infected plants disintegrates and becomes soft. When this

Although wilting may start in a single branch, a carnation plant affected by bacterial wilt eventually wilts uniformly and completely.

decayed bark is broken away, the discolored wood of the inner stem is sticky to the touch.

The root systems of wilting plants are rotted and most of the roots remain in the soil when the plant is lifted. The inner tissues of affected roots are discolored yellowish to brown like the stem. The root tissues gradually disintegrate and soften, exhibiting the same sticky character as the stem tissues.

The stickiness of disintegrating root and stem tissues is an important characteristic in distinguishing bacterial wilt from the other wilt and root-rot diseases.

Control. The causal bacteria enter the carnation plant through the roots and the base of the stem. Because the disease is spread in much the same way as Fusarium wilt, the control measures outlined for Fusarium wilt will also control bacterial wilt. If cuttings are treated with root-promoting substances, powdered rather than liquid forms should be used.

BOTRYTIS BLIGHT

Symptoms. The spores of *Botrytis cinerea* are produced in large numbers when the atmosphere is warm and damp. Under such conditions, moisture collecting in the opening bud forms an ideal environment for germination of the spores and growth of the fungus. Petals of affected flowers

Botrytis blight on carnation variety Northland. The petals were matted together by the fungus.

turn brown while still in the buds, or after the flowers have opened. Frequently a number of petals are matted together by the growth of the fungus. If the weather remains warm and moist, the affected petals soon become covered with the gray fungus growth and a powdery mass of spores may be seen on the surface of the fungus. If the weather suddenly becomes dry the fungus usually will not develop further, but the affected parts of the petal become brown, dry, and brittle.

Control. Botrytis blight occurs only during periods of extremely high humidity. Control measures usually are unnecessary, but in houses where the disease has become troublesome it is advisable to cut and destroy affected buds as soon as they are noticed. Careless splashing of water and drips from the roof should be avoided. Anything that can be done to reduce the humidity in the greenhouse will help control Botrytis blight. Spraying with Bravo or Botran may be advisable.

CENTRAL BUD ROT

Symptoms. Central bud rot is caused by the fungus *Fusarium tricinctum* f. *poae* and is spread from diseased to healthy buds by the mite *Siteroptes graminum.* Infected young buds may outwardly appear normal, but when opened show a moist, brownish, decayed mass of the inner floral organs. Pistil, stamens, styles, and petal bases may be rotted through by *Fusarium,* which is generally visible as a heavy or sparse, white, cottony growth. The glistening, white, ellipsoidal bodies of the pregnant female mites are embedded in this decayed, moldy mass of tissue.

Young, severely infected carnation buds usually do not open. Medium-sized and large buds may open, even after heavy infection by *Fusarium.* Such buds, when dissected, show a central decay, a cottony growth of the fungus, attached bodies of pregnant mites, and an accumulation of water droplets in the rotten mass. Unlike the diseased young buds, large buds show external symptoms of the disease. They are extremely soft or mushy at the base, and generally fail to unfold at one side as they expand, so that the flower has a peculiar, lopsided appearance. White varieties of carnation are most susceptible to this disease, and crimson and dark-red varieties are least affected.

Control. Control of central bud rot is largely a matter of eliminating the mite from the greenhouse. All infected buds should be picked off and burned as soon as they are noticed. The plants should then be sprayed with a good miticide.

FAIRY RING SPOT

Symptoms. In fairy ring spot, minute black fruiting bodies of the fungus *Heterosporium echinulatum* appear in ring formation on the leaves.

Control. Control measures are the same as for Alternaria blight.

FASCIATION

Symptoms. Many short, spindly branches develop at a node of a main stem. The masses of fasciated growth, which resemble small brooms, most commonly occur on the lower parts of the stems.

Control. Destroy affected plants. Propagate only from healthy plants.

FUSARIUM STEM ROT

Symptoms. Carnations are most susceptible to attacks by the stem-rot fungus, *Fusarium roseum* f. *cerealis,* in the propagative stage and, to a lesser extent, immediately thereafter. Thus, the most important losses from this disease occur in young stocks. Infected plants wilt and die from a stem rot at the base. Lesions at the soil line or below develop inward from the outside. Often there are pink or red discolorations on the edges of the lesions. There is no internal stem discoloration.

In older plants the symptoms are similar but may be complicated by symptoms caused by other pathogens frequently associated with the stem-rot organism. In older plants it is not uncommon to find the roots rotted and sloughed away to the root head.

An abnormally large number of small shoots at a lower node on a carnation stem is typical of fasciation.

Carnation plant affected by Fusarium stem rot and root rot. The roots are almost completely rotted away.

Control. Use healthy, vigorous propagating material. Likelihood of carnation cuttings to attack by *F. roseum* f. *cerealis* is altered by nutrition of the mother plant. Reduced nitrogen levels while maintaining relatively high phosphorus and calcium levels prior to harvesting the cuttings will reduce the hazard of epidemics.

Steam sterilize the propagation medium, benches, and tools. Use inert materials, such as perlite, for soil amendments or mulches that will not provide a food base for further growth and development of *F. roseum.* Straw amendments and mulches should be avoided. The depth of planting is particularly important because deep planting results in death of the lower foliage and provides an avenue of invasion for the pathogen. Good drainage should be provided in the planting medium and overwatering should be avoided because excessive moisture is conducive to disease development.

Fungicides should be applied properly, to cover open wounds from recent planting and cutting harvest and thus prevent invasion by the pathogen. Good sanitation practices should be followed in and around greenhouses to prevent accumulation of plant debris which can harbor the pathogen. Watering should be done carefully to prevent unnecessary spread of the pathogen by means of splashing water. Stock plantings should be examined weekly, during and after propagation, and diseased plants should be rogued as soon as possible.

Significant control of Fusarium stem rot of carnations by use of an antagonistic microorganism, *Bacillus subtilis,* has been reported. Incorporation of the antagonist in the perlite rooting medium resulted in better control than that obtained when cuttings were dipped in the suspension.

FUSARIUM WILT

Fusarium wilt, caused by *Fusarium oxysporum* f. *dianthi,* has caused greater losses to carnation growers than any other disease. Although it is much more serious in some areas than in others, Fusarium wilt occurs nearly everywhere carnations are grown.

Symptoms. Plants may show symptoms at any stage of development. The first indication of Fusarium wilt is a slow withering of the shoots, often apparent on only one side of the plant. In young plants this results in distortion because the plant tends to curl to one side. The wilting and withering of the roots often is accompanied by a change of color. The normal deep green of the leaves and stems changes first to a lighter gray-green and finally to a pale straw yellow. If the stem of a diseased plant is split, a brown, discolored streak may be seen in the vascular tissues. Such streaks often extend from the roots to the uppermost parts of the stem.

The presence or absence of vascular discoloration in a cutting is not a completely reliable indicator of the presence or absence of *F. oxysporum* f. *dianthi.* If a cut-

A young carnation plant affected by Fusarium wilt. The tendency of an affected plant to curl to one side is typical of this disease.

ting exhibits obvious vascular discoloration, the fungus can be recovered readily in cultures from that cutting. The fungus, however, sometimes can be recovered from cuttings that have no vascular discoloration. The root system remains intact unless the plant has been attacked by one of the root-rotting organisms or the bacterial wilt organism. Symptoms of Fusarium wilt develop most rapidly and become most severe during the high temperatures of summer.

Control. Control of this disease is difficult but far from impossible. The first step is to make certain that the plants from which cuttings are taken are absolutely free of the disease. This is sometimes difficult because symptoms of wilt are usually not much in evidence during the cooler months when cuttings generally are taken.

One of the best ways to obtain healthy cuttings is to establish and maintain disease-free mother blocks. Once such blocks are established, a source of healthy cuttings is always available if reasonable care is taken to avoid recontamination. The problem, of course, is to establish a completely healthy mother block. The most reliable and effective way is to use the cultured-cutting method, which utilizes laboratory culturing techniques to determine if the cuttings are free of the wilt organisms. Growers who have neither time nor facilities for using the cultured-cutting method of obtaining disease-free stock, and who cannot buy cultured-cutting stock from a specialist, can best establish healthy mother blocks by the indexing method. By this method all plants used for propagation purposes are numbered, and complete records are kept so that all cuttings can be traced back to their mother plant. Any line of plants that develops disease is discarded, including the mother plant.

The second step in controlling Fusarium wilt is to eliminate the causal fungus from the propagating benches and from the soil in which the carnations are finally planted. The most satisfactory method is by steam sterilization. Most of the methods that have been substituted for steam sterilization are usually unsatisfactory and should be resorted to only when steam is unavailable.

Year-round indoor culture is the only method for growing the plants in disease-free soil at all times. Many field soils contain the Fusarium wilt organism, as well as other pathogens, especially after carnations have grown there, so growers who use the summer field-culture method must expect to lose part of their plants each year.

To cope successfully with the Fusarium wilt problem the carnation grower should remember these points: (1) *Fusarium oxysporum* f. *dianthi* can live in the soil as well as in the carnation plant; (2) plants may be infected for some time before they show disease symptoms; (3) the fungus can be carried from one crop to the next in the cuttings; (4) a carnation plant can become infected in any stage of its development; (5) control of the disease consists of eliminating the causal fungus from the planting stock as well as from all soil in which plants are grown; (6) after the causal fungus has been eliminated, the grower must be constantly on guard to avoid recontamination.

GREASY BLOTCH

Symptoms. In plants affected with greasy blotch, caused by the fungus *Zygophiala jamaicensis*, the basal leaves lose their glaucous or frosty, waxy bloom and appear greasy or shiny green. The middle leaves have greasy blotches with fibrous extensions radiating from the edges. Yellowish pimples develop in affected areas of stems and leaves. Under moist conditions tiny, thin, black fungus masses (stromata) are formed on the surface.

Control. Since the disease occurs only under conditions of high humidity, control is achieved by eliminating these conditions.

PETAL BLIGHT

Symptoms. Early symptoms of carnation petal blight, caused by the fungus *Stemphylium floridanum,* consist of small cinnamon-colored lesions at the petal margins or wound sites. The lesions enlarge to cover the entire petal and the fungus spreads to adjacent petals. When the fungus sporulates in the older areas of the lesion those areas are a darker brown to black. In advanced stages, the entire flower wilts and shrivels.

Control. Pick off and destroy affected flowers as soon as they are noticed. Reduce the relative humidity in the greenhouse.

PIMPLE

Symptoms. Pimple-like spots, thought to be caused by a form of the bacterium *Xanthomonas oryzae,* sometimes appear on leaves and stems of carnations. The pimples are about 1 millimeter in diameter and appear first near the base of the leaf on the upper surface. More pimples form nearer the tips of the leaves. The pimples make their appearance first on the upper portions of the plant. Leaves of severely infected plants may shrivel.

Control. Use cuttings only from healthy plants. Avoid wetting the leaves when watering the plants.

RHIZOCTONIA STEM ROT

Symptoms. Foliage of plants affected with stem rot, caused by the fungus *Rhizoctonia solani,* gradually becomes pale and wilted. A slimy, wet rot of the bark takes place at the soil line. The fungus passes into the woody tissues to the pith. The rot in the cortex is more or less dry or corky. Sclerotia may be formed in the center portions of the stem.

Control. Growers who practice year-round indoor growing, and who steam sterilize their soil, rarely have trouble with Rhizoctonia stem rot. Terraclor, applied at the rate of 1 pound of 75-percent wettable powder to 800 square feet, is effective in preventing sterilized soil from becoming re-infested with *Rhizoctonia* or in halting the further spread of established infestations.

RUST

Symptoms. Reddish-brown pustules form on the leaves and stems. The pustules are caused by numerous spores of the fungus *Uromyces caryophyllinus,* which form below the epidermis and break through. Individual leaves may be killed by the rust, or entire plants may be injured to the extent that they are unprofitable.

Control. Rust spores require water to germinate; therefore, keeping the foliage

At right, rust pustules on carnation leaves, as seen with the naked eye. Below, a highly magnified cross-section through one of the pustules, showing the ruptured epidermis with the rust spores beneath.

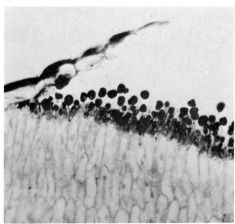

dry is the most important factor in rust control. Examine cuttings to be sure they are free of rust, because conditions in a cutting bench favor its development and spread. In severe outbreaks of rust a fungicide spray of zineb or captan becomes advisable. It may be necessary to spray once a week to stop the spread of the disease.

Drenches containing 20 parts per million Plantvax or Vitavax applied at 10-day intervals have been reported as giving good control of carnation rust. Plantvax at 5 parts per million injected by liquid proportioners into modern feed systems along with nutrient solutions has given excellent control of rust when treatments were started immediately after planting.

SEPTORIA LEAF SPOT

Symptoms. The fungus *Septoria dianthi* produces light-brown spots with purple margins on the leaves and stems, especially on the lower portions of the plant. Small black specks, the fruiting bodies of the fungus, may be seen in the centers of these spots. Individual spots may enlarge or coalesce with other spots, causing death of the tip of the leaf.

Control. Control measures are the same as for Alternaria blight.

VIRUS DISEASES

Symptoms. Four virus diseases are commonly found in commercial carnation ranges. These are mosaic, streak, mottle, and ring spot. Etched ring and latent viruses also may be found. Because the same plants may be carrying more than one of these viruses, the symptoms are not always clearly defined. The virus diseases often are disregarded by commercial growers because the plants rarely are destroyed by these diseases. Losses result from reduced flower production and poor-quality flowers.

Plants affected by streak do not show strong symptoms without the presence of other viruses. With the help of the other viruses, the streak virus produces yellowish or reddish spots and streaks which parallel the leaf veins. These spots are red on dark-colored varieties and yellowish or light pink on the white varieties. On dark-red varieties the outer portions of the spots become purple. Many of the lower leaves on affected plants may become severely spotted, turn yellow, and die. Feeding injury caused by the aphid *Myzus polaris* closely resembles symptoms of streak and the two often are confused.

Control. The mottle and ring-spot viruses are transmitted on the knife used in cutting flowers or in making cuttings. The mosaic virus is transmitted by aphids. Practices such as breaking the cuttings from stock plants instead of using a knife, refraining from trimming the cuttings, controlling insects, and establishing mother blocks from indexed plants, will help control these diseases by interfering with trans-

Color breaking in a carnation flower affected by mosaic. The streaks in the petals are evident before the flower opens.

The two carnation leaves on the right show the mottling that is characteristic of mosaic. The leaf on the left is healthy.

Carnation leaves showing symptoms of streak.

mission of viruses from diseased to healthy plants.

Growers who receive virus-free carnations should keep them in a separate block or preferably in a separate greenhouse. In pinching, disbudding, and cutting, the virus-free block should be handled first. Hands should be scrubbed and tools flamed before moving from a contaminated planting to the virus-free carnations.

The carnation viruses can be eliminated in 2 months by dry heat at 100.4°F. The more heat-tolerant carnations withstand this treatment. Less heat-tolerant varieties survive better if the temperature is dropped to 86°F for about 5 days near the middle of the run, then returned to 100.4°F, with a few extra days added to compensate for the drop in temperature. Short stem tips are taken at the end of the run. These root in a week or less. Approximately another week is required for the carnation tips to grow to sufficient size for indexing. Indexing to detect presence of the mottle virus should be done by a person trained to run this test. Because mottle virus is the most difficult to elimi-

nate, mottle-free carnations are essentially free from other viruses, but visual checks should be made for streak and etched-ring viruses as the carnations grow. Heat-treated carnations should be flowered before release, to be sure no change has occurred.

CHRYSANTHEMUM

The chrysanthemum (*Chrysanthemum morifolium*) is susceptible to a number of diseases that can result in serious losses to growers. With year-round chrysanthemum growing now being generally practiced, recognition and control of diseases becomes more important than ever.

ASCOCHYTA DISEASE

Symptoms. The Ascochyta disease caused by the fungus *Mycosphaerella ligulicola* (*Ascochyta chrysanthemi*), is commonly known as ray blight because of its conspicuousness on the flowers, but it also attacks other parts of the plant. The flower clusters usually are attacked on one side, either in the bud or during various stages of blooming. The affected flowers turn straw color or brownish, cease to develop, and wither, with the discoloration proceeding from the base toward the tip on each flower. If a bud is attacked while still young, no rays develop and the head does not open. If the attack comes later, a portion of the head may develop normally. The disease usually progresses rapidly. The receptacle turns black, and stems may also become black for some distance below the flowers.

In both propagation and flower-production beds the fungus often causes stem cankers. These lesions may start at the cut ends of stems several inches above the soil, some at the point of attachment of leaves decayed by the fungus, or at the base of the cuttings. The cankers are irregular in shape, up to 1 inch long, reddish brown at first, then deep brown to black. Pycnidia and perithecia may develop in the cankers.

Control. The ray blight fungus is difficult to control after it is established. Control is logically through the production and distribution of pathogen-free stock. Commercial cutting production is seriously complicated by the presence of the ray blight fungus. Cuttings produced in an area near which the fungus is developing are almost certain to be infected or infested. Propagation specialists should not be located in an area closely surrounded by commercial chrysanthemum growers. Neither should cuttings be taken from beds or houses where the disease is known to occur.

Stock plants in mother blocks should be sprayed thoroughly every 7 to 14 days with benomyl, ferbam, maneb, or zineb at 1 pound per 100 gallons of water. A suitable spreader must be used to ensure coverage. Cuttings should be dipped in a suspension of benomyl (1 pound Benlate 50W in 100 gallons of water) before sticking them in the rooting bench. The sprays should be continued in the cutting bench, where, if overhead misting is used, the frequency of application must be increased. When cuttings are planted in beds for flower production, ferbam sprays should be continued until the flower buds begin to develop. At that time applications of zineb or captan at one-half to three-fourths pound commercial wettable powder per 100 gallons of water should be started. A suitable wetting agent should be added. Application should be made with a multiple-nozzle boom that delivers a fine mist spray from above so as to protect flowers from the ray blight phase. During wet weather 2 or 3 applications per week may be necessary, and in an epidemic area or season, daily applications may be needed.

BACTERIAL BLIGHT

Symptoms. Bacterial blight, caused by *Erwinia chrysanthemi*, is a relatively new disease. The first evidence of the blight on established plants is the dull, grayish, water-soaked appearance of the stem at a point one-half or two-thirds of the way up to the tip. The affected stem is easily flattened by squeezing with the thumb and fingers. Within a day or two the affected area becomes blackish, and the terminal portion of the stem may wilt and fall over. If conditions remain favorable for the disease, the rotting may progress down the stem. The internal tissues are usually either completely dissolved, or partially digested and converted into a jellylike mass. In some instances the stem may split open; in other cases reddish-brown, sticky drops may exude from the infected tissues. Part or all of the water-conducting tissues just beneath the bark are reddish brown down to the root zone.

Although the first evidence of rot on older plants is usually well up on the stem, it is not uncommon to find infection developing first at the base of the plant. When such plants are not definitely blighted they remain stunted and are slow to mature. Often the tissues first start to rot back from the point where the tip has been pinched out. The roots of affected plants usually are not conspicuously rotted, although in some cases the rotting may be extensive.

The degree of damage to an individual plant depends upon the variety and upon environmental conditions. Often only one branch of the plant is affected, the other branch or branches remaining apparently healthy and flowering normally. Frequently the obvious rot may be confined to the upper part of the stem, and apparently healthy shoots will break from the base and produce normal flowers.

Cuttings infected with blight may show a slight brown to black rotting at the base. The pith tissues in the center of the stem may be partially rotted and reddish brown in color. Often the pith is completely dissolved, leaving the base of the stem hollow. If the outer bark is peeled back, reddish streaks sometimes are seen in the stem. Infected cuttings occasionally root and develop into apparently normal plants but more often they wilt and die.

Control. Since plants can be infected and yet show no symptoms, diseased cuttings may unknowingly be taken from such plants, thereby spreading the disease from one location to another. Thus, the most important step in control of bacterial blight lies in guarding against carry-over in cuttings. Soil should be sterilized before being planted with chrysanthemums. In pinching, taking cuttings, or picking blooms, the stems should be snapped off and not cut with a knife or the fingernails. If cuttings are to be dipped in a root-promoting solution, the solution should contain a bacteria-destroying additive such as streptomycin, which has shown much promise for this purpose.

Since bacterial blight is extremely responsive to environmental conditions, much can be done to control the disease by regulating temperature and humidity. Serious development of blight in an infected plant depends upon high temperature and high humidity. Cultural factors that favor lush growth — heavy nitrogen fertilization, high soil moisture, and prolonged high humidity — favor development of blight.

BACTERIAL LEAF SPOT

Symptoms. The leaf spot, caused by the bacterium *Pseudomonas cichorii,* is usually found on the lower, older leaves first but eventually the top leaves and flower buds may be blighted as the plant matures. In new plantings the disease often appears 4 to 5 weeks after planting. The spots are more or less circular to elliptical at first, and only a few millimeters in diameter but later may increase in size to approximately 1 centimeter. Several lesions may coalesce to form large, irregular necrotic areas on the leaf. The lesions are dark brown to black. When moist the spots are soft and mushy, but when dry they are slightly sunken and brittle, and show characteristic zonations. Often the centers of the spots fall away and leave areas that resemble those eaten by certain insects. A clear line of demarcation, without yellowing, separates diseased from healthy tissue.

Occasionally leaf infections spread down the petiole and cause a dark-brown to black stem necrosis which results in a blighting of the parts above. If the disease is not controlled on the foliage, flower bud infections often result. The buds turn dark brown to black, and the necrosis usually extends down the stem for 1 to 2 inches. Affected buds wither and die prematurely.

Control. Weekly sprays of Tribasic copper sulfate at 4 pounds in 100 gallons of water or Agri-mycin 500 at 3 pounds in 100 gallons have given good control.

BOTRYTIS BLIGHT

Symptoms. Botrytis blight, caused by the fungus *Botrytis cinerea,* first appears on the

Early stage of Botrytis blight on chrysanthemum flower. The rot may eventually involve the entire flower.

petals as small, water-soaked, brown spots that enlarge rapidly. The tips of unfolding flowers are attacked first in many instances. The entire blossoms and some of the leaves may become covered with a grayish mold.

Control. To keep Botrytis blight under control, avoid excessive humidity, and allow generous space between plants and good ventilation in the greenhouse. Mist-spray the buds and blooms with zineb or captan 2 or 3 times a week during periods of high humidity or abundant condensation. High levels of nitrogen increase the susceptibility to infection by *B. cinerea*.

FUSARIUM FLOWER AND BUD ROT

Symptoms. The fungus *Fusarium tricinctum* f. *poae* causes a brown to brownish-black dry decay of the petals. Often a sparse, cottony fungus growth can be found between the petals. The sepals and receptacles are not affected. Some infected flowers have a rot of the central floral parts which are distorted because of an uneven distribution of outer expanded petals. Severity of damage depends on the stage of flower development when infection occurs. Petal tissues of flower buds may be completely rotted and killed if infection occurs before petal expansion starts. Distorted flowers with dead centers result when buds become infected after petals start to expand. Infection at still later stages of flower expansion results in rot of the flower center, but there is near normal development of the outer petals.

Control. Mist-spray the buds and blooms with captan at weekly intervals.

FUSARIUM WILT AND STEM ROT

Symptoms. Fusarium wilt of chrysanthemums is caused by two races of *Fusarium oxysporum,* each of which attacks specific chrysanthemum varieties. Disease development depends on the chrysanthemum variety, the race of *Fusarium* present, and environmental factors such as temperature, nitrogen nutrition, and soil reaction. When conditions for disease development are optimum, the first symptom is chlorosis or yellowing of one or more leaves on one side of the stem tip. There

may be a slight to pronounced cupping and curvature of the chlorotic leaves. The stem often curves toward the affected side of the plant, especially if one side of the vascular system happens to be more affected than the other. This is common on young, rapidly growing, susceptible plants.

As the disease progresses, chlorosis of the affected leaves becomes more general and severely affected leaves wilt. Wilting leaves occur initially on the most severely affected side of the plant, but as the disease progresses the entire plant wilts and dies.

Symptoms on the more resistant varieties include leaf chlorosis, stem necrosis, stunting of the leaves, and reduced rate of plant growth. These symptoms may be so mild that they resemble a nutritional disorder, or they may be so severe that death of the plant follows extended periods of leaf chlorosis and stem necrosis. Black necrosis of the stem sometimes extends from the roots into the upper parts of the stem. In some instances this black necrosis occurs only in the upper part of the stem and has no externally visible connection with the base or tip of the plant. This black streak symptom is easily confused with Pythium root and stem rot.

Vascular discoloration always occurs in the stems when there are leaf symptoms. It also occurs in the leaves of some varieties. In the stem, various intensities of brown to reddish-brown discoloration are associated with the portion of the vascular system leading to affected leaves.

Externally visible vascular discoloration in leaf veins occurs on some varieties but is uncommon.

Disease development is extremely dependent on temperature. Severe symptoms develop at constant temperatures of 80° and 90°F. They are mild at 70°F and absent at 60°F and below.

High nitrogen nutrition tends to make chrysanthemums more susceptible to this disease.

Control. The control measures recommended for Verticillium wilt (pages 53 and 54) will also control Fusarium wilt and stem rot. Benomyl drenched on potted chrysanthemums grown on a high-lime all-nitrate nitrogen cultural regime has been reported to provide complete control of Fusarium wilt in a highly susceptible variety.

The Fusarium wilt pathogens of chrysanthemum may be disseminated on plants, stems, leaves, and cuttings irrespective of the presence of foliage symptoms or vascular discoloration.

LEAF SPOTS

Symptoms. Leaf spots are caused by the fungi *Septoria chrysanthemi, S. leucanthemi,* and *Cylindrosporium chrysanthemi. Septoria* produces small, dark-brown spots that gradually increase in size until they coalesce or unite. Numerous tiny, black fruiting bodies of the fungus are usually visible in the infected parts. The affected leaves drop off prematurely.

Cylindrosporium leaf spot is characterized by the appearance of dark blotches ½ to ¾ inch in diameter. Infected leaves soon die and shrivel, but cling to the stem. The lower leaves are usually affected first.

Control. Dip cuttings in ferbam suspension (2 tablespoonfuls to a gallon of water) before sticking them in the sand. Dip them again, roots and all, just before planting out.

Spray plants with ferbam, captan, or zineb (1 ounce to 4 gallons of water) several times during the growing season. Pick off and burn diseased foliage. Avoid high humidities and splashing water.

PYTHIUM ROOT ROT AND STEM ROT

Symptoms. Several species of *Pythium, P. aphanidermatum, P. carolinianum, P. polytylum,* and *P. spinosum,* have been reported as causing root and stem rot of chrysanthemums. Infections are characterized by dark-brown to black lesions at the soil level. In advanced stages of the disease, lesions may extend to the top of the plant and involve the main stems, lateral branches, and leaf petioles. Red coloration of the cortical tissues frequently occurs in advance of the lesions. Root rot commonly precedes or accompanies stem symptoms when the disease is initiated below ground. Severe wilting accompanies necrosis except where lesions are restricted to one side of the stem, or when new roots are formed from noninvaded stem tissue above arrested, below-ground infections.

Control. Several materials have been used successfully to control this disease. A mixture of thiram and captan applied to the soil before setting either rooted or unrooted cuttings or immediately after the cuttings have been set, followed by 1 to 5 weekly applications, has given good control. The fungicide mixture may be applied in conjunction with a liquid fertilizer application or during normal irrigation procedures.

Truban is an effective fungicide for the control of Pythium disease on chrysanthemums. Either the wettable powder or the emulsifiable concentrate formulations may

Septoria leaf spot of chrysanthemum. As the spots enlarge and coalesce the leaf tissue withers and dies, giving the leaf a ragged appearance.

be mixed with water and applied to the soil as a drench.

Dexon, when mixed with soil at 45 parts per million active ingredient will control the disease. The chemical is not toxic to chrysanthemums at this level.

POWDERY MILDEW

Symptoms. The fungus *Erysiphe cichoracearum* covers the leaves with a white powdery growth. In severe infections the leaves may be deformed and stunted.

Control. Watering so as to keep the foliage dry, and ventilation to keep the humidity down, will aid in preventing this disease in greenhouses. If the disease gets a start, dust the plants with dusting sulfur, or spray with wettable sulfur (1½ pounds in 100 gallons of water) or benomyl.

RUST

Symptoms. Rust, caused by the fungus *Puccinia chrysanthemi,* is characterized by the appearance of small blisters about the size of a pinhead on the underside of the leaves. The blisters also appear to some extent on the upper surface. These soon break open and expose a dark-brown, powdery mass of spores.

Control. Remove diseased leaves from the plants as soon as noticed and burn

A healthy chrysanthemum leaf and a leaf that is covered with the white, powdery growth that is characteristic of mildew.

Below, chrysanthemum rust pustules on underside of leaves at left and right, and upper side of leaf in center. The small, light-colored spots on the leaf at right are new infections.

them. Keep the tops of the plants dry. Dusting with sulfur or spraying with zineb (1 ounce to 4 gallons of water) is advisable if the plants become generally infected. Infected plants should be avoided when taking cuttings.

STEM ROT

Symptoms. The fungus *Rhizoctonia solani* may cause stem rot in young plants. The stem turns dark at the soil level and soon the entire stem is girdled and the plant turns yellow and dies.

Control. A thiram-captan drench applied to the soil immediately after the plants have been set has given excellent control of this disease.

STUNT

Symptoms. The symptoms of the virus disease known as stunt vary greatly among different chrysanthemum varieties. The most common effects are reductions in size of plant, leaves, and flowers. These differ-

Chrysanthemum stunt (center plant) with normal plants of the same age on either side. Differences between normal and stunted plants are not always this great.

ences are best recognized when healthy and diseased plants of the same age are grown side by side. In many varieties stunt cannot be diagnosed with assurance without a normal plant for comparison. The bronze or red flowers on diseased plants of some varieties are bleached to lighter shades. Diseased plants commonly bloom earlier than normal plants of the same variety.

Specific leaf symptoms accompany stunt in some varieties. The leaves of normal Rusticon variety are large, with segments arched so as to produce a ruffled effect, whereas in diseased plants the leaves are not only smaller, but nearly flat. Lower leaves of diseased Indianapolis varieties curl upward sharply at the margins, while only a trace of such curling appears in normal plants. Small, round, pale, diffuse spots near the margins of the leaves characterize stunt in Vibrant and some other varieties. In Blazing Gold, the leaves of infected plants have diffuse yellowish bands along the veins.

The most striking leaf symptoms of stunt are the crinkle found in Blanche and Yellow Garza, and the measles pattern in the Mistletoe varieties. On crinkled plants, the leaves are smaller than on healthy plants, their surfaces are wavy or crumpled, and at the crumpled areas there are irregular, yellowish-green patches. When Mistletoe varieties are affected by stunt the leaves are sprinkled with bright-yellow, roughly circular spots, up to one-fourth inch across in summer but much smaller in winter.

Leaf symptoms may be useful for recognizing stunt when mums are in vegetative condition. However, some chrysanthemum varieties can carry the stunt virus without showing distinct symptoms and perhaps without showing symptoms of any kind.

Control. The only method of controlling stunt is the reselection of healthy stock with suitable precautions against further contamination.

In commercial operations, cuttings from diseased plants represent the chief means of perpetuating stunt. The virus is transmitted by the knife used in taking cuttings, the hands in making the soft pinch, and the shears used in cutting flowers. The virus invades all parts of the affected plant except the seeds. Thus crop residues may serve as a source of contamination, and soil should be steamed before being replanted with chrysanthemums.

Specialists in the production of chrysanthemum cuttings have developed effective indexing methods for eliminating stunt from their propagating stock. These methods also have generally eliminated the other virus diseases from their stocks. Usually it will be advantageous for the commercial grower to purchase cuttings from one of these specialists rather than do his own propagating.

VERTICILLIUM WILT

Symptoms. The fungus *Verticillium albo-atrum* produces two kinds of symptoms in chrysanthemum plants. In some cases a general wilting of the plants occurs. The leaves become paler green, then turn brown and die, but remain attached to the stem. In severe cases all foliage wilts and the plants die before the blossom buds open.

In some cases general wilting does not occur. The first symptoms appear on the lower leaves, with the areas between the veins turning pale or yellowish green and finally brown. Brown areas appear on the petioles soon after the symptoms first appear on the leaves. Infection may vary in severity from a condition in which only a few of the lower leaves are affected, to the extreme in which all the leaves are killed and the blossoms turn brown and die.

Infected plants are stunted and the flowers are reduced in size. In severe cases the petals turn brown and die.

Control. Verticillium wilt is transmitted from one crop to the next in two ways. The fungus may be carried in the cuttings taken from diseased plants, or the plants may be attacked by the fungus harbored in the soil. The best safeguard against disease-carrying cuttings is the purchase of disease-free cuttings produced from cultured stock.

Verticillium wilt of chrysanthemum. The plant at left shows typical killing of lower leaves of the older flower stalk from the base upward, and development of a number of apparently healthy basal shoots. The center plant shows similar symptoms plus stunting. The plant at right was killed before flowering.

The fungus can be eliminated from the soil by steaming. All soil in which chrysanthemums are to be planted should be steamed if facilities are available. *V. albo-atrum* has been found in virgin soil. It persists in the soil for an unknown period of time and attacks over 100 kinds of plants including tomato, potato, strawberry, rose, dahlia, snapdragon, and many kinds of trees and shrubs. Certain weeds, especially members of the nightshade family, are also hosts.

In chrysanthemums grown out-of-doors in soil that cannot be steam sterilized, effective control of Verticillium wilt may be achieved by soil fumigation. Chloropicrin, or tear gas, is the most effective fumigant known at the present time. For best results the soil should be loose and friable at the time of application. Rototilling should be done several days in advance of fumigation to allow the soil to settle. Large clods must be broken up and all large roots removed. The soil mixture should be about the same as for planting. Do not treat when the soil is wet and cold.

Chloropicrin should be applied at the rate of 3 milliliters per injection on a 12-inch staggered spacing to a depth of 6 inches. Immediately after the chloropicrin is applied, each hole should be closed and a water seal applied. A light sprinkling sufficient to wet the soil to a depth of one-half inch is an adequate water seal. Usually it will be safe to plant 2 weeks after fumigation, provided the soil is cultivated a day or two before planting.

Do not apply chloropicrin in a closed area near growing plants. Do not apply chloropicrin during windy periods, because the gas will escape from the soil too rapidly for effective fumigation. A plastic cover may be used to retain the gas when the use of a water seal is inconvenient. Avoid contaminating a fumigated area with diseased plants, nonfumigated infested soil, or dirty tools.

Good control of Verticillium wilt has been obtained by treating the planting site with Vapam at the rate of 1 gallon per 800 square feet.

Benlate 50W applied at the rate of 1 pound per 1,000 square feet of chrysanthemum bed has given good control of Verticillium wilt. The fungicide suspended in water can be drenched over established 4-week-old plants with a garden sprinkler can.

Chrysanthemum plants can be immunized against infection by *V. albo-atrum*

by thoroughly spraying or dipping in benomyl suspensions (4 pounds Benlate 50W in 100 gallons of water). The plants must be treated within 4 weeks of being planted into infested soil.

Many varieties of chrysanthemums are resistant to Verticillium wilt and are recommended whenever possible.

YELLOWS

Symptoms. The aster yellows organism produces several symptoms in chrysanthemums, green flowers being the most distinctive. Instead of being the normal color for the variety, the flower is a sickly green, although the entire flower may not show the green color. The same plant may produce both normal-colored and green blossoms.

The foliage of badly diseased plants is affected in varying degrees. Sometimes the lateral shoots on flowering stems are weak, pale, and upright. Thin, weak basal shoots bearing very small leaves often develop in large numbers. Affected plants of many hardy outdoor varieties may die within a year, but some will survive and show well-defined symptoms for several years.

Control. All plants showing symptoms of yellows should be destroyed as soon as noticed. Since the causal agent is spread by leafhoppers, sprays to reduce leafhopper populations are advisable.

OTHER VIRUS DISEASES

Several other virus diseases of chrysanthemums are known, but the symptoms vary greatly among different varieties.

Tomato spotted-wilt virus produces ring and line patterns, pale areas, mottling, and necrotic spots in the leaves. Symptoms are not well defined, but are more pronounced in young plants than in older ones.

Blanche or Good News mosaic virus produces no symptoms in the Blanche variety, but produces typical mosaic symptoms in Mistletoe and Good News varieties. In Mistletoe, symptoms range from veinclearing, mottling, and leaf-dwarfing to leaf- and bud-blasting and dark-colored blighting of young stems.

Ivory Sea Gull mosaic virus causes no symptoms in the Ivory Sea Gull source variety, but produces yellow veinbanding and marked crinkling and dwarfing of leaves in the Blazing Gold variety.

Tomato aspermy virus typically produces no symptoms in chrysanthemum leaves but causes an irregular curling or waviness of the ray florets, with flowers 10 to 15 percent smaller than normal ones.

The chlorotic mottle virus produces mild mottling or variegation of the young leaves and occasional distinct chlorotic spotting. General chlorosis of new leaves often follows mottling of early-formed leaves. Dwarfing of leaves, flowers, and the entire plant may occur and there is a delay in development of blossoms. Symptoms vary at any given time and from time to time. Plants may at one time be chlorotic, later appear to recover, then again exhibit severe symptoms.

The flower-distortion virus produces no distinctive leaf symptoms but causes extreme dwarfing and distortion of the flowers of some varieties. Ray flowers are shorter and narrower than normal and are incurved or irregularly curled.

Control. Control of these virus diseases is largely the responsibility of the propagation specialist. In commercial plantings, all plants showing symptoms of any of these diseases should be removed and destroyed promptly.

CINERARIA

The florist's cineraria, *Senecio cruentus,* is relatively free of serious diseases but occasionally the two virus diseases, mosaic and streak, are responsible for many unsalable plants.

MOSAIC

Symptoms. The foliage of plants affected by mosaic is mottled with irregular, light- and dark-green areas. Crinkling, ruffling, and dwarfing of leaves, shortening of leaf petioles, and dwarfing of plants commonly occur.

STREAK

Symptoms. Roughening and curling of leaves of young plants are the first evidences of streak. Reddish-brown areas in

Cineraria leaves with mosaic symptoms. (Photograph courtesy of Washington State University.)

leaf veins, petioles, and stalks of middle-aged plants may be observed when strong light is transmitted through those areas. These areas may enlarge and constrict the affected tissue, causing death of large triangular areas in the leaves, or death of entire leaves or the whole plant. Wilting, rolling, yellowing, and death of leaves commonly occur as the affected plants approach blooming.

Under some conditions, numerous small, brown, necrotic spots on the leaves are associated with the disease. The necrosis often develops to the extent that most of the leaves die progressively up the stem, and few leaves are left on the plant at blooming time. Affected plants wilt more easily than healthy plants and do not recover from wilting as readily.

When streak and mosaic occur in the same plant, a combination of symptoms appears. These plants are more severely

Rolling, wilting, and death of cineraria leaves following inoculation with the streak virus. (Photograph courtesy of Washington State University.)

The cineraria leaf at left below shows the scattered, brown, necrotic spots associated with streak; the leaf at right shows the mild mottling caused by the mosaic virus. (Photograph courtesy of Washington State University.)

dwarfed than are plants affected with either disease alone. Necrosis often appears in the light areas of the mosaic pattern in the middle-aged leaves, and in the older leaves before yellowing.

Control. Mosaic and streak diseases are transmitted in seed; thus great care in selecting disease-free plants for seed production is of utmost importance. Control of aphids and thrips is also important because mosaic is transmitted by aphids, and streak is transmitted by thrips. Handling diseased plants previous to working with healthy plants should be avoided. It is best to discard diseased plants as soon as they are noticed.

CLEMATIS

Clematis (*Clematis* spp.) is affected by a leaf-spot and stem-rot disease caused by the fungus *Ascochyta clematidina.*

LEAF SPOT AND STEM ROT

Symptoms. Leaf-spot and stem-rot disease appears differently on the various clematis species and hybrids and under different growing conditions. On hybrids grown in the field it is primarily a stem rot, while in the greenhouse, where cuttings are propagated, it is a leaf spot as well as a stem rot.

The leaf spot first appears as a mere dot or as a water-soaked area. On drying, the water-soaked spot becomes tan with a red margin. The causal fungus may grow down the petiole to the stem. Reddish lesions are formed on the stem and in time the stem may be girdled. Older spots become gray, and pycnidia of the fungus develop in these spots. The downward progress of the fungus ultimately kills the plant if the diseased tissue is not removed.

Control. Matting of the vines produces a condition most favorable for spread of the disease. Ventilation by supporting the vines or planting them far enough apart to prevent matting will aid in checking leaf spot and stem rot. Spraying with a sulfur fungicide checks the disease. Removing diseased leaves and vines before spraying is of practical value. Select cuttings from disease-free plants and grow young stock in new beds.

Coleus mosaic. The infected, stunted plant at the left with crinkled, distorted, and mottled leaves is the same age as the healthy plant shown at right.

COLEUS

The only disease that seriously affects commercial production of coleus (*Coleus blumei*) is the virus disease known as mosaic, shown below and on page 57.

MOSAIC

Symptoms. The most striking symptoms of coleus mosaic are those connected with changes in foliage color. Since there are so many varieties of coleus, each with its own color pattern, the color changes resulting from coleus mosaic differ among varieties and often are overlooked or unrecognized.

Mottling, splotches, ring spots, oak-leaf patterns, and other abnormal markings are formed on the leaves. Affected leaves are often puckered, asymmetric, and rugose or wrinkled. Puckering and crinkling are often associated with the oak-leaf markings, large ring spots, and other strongly marked patterns. Affected leaves frequently are stunted, and occasionally branches are stunted. Entire plants are sometimes stunted and distorted. If diseased stock is used for propagation, the symptoms become more pronounced with each succeeding propagation.

Control. Discard diseased plants and select healthy plants for making coleus cuttings.

COLUMBINE

Like many other kinds of plants, columbine (*Aquilegia* spp.) is affected by crown rot or wilt caused by the fungus *Sclerotinia sclerotiorum*.

Coleus leaves showing various markings caused by mosaic; a healthy leaf is shown at top.

CROWN ROT OR WILT

Symptoms. Crown rot or wilt is characterized by general wilting of the leaflets and tender shoots, accompanied by a slow drying of the affected branches. Usually the disease progresses slowly, affecting one by one the main branches of the plant. Close examination of newly infected plants shows the presence of a web of white fungus strands on the diseased stems. The interior of an infected stem is usually filled with white fungus threads and numerous small, dark, hard bodies. These are resting bodies, or sclerotia of the fungus.

Control. Keeping the soil well cultivated around the crown so that it will dry rapidly helps to prevent the disease. Replacing the heavy top soil with sand is a good practice. Remove and destroy badly diseased clumps. Also, remove the old soil and replace with new soil before setting other plants in the vacant spot. Treating the soil with Terraclor should be helpful in retarding growth of the fungus.

COSMOS

Cosmos (*Cosmos bipinnatus*) is relatively free of serious diseases but is subject to a few diseases that become troublesome occasionally.

BACTERIAL WILT

Symptoms. Bacterial wilt, caused by *Pseudomonas solanacearum,* is characterized by sudden wilting and collapse of the plants. The plants usually dry up in a few days with many leaves still attached.

Control. Destroy all affected plants as soon as noticed. The causal organism overwinters in the soil, so cosmos should not be replanted where the disease has occurred.

LEAF SPOTS

Symptoms. Dead areas develop on the leaves as a result of attacks by the fungi *Cercospora* sp. and *Septoria* sp.

Control. Control measures are seldom necessary. Spraying with a good foliage fungicide may be helpful.

POWDERY MILDEW

Symptoms. A grayish-white growth of the fungus *Erysiphe cichoracearum* develops on the leaves and small branches.

Control. Because the disease usually does not appear until late in the growing season, control measures are seldom necessary. The plants may be sprayed with wettable sulfur, Karathane, or Acti-dione PM.

STEM BLIGHT OR CANKER

Symptoms. Stem blight or canker, caused by the fungus *Diaporthe stewartii,* is a disease of mature cosmos plants. The point of attack may be anywhere on the stems or branches but never on other parts of the plant. Brown spots appear on the green stem and enlarge until they nearly or completely encircle the stem. Stem sections several inches long may be affected. The parts above the diseased area wilt suddenly and die. As the diseased areas become older they change from brown to ash gray. The diseased section of the stem is hollow, while the parts above and below the lesions are nearly or quite solid. This causes the affected stems to break over easily.

Control. Remove and destroy diseased plants. Burn all plant parts in the fall.

CYCLAMEN

Because of the substantial investment in time and labor required to produce a finished crop of cyclamen plants (*Cyclamen persicum*), disease control is extremely important if a profit is to be realized. Although the number of diseases affecting this crop is comparatively small, some of the diseases are quite devastating.

BOTRYTIS BLIGHT OR GRAY-MOLD DISEASE

Symptoms. Under conditions of continued high humidity, the fungus *Botrytis cinerea* causes a soft decay of flowers and leaves. The affected parts soon are covered with a downy gray mold and later dry and become gray-brown.

Control. The disease is quickly checked if the relative humidity is reduced below

85 percent. The humidity may be controlled by heating and ventilating to reduce moisture as well as to control temperature. Give plants adequate space to improve aeration and reduce humidity. Spraying with Botran, Bravo, or benomyl may be beneficial.

FUSARIUM WILT

Symptoms. Symptoms of wilt caused by *Fusarium oxysporum* f. *cyclaminis* occur on roots, corms, and aerial parts of diseased seedlings. On young plants with 2 to 6 leaves, the first visible symptom is a color change from normal green to vivid yellow in the leaf blades. Usually the discoloration begins at the base of the blade as a small, sharply defined area adjacent to the point of attachment of the petiole. This discoloration may enlarge vertically and horizontally until only a narrow band of normal tissue remains along the periphery. Eventually the entire blade may turn yellow, although it remains turgid. Often, instead of basal color change, one or more yellow, irregular-shaped spots may develop on any part of the blade or along its edge. Later these spots may enlarge and coalesce.

Internal vascular discoloration occurs in the young roots. At first there is no visible change in the color or condition of the root system, but as the disease progresses, some roots may turn brown to brownish black.

In the corms of young affected plants, the vascular bundles which are sufficiently close together to form closed rings are brown to brownish black. As the corms enlarge these symptoms become more intensified.

In commercial practice, no symptoms of the disease may be seen until the flowering, or mature, stage of growth. Then plants develop sudden wilting and they never recover. The leaves and flowers wither and the plant dies.

Control. Seed should be planted in sterilized soil. When the seedlings are transferred to pots they should be planted in sterilized soil.

LEAF SPOTS

Symptoms. Dead spots on the leaves may be caused by the fungi *Glomerella cingulata*, *Phyllosticta* sp., and *Ramularia cyclaminicola*. In severe cases partial defoliation may result.

Cyclamen leaf spot. The plant on the left is being defoliated by a severe attack; a healthy plant is on the right.

A leaf infected with cyclamen leaf spot.

Control. Remove and destroy all infected leaves. Humidity should be kept no higher than necessary to produce good plant growth. Spray the young plants with ferbam at 2- to 3-week intervals, or turn potted plants upside down and dip them in the ferbam suspension.

PETAL SPOT

Symptoms. *Botrytis cinerea* causes a petal-spot disease in addition to the gray mold described above. It is not known whether this disease is caused by a different strain of the fungus, or whether the difference in the two diseases is the result of different environmental conditions.

The petal spots are small, round to oval, few to many, and scattered at random between the veins of the petal. On pink, red, and salmon-colored varieties, the spots consist of an outer band of living tissue of a deeper color than the normal color of the petal, and a very small center which at first is normal in color but soon becomes water-soaked, and finally tan and necrotic. On white-flowering varieties, the outer band of the spot first appears water-soaked while the center is necrotic; later the entire spot becomes necrotic. When heavily spotted, petals may be distorted.

Leaf infection may occur occasionally in conjunction with petal spot, but it is generally confined to older leaves and is of minor importance.

Left, wilted cyclamen plant affected by soft rot. Sectioned corm of a diseased plant is shown at right. The rot has invaded the tissues at the top of the corm and is progressing through the corm. The roots are free of rot.

Control. This disease can be controlled by adjusting heat and ventilation to reduce the relative humidity, especially during the evening hours. All flowers with spotted petals should be removed promptly and destroyed.

SOFT ROT

Symptoms. Soft rot, caused by the bacterium *Erwinia carotovora,* is probably the most common and most destructive disease affecting cyclamen. Often the first visible symptom is a sudden wilting and collapse of the plant. In such plants, portions of the corms usually have broken down into a soft, slimy mass although the roots may remain intact. In some instances individual leaf petioles and flower stems become affected by a soft, slimy rot and soon wilt and droop. Such plants may become stunted and unsightly from loss of leaves. The rot progresses most rapidly during the high temperatures of summer.

Control. Use extreme care when watering because the causal bacteria may be spread from plant to plant by splashing water. Affected plants should be removed and destroyed as soon as they are detected. The plants should be spaced so there will be good air circulation around them. All soil, flats, and pots should be sterilized before being used to grow cyclamen.

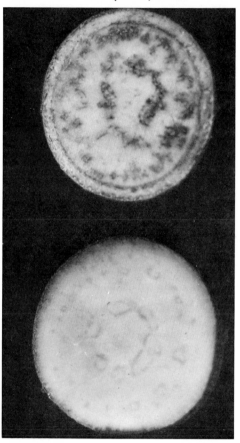

Cross section of a diseased cyclamen corm (top) showing the dark spots typical of the stunt disease. A healthy corm, below.

Cyclamen stunt. A diseased plant is at left, a healthy plant at right. Flowers open below the leaves on diseased plants.

STUNT

Symptoms. Plants infected with the fungus *Ramularia cyclaminicola* are conspicuously stunted but not quickly killed. Leaves are small and may be yellow. The petioles and flower stalks are shorter than normal and the flowers characteristically open below the leaves. Reddish-brown, necrotic areas occur in the tissues of the corm. These areas are particularly evident at the crown but also extend for short distances into the petioles, peduncles, and large roots.

A leaf disease and a wilt sometimes are produced by the same fungus that causes stunt. Brown, irregular areas of varying size and with indefinite margins are produced on the leaves. Severe wilting and yellowing of the basal leaves may occur. Many or all of the flowers and upper leaves may wilt also.

Control. Seed from healthy plants should be planted in sterilized soil. Seedlings should not be grown near old, infected plants. Spraying young plants with a fungicide such as ferbam may be helpful, especially if the leaf disease phase is prevalent.

DAHLIA

Dahlias (*Dahlia* spp.) are affected by a number of diseases caused by fungi, bacteria, and viruses.

BACTERIAL STEM ROT

Symptoms. Bacterial stem rot, caused by *Erwinia cytolytica*, is externally recognizable as a blackening and softening of the stem. When cut lengthwise, stems show a moist and advanced decay of the layer of pith that lines the hollow stem. The decay extends into the cortex, which becomes blackened. The decay generally starts at the crown, and may or may not progress into the tuber. The rot is accompanied by a foul odor.

Control. Remove and destroy affected plants promptly. Do not plant dahlias where the disease recently has occurred.

BACTERIAL WILT

Symptoms. Bacterial wilt, caused by *Pseudomonas solanacearum*, has symptoms similar to those caused by *Verticillium* and *Fusarium*. The causal bacterium produces a soft, wet rot within the stem, and a browning of the vascular system which shows a yellow-orange bacterial ooze when cut.

Control. In general the control measures given for Verticillium and Fusarium wilts should be used for bacterial wilt, but soil treatments may not be as effective against bacterial wilt.

BOTRYTIS BLIGHT

Symptoms. Blight, caused by the fungus *Botrytis cinerea*, can be identified by the gray masses of spores that form in abundance on dark-gray or brown spots appearing on affected buds, leaves, or stems. The open flowers are especially subject to attack when atmospheric humidity is high for prolonged periods. The causal fungus develops rapidly on the old, fading, and falling petals, and spreads to other portions of the plant. Buds in various stages of development may be attacked. An attack may result in a soft rot in unseasonably wet weather; under less humid conditions it may produce injury that causes blasting, or various degrees of bud distortion.

Control. Remove and destroy all faded flowers. Spray the plants with Botran, Bravo or benomyl. In normal seasons, little or no spraying may be necessary. In wet seasons, repeated spraying may be needed to keep the disease in check. Destroy all old, above-ground parts of dahlia plants in the fall or early spring.

HOPPERBURN

Symptoms. Hopperburn, an insect injury caused by the leafhopper *Empoasca fabae*, is sometimes confused with stunt or mosaic because stunt is also a symptom of this condition. The leaves turn yellow and then brown along the edges, and the central green area becomes puckered because it continues to grow after the edges of the leaf are dead. The stunted plants start to grow again after the leafhoppers have been eliminated, whereas plants affected by mosaic never grow properly.

Control. The insects may be controlled by spraying with malathion.

LEAF SPOTS

Symptoms. Leaf spots, caused by the fungi *Phyllosticta dahliaecola* and *Cercospora* sp., may appear at any time during the growing season but usually are not seen until late summer.

Control. Leaf spots usually are not serious enough to warrant control measures. Bordeaux mixture or some other foliage spray may be used to protect the plants. Gathering and burning all above-ground plant parts in the fall will aid in holding these diseases in check.

MOSAIC, STUNT, OR DWARF

Symptoms. The most consistent evidence of mosaic, a virus-caused infection, is the occurrence of pale-green bands of tissue along the midribs and larger secondary veins of the leaves. The chlorotic tissue may be clear yellow and easily recognized, or pale green and not readily distinguished without close examination. Some varieties show little if any evidence of chlorosis along the veins, so absence of this symptom is no proof that the plant is healthy. Mosaic-affected plants usually are dwarfed and tend to produce lateral shoots that are much shortened, resulting in a bushy plant.

Plants that show dwarfing should be examined carefully for evidence of veinclearing symptoms. These two characteristics, dwarfing and veinclearing, constitute the most important visible evidence of mosaic infection. The tubers of stunted plants frequently are thickened and much shorter than those of normal plants. The mosaic virus is spread from plant to plant by *Myzus persicae*, a species of aphid.

Control. Remove and destroy infected plants as soon as noticed. Discard tubers from infected plants. If there is any question of accurate diagnosis of this disease, plant the tubers from suspected plants in an isolation plot away from the main planting. If the disease appears on these plants the following year they should be destroyed.

POWDERY MILDEW

Symptoms. *Erysiphe cichoracearum*, the causal fungus of powdery mildew, grows over the surface of the leaf, forming a cobwebby mat of delicate threads or hyphae. The summer spore stage of the fungus is seen as white powdery masses on the leaf surface. More or less defoliation may occur, depending upon the severity of the attack. Late in the season the overwintering form of the fungus is seen as small, brown to black specks entangled in the webs of hyphae.

Control. Spray with wettable sulfur, Karathane, or Acti-dione PM when mildew first appears, and repeat every 7 to 10

Mottling and veinclearing are the most consistent symptoms of mosaic in dahlia leaves, although yellowing along the veins is not seen in diseased plants of some varieties. Mosaic-affected plants are usually dwarfed.

days thereafter until the end of the growing season.

RING SPOT OR SPOTTED WILT

Symptoms. This virus disease is characterized by conspicuous rings of light-green
or yellow tissues in the leaves. In the beginning the spots, which later develop a
ring pattern, appear as scattered areas of
yellow or light-green tissue. They usually
are seen on the older leaves. As the spots
age, the ring pattern appears and may become decidedly conspicuous. The old spots
may be brown and include a number of
rings. Affected plants apparently are not
noticeably dwarfed.

Control. In general, control measures
are the same as for mosaic. Spotted-wilt
virus has been eliminated from severely
infected plants by rooting small stem-tip
cuttings. Plants developed from such cuttings are free of the virus.

STEM ROT

Symptoms. Plants infected with the fungus *Sclerotinia sclerotiorum* wilt and die
suddenly. This disease may be distinguished
from the true wilt diseases by the more
sudden wilting and death caused by the
stem-rot fungus. Water-soaked areas or
cankers are formed on the stems near the
soil level. The stem may be completely
girdled and the shoot above the affected
region wilts and dies. The affected areas
are covered with a white mold. After the
plant dies, black sclerotia or resting bodies
are formed within the hollow stem and
on the stem below the soil level. Because
sclerotia are highly resistant to drying and
freezing, they serve to carry the causal
fungus over unfavorable conditions.

Control. The use of well-drained soil is
the best insurance against damage from
stem rot. Wide spacing of the plants to
prevent excessive shading of the soil is also
helpful. If mulches are used they should
not be placed in contact with the stems.
Remove and destroy diseased plants at
once, to prevent formation of sclerotia.
Treating the soil with Terraclor before
planting dahlias will aid in preventing stem
rot.

STORAGE ROTS

Symptoms. Dahlia tubers may be destroyed in storage by various fungi. The
type of decay depends upon the causal
fungus and upon the storage conditions.
Most tuber rots start in wounds made
during digging or handling, and they develop most rapidly under moist, warm
conditions.

Control. The prevention of storage rots
depends upon fully matured tubers, care
in digging and handling to avoid injuries,
avoidance of frost damage both before
and during storage, maintenance of storage temperatures at about 40°F, and
avoidance of high humidities in storage.
Following heavy losses from tuber rot,
thoroughly clean and wash the storage
space with a solution of formaldehyde, 1
gallon to 50 gallons of water.

VERTICILLIUM AND FUSARIUM WILTS

Symptoms. In either of the wilt diseases,
caused by *Verticillium albo-atrum* or *Fusarium* sp., a single branch or the entire
plant gradually wilts from the tip downward and eventually dies. Partial recovery
may occur at night for a short time, but
eventually the plant is killed. Cross-sec-
tions of the stem, taken near the soil level,
or sections through the stem end of the
tuberous roots, aid in identifying the disease. The vascular bundles of stems and
roots of wilted plants are discolored, being
either dark brown or greenish brown. Affected tubers decay in storage, especially
if kept moist.

Control. Plant only healthy tubers, in
soil where the disease has not occurred.
Wilting plants should be removed and destroyed promptly. Infested soil may be
treated with chloropicrin or Vapam before
planting dahlias.

DELPHINIUM AND LARKSPUR

The genus *Delphinium* includes both
annual and perennial species. By common
usage the name "delphinium" is generally
applied to the perennial species, and the
name "larkspur" to the annual species.

There is, however, no botanical basis for such a separation. Most of the diseases that attack plants in the genus affect both groups, although the symptoms may differ.

ASTER YELLOWS

Symptoms. This disease of delphinium, which gets its name from being first observed and studied on aster, has also been called stunt, greens, or witches'-broom. The most characteristic symptoms of this disease on almost all hosts are a conspicuous greening of all or part of the flower, changing it to a leafy, sterile structure, and the development of yellowish, upright, and more or less dense clusters of succulent leaves or shoots.

Delphinium shows the greening of some or all of the flowers in a striking manner. The color change may involve the flowers on only one side of the spike. One or more basal shoots may be diseased following the production of a healthy main spike, or the lower flowers on a spike may be healthy and the upper ones diseased. The parts of individual flowers on a spike may be converted in varying degrees to sterile leaf-like members. A portion of the petal may be green and the rest normal, without alteration of shape or size. In other cases the petals may be much reduced in size and entirely green. The sepals may be enormously enlarged and leaflike, or severely dwarfed. The carpel, which normally forms the follicle, may be strikingly transformed. The stamens may be greatly lengthened and have straplike sterile tips, or may retain a nearly normal appearance.

The entire flower spike may become a dense cluster of compressed and leafy flowers. This condition has given rise to the name "stunt."

An infected seedling may form yellow leaves on erect petioles, and may either die without flowering or produce a green spike. Flowers initiated at any time after infection are green, and this suggests the approximate time when infection occurred. A plant infected after the first flowering and before the next spring will develop only into a leafy clump, and probably will not survive the winter months. The dense basal cluster of shoots is characteristic in infected plants. The shoots are yellow, 6 to 12 inches high, produce no flower spikes, and generally have yellow leaves on long, slender petioles. This symptom has given rise to the name "witches'-broom."

Control. Control measures consist of using disease-free planting stock, prompt removal of infected plants, weed control, and insect control. The aster-yellows organism has many weed hosts and the disease is spread by leafhoppers.

BACTERIAL BUD ROT, CROWN ROT, AND STEM ROT

Symptoms. Characteristic symptoms of the rot diseases, caused by the bacteria *Erwinia atroseptica* and *E. chrysanthemi*, are yellowing of the leaves, blackening of the stems, and stunting of the plants. Infection of delphinium occurs through wounds, primarily the lengthwise cracks that develop at the base of normally growing spikes. In larkspur, infection commonly occurs in the flower buds or growing points as well as in the growth cracks.

In delphinium, a blackened area at the base of the stem develops in and around the cracks, but generally does not progress far up the stem in most varieties. Under continued moist conditions, the stem may be girdled rapidly, and an abundant, white to light-tan, frothy, frequently odoriferous, ooze appears from the cracks. The flower stalks soon die and the leaves turn brown. Under somewhat drier conditions the ooze may be inconspicuous or lacking, and the stem is killed more slowly; the leaves then turn yellow and wilt, later becoming brown. In either case the stems may fall over. If moist conditions do not continue, the disease may be checked and new sprouts may arise from the crown below soil level. This sequence commonly occurs with overhead irrigation; the wet conditions favor the disease, but, as the soil dries and the pathogen is checked, new shoots appear. Whether these shoots escape subsequent infection depends largely on the soil moisture conditions.

In larkspur, the rot may start at the

basal stem cracks, appearing first as water-soaked areas which quickly blacken and gradually progress up the stem for a considerable distance. Black streaks on the outside and in woody parts of the stem are common. The pith in the stems is blackened and may contain sticky bacterial masses. The plant may be killed quickly and turn brown, or, under drier conditions, it may develop yellow leaves and gradually wilt and die. It may survive to produce some seed. Infected plants generally are stunted and may fall over from weakening of the stem base. Under moist conditions, the bacteria also infect the growing points and flower buds, without obvious injuries; the soft, slimy rot is produced quickly under these conditions and may spread downward almost to the soil level. No frothy exudate, such as appears on delphinium, has been observed on larkspur. Healthy new shoots starting from diseased crowns also are lacking.

Control. There is evidence that the causal bacteria are carried in the seed.

Bacterial leaf spot of delphinium. (Photograph courtesy of Division of Plant Pathology, University of California, Berkeley.)

Seeds suspected as carriers should be treated in water heated to 122° to 129°F for exactly 10 minutes. For such treatment, place the seeds in cheesecloth bags and submerge them in the hot water. The seeds should be agitated in the bags and the water kept in motion to prevent cold-pockets. After 10 minutes remove the bags and immediately plunge them into cold water to terminate the treatment. Spread the seed on clean screens or newspapers in the sun or in a warm room so they will dry within a few hours.

Avoid planting in low, poorly drained areas. The plants should be set on ridges in order to keep the crowns dry at all times. Avoid overhead irrigation, especially after stem cracks begin to appear in the elongating flower spikes. Drenching the plants and adjacent soil with bordeaux mixture will help to check the disease.

BACTERIAL LEAF SPOT

Symptoms. Bacterial leaf spot, also known as black spot or black disease, is caused by a bacterium, *Pseudomonas delphinii*. Irregular, tarry, black spots appear on the leaves, and sometimes on stems and buds. These spots may remain numerous and small, or they may enlarge, sometimes uniting to form large blotches that distort the leaves. The disease frequently causes serious losses among seedlings at the 2- to 3-leaf stage of development. The tiny leaves show numerous minute, black spots that may unite and, under moist conditions, completely rot the leaf. Such seedlings may have all the leaves rotted, leaving only the growing point, and in some cases that may be destroyed also.

Control. The causal bacteria overwinter in infected crowns or in plant remains distributed through the soil. When spring growth is renewed, the bacteria are spread to the new leaves by the spattering of rain. Cutting the spotted leaves in late summer or fall and drenching the crowns with bordeaux mixture, followed by spraying of young shoots with bordeaux mixture in the spring, should control the disease. The disease in the seedbed may be controlled effectively by a thorough spraying with 2-2-50 bordeaux mixture, applied when the disease first appears.

DIAPORTHE BLIGHT

Symptoms. In delphinium blight, caused by the fungus *Diaporthe arctii,* the lower leaves of plants that have reached the flowering stage become brown and dry but remain attached. Brown lesions occur near the base of the stems. By the time these lesions completely girdle the stems, the entire foliage gradually will have withered and dried. Eventually the lesions extend upwards for several inches above the surface of the soil, and downward into the root systems. Small, black pycnidia develop on the leaves, stems, and seed capsules. The crown and uppermost roots are involved in a cottony weft of mycelium during rainy periods.

Control. Remove and destroy the diseased plants. Since the causal fungus is seedborne, plant seed that is known to be from healthy plants.

DIPLODINA DISEASE

Symptoms. The disease caused by the fungus *Diplodina delphinii* occurs most often as a crown and root rot but also appears as cankers or local stem lesions, as leaf spots, as shoot or petiole soft rot, and as inflorescence and seed pod blight.

On the stem, localized lesions are brown to black, and variable in size and shape. Fruiting bodies of the causal fungus, which are imbedded beneath the epidermis of the host, appear as small pinpoint dots arranged in rings over the surface of the infected area. When the mature pycnidia are moistened, large numbers of spores ooze out in long, gelatinous coils.

Petiole symptoms vary, depending on the succulence of the tissue at the time of infection. Diseased tissues of young green petioles appear brown and water-soaked as if affected with a soft rot; the fungus travels rapidly down the petiole, and a brown, water-soaked area soon forms around the base. It is not uncommon to find the base of almost every petiole of an individual stem affected. In less succulent tissue the fungus is confined to local lesions and the invaded area is usually black. Pycnidia may develop on any infected tissue, but especially on lesions formed at the point of attachment of petiole and leaf blade.

Following wet weather the Diplodina fungus attacks the young, tender basal shoots arising from the crown, producing a rapid, brown to black, watery, soft rot similar to the petiole rot described. Such rots occur throughout the season when moist conditions prevail. In the spring, basal shoots of plants in an advanced stage of crown decay usually wilt suddenly.

Symptoms on leaves are difficult to distinguish from those of bacterial leaf spot.

Crown and root symptoms resemble those caused by other crown rot organisms. A black or dark-brown discoloration of the vascular tissues is characteristic of the Diplodina disease, in contrast to the brown discoloration associated with Fusarium wilt. In an advanced stage of Diplodina disease, the invaded outer tissues undergo a general necrosis, evident as a rather soft, moist, black rot. In the spring, badly decayed crowns send up a few weak, sickly shoots from uninvaded buds, but these soon wilt and die because the remaining root system is not sufficient to support them.

The fungus may also be found on the terminal portions of the flower spike, especially during the latter part of the season. With prolonged moist weather the flowers and seed pods may exhibit a blackish decay.

Control. Plant in raised beds, and avoid overhead irrigation. An area that has had an outbreak of the disease should not be replanted to delphinium for several years. Burn all refuse from infected plants. Spray with bordeaux mixture 4-4-50 to protect the new growth during wet weather.

FUSARIUM CANKER AND WILT

Symptoms. The first symptoms of stem canker and wilt, caused by the fungus *Fusarium oxysporum* f. *delphinii,* are small, brown to brownish-gray spots on the stems.

These spots gradually enlarge, and several may coalesce to form one or more large spots. Brown, sunken, water-soaked lesions may appear on the petioles and spread to the stem. The lesions enlarge, both cross-wise and lengthwise, but the lengthwise spread is the more rapid. The cankered area is chocolate brown and character-istically moist or water-soaked. On large plants, cankers may be over a foot long. In the advanced stages of canker develop-ment, the diseased tissue in the center of the canker may rupture. Eventually the tissue in the central part of the canker shrinks or collapses while the thin epi-dermis remains intact and appears white or bleached. Numerous salmon-colored sporodochia or clumps of spores of the *Fusarium* are distributed irregularly over the bleached area. The pith cavity of a cankered stem is almost completely filled with white mycelium. In time the fungus reaches the crown, where it causes a local necrosis or dead patches. After passing into the crown the fungus invades and dis-colors the vascular tissues, and the young shoots commonly present at the base of the plants soon wilt. In late stages of the dis-ease the parts of the stem above the canker may wilt. When a mature plant with symptoms of Fusarium wilt is cut, a typical brown vascular discoloration is evi-dent. The discoloration may extend from the crown into the main root and for some distance upwards into the main stem and young shoots. Yellowing of the leaves, and

wilting and drooping of the flower head may occur.

Control. An area where the disease has occurred should not be replanted to del-phinium for several years unless the soil can be sterilized. All refuse from diseased plants should be destroyed by burning.

PHOMA CROWN ROT

Symptoms. Crown rot caused by the fungus *Phoma* sp. produces cankers, usu-ally near the crown, causing one or more cracks in the stem. The cracks may extend upward for a considerable distance. Pyc-nidia or spore-producing bodies of the fun-gus can be found in the blackened tissue adjoining the edges of these cracks, and also on irregular black or brown necrotic areas along the stem. Another character-istic symptom is the blackening of tissue at the base of each petiole; pycnidia develop in abundance on these areas. On old stems, reddish-brown masses of pycnidia may appear near the top.

Control. The control measures suggested for Sclerotium root and crown rot (page 70) should be effective for this disease also.

POWDERY MILDEW

Symptoms. Grayish-white, moldy patches appear on the surface of leaves attacked by the fungus *Erysiphe polygoni*. Small black fruiting bodies of the fungus may develop on these patches in late summer. Leaves and flower shoots may be deformed

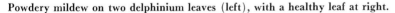

Powdery mildew on two delphinium leaves (left), with a healthy leaf at right.

and stunted. Basal leaves may turn yellow, then brown, and die progressively up the stem.

Control. Avoid overcrowded planting. Use dusting sulfur or wettable sulfur spray at 10- to 14-day intervals or as often as needed to hold the fungus in check. Clean up and burn all fallen leaves and other plant debris.

SCLEROTIUM ROOT AND CROWN ROT

Symptoms. The first indications of root and crown rot, caused by the fungi *Sclerotium rolfsii* or *S. delphinii,* are a discoloration of the lower leaves and a wilting of the young shoots, commonly followed within a few days by the death and drying up of the entire plant. Roots of affected plants are black or dark brown and rotted. White strands of the causal fungus usually can be found on some of the rotted parts.

The fungi are especially active during wet weather, and under such conditions, small, egg-shaped bodies or sclerotia are formed around the infected plant parts and in the adjacent soil. These sclerotia are at first white to cream colored. They change to buff, then reddish brown, then finally to dark red or chocolate brown. The sclerotia are resistant to drying and freezing so they are able to carry the fungus over unfavorable conditions.

Control. Treating the soil with Terraclor before planting is effective in preventing the disease. Any plants that develop the disease should be removed and destroyed.

SCLEROTINIA WILT AND STEM ROT

Symptoms. Wilt and stem rot, caused by the fungus *Sclerotinia sclerotiorum,* is characterized by a general wilting of the leaflets and tender shoots, accompanied by cankered areas on the stem. Individual branches, especially those near the ground line, soon wilt. As large portions of the stems and branches become involved, entire plants wilt and may fall over. Areas near the ground line on diseased stems become covered with a white, cobweblike

Sclerotinia wilt and stem rot of larkspur. Sclerotia of the causal fungus have formed in the stem pith of the plant at left, and on the outside of the crown of the plant at right.

growth of the wilt fungus, and numerous large sclerotia are formed on the outside and inside of the affected stems.

Control. The control measures suggested for Sclerotium root and crown rot are equally effective against this disease.

Wilting of leaves, canker formation, and dieback associated with Sclerotinia wilt and stem rot of larkspur.

DIEFFENBACHIA

Dieffenbachias (*Dieffenbachia picta*) occasionally are affected by leaf spots and a stem rot disease.

BACTERIAL LEAF SPOT

Symptoms. Circular, reddish-brown spots, surrounded by light-yellow, water-soaked margins, are produced on the leaves affected by bacterial leaf spot, caused by *Xanthomonas dieffenbachiae*. As the spots enlarge or coalesce, their centers become brown and dry. Often the area between the spot and the leaf margin turns yellow and dies. A bacterial ooze usually occurs in the spots on the lower leaf surface, and eventually dries into a thin waxlike layer that peels off readily.

Control. Separate the infected plants from the healthy ones. If possible, lower the temperature, and avoid syringing the plants.

BACTERIAL STEM AND LEAF ROT

Symptoms. The disease caused by *Erwinia dieffenbachia* is characterized by brownish, water-soaked, sunken, soft areas on the stems, and irregular, brownish, soft spots on the leaves. Favored by high temperature and moisture, the pathogen may attack plants of any age. Detection of the disease is difficult because plants may be infected but show no visible symptoms.

Stem lesions may occur above or below the soil surface. When below the soil surface, lesions may not be noticed until the rot becomes advanced. Stem lesions are water-soaked, soft, and grayish at first, later becoming tan to pale brown, sunken, and irregular in shape but with a distinct line separating the diseased and healthy tissues. Affected plants characteristically produce small, pale-yellow terminal leaves. Under favorable conditions, the stem lesions advance rapidly and cause the lower leaves to turn yellow and die prematurely. Frequently the bacteria invade the petioles and midribs. Such areas become water-soaked and brown; the leaves collapse and become soft and mushy.

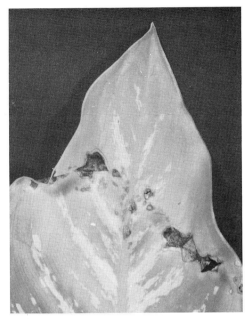

Bacterial leaf spot of dieffenbachia. The young leaf was infected near the tip before reaching the stage where it unrolled.

Leaf infections are characterized by small pinpoint, water-soaked, pale-brown spots surrounded by diffused yellow margins. Under favorable conditions, the spots enlarge slowly and become irregular, water-soaked and sunken with light-tan centers and darker brown borders. The yellow, diffused margins enlarge around the spots; under humid conditions the spots are soft and full of water. When the pathogen invades the large veins and midrib, advancement into the petiole and stem often follows, resulting in yellowing and total collapse of the leaf. Occasionally large, water-filled blisters form on the underside of the leaf. Under less favorable conditions the spots become dry and brittle and develop a torn or ragged appearance.

Control. Agri-mycin 100 used as a 30-minute preplanting liquid dip treatment at 200 parts per million has given satisfactory control of this disease without causing injury. A 15-minute cane soak in Agri-mycin 100 at 200 parts per million, followed by immersion in hot water at 120°F for 40 to 60 minutes, depending on cane diameter, also has been effective.

Extreme care to avoid recontamination is needed in handling the canes after treatment. Disinfected trays, tools, gloves, and so on should be used in handling treated canes, and the canes should be planted directly in a sterilized medium. The application of Agri-mycin 100 at 200 parts per million active ingredient at 10-day intervals may help reduce leaf infections.

BROWN LEAF SPOT

Symptoms. The fungus *Leptosphaeria* sp. may infect leaves so they have 50 or more lesions with diameters less than 1 millimeter or only a few circular spots of greater size. Lesions are not delimited by veins and occasionally they may occur on the midvein, petiole, or flower spathe. Mature lesions on some varieties have strong yellowish-brown centers surrounded by a ring of grayish brown and an outer halo of dark orange-yellow. Fruiting bodies of the causal fungus may appear as black specks just within the gray-brown center. Spots on some other varieties may be surrounded by a water-soaked halo. Leaves gradually become chlorotic and die when severely infected.

Control. Spray with maneb or basic copper sulfate.

CEPHALOSPORIUM LEAF SPOT

Symptoms. The initial infections by *Cephalosporium dieffenbachiae* appear on the young, convolute, or rolled, leaves as tiny, reddish-brown, circular to elongate lesions. As these leaves unroll and expand, the lesions increase in diameter. At this stage they are mostly circular in outline, and rather sharply delimited by a dark-brown border. The central portion is grayish. Elongated lesions are found occasionally on the petioles, midribs, and even on the stems. Coalescence of the lesions or yellowing and death of entire leaves rarely occur.

Control. The control measures suggested for bacterial leaf spot are also recommended for this disease. Control of mealybugs is also highly desirable as there is evidence that they may spread the disease.

STEM ROT

Symptoms. The first visible symptom of stem rot, caused by the fungus *Phytophthora palmivora,* is a small, irregular-shaped, water-soaked lesion on the main stem at the soil level. Usually the lesion rapidly increases in size and ultimately may extend as much as 1 inch above and below the soil level. The affected stem tissues become soft and watery. Coincident with infection of the basal part of the main stem of young plants, the leaves and petioles usually turn yellow and wilt suddenly. Soon the main stem breaks at the point of infection and falls over, and the plant dies.

In older or larger plants, invaded tissues collapse, forming a brown cavity which, as it continues to enlarge, weakens the structural stability of the main stem and soon causes breakage and lodging. In contrast to young plants, the foliage of older infected plants does not wilt, either before or after the main stem collapses. The leaves and petioles retain their normal turgidity and color, probably because of the rapid spread of the disease in a relatively restricted area, and because of the high water content of the succulent main stem. Internally the invaded tissues are water-soaked and turning dark gray, and frequently a definite, narrow, black band separates the diseased from the healthy tissues. The roots are not affected.

Control. Stem rot is favored by relatively high air temperatures, high humidity, poor soil drainage, excessive irrigation, and crowding of the potted plants on greenhouse benches. Correcting these conditions will aid in controlling the disease. The disease can be avoided by rooting cane cuttings (previously dusted with ferbam, Phygon, or Spergon) in small pots of steam-sterilized sand. Subsequently, in shifting the rooted cuttings to larger pots, steam-sterilized soil should be used. Care in watering the plants and good drainage are essential.

Bacterial leaf spot on English ivy. The margins of the spots are red and the centers are brown to brownish black. The spots may occur anywhere on the leaf.

Amerosporium leaf spot develops on the edges of English ivy leaves. The spots are tan to brown but without the red margins seen in bacterial leaf spot.

ENGLISH IVY

Leaf spots are the most common diseases on English ivy (*Hedera helix*). In some cases stem cankers are produced by the same organisms that cause leaf spots.

BACTERIAL LEAF SPOT AND CANKER

Symptoms. Bacterial leaf spot, caused by *Xanthomonas hederae,* is most prevalent on English ivy in greenhouses. The spots at first are light green, water-soaked, and circular. As the spots enlarge, the centers become brown to brownish black and eventually they dry and crack. The margins of the spots on mature leaves are red, and the water-soaked appearance usually disappears. Infection on the petioles produces a blackening and shriveling of the tissue, or lengthwise cracking. The tips of young twigs may turn black from the tip downward into the old wood, and distinct cankers may form on the stems. When cankers form on the stem the plant fails to grow normally, remaining dwarfed and having sickly, yellow-green foliage.

Control. Avoid wetting the foliage when watering; avoid unnecessary syringing and high temperatures. If infections are light the diseased leaves may be picked off and burned.

FUNGUS LEAF SPOTS

Symptoms. *Amerosporium trichellum* produces large, diffuse tan to brown spots on the edges of the leaves. Black pycnidia or fruiting bodies of the causal fungus form in the dead tissue. As the spots age, the affected tissues may shred and fall away.

Other leaf spots are caused by *Glomerella cingulata, Phyllosticta concentrica, P. hederae,* and *Ramularia hedericola.*

Control. Pick off and burn the infected leaves. Spray the plants with a copper or a carbamate fungicide.

FERNS

The various genera and species of ferns are subject to a number of diseases. Only the two most serious troubles are treated in this publication.

ANTHRACNOSE

Symptoms. Anthracnose, a disease of Boston fern (*Nephrolepis exaltata* var. *bostoniensis*) is caused by the fungus *Glomerella nephrolepis*. Symptoms first appear on the growing tips of the fronds and on other succulent leaf tissue that has not become hardened. The first symptom is a slight browning of the infected tissue. Attached tissues shrink rapidly. When the plant is kept under humid conditions, small white patches begin to appear over the surface of the brownish lesions. Seldom does the infection appear over the entire frond, but two or three separate lesions on the same frond are not uncommon. The infection of older fronds is limited to the young tissues near the apex of the leaves. As a whole, infected ferns appear blighted, with their numerous dead fronds far outnumbering the isolated, partially diseased ones that have been able to develop a few pinnae.

Control. Remove all infected tissue as it appears; destroy badly diseased plants. Use care in watering to avoid wetting the foliage. Unnecessarily high humidity should be avoided.

BACTERIAL LEAF BLIGHT

Symptoms. The bird's-nest fern (*Asplenium nidus*) is subject to a leaf blight caused by the bacterium *Pseudomonas asplenii*. The disease starts as small, water-soaked, translucent spots on any part of the frond, but usually on the upper surface. Infection may also occur through the water pores on the tip of the frond. Under warm and humid conditions the spots enlarge rapidly and soon involve the entire frond. Frequently the bacteria invade the crown and quickly kill the plant.

Control. Control of this disease depends entirely upon sanitation and good cultural conditions. In propagating, spores should be taken only from healthy plants. All growing media, flats, and pots should be steam-sterilized. When the prothallia and young plants are being transplanted, they should be handled with forceps that are frequently dipped in alcohol and flamed. Where the disease is present it is important to destroy all diseased plants and to grow the healthy plants under drier conditions.

FREESIA

The most serious disease of freesia (*Freesia refracta*) is wilt and corm rot.

WILT AND CORM ROT

Symptoms. Plants infected with *Fusarium oxysporum* appear yellowish, then gradually wilt, die, and collapse. After collapse of the affected plants the yellow color of the leaves changes to straw white or papery white. The dead leaves gradually decay as they lie on the ground and in time disappear.

The causal fungus invades the main roots, the larger laterals, and the feeding rootlets, all of which take on a characteristic pink color. These roots finally decay and assume a dark-brown color that soon may become obscured by a superficial coating of the mycelium and spores of *Fusarium*. From the infected and dead roots the disease spreads to the corms, which may be found in various stages of infection. With relatively mild infection the husks may conceal superficial to deep, pink lesions on the outside of the corms. The tissues of diseased corms first become yellowish and, as decay progresses, they become a definite dark brown. In well-advanced stages the browned vascular system is usually surrounded by a pink discoloration. As decay spreads and involves the entire corm, the affected tissue becomes a uniform chalky white and is hard, dry, friable, and gritty in texture, crumbling readily under light pressure.

Control. Areas where the disease has occurred should not be replanted to freesias for several years. Sterilize the soil used in greenhouses. Inspect the corms before planting. Discard all those showing lesions and treat the healthy-appearing corms with a fungicide such as Arasan before planting.

GARDENIA

The florist's gardenia (*Gardenia jasminoides*) is subject to a few diseases, the most serious being canker.

BACTERIAL LEAF SPOT

Symptoms. Bacterial leaf spots of gardenia are caused by two distinct species of bacteria, *Pseudomonas gardeniae* and *Xanthomonas maculifoliigardeniae*. Because symptoms produced by the two organisms are so similar, the two leaf spots will be considered here as one disease.

The disease starts on tender leaves as minute dots that gradually enlarge, showing at first a pale-yellow center, which later becomes reddish brown, surrounded by a yellowish halo. The margins of the lesion are somewhat thickened and appear greasy. Several spots may coalesce to form a large one. Abundant infections may cause premature dropping of leaves. Flower buds and sepals are affected sometimes but this is relatively uncommon.

Control. The disease may be spread by taking cuttings from infected plants, and especially by syringing the plants. When gardenias are forced for flower production, the high humidity and air temperature that are usually maintained provide excellent conditions for the spread of leaf spot organisms and subsequent epidemics. The disease seldom becomes serious, however, unless syringing is practiced.

BUD DROP

Symptoms. Bud drop first becomes evident as a gradual discoloration of the pedicel and bud. The disease develops on the exterior of the calyx where there are five porelike structures known as the extrafloral nectaries. The bright-green color of

Below, leaf spot of gardenia, caused by **Phomopsis gardeniae**, is characterized by concentric zones and pycnidia of the causal fungus in the lesions. The same fungus causes canker. At right, bacterial leaf spot of gardenia caused by **Xanthomonas maculifoliigardeniae**.

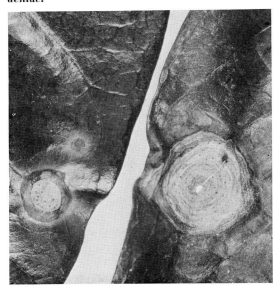

the buds becomes dark cream, then yellow, and finally dark brown. The bud gradually becomes moist and rotten, and eventually drops off within 4 to 30 days.

Bud drop is probably caused by excessive soil moisture and temperature fluctuations. Bacteria and *Botrytis* are often associated with bud drop but these are probably not primary causes of the disease.

Control. Avoid high temperature and humidity, which tend to increase the dropping of buds. The bacteria and *Botrytis* associated with the disease may be spread from plant to plant by mealybugs and ants, which usually infest the beds in which gardenias are grown. Control of these pests often helps to control bud drop.

CANKER

Symptoms. The stem is cankerous near and below the soil line and becomes considerably enlarged. A large amount of cork, containing numerous longitudinal cracks, is formed on the surface of the cankered area and gives the canker a rough, corrugated appearance. The corti-

Swollen canker at the base of a gardenia stem.

cal tissue below the cork, as well as for some distance beyond the cankered area, is bright yellow. Even after the canker has completely circled the stem the plants are slow to die and may live for several weeks, although they are more or less stunted. Upon close examination, small black pycnidia of the causal fungus, *Phomopsis gardeniae,* can be found half-buried in the cortex near the point where the canker started. If humidity is high, a yellowish mass of spores exudes from the fruiting bodies.

A leaf spot is sometimes produced by the same fungus.

Control. Since infection occurs only through wounds, the grower should avoid injuring the plants during handling and potting. Sterilize the pots and soil if they have been in contact with diseased plants. Destroy all diseased plants so that they will not serve as a source of infection, and use completely disease-free plants as stock for cuttings. Sterilize the rooting medium, preferably with steam. If steam is unavailable, mix ferbam with the sand in the cutting bench, at the rate of ½ pound ferbam to 100 pounds of sand. If plants are accidentally wounded they should be sprayed immediately with ferbam, 2 pounds to 100 gallons of water.

CHLOROSIS

Symptoms. When leaves become chlorotic they lose their healthy dark-green color and change to a sickly yellow. The plants develop slowly and have a generally unthrifty appearance.

Control. In order to control chlorosis the causal factors must be corrected. Perhaps the most common causes are cold, wet soil; a soil that is too alkaline; too cold or too dry an atmosphere; or excesses or deficiencies of some of the necessary plant nutrients. Soils that are kept below 70°F are likely to produce chlorotic plants. No deficiencies or excesses of chemical nutrients should occur if the soil is properly prepared. Test the soil reaction frequently during the season.

DIEBACK

Symptoms. Defoliation usually is the first noticeable symptom of dieback but bright-yellow veinbanding and brown necrotic lines sometimes appear before or after the leaves fall. Black, necrotic areas develop slowly on the twigs and often enclose islands of apparently normal tissue. Plants die when the main stem is girdled. Roots typically remain white and normal in appearance until late stages of dieback.

Control. Dieback is caused by root smothering as a result of overwatering. Root smothering may develop in gardenias long grown in pots when roots clog the drainage hole. Good drainage should be provided, and overwatering should be avoided to prevent dieback.

RHIZOCTONIA LEAF SPOT

Symptoms. The fungus *Rhizoctonia* sp. causes leaf spots that vary in color from tan to dark brown. They are from ¼ to ½ inch in diameter, more or less circular, and in many cases marked by zones. Young spots appear water-soaked under moist atmospheric conditions favoring rapid spread of the causal fungus in the leaves. A translucent ring usually surrounds the spots when further growth of the fungus is checked by a dry atmosphere. The spots first appear on the lower leaves and spread upward only when plants are kept excessively wet or overcrowded. In most instances fungus infection is confined to the leaves. Occasionally, however, it spreads down the midrib, killing the entire leaf, and continues down the petiole and stem, killing these parts.

Control. Pick off and burn all infected leaves. Give the plants plenty of space and adjust the ventilators to allow free movement of air. If syringing is practiced it should be done only in the morning on clear days so the plants will dry off as rapidly as possible.

ROOT KNOT

Symptoms. Root knot is caused by nematodes that penetrate the root tissues

Root knot on gardenia. The swollen roots are characteristic of this disease, which affects many kinds of plants in a similar way.

and cause the formation of knots or swellings of various shapes and sizes. Plants with badly infected roots present a more or less sickly appearance of the above-ground parts. They are dwarfed, and wilt more readily in hot dry weather than plants with healthy roots, and the foliage is usually paler green.

Control. Steam sterilization of the soil is the most effective method of control. Chloropicrin, D-D, Nemacur, Dasanit, and Mocap are highly effective in ridding soil of nematodes. Chloropicrin and D-D are fumigants; the other materials are obtainable as liquids or granules. Follow the directions of the manufacturer when using any of these materials.

GERANIUM

Geraniums (*Pelargonium hortorum*) are plagued by a number of diseases caused by bacteria, fungi, viruses, and unfavorable environmental conditions.

ALTERNARIA LEAF SPOT

Symptoms. The symptoms of leaf spot, caused by the fungus *Alternaria tenuis,* are quite variable. The spots are most prevalent on the undersides of the older leaves on the plant, but the uppermost young leaves may be infected also. At first the infection appears as a water-soaked area, less than 1 millimeter in diameter, on the lower surface of the leaf. Such spots may enlarge to form necrotic areas 2 to 3 millimeters in diameter with slightly sunken centers. When viewed by transmitted light the spots have small, brown centers surrounded by yellow, diffuse bands. These spots may either enlarge or remain this size. Those that enlarge become irregular necrotic areas, 6 to 10 millimeters in diameter. Some of these large spots may be localized and isolated, and have several rings of darker brown tissue surrounding a dark center. Often the spots coalesce and form very irregular necrotic spots, usually limited by the large veins of the leaf. The leaf blade does not wilt. Severe infections may kill the leaf or cause considerable leaf fall. Dead leaves shrivel and blacken, and the fungus produces spores abundantly on the fallen leaves.

Control. Alternaria leaf spot is common on field-grown geraniums in certain parts of California, so imported cuttings may carry the disease into other localities. Since the fungus rarely produces spores on intact leaves but commonly does on fallen ones, prompt removal and destruction of infected leaves should prevent the disease from spreading.

BACTERIAL BLIGHT

Symptoms. The bacterium *Xanthomonas pelargonii* attacks leaves, stems, and cuttings of geraniums. Infection either produces round leaf spots, or large, angular, dead areas, depending upon the variety. The first symptoms are small, water-soaked spots on the underside of the leaf. In two or three days the spots become well defined, slightly sunken, and about $\frac{1}{16}$ to $\frac{1}{8}$ inch in diameter. They rarely coalesce. This stage is followed rapidly by necrosis and wilting of the leaf, which either falls off or droops and hangs on the plant for a week or two. The original spots turn dark brown to black and become hard and dry. If there is no secondary spread of the bacteria, the other leaves on the plant do not develop the spotting symptom observed in the initial infection.

Another leaf symptom is the wilting of the margins. Infected areas rapidly become necrotic in angular patches bounded by the veins. Angular necrosis of this type is common on geraniums and may be caused by several factors, but the limp condition of the leaf is always associated with bacterial infections. Leaves soon fall off, or hang on the plant, as is observed in connection with the spotting. After the leaves fall, the vascular tissues of the stems may be discolored.

The stem-rot symptom is commonly known as "black rot." Vascular bundles in stems and branches of plants infected with the bacteria become brown to black 2 to 4 weeks after infection. At this stage one or more leaves on a branch usually will wilt and exhibit the angular necrotic symptom. Soon the bacteria infect the pith and cortex of the stem, causing a black, sharply limited discoloration. At this stage the exterior portions of the stem appear gray and dull, and only the ends of the branches are left with leaves. The stem rapidly blackens and shrivels into a dry rot, leaving the fibers and epidermis intact, and the rest as a disorganized crumbly mass. At this stage the plant consists of almost completely defoliated, blackened branches with only a few tufts of leaves on the tips. The roots are blackened but not decayed. Occasionally a plant will recover and produce new, healthy-appearing branches, but in 3 to 6 months these branches usually die.

Cuttings infected with *Xanthomonas pelargonii* fail to root, and slowly rot from the base upwards. The leaves wilt and often show the typical angular necrosis and wilt symptoms. In 2 to 4 weeks after the cuttings are placed in sand, the stems become dull blackish brown, as they do with the typical stem rot.

Control. Control measures must be based upon establishing disease-free planting stock and practicing strict sanitary measures. The vascular-inhibiting bacteria are carried over in infected cuttings taken from symptomless infected plants, from obvi-

Geranium leaf affected by bacterial leaf spot.

Geranium cuttings affected by bacterial stem rot caused by *Xanthomonas pelargonii*. Some of the cuttings in this lot had been attacked by *Pythium* also, as sometimes occurs.

Geranium plant affected by bacterial stem rot. Tissues of stem and upper roots are blackened.

Geranium leaf with angular necrosis caused by potash deficiency. Leaves affected by bacterial leaf spot may have the same type of lesion.

ously diseased plants, or from recently infested soil. The bacteria may carry over for at least 3 months in moist soil. They are extremely infectious and may be spread by contact and by splashing water, but primarily by contaminated cutting knives. Infected cuttings carry the disease to adjacent healthy cuttings in the rooting bed. *X. pelargonii* is transmitted from diseased to healthy plants by white flies (*Trialeurodes vaporariorum*) so control of this insect is extremely important.

BLACKLEG

Symptoms. Blackleg, caused by species of fungi belonging to the genus *Pythium,* is a disease of cuttings and young plants. Usually entire stems and petioles blacken, shrivel, and rot. The rot starts at the base of the stem and the affected plant soon wilts and dies.

Blackleg is sometimes confused with the cutting-rot phase of bacterial stem rot, and in some instances cuttings may be affected by both diseases at the same time. Pythium rot progresses rapidly, often killing within a week, and the cuttings have a shiny, coal-black, wet appearance, whereas bacterial rot often takes several weeks to kill and the cuttings are dull black and have a drier appearance.

Control. Sterilization of the sand used in the cutting bench is essential. Rot that develops soon after the cuttings are inserted in the bench may be partially checked by watering heavily with a solution of 2 ounces of copper carbonate in 3 gallons of water.

BOTRYTIS BLIGHT

Symptoms. The fungus *Botrytis cinerea* causes blossom blight, leaf spot, and cutting rot in geraniums. Blossom blight is characterized by premature fading and drying of the petals. At first the petals turn dark at the margins and wilt as though they were fading with age. Usually the central florets are the first to show infection. In red-flowered varieties, infected petals turn very dark. This usually occurs several days before the petals would naturally drop. If sufficient moisture collects on the blossoms the causal fungus will form masses of spores on the infected tissue, and the florets may be matted together.

Infected petals may drop onto healthy leaves and initiate leaf lesions. The spots on the leaves are irregular, brown, and water-soaked, becoming dry, wrinkled, and in many instances covered with powdery fungus spores.

If cuttings are taken from infected plants, spores may be present and a cutting rot may develop after the contaminated cuttings are put in the propagating bench.

Below, geranium leaves with lesions caused by Botrytis blight. Such lesions develop where infected petals fall on healthy leaves. At right, stem of a geranium cutting, showing rot caused by *Botrytis* in the propagating bench.

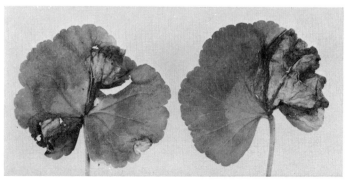

Geranium flower, blighted by *Botrytis*. The florets have been matted together by the fungus.

Control. Sanitary measures will go far in controlling Botrytis blight in the greenhouse. Prompt removal and destruction of the infected parts, and careful watering and syringing of the plants are essential in checking the disease. Proper ventilation must be provided to prevent the leaves and flowers from remaining moist for long periods. Geranium plants should be separated sufficiently on the bench to allow adequate air circulation and sunlight. Debris should be kept off the floors and benches.

The fungicide Bravo has given excellent control of Botrytis blight on geraniums. This material may be applied as a spray or as a method of fungicide application that has been termed "thermal dusting." The fungicide vaporizes when heated to a temperature of 600° to 800°F and condenses to form ultrafine particles which are deposited on all plant surfaces, resulting in an almost invisible layer of protection against Botrytis. A tablet formulation sold under the name Termil is available for this purpose.

Benomyl in combination with Surfacant F appears to be a promising fungicide for use under greenhouse conditions, particularly as a spray, for the prevention of the Botrytis blight of geranium cuttings and cutting stubs on stock plants.

Spraying with captan, 1 pound to 50 gallons of water, or Botran, one-half pound to 50 gallons, at 5- to 7-day intervals is helpful in cleaning up severe outbreaks of the disease.

Cutting beds should be steam sterilized and the rooted cuttings should be planted in sterilized soil.

CERCOSPORA LEAF SPOT

Symptoms. The fungus *Cercospora brunkii* produces light-brown or pale, brick-red spots, circular or oval, with a narrow, slightly raised, and somewhat darker border that is more prominent on the lower side of the leaf. The spots may unite and occupy a considerable area of the leaf.

Control. Control measures are the same as for Botrytis blight.

CRINKLE OR LEAF CURL

Symptoms. The young leaves are wrinkled and deformed, with hyaline or colorless spots that are slightly thickened. With age the spots may yellow and develop small necrotic areas. When examined from below, the hyaline spots transmit light like tiny windows. The centers of the chlorotic spots may become brown with a chlorotic border, and severely affected leaves may turn yellow and drop. Brown, elongated, corky, raised, necrotic areas often develop on the petioles and stems. In extreme cases the entire top portion of the plant may turn brown and die. The disease is ordinarily severe during the spring months,

Geranium plant with fasciation at the base of the stem. The gall-like formation is composed of many short, fleshy, and aborted stems and misshapen leaves.

Necrotic spots and crinkling of the foliage are symptoms of the geranium crinkle disease.

often disfiguring and dwarfing the plants. Severely affected plants usually outgrow the disease during the summer and appear healthy, but cuttings taken from such plants carry the causal virus and will show the disease the following spring.

Control. Control measures are the same as for leaf breaking.

FASCIATION

Symptoms. The bacterium *Corynebacterium fascians* produces a condition known as fasciation. Many short, fleshy, thick, and aborted stems with misshapen leaves develop on the main stem at or below the soil line. A normal green color develops in the portion exposed to the light. The main stem of an affected plant apparently grows normally, but may be dwarfed.

Control. Use cuttings from disease-free plants and plant them in sterilized soil.

LEAF BREAKING

Symptoms. Leaf breaking, caused by a virus, sometimes is called mosaic but does not produce a true mottle typical of mosaic diseases. It completely rearranges or reduces the anthocyanin pigments in the leaves. The purplish zones or horseshoe patterns normally found in healthy geraniums of many varieties disappear and are replaced by purple spotting along the veins. In some cases formation of anthocyanin pigments is completely suppressed. The leaves are reduced in size during severe stages of the disease. There is also a slight reduction in the chlorophyll-green coloration. The disease is seasonal, severe symptoms being apparent in the short-day months, followed by nearly complete recovery during the long-day months. Usually the new foliage is without symptoms by the time the plants bloom.

Control. Use of virus-free cuttings is the only known means of control. Diseased plants should be rogued out as soon as they are noticed.

The geranium leaf farther left is affected by the leaf-breaking disease; the other leaf is healthy.

Geranium plant affected by the leaf-breaking disease. The anthocyanin pigments have been completely suppressed.

LEAF CUPPING

Symptoms. Leaf cupping, thought to be caused by beet curly-top virus, is probably the most distinctive and destructive virus disease affecting geraniums. The disease is so destructive that affected plants are rarely found to any extent in commercial stocks. The disease changes the plant to a shape that no longer has the appearance of a geranium. Normal, flat, pubescent leaves are changed to incurved, hairless cups with sinuous veins, cleared veinlets, and sometimes protuberances on the lower surface. The older leaves sometimes are chlorotic between the veins, while the area in the vicinity of the veins remains green. The entire plant may become yellow in an advanced stage of the disease.

Control. Control measures are the same as for leaf breaking.

OEDEMA

Symptoms. Oedema is a nonparasitic disease associated with excessive soil moisture and retarded transpiration. Water-soaked spots, which later become brown and corky, develop on the leaves. The leaves turn yellow and drop off. Corky ridges may develop on the petioles and stems. Oedema is likely to develop when the soil is moist and warm and the air is moist and cool. This environment results in rapid water absorption from the soil, and slow water loss from the leaves, which in turn results in an overturgid or swollen

Corky spots and ridges on petioles and leaf blades are characteristic of oedema in geraniums. The spots are usually more numerous on the underside of the leaves.

condition in the plant and the bursting of some cells, followed by development of the corky swellings. The trouble is usually most severe in late winter and early spring during cloudy weather.

Oedema is not fatal, nor is it known to be detrimental to the vigor of the plant, but it is somewhat unsightly and, when severe, lowers the value of the plant.

Control. If plants are given sufficient air and light without excess water, oedema does not become a problem. Once a leaf has oedema, it will never recover — that is, the symptoms on that leaf will never disappear. However, when plants are given good growing conditions or when set out-of-doors, the new growth that will be affected by any beneficial change in the environment usually will be free of oedema.

RUST

Symptoms. Zonal geranium rust, caused by the fungus *Puccinia pelargonii-zonalis,* first appears as a small yellow spot about 1/25 inch in diameter and continues to increase in size to as much as ¼ inch. Spots are visible on the top side of the leaves but they are much more conspicuous on the underside. A rust-colored pustule develops in the center of the spot on the underside of the leaf. The pustule may break and sporulate almost immediately, or it may

remain capped-over for weeks. One to more than 100 pustules may occur on a single leaf. The characteristic expression of zonal rust usually appears from a week to several weeks after the first pustule appears. A partial or entire circle of pustules will develop around the original. Occasionally, the entire circle will fill with pustules, and, less often, a second circle will form around the first. Heavily infected leaves turn yellow and drop prematurely, leaving the plants partly defoliated.

The orange-colored spores produced in the pustules on the lower surface of the leaves are spread by wind. They germinate in presence of water and infect geranium leaves through stomata. The rust fungus survives in infected leaves.

Control. Rust can be avoided; or, when an infection does occur, it can be eradicated within 30 days if treated immediately. If allowed to spread uncontrolled, it can become a total disaster. Since the spores require water for germination and infection, anything that can be done to keep water off of the foliage will aid in controlling the disease.

Spraying with zineb or maneb will protect the plants from rust infection but this is effective only when the leaf is completely covered. The same spray mixture can be used for protective spray programs and for curative spraying or dipping. Protective spraying should be done at least every 10 days. Curative spraying should occur at least once a week. Although good spraying will be effective, most growers who have had rust have found that the best practice is to remove all infected leaves and put them in a container so they can be destroyed. Then the whole plant is plunged into a bucket of the spray mixture. The plants should be inspected regularly for at least 2 months, and any leaf that develops symptoms of rust should be destroyed. Imported plants should be kept isolated for a considerable time and inspected frequently for any possible appearance of the disease.

Because conditions in propagating beds are ideal for rust development, cuttings should be dipped in a preparation contain-

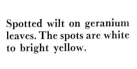
Spotted wilt on geranium leaves. The spots are white to bright yellow.

ing 3 ounces of 35 percent zineb wettable powder and ¼ teaspoonful of spreader-sticker to each 5 gallons of water. Prepare the cuttings for planting, then submerge the cuttings in the solution for 3 to 5 minutes. Drain and plant.

SPOTTED WILT

Symptoms. A disease thought to be caused by the spotted-wilt virus is characterized by bright-yellow or white spots, often arc- or ring-shaped, on the leaves. Usually an occasional leaf shows the symptoms. Some stages of this disease can be confused with crinkle because of the bright appearance of the chlorosis; also both viruses often are present in the same plant. However, the spots produced by spotted wilt do not transmit light as do the spots produced by the crinkle disease.

Control. Control measures are the same as for leaf breaking.

GERBERA (TRANSVAAL DAISY)

The one serious disease that affects gerbera (*Gerbera jamesonii*) is foot rot, caused by the fungi *Phytophthora cryptogea* and *P. drechsleri*.

FOOT ROT

Symptoms. The leaves wilt suddenly and their color changes from the normal green to a violet carmine. Plants of all ages may be attacked but the principal damage occurs during flowering time. The fungus invades the crown tissues near the soil level and progresses downward into the roots. Diseased crown and root tissues are soft, water-soaked, blackish brown, and odorless. When infected plants are dug, the cortex of the roots usually sloughs off, exposing the discolored central cylinder or stele. If an attempt is made to pull the plant before digging, breakage occurs at

At left, a healthy gerbera plant is contrasted with one that is affected by Phytophthora foot rot.

the crown and most of the roots remain in the soil.

Control. Use healthy plants for propagating stock, or propagate from seed. Outdoor plants should be placed on well-drained sites. Avoid overwatering. Plants grown in the greenhouse should be planted in sterilized soil.

GLADIOLUS

Gladiolus (*Gladiolus hortulanus*) are affected by many diseases caused by bacteria, fungi, and viruses. The successful gladiolus grower, whether he is a large-scale commercial grower or a backyard gardener, must be able to recognize and control these diseases. Much research has been done on gladiolus diseases, and effective control measures have been developed for most of them.

BACTERIAL LEAF BLIGHT

Symptoms. The first symptom of the disease caused by the bacterium *Xanthomonas gummisudans* is the appearance of water-soaked spots on the leaves. These

Bacterial leaf blight of gladiolus. The spots are first water-soaked and dark green, later becoming tan or brown. The rectangular shape of the spots is characteristic.

spots are at first narrow, horizontal, translucent, and dark green, becoming more or less regularly square or rectangular and brown. Single lesions may unite to form larger ones so that an entire leaf may be covered. When the spots are numerous a leaf may be partially or completely killed. Bacterial slime exudes from blighted leaves and, under moist conditions, a sticky film covers portions of the leaves. Soil particles and small insects may become embedded in this film. Plants developing from cormels are much more severely attacked than are larger plants developing from corms. The disease occurs sporadically and is most severe in wet seasons. It may not occur at all in dry seasons.

Control. Specific control measures for this disease have not been developed. Spraying frequently with one of the streptomycin plant sprays may be beneficial in wet seasons.

BOTRYTIS LEAF SPOT, STEM ROT, AND CORM ROT

Symptoms. The fungus *Botrytis gladiolorum* causes leaf spots, flower spots, stem rot, and corm rot. Leaf spots are remarkably variable in shape and size. They may be oval or circular, and pinpoint in size, or large and irregular. They usually have brown or grayish-brown centers that often are covered with gray masses of spores. The margins of small spots usually are definite and dark brown, reddish brown, or even red, but large spots more often have indefinite margins. When large spots occur on leaves or stems the tips of the leaves may turn yellow and die prematurely.

If infection occurs at or near the soil level it may progress inward through the leaf bases and rot the stem. Vascular bundles leading downward from the lesions may have a discoloration that often may be traced into the bundles of the newly developing corm. Above, the outer leaves turn yellow and die.

Under extremely wet conditions most of the tissues at soil level may be killed, causing the plant to fall over and die. Under moist conditions the rot is wet and

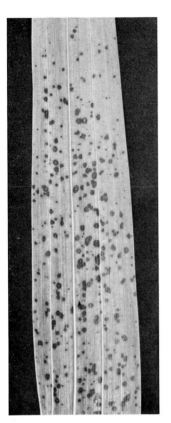

The Botrytis disease of gladiolus. At left, small leaf spots; bottom, flowers partly and completely destroyed by the fungus, which produces abundant spore masses on the rotted tissue. Below, corms in various stages of rot. The husks have been removed from the corm at upper left to show the brown, decayed tissue. Black sclerotia may be seen protruding through the husks of the other corms.

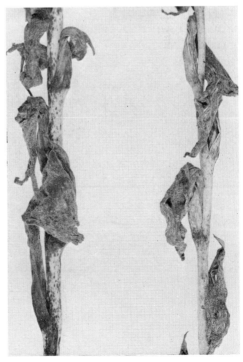

brown; under dry conditions it is dark brown and firm, with a definite margin. The outer leaf bases may become shredded and break off easily at the junction with the corm. Botrytis spores develop on the dead tissue at soil level, and several inches upward on dead or living shoots. Sclerotia generally are produced below-ground on the more extensive lesions and may remain attached to the dead tissue until it disintegrates. In stem rot the infection may come from diseased corms, in which case it usually appears soon after the plants emerge, or it may come from airborne spores, with the time of infection dependent on suitable weather conditions.

Infections on flowers often begin as small, water-soaked spots, usually near the edges of the petals. The spots may enlarge rapidly and become rather slimy. They vary in color from white to brown and are sometimes white with a light-brown or violet border. The fusion of several spots rapidly converts the flower into a drooping mass of tissue that, under moist conditions, is soon covered with a gray mass of spores.

Several types of symptoms occur on corms infected with *B. gladiolorum*. Slightly sunken, round, straw-colored or greenish-brown to dark-brown spots occur on the corm surface. These spots often appear water-soaked, and vary from pinhead size to one-half inch or more in diameter. Occasionally a brown discoloration of the basal plate may be seen. One or more brown vascular bundles may extend up to the stem area. The core may be partially or completely rotted, with or without surrounding tissue also rotted, and with or without infected brown vascular strands radiating to the surface. The core may fall out or become completely covered, leaving a doughnutlike appearance.

In other instances there is a general spongy decay that varies in texture from soft to rather fibrous and firm. Sometimes the husks appear normal, but the corm underneath will be completely rotted. At an early stage water can be squeezed from such a corm, but in the advanced stage the decay becomes spongy or corky, and tan to chocolate brown in color. By this time so much of the corm has decayed that the whole mass is unusually light in weight. Removal of the husks will reveal either a dark, punky mass interspersed with pockets of mycelium, or a rock-hard, mummified corm. Black sclerotia are often found on the corm surface or intermingled with the rotted tissues and mycelium.

When infected corms are planted some of them decay in the soil. Others give rise to weak, yellow shoots that soon die, and only a few produce healthy shoots.

Control. Botrytis infection on plants in the field occurs only under excessively moist atmospheric conditions, accompanied by temperatures between 50° and 65°F. Fogs or dews, which deposit fine droplets of water on the leaves, provide ideal conditions for leaf infections. When such conditions prevail the plants should be protected with a fungicide such as benomyl, Bravo, Botran, maneb, zineb, ferbam, or nabam. Spraying or dusting every few days may be necessary as long as conditions favorable for Botrytis infection persist. Roguing of diseased plants and removal of old flower spikes will do much to reduce the amount of infection. Plants in locations with good soil and air drainage are less likely to be infected than are plants in locations with poor drainage. Digging corms in dry weather and as early as possible is one of the best methods of reducing Botrytis corm rot. After being dug, corms should be cured promptly at 85° to 95°F with a relative humidity of about 80 percent for 7 to 10 days. After being cleaned the corms should be returned to the curing chamber for 4 to 7 days longer. Because the fungus spreads more rapidly at temperatures of 38° to 45°F than at higher temperatures, corms that were cured at higher temperatures do not usually rot under normal storage conditions. Cured corms usually can be stored safely at 40° to 50°F and a relative humidity of 70 to 80 percent with little danger of loss from Botrytis rot.

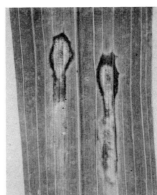

Above, left and center, brown vascular strands extending through the flesh of *Curvularia*-infected gladiolus corms. Right, Curvularia lesions on gladiolus leaf, with black spore masses in the center of the spots.

CURVULARIA LEAF SPOT AND CORM ROT

Symptoms. In the Midwest the disease caused by the fungus *Curvularia trifolii* f. *gladioli* is usually a corm rot, but foliage and flower infections occur occasionally. In certain other areas it is primarily a foliage and flower disease. Lesions on the corms are brown to black, round, elongated or irregularly shaped, and vary in size from pinpoints to three-fourths inch in diameter. Penetration may be slight to deep, and many lesions are completely walled off by a layer of periderm (protective tissue). Many corms have a dark-brown, corky core rot. Frequently brown vascular strands extend from the core through the flesh to the surface of the corm.

On the leaves the spots are at first pinhead-size and round, but grow rapidly, mainly in the direction of the veins. The spots are tan, surrounded by a darker reddish-brown ring and a yellowish halo. Black spore masses develop in the center of the spot. Small leaves on plants grown from cormels often are curled and twisted at the tips. The fungus may girdle small plants near the soil level and cause them to die in sections of a row.

On the stem and bud sheath the spots are brown and oval with sunken edges. They enlarge rapidly, and spores are produced abundantly. The brown color changes to black when the spores appear.

On the opened and unopened flowers, spots appear first as small, colorless, water-soaked areas, enlarging to form irregularly circular or elongated blotches that are light yellow, then brown, and finally black when the spores develop.

Control. Before planting, the corms should be inspected carefully and all those with rot lesions should be discarded. The healthy-appearing corms should be given one of the following treatments before

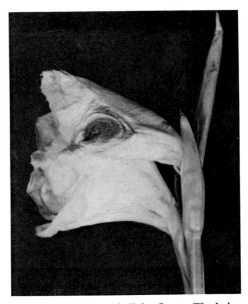

Curvularia lesion on gladiolus flower. The lesion is covered with a black mass of spores.

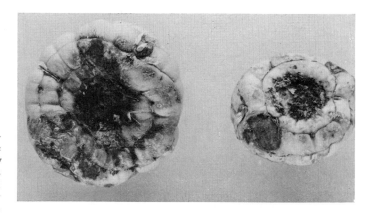

Curvularia corm-rot lesions are variable in size and shape. On the Picardy corms (above) the lesions vary from small, round spots to large, irregular areas. The rot has also extended into the base of the core. On the Leeuwenhorst corms (below) all of the spots are small and may be confused with scab lesions.

planting: Dip the corms 15 to 30 minutes in a 1:1,000 dilution of Busan 72; dust the corms with Arasan; dip the corms for 15 to 30 minutes in a solution of 3 pounds Dowicide B in 100 gallons of water.

In some areas the leaf and flower infection phases of the Curvularia disease have not become serious enough to warrant special control measures. If spraying is indicated, maneb should be used.

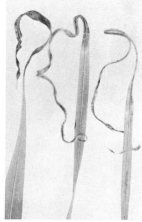

Small gladiolus plants grown from cormels may be killed in sections of rows when attacked by *Curvularia.* The leaves are often curled and twisted at the tips.

FUSARIUM ROT

Symptoms. Although the disease caused by *Fusarium oxysporum* f. *gladioli* is primarily a corm rot, the foliage, flowers, and roots also are affected. Three forms of the disease have been distinguished, mainly by their effects on the corms, and are known as the vascular, the brown-rot, and the basal dry-rot forms of the disease. The symptoms common to all three forms are a brownish to black dry rot of the corm tissues; yellowing, browning, and death of the foliage; and browning and destruction of the roots.

In the vascular form of the disease a sectioned corm will reveal a brown discoloration of the core, and dark vascular bundles extending laterally into the flesh. In an advanced stage of the disease the infected strands reach the surface of the corms at the nodes, and brown lesions develop at these points.

In the brown-rot form of the disease, tan, brown, or blackish lesions may appear anywhere on the corm but are most common near the base. The rotted tissue often is quite thick and may extend all the way through the corm. Vascular discoloration is not associated with this form of the disease.

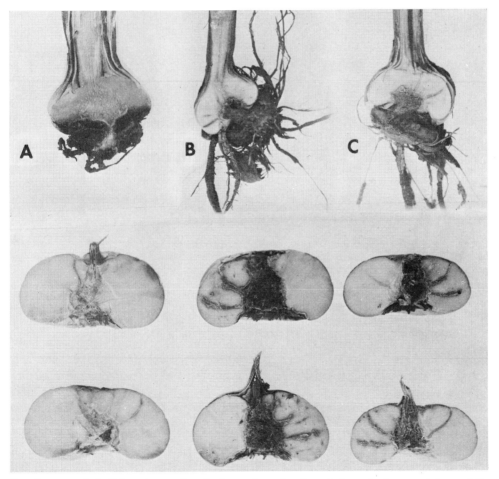

Fusarium rot of gladiolus. At top, lengthwise sections showing, A, how the brown-rot form of the disease progresses from the mother corm to the daughter corm; B and C, how the vascular form progresses from the mother corms into the core and vascular tissues of the daughter corms. Center and below: older corms showing rotted cores and discolored vascular streaks associated with the vascular form of the disease.

The basal dry-rot form of the disease differs from the brown-rot form mainly in the thickness and position of the lesions. Basal dry-rot lesions occur only on the base of the corms and usually are restricted to the first and second internodes. The lesions are visible when the corms are dug and, under favorable curing condi-

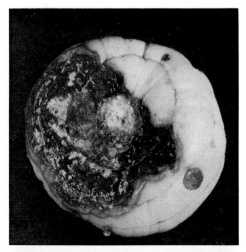

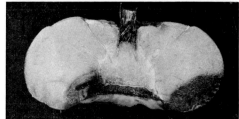

Gladiolus corms affected by the brown-rot form of the Fusarium disease. At top: bottom view of corm. Below: section of corm showing thickness of rotted tissue.

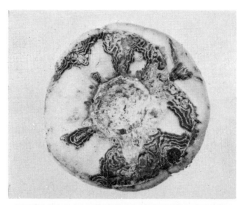

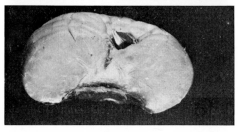

Corms of three gladiolus varieties affected by the basal dry-rot form of the Fusarium disease. Top, variety Gold Eagle; center, Lake Placid; bottom, Spotlight. The sectioned Spotlight corm shows the extreme thinness of the rotted tissue, in contrast to that of brown rot.

tions, do not enlarge after harvest. They rarely, if ever, extend deeper than 2 to 4 millimeters into the flesh. The diseased tissue is dark brown to black, hard, rough, and usually somewhat scaly after the corms are dug. The affected area is sunken, and there is a sharp line between diseased and healthy tissues.

When infected corms are planted the more severely diseased corms rot without sprouting, or produce feeble shoots that soon die. The less severely infected corms may produce plants that grow normally until late in the season. Eventually, however, the tips of the leaves turn yellow and begin to die back gradually until the entire plant is dead.

Distinct flower symptoms often appear on *Fusarium*-infected plants. In colored varieties the petal color is darker than normal, and the petals are narrow, with less ruffling of petal edges. The florets are smaller than normal, often tulip-shaped, and tilt upward and do not open as fully as normal florets.

Control. Before planting, the corms should be inspected carefully and all those with rot lesions should be discarded. The healthy-appearing corms should be given one of the following treatments before planting: Dip the corms for 15 minutes in a 1:1,000 dilution of Busan 72; dust the corms with Benlate 50W; dip the corms for 15 minutes in a suspension of 1½ pounds Benlate 50W in 100 gallons of water; dust the corms with Arasan; dip the corms for 15 minutes in a solution of 3 pounds Dowicide B in 100 gallons of water.

Gladiolus should not be replanted in locations where this disease was present the previous year.

Corms should be dug before the onset of cold, wet weather. Dry the corms as soon as possible after digging. This is best done by using heat and fans to circulate warm air through the crates. The temperature should be kept between 85° and 95°F during the drying period. The average relative humidity should not be allowed to fall below 50 percent at a temperature of 80°F or below 80 percent at a temperature of 90° to 95°F. Dirty or muddy corms should be washed before drying. The corms should be turned in the trays at least once or twice during the initial drying period so that all corms will be exposed to the circulating air. Clean the corms as soon as old and new corms separate readily, then hold them at curing temperatures for several days before stor-

ing. Corms should be stored at 40° to 50°F.

Treating cormels in hot water will greatly reduce the rot-producing pathogens in an infected lot. This treatment, however, can be used only on fully dormant cormels. Dormancy varies with variety and temperatures under which they were grown and stored. Cure the cormels for 1 week or longer at 95°F. Presoak them for 2 days in water at shed temperature. For the last 2 to 5 hours of this period, hold them in diluted commercial 38 percent formaldehyde, 1 part to 200 parts of water. Remove the cormels from the solution, drain well, and immerse in water at 135°F for 30 minutes. Immediately after removing them from the bath, cool the cormels rapidly and dry them thoroughly. Place in cool storage until ready to plant.

INK SPOT

Symptoms. Cause of the ink-spot disease of corms is not known but it appears to be physiological rather than parasitic. In one instance of this disease, black spots developed on the corm husks of corms that were placed in a metal container when they were slightly damp. The spots formed where the husks made contact with the container. Similar spots have been found on corms stored in wooden containers. The stained areas usually are confined to the husks.

Control. If the corms are cured properly and stored in cool, dry quarters, ink spot should not be a problem.

Ink-spot disease may develop on gladiolus corms where they come in contact with a moist container. The stained areas usually are confined to the husks.

PENICILLIUM CORE ROT

Symptoms. Infection by the fungus *Penicillium funiculosum* occurs most frequently through the corm base. Infected core tissue becomes dark brown or black. Core rot may progress until the central portion of the corm is destroyed, leaving a hole so that the resulting corm resembles a doughnut. Decayed corm tissue gradually becomes dry, corky, and light brown, and can be separated easily from the adjacent healthy storage tissues. Careful removal of the decayed core leaves a smooth inner surface with occasional depressions corresponding to conical decayed projections. Corm tissues other than the core and lateral vascular traces usually are not invaded by the pathogen. Corms in which decay is less advanced show only an internal darkening of lateral or longitudinal vascular tissue. A pronounced depression of the basal callus layer or a darkening of the top of the corm is usually the first external symptom, but internal decay is well advanced by this time. Dull-green spore masses develop on corm bases in storage at high temperature and humidity.

During the period of corm maturation, following flower harvest, spike stubs may become infected and the pathogen can progress into the top of the corm. Infected stubs soon become brown and leaf blades develop brown necrotic areas at points of contact with the stub tips.

Control. This disease is generally of minor importance. All affected corms should be sorted out and destroyed.

PENICILLIUM ROT

Symptoms. The rot caused by the fungus *Penicillium gladioli* occurs primarily in storage, after infection has taken place through injuries or breaks in the corm surface. The rot appears as rather firm, but not hard, reddish-brown, sunken spots that are more or less irregular in size and shape and sometimes slightly roughened by irregularly concentric wrinkles. At low temperatures a green mold grows over the lesions. Numerous egg-shaped, tan sclerotia may be found embedded in the rotted tissues.

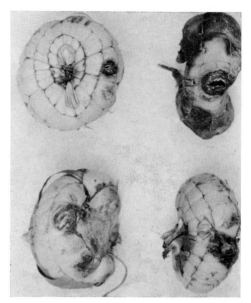

Corm lesions caused by *Penicillium gladioli* are reddish-brown, sunken spots with numerous egg-shaped, tan sclerotia in the rotted tissues.

Control. Corms should be well cured and handled carefully to avoid injuries. Damp storage conditions should be avoided.

PROTRUSIONS

Symptoms. Cone-shaped protrusions appear on the back side of the petals. When the protrusions are examined from the front side of the petals they appear as short, hollow cones. One or more florets of a spike may be affected. The disorder is transmitted from the parent plants to the progeny through corms and cormels.

Control. Dig out and destroy affected plants.

RHIZOCTONIA NECK ROT

Symptoms. A disease caused by the fungus *Rhizoctonia solani* occurs in plants grown from cormels, and destroys the plants in long sections of the rows. Infection occurs in the basal parts of the leaves about 1 inch below the soil surface, causing lesions that are at first soft and water-soaked, later brown and necrotic. Eventually the bases of infected leaves are shredded. Infected plants usually wilt,

One or more florets may have cone-shaped protrusions on the back side.

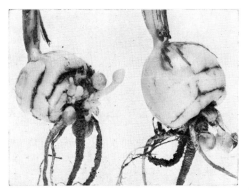

Rhizoctonia lesions give gladiolus corms a horizontally striped appearance.

and ultimately the entire above-ground portions of the plants die. Occasionally leaf sheaths and corm scales on affected plants are destroyed, and long, narrow, brown lesions develop on the corms where the infected scales are attached. These lesions give the corm a horizontally-striped appearance. A characteristic cobweblike mycelial growth to which soil particles cling is usually found if the dead tops are carefully lifted from the soil.

Control. Before planting, treat the soil with Terraclor at the rate of 150 pounds per acre.

A shredded condition at the base of the leaves is an additional symptom of Rhizoctonia infection of gladiolus.

Rhizoctonia destroys small gladiolus plants in long sections of the row.

SCAB

Symptoms. Scab, caused by the bacterium *Pseudomonas marginata,* is easily recognized by the lesions on the corms. The lesions begin as definitely outlined, water-soaked, circular spots. As the spots age they become light brown, dark brown, or almost black. Eventually the lesions become shallow depressions surrounded by definite and somewhat elevated margins. The individual spots vary in size from pinpoints to one-fourth inch in diameter. They may be few or numerous and usually are most abundant on the lower half of the corm. The scabs do not extend deeply into the flesh of the corm and are rather easily removed, leaving a clean, saucer-shaped cavity. A gummy ooze from the corm lesions is characteristic. At first colorless, the ooze changes to yellow brown or dark brown and, when dry, is brittle and shiny like varnish. The diseased husks may be glued together and to the corm by this sticky material and masses of soil may be glued to the corm.

Lesions on the husks are elongated and dark brown to coal black. Holes with rough, blackened margins are left where the causal bacteria destroy some of the husk tissue.

When the plants are growing in wet soil, a stem- or neck-rot stage of the disease may develop. This form of the disease begins with numerous tiny spots that enlarge and coalesce to form elongated lesions that become soft and watery. These lesions occur most frequently near the base of the leaves and may spread upward

The neck-rot phase of gladiolus scab occurs only when the plants are growing in wet soil.

for several inches. Later the lesions turn yellow, then gradually brown, and affected tissues may become shredded. In severe cases the plant may be so weakened that it breaks over and dies.

Control. Although the scab disease is caused by a bacterium, a vector or carrier appears to be instrumental in bringing about infection. One such vector is the bulb mite *Rhizoglyphus echinopus,* common in many gladiolus fields. The insecticides aldrin and heptachlor, applied at the rate of 3 pounds active ingredient to 14,500 feet of row, have given excellent control of scab. The insecticide should be applied in the furrows just before the corms are covered at planting time. Granular and liquid forms are equally effective. Dasanit, Di Syston, Dyfonate, and Thimet used at the same rates also have been effective.

SEPTORIA LEAF SPOT AND CORM ROT

Symptoms. The fungus *Septoria gladioli* causes a leaf spot, and a corm rot commonly known as "hard rot." The leaf-spot phase is much more common than the corm rot. The spots on the leaves are small, brown or purple brown, and almost round.

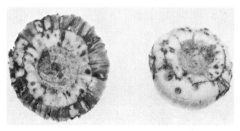

Gladiolus scab is easily recognized by the characteristic round, sunken lesions on the flesh of the corms and by the elongated, dark lesions in the husks, which may also be marked with holes.

Septoria leaf spot of gladiolus. The black, pimplelike structures in the center of the spot are pycnidia of the causal fungus.

As the spots enlarge the affected tissue becomes darker and is finally dark brown with a lighter center. In the centers of the older, more mature spots, the lighter area is dotted with small, black, pimplelike structures — the pycnidia of the causal fungus. In severe infections entire leaves or plants may be killed. This is most likely to occur in young plants in dense stands.

Corm lesions appear in the fall as water-soaked, circular, reddish-brown to brownish-black spots. It usually is necessary to remove the husks to find these lesions. As the spots enlarge the centers become sunken, the color deepens to dark brown or almost black, and the margins become more definite, irregular, and somewhat angular in outline. The diseased tissue is very hard. Frequently the corm is reduced to a hard, wrinkled mummy. Plants from diseased corms usually are dwarfed, often fail to bloom, and may die prematurely.

Control. The Septoria disease seldom becomes serious enough to warrant special control measures. Spraying with one of the fungicides recommended for Botrytis control should be effective against *Septoria* also. Sort out and discard diseased corms before planting.

STEMPHYLIUM LEAF BLIGHT

Symptoms. Small, circular lesions that are light green to yellow with a small prominent red spot in the center occur on leaves attacked by the fungus *Stemphylium* sp. Two or more lesions may coalesce to form irregularly shaped spots, usually with an equivalent number of red spots in the affected area. The presence of these red spots is a distinguishing characteristic of the Stemphylium disease and has given rise to the name "red spot disease." Leaves may be so severely spotted that they are killed, and under favorable weather conditions all of the above-ground parts are killed. The most severe outbreaks of Stemphylium leaf blight occur during or near flowering time.

Control. If infection starts in a field, spread of the disease can be checked by spraying with maneb or Dyrene, 2 pounds to 100 gallons of water. The disease is favored by high atmospheric humidity with warm days and cool nights.

Stemphylium spots on gladiolus leaves are small and light green to yellow, with a distinctive red spot in the center.

STORAGE BREAKDOWN

Symptoms. Various kinds of discolored areas appear on the corms during storage. In some cases only the outer tissues are affected, with thin, hard, brown areas appearing on the lower half of the corm. In other cases distinct pitted areas appear on the corms, often extending deeply into the flesh and sometimes developing into hard, irregularly shaped masses.

Control. Storage breakdown is a physiological condition associated with improper curing and storage conditions. When corms are cured and stored properly, storage breakdown is no problem.

STROMATINIA DRY ROT

Symptoms. All below-ground parts of the plant may be affected by dry rot, caused by the fungus *Stromatinia gladioli*. A rot on the lower inch or two of the leaf bases may be seen at the soil surface. This

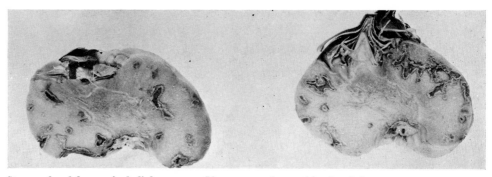

Storage breakdown of gladiolus corms. Uppermost photo, thin, hard, brown areas may appear on the lower half of the corm (healthy corm at top); center photo, distinct, pitted areas may extend deeply into the flesh; bottom photo, hard, irregular masses may be found embedded in the flesh of the corm. This condition is related to improper curing and storage practices.

rotting often results in premature yellowing and death of the tops. Small, black sclerotia usually are present on diseased leaf bases.

Diseased corms characteristically bear many small lesions ranging in size from mere dots to about one-half inch in diameter. The individual lesions are approximately circular and appear first as minute, reddish-brown spots, usually on the side and lower half of the corm, but frequently on the upper half as well. The line of demarcation between healthy and diseased tissue is rather sharp. As the lesions increase in size the centers become sunken, the color usually deepens to black, and the margins become definite. The margins of the lesions, especially noticeable in the larger and older diseased areas, are slightly elevated. The consistency of diseased tissue is characteristically corky. Mummification of the corms often occurs in storage.

If diseased corms are sectioned, blackened vascular strands often may be seen extending from the core to the surface of the corm.

Control. Badly diseased corms should be sorted out and discarded. Low, wet planting sites should be avoided. Corms that are dug before the onset of cold, wet weather usually are not troubled with this disease. Stromatinia rot usually will not develop in soils having a temperature of 80°F or higher. Corms dug from cold, wet soil should be dried as quickly after digging as possible. Treating the soil with Botran or Terraclor before planting is beneficial. Vapam or Vorlex may be used to fumigate the soil but planting cannot be done until all traces of the fumigant have disappeared.

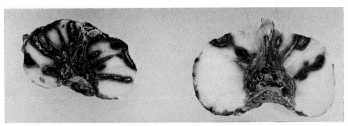

Left, gladiolus leaf base infected with **Stromatinia.** Rotting of the tissues gives the leaf a shredded appearance. The tiny, black dots on the tissue are sclerotia of the causal fungus. The bottom photo shows Stromatinia lesions on gladiolus corms. All of the husks except the bud scales have been removed to show the lesions in the flesh of the corms. Photo immediately below shows blackened vascular strands extending through the flesh of **Stromatinia**-infected corms.

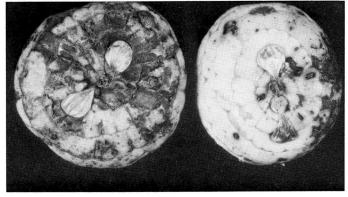

VIRUS AND VIRUS-LIKE DISEASES

A number of virus diseases affect gladiolus but the individual diseases have not been clearly differentiated. Often several strains, or even different viruses, may be responsible for a given condition. Different gladiolus varieties often react differently to the same virus. The following descriptions are, therefore, only general and are subject to variations.

Mild mosaic. A mild mosaic in gladiolus is produced by the bean yellow-mosaic virus. This disease is characterized by angular light- and dark-green mottling in the leaves and flower stems. It is most readily detected in early summer when the plants are growing rapidly and before air temperatures become high enough to cause symptoms to disappear. The pencil-stripe break patterns in the flowers of some varieties are sometimes lighter, sometimes darker than the normal flower color, and are often inconspicuous and seldom

so unattractive that they affect the sale of the blooms. In other varieties both the leaf markings and the flower breaks are so conspicuous as to be objectionable.

The mild mosaic virus is spread by aphids. Plantings of gladiolus adjacent to bean or clover fields may be heavily inoculated with the virus as a result of insect migrations. The virus is much more destructive to beans than to gladiolus.

White break mosaic. The white break mosaic disease in gladiolus is caused by one or more strains of the cucumber mosaic virus. This virus produces contrasty white or yellowish blotching of flowers accompanied by crinkling, shrinking, and other flower deformations. Flower bracts are often strongly yellowed and may wither early. Affected flowers open slowly and imperfectly, and fade early.

White break symptoms usually cannot be detected in the leaves during the season in which the plants become infected. The following season, however, conspicuous symptoms appear on the leaves of some varieties. Other varieties never show leaf symptoms. Typical leaf symptoms consist of small, chlorotic squares between two leaf veins. The spots may be gray, yellow,

The bean yellow-mosaic virus produces pencil-stripe break patterns in the flowers of some gladiolus varieties. This symptom is often so mild that it is unnoticed.

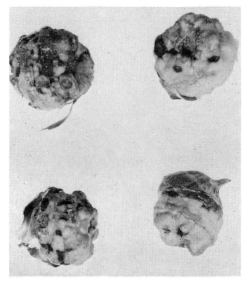

Warty corms from gladiolus plants, variety Innocence, affected by the white break disease. Only a few varieties develop this symptom in the corms.

White or yellow blotching of gladiolus flowers is the first symptom of white break. Gray, yellow, brown, or reddish spots that develop on the leaves usually do not appear until the season after the plants became infected.

brown, or reddish. Severe cases can be recognized readily because of the overall yellow appearance of the plant, while mild cases may be detected only if the leaf is held against light. Affected plants are commonly much shorter than normal.

In some varieties affected by white break the corms are typically warty.

Aster yellows. The aster yellows organism produces varying symptoms in gladiolus depending on when infection takes place. When plants are infected early in the season they usually die before reaching maturity. The flower parts remain green, eventually turn yellow, and shrivel without developing the normal flower coloration. Young leaves may be uniformly yellowish green and the flower spikes spindling and green. The plants turn yellow and shrivel prematurely, and in some varieties a severe twisting of the flower spike occurs and the florets open incompletely or not at all. Plants that become infected later in the season and survive to the following season then express the symptoms known as "grassy top." The plants have spindly, weak, yellow leaves and short, thin roots.

Discoloration or degeneration of vascular tissue occurs near the base of the affected corms. In cross-section the core is larger and more irregular in shape than the core from a healthy corm of similar

Severe twisting of a gladiolus flower spike, caused by the aster yellows organism.

The weak spindly gladiolus plants on the right were produced by corms carrying the aster yellows organism. A healthy plant is shown at left. All plants were the same age.

Necrotic ring spot on gladiolus leaf infected with the tobacco ring-spot virus.

size. The storage tissue at the basal part of diseased corms is pale in color and coarse in texture in comparison with healthy tissue. The base of the core is rough, hard, and black in many cases. Primordial roots are dark and prominent, and extend rather deeply into the corm.

Ring spot. Necrotic ring-spot patterns on the leaves are produced by the tobacco ring-spot virus and probably by other viruses. Flowers are not affected.

Stunt. Although the virus nature of the stunt or stubhead disease has not definitely been established, there is some evidence that the tomato ring-spot virus may be the causal agent. Entire plants are stunted. The flower spikes are short, often consisting of only four or five florets per spike. Leaves of affected plants are somewhat smaller than normal and usually are rather stiff and erect.

Notched leaf. Gladiolus notched leaf is caused by tobacco rattle virus and is transmitted by two species of nematodes. Affected plants have seriously distorted growth and notches along the margin or along the veins of one or more leaves, in most cases combined with chlorotic or brown necrotic stripes and spots. The flower stem and bud may stop growing and show deformities and necrosis as well. These plants are highly susceptible to infection by *Botrytis gladiolorum* and often die prematurely. In infected stocks, less serious deviations from normal growth often occur. Even a crumpling of the leaf tissue between the veins may indicate that the plant is not healthy.

Control of virus diseases. Affected plants should be rogued out as soon as noticed. Insects should be kept under control throughout the growing season. Gladiolus should not be planted near beans, clover, cucumbers, melons, or tomatoes.

GLOXINIA

The diseases of gloxinia (*Sinningia speciosa*) are few, but those that occur may cause serious losses.

BORON-DEFICIENCY DISEASE

Symptoms. On young seedlings the first symptoms of boron deficiency are small,

Boron-deficiency disease of gloxinia. Blackened leaves and petioles of plant on left show boron deficiency; healthy plant on right. Photograph courtesy of the Division of Plant Pathology, University of California, Berkeley.

brownish-black, irregularly shaped areas at or near the base of the leaf blade. Within a few days the discoloration spreads toward the tip of the leaf and downward into the crown of the plant. At the same time there is a marked wilting of the leaves. Frequently, the growing point of a plant is killed prematurely. On older affected plants in pots, the flowers and peduncles are considerably reduced in size and appear wilted. Eventually the above-ground parts of the plant become brown and the plant dies.

Control. This disease occurs when the culture medium is deficient in available boron, needed for normal growth of the plants. This deficiency can be corrected by several applications of a 6-percent solution of boric acid at intervals of 2 weeks.

LEAF AND STEM ROT

Symptoms. In plants attacked by the fungus *Phytophthora cryptogea* the leaves become water-soaked, dark brown, and quite flaccid. Infection may progress from the leaf blade to the petiole, causing death and collapse of the leaf. In badly diseased plants the stems may be attacked; quite often stem infection is noted in the absence of leaf infections. Infected plants at first appear stunted and wilted, but later they may become chlorotic, collapsing as infection spreads into the petioles. Diseased stems bear sunken, water-soaked lesions that may be rather narrow and run lengthwise on the stem, or may be quite large and encompass the stem. Infected corms exhibit soft, sunken, surface lesions. Severely diseased corms usually have dark-brown, soft, internal, necrotic areas. Infected roots are darkly discolored and flaccid.

Control. Plant gloxinias in steamed soil. Remove and destroy infected plants as soon as they appear.

MYROTHECIUM ROT

Symptoms. The fungus *Myrothecium roridum* produces dark necrotic areas on the leaf blades of young plants and a water-soaked appearance of the petioles; it girdles the stem near the soil surface. Severe infection often results in distortion and stunting of the apical stem region. An infected mature plant characteristically has a large black sunken lesion at the soil surface, at which point the stem is easily broken. Under moist conditions black sporodochia (spore-producing structures of the causal fungus) fringed with white mycelium appear on the lesions and on the underside of infected leaf blades.

Control. Excessive moisture favors the spread and destructiveness of the disease. Control is largely a matter of sanitation and proper culture. Water should not be used in excess, and overhead syringing or sprinkling should be avoided. Sterilized soil should be used consistently. Infected plants should be removed and burned.

HOLLYHOCK

Hollyhocks (*Althaea rosea*) are subject to several diseases, the most common being rust, and the most destructive, anthracnose.

ANTHRACNOSE

Symptoms. Veins and leaf blades are attacked by the anthracnose fungus, *Colletotrichum malvarum*. Black blotches, the principal symptom, also are produced on the petioles and stems. This disease is especially destructive in the greenhouse, where it may cause heavy losses to seedling plants.

Control. Spray with bordeaux mixture. Remove and burn all plant parts in the fall.

LEAF SPOTS

Symptoms. The fungus *Cercospora althaeina* causes small, angular, ashy-white spots with a dark border. In many places the dead tissue cracks and falls away, giving a shot-hole effect to the leaf. *Phyllosticta althaeina* causes much larger spots, but of the same character. In the center of such spots, a few pycnidia may occur, appearing as black, pinpoint dots. The tissue becomes brittle and may fall away, leaving irregular, jagged holes.

Control. Control measures are the same as for anthracnose.

RUST

Symptoms. Brown pustules on the undersides of the leaves are characteristic signs of rust, caused by the fungus *Puccinia malvacearum*. These pustules may

Hollyhock rust. The numerous brown pustules on the underside of the leaf are unmistakable signs of this disease.

also occur to a lesser degree on the upper side of the leaves or on the stems and green flower parts.

Control. Picking the first rusted leaves in the spring, and dusting the plants with sulfur or spraying with zineb, will aid in controlling the disease. It is important to keep the new foliage covered with the fungicide. Destroy all the common mallow plants (*Malva rotundifolia*) that may be growing in the vicinity, as this weed also may be attacked by this rust and is a means of spreading it to hollyhocks. Old plants should be cut down and the old parts burned as soon as flowering is over.

STEM CANKER

Symptoms. Black to dark-green, water-soaked, rapidly enlarging cankers appear on the stem near the ground line when plants are attacked by the fungus *Sclerotinia sclerotiorum*. The centers of the cankers later dry and turn white or light brown. Often the stems are completely girdled. Shredded fibers project from the cankers, and sclerotia are formed on the cankers and in the stems made hollow by the causal fungus.

Control. Infected plants should be removed and destroyed as soon as noticed. If practical, sterilize the soil and replace with new soil before replanting to hollyhocks. Treating the soil with Terraclor before planting will aid in preventing this disease.

HYACINTH

Hyacinths (*Hyacinthus orientalis*) are not often troubled with serious diseases. The most common disease on this crop is yellow rot.

BOTRYTIS BLIGHT

Symptoms. Leaf tips turn brown. The affected areas may enlarge and become covered with a gray mold. Additional brown spots may develop further down the leaves. Flowers may rot and become covered with the causal fungus, *Botrytis hyacinthi*. Small, black sclerotia develop in the rotted tissues.

Control. Promptly remove and destroy all infected leaves and flowers. Spray frequently with ferbam, thiram, zineb, benomyl or Bravo.

MOSAIC

Symptoms. Mosaic is a virus-caused disease resulting in blue-green mottling, streaking, and blotching of the leaves. Flowers may be withered.

Control. Destroy affected plants.

ROOT ROT

Symptoms. Plants affected with Pythium root rot show retarded growth, and on sunny days their leaves become less turgid. In a more advanced stage the leaf tissue dies, starting at the tip. This often occurs several weeks before the end of the growth period. Many of the roots of plants with withering leaves no longer show the normal white color; they first become glassy and soon turn gray and limp.

Control. Apply Dexon to the soil 1 month after planting.

SOFT ROT

Symptoms. When plants are affected by soft rot, caused by the bacterium *Erwinia carotovora*, the bulbs fail to produce flowers, or if a flower stalk does develop, the buds open irregularly and eventually the flowers rot. The stalk commonly rots off at its base and falls over. The rot involves the top of the bulb, and after a few days the leaves and flower stalks, if there are any, can be lifted from the rotted bulb.

Control. Planting sound, vigorous bulbs and growing them properly will overcome the disease. Excessive watering, unduly high temperatures during forcing, heating of the bulbs in storage or in shipment prior to planting, and repeated freezing and thawing, all encourage development of soft rot.

YELLOW ROT

Symptoms. Yellow, water-soaked stripes appear on leaves attacked by the bacterium *Xanthomonas hyacinthi*. The tissue in these stripes dies and leaves brown streaks down the leaf. Infected flower stalks appear water-soaked, then become brown and shriveled. The vascular bundles in the infected leaves, flower stalks, and bulbs are filled with yellow bacterial slime that oozes out when these parts are sectioned. Rotted areas or pockets appear in the bulbs and slimy yellow masses of bacteria ooze from them. The rot usually progresses until the bulb is completely destroyed.

Control. Plant only disease-free bulbs and destroy all plants that become infected.

HYDRANGEA

Hydrangea (*Hydrangea macrophylla*) is subject to two or more ring-spot diseases caused by viruses. Mildew also can be quite troublesome.

BOTRYTIS BLIGHT

Symptoms. The Botrytis fungus may be a serious problem on maturing plants because it can cause complete blighting of developing flower buds. Later, the senescent flowers may drop on leaves and become focal points of Botrytis leaf spot. In the propagating bench the cut or injured leaves may become completely blighted by the fungus. The affected parts soon are covered with a downy, gray mold and later they dry and become gray-brown.

Control. See control of this disease on geranium.

CHLOROSIS

Symptoms. Chlorosis is the condition in which the leaves lose their normal green color and become yellow. In severe cases the plants may be stunted.

Control. This condition may be corrected by growing the plants in a slightly acid soil. Aluminum sulfate may be used to acidify the soil.

POWDERY MILDEW

Symptoms. The mildew fungus, *Erysiphe polygoni,* usually appears first on the lower

Powdery mildew on a hydrangea leaf.

leaf surfaces, where it produces a white, loose, cottony mycelium. Yellowish blotches usually appear on the upper surface of the leaves over these infected areas. Purple-brown blotches with mycelium also appear on the upper surface of the leaf when conditions are favorable. If the disease is allowed to progress, the fungus not only may cover the entire leaf surface, but also will advance into bud clusters and flowers. Severely infected plants often are badly stunted.

Control. The use of dusting sulfur or wettable sulfur spray will control this disease. Benomyl spray applied at 21-day intervals has been reported to completely control the disease.

RING SPOT

Symptoms. Hydrangea varieties vary greatly in their tolerance to the hydrangea ring-spot virus. Only Charm and Sainte Speer are known to be unsalable when infected.

The leaves of Charm are conspicuously distorted. Development of the midrib is checked about midway from the base to the tip of the leaf, and the lamina becomes strikingly curled or waved at this point. The lower leaves are more nearly flat and have irregular blotches or rings. The upper leaves of Sainte Speer show milder curling and no characteristic ring patterns. This variety is severely dwarfed and produces few florets per head, but those are normal in size and shape. Except for the suppression of floret number, no recognizable flower symptoms are associated with the hydrangea ring-spot virus.

Rose Supreme and Sainte Therese occasionally develop yellowish blotches or rings on the lower leaves before flowering. Merveille frequently shows conspicuous yellow blotches and chlorotic rings in green leaves, and occasionally reddish-brown rings also. Shaded or retarded leaves of Merveille and other varieties often show a reversal pattern, green rings on a yellow ground.

The more tolerant varieties, Strafford, Engel's White, Todi, and Monte Forte

Perle, generally show no symptoms during the forcing period.

The tomato ring-spot virus also affects hydrangea, causing dull-yellow chlorosis of leaves with diffusely bordered, dark-green blotches superimposed. Plants are dwarfed and the leaves are smaller than normal, often irregular in shape, frequently narrow, occasionally but not typically rugose or wrinkled, and sometimes stiff and brittle. Flowers are generally smaller than normal. They tend to open irregularly, and the same flower cluster may contain green flowers along with those that have developed the wanted color of pink or blue. The color of the sepals is paler than normal. A shoot dieback is sometimes associated with this disease.

Control. Badly diseased plants should be destroyed. Culture of the florist's hydrangea in the United States is based on use of varieties tolerant to hydrangea ring-spot virus. The so-called "running-out" or "slow decline of some varieties appears to represent gradual contamination of intolerant sorts during propagation and subsequent build-up of the virus. There is so far no evidence that the more tolerant varieties are significantly damaged by hydrangea ring-spot virus, and consequently there is little incentive for a shift in propagation practice to protect the less tolerant new varieties against contamination.

IRIS

Irises (*Iris* spp.) are generally divided into two groups, those grown from rhizomes and those grown from bulbs. The rhizomatous irises usually are grown out-of-doors and the bulbous irises are more often grown in greenhouses. Each type is subject to a number of diseases, some of which affect both groups.

BACTERIAL LEAF SPOT

Symptoms. Usually the first indications of bacterial leaf spot, caused by *Xanthomonas tardicrescens,* are rather large, dark-green, water-soaked spots on the leaves. These areas are conspicuous in early morn-

ing or after a period of moist weather. A few hours of dry weather may cause a large part or even all of these areas to disappear, leaving only small, yellow-green spots. With a renewal of moist conditions, the dark, water-soaked areas reappear.

Streaks that are 1 to 6 inches long and fairly uniform in width, and large irregular spots are common. Lesions occur on all parts of the leaves above the extreme base but they are most frequently found on the margins. Tiny, pale spots, at first visible on one side only, enlarge, become translucent, and extend through the leaf. In a dry or even moderately dry atmosphere the spots increase in size slowly or not at all, and the water-soaked margins are lacking. Under such conditions the infection may be unnoticed, or mistaken for the leaf spot caused by the fungus *Didymellina macrospora.*

The organisms that cause bacterial leaf spot remain alive, though inactive, as long as the leaf lives, and in any period of sufficient atmospheric humidity they renew growth and produce the characteristic lesions. There is usually considerable bacterial exudate from large, active lesions, with drops sometimes forming at the lower edge of the spots.

Control. Clean culture and exposure of the soil to sun and drying conditions, and removal of all leaves in late fall or winter should aid considerably in preventing infections that probably arise from bacteria that have overwintered in the soil or in old infected leaves. Spraying with bordeaux mixture may be beneficial.

BLACK SLIME DISEASE

Symptoms. The nature of the black slime disease, caused by the fungus *Sclerotinia bulbarum,* is usually that of an "all or none" type of infection. Most bulbs are infected so early in the spring that they are completely decayed by harvest time, leaving only a shell which is eliminated in the cleaning process. The percentage of partially infected iris bulbs harvested is small. Typical symptoms on such bulbs are blackened tips or bases.

Control. The causal fungus is primarily bulb-borne, and is easily controlled in this stage by a hot water and formalin treatment. Another effective control measure is dipping the bulbs in a 7.5 percent suspension of Terraclor 75 percent wettable powder, followed by dusting the bulbs and the sides of the furrows with Terraclor at 200 pounds active ingredient per acre.

BLACK TIP

Symptoms. A black, powdery layer develops on the tips of iris leaves attacked by the fungus *Didymellina poecilospora*.

Control. Because the fungus usually attacks only foliage that has been frosted or otherwise injured, control measures are usually unnecessary. Spraying with bordeaux mixture may be of benefit.

BLUE MOLD

Symptoms. Blue mold of bulbous iris is caused by various species of *Penicillium*. Symptoms vary with time of attack, iris variety, and species of *Penicillium*. The husk may be normal in color but sunken and sometimes split at the center. The infected fleshy scales at first may be soft, watery, and white to greenish gray, later becoming rather firm and yellow or brown. Mature spots on the sides of the bulbs are often more or less oval, sunken, and dry, and sometimes have a cavity under the husk. The centers of the spots are often partially covered with a blue-green, powdery mold. Infected bulbs may decay completely, leaving nothing but the husk and a little debris. Infection often enters at a bruised area or at a wireworm puncture, and may be only one scale deep. Many bulbs infected on the sides or tip will grow, but when the rot begins at the base the bulbs usually decay completely.

Control. Avoid bruising the bulbs when digging. Cure bulbs rapidly, clean, and store them in thin layers. Discard all infected bulbs. Treat bulbs with Arasan or Spergon dust and avoid overheating them in storage. Prevent excessive dampness in the warehouse and provide good ventilation during cold storage.

CROWN ROT

Symptoms. On rhizomatous iris the first noticeable symptom of crown rot, caused by the fungus *Sclerotium rolfsii*, is a gradual dieback of the tips of the outer leaves. Further examination will reveal that the bases of these leaves have rotted near the soil line. As the disease progresses toward the center of the clump, the inner leaves begin to exhibit the dieback symptom and the entire plant is soon dead. The rhizomes are not attacked. White, fanlike mats of the causal fungus can be found between the rotted leaf bases. Numerous light-brown sclerotial bodies usually appear on the rotted leaf bases.

When the disease attacks bulbous iris, infected plants are yellow and stunted, and die prematurely, either from rot of the bulb, or of the stem and leaves just above the bulb. The bulbs appear soft and crumbly or fibrous. The outer leaves usually turn yellow before the inner ones, yellowing from the top downward. Under warm, moist conditions the surrounding ground may become covered with sclerotia that are white at first and later tan or reddish brown, and up to one-quarter inch in diameter. Sclerotia may also develop on the stem and in the bulb. A mass of soil often clings to infected bulbs when dug and sclerotia are sometimes present in the soil and on the bulb. The husk adheres tightly to the bulb at the point of infection and may be partly shredded. After infected bulbs have dried, the color of the husk is a dead-looking light tan.

Early infection of the fleshy bulb scales usually appears as a soft, white, cheesy rot with a sharp margin but with no change in color from the normal bulb. As the bulbs dry, the infected tissues become dry, sunken, and tan. Scattered, dark, grayish lines are sometimes present within the sunken areas. Sclerotia are often found on or between the scales. Bulbs may be rotted completely with nothing but the husk and sclerotia left. Infection usually occurs at the bulb tip but may be elsewhere. Under suitable storage conditions, the infected area dries up, but under warm, moist conditions the fungus can spread to adjacent bulbs in the tray.

S. rolfsii also attacks many other kinds of annual and perennial plants.

Control. Do not allow irises to become overcrowded because the disease is most serious when plants are growing under crowded conditions. If the disease appears suddenly during the early summer, remove and destroy severely infected plants.

When crown rot occurs in bulbous iris, discard all affected bulbs and soak the remaining bulbs for 3 hours in a 0.5 percent formalin solution (1 part commercial USP formaldehyde in 200 parts water). Infested soil can be drenched with formaldehyde before replanting to iris. Drench loosened soil with ½ pint commercial formaldehyde in 3 gallons of water; apply at the rate of ½ gallon per square foot. Treating the soil with Terraclor has effectively controlled *S. rolfsii* in some areas. Soil fumigation with chlorobromopropene also has given some degree of control.

FUSARIUM BASAL ROT

Symptoms. Basal rot of bulbous iris, caused by the fungus *Fusarium oxysporum,* is characterized by infected, sunken areas at the base of the bulb, with husks adhering firmly and sometimes matted with a white or reddish-tinged mass of the fungus. The basal plate and fleshy scales are brown or reddish brown and shrunken, with a fairly definite margin between decayed and healthy tissue. The rot is rather firm.

Control. Avoid bruising the bulbs when digging or cleaning them. Sort the bulbs, discarding all diseased ones, immediately after digging and again before planting. Treating the bulbs as soon as they are harvested is the most important factor influencing control of Fusarium basal rot of iris. The bulbs should be treated with benomyl within 1 or 2 days after harvest. Dusting the bulbs is usually more effective than soaking or spraying them. Other materials that may be used to treat the bulbs are thiabendazole and Tersan. Avoid planting in infested soil.

GRAY MOLD ROT

Symptoms. The rot caused by the fungus *Botryotinia convoluta* destroys the plants during the winter and spring. Its presence is first noticed when the plants fail to grow in the spring, or when they put forth a few weak shoots that later turn yellow and die by midsummer. Such plants are easily removed from the soil because of the death and decay of the roots. The rhizomes are shrivelled and partially or completely decayed. Diseased tissue is gray brown in color and pithy in texture. There is no foul odor as in soft rot.

Early in the spring, large numbers of spores are formed by the causal fungus on the exposed portions of the rotted rhizomes and at the base of the leaf sheaths of the previous year's growth. At the same time large masses of characteristically convolute, shiny, black sclerotia may be found on the undersides of rotted rhizomes and along the roots.

Control. Any plants that appear to be sickly or fail to grow in the spring should be dug up, together with some of the surrounding soil. If the rhizomes and roots are rotted and the characteristic black sclerotia are present, destroy the plants and the immediately surrounding soil.

INK SPOT

Symptoms. Ink spot is a disease of bulbous iris that causes irregular, black patches or blotches on the leaves soon after they push through the ground. Such spots sometimes are surrounded by a reddish area. Under moist conditions the attack may be so severe that the foliage withers and dies prematurely. On the bulbs, the disease is characterized by irregular, inky-black stains on the husks, sometimes in the shape of rings, and varying in size and number. The fleshy scale beneath the husk may exhibit small yellow dots or irregular, elongated, sunken, black craters with distinct margins. Infected bulbs sometimes rot, leaving only the husk and a mass of black powder. The causal fungus, *Mystrosporium adustum,* may spread through the soil and attack adjacent healthy bulbs.

Control. Sort out and destroy all diseased bulbs. Treat healthy-appearing bulbs for 3 hours in water at 110°F to which formaldehyde has been added in the proportion of 1 pint to 25 gallons of water. Plant immediately, or dry and cool the bulbs properly by spreading them in thin layers in a cool place with good air circulation. Spray with bordeaux mixture.

LEAF SPOT

Symptoms. Leaf spot, caused by the fungus *Didymellina macrospora,* usually is confined to the leaves, but symptoms may appear on stems and flower buds also. The first evidence of the disease is the appearance of minute, brown spots surrounded by water-soaked margins that later turn yellow. The spots occur on either surface of the leaf and enlarge slowly during the spring and early summer. After the plants bloom, the spots enlarge more rapidly and coalesce. Many

Iris leaf spot, caused by the fungus *Didymellina macrospora,* is easily confused with bacterial leaf spot. The spots caused by *Didymellina* (below) are usually more clearly defined by their reddish-brown borders with dark spore masses in the center. In spots of bacterial origin (right), a bacterial ooze is often displayed.

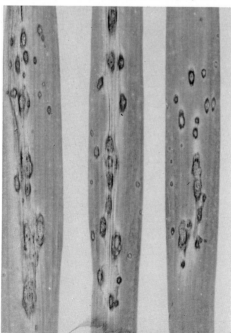

leaves are killed prematurely. The older spots have gray centers surrounded by reddish-brown borders. Repeated severe attacks may kill the plants after a few years, since premature death of the leaves gradually weakens the rhizomes or bulbs.

Control. The causal fungus passes the winter on old iris leaves. Removing and burning all diseased leaves in the fall is usually all that is necessary to control the disease. Bordeaux mixture 4-4-50 will control the disease, even under conditions favorable for the fungus. A good spreader should be added to the mixture to make it adhere to the foliage. Zineb and benomyl have been reported as giving good control of Didymellina leaf spot.

MOSAIC

Symptoms. Irises are afflicted with several mosaic diseases, caused by different viruses but having similar symptoms. Mosaic is more severe on bulbous iris but rhizomatous iris may be attacked also.

Leaf symptoms consist of a characteristic mottling of the foliage with light, yellowish-green areas alternating with the normal green. On bulbous iris, dark, teardrop markings occur on white, blue, and lavender flowers, and clear, featherlike markings appear on yellow flowers. The bud sheaths may develop yellow streaks or, more often, bluish-green blotches on a pale-green background. Not all infected plants show both leaf and flower markings.

Control. Since the virus is carried in the bulbs or rhizomes, control measures must be directed toward removing all infected plants. A disease-free foundation stock, from which all planting stock can be selected, should be established where irises are propagated on a large commercial scale.

RHIZOCTONIA NECK AND BULB ROT

Symptoms. The fungus *Rhizoctonia solani* causes a soft, light-brown rot at the neck of the bulb, resulting in death of all above-ground parts without any dieback of the leaf tips, as may occur in soft rot. In severe cases of neck and bulb rot, dark-brown lesions occur on the outer scales, and the bulbs may be almost completely rotted away.

Control. Treat the soil with Terraclor before planting.

RUST

Symptoms. Rust, caused by the fungus *Puccinia iridis*, can be recognized by the large numbers of orange-brown, powdery pustules of spore masses on the leaves. If infection is severe the foliage may be killed prematurely.

Control. Remove and burn all infected leaves in the fall. The following season, dust the plants several times with dusting sulfur in areas where this disease has occurred.

SCORCH

Symptoms. Symptoms of the scorch disease of rhizomatous iris, caused by *Pseudomonas* sp., include a gradual dying back of the plants starting at the leaf tips, with the dead leaf tissues turning brown or reddish brown and eventually dying back to the rhizome. The roots also start to rot or become digested. This rot continues until it reaches the rhizome. Plants that survive the initial attack may persist but seldom regain full vigor.

Control. Diseased plants should be dug, placed in a container, carried from the planting, and destroyed. When replanting rhizomes from plants taken from a planting where diseased plants are present, the newly cleaned and trimmed rhizomes should be dipped in sodium or calcium hypochlorite, in the form of household bleach — diluted before use to ½ percent of the active material. The dip rapidly loses strength and should be renewed regularly. Dipping rhizomes in a bath containing 200 parts per million streptomycin may also prove beneficial.

SOFT ROT

Symptoms. Soft rot, caused by the bacterium *Erwinia carotovora,* results in a soft, ill-smelling rot of the rhizomes and the lower leaf sheaths. Leaves on infected plants may wilt and eventually collapse completely because of rot at the base. In plants where the decay is progressing more slowly, the leaves may die back gradually from the tips. Finally all of the internal structure of the rhizome is disintegrated except the tough outer skin, which remains intact. Infection takes place almost entirely through wounds, especially those made by the iris borer *Macronoctua onusta.*

Control. All rotted portions of the rhizomes should be carefully cut out and destroyed when the plants are divided. After the rhizomes have been cleaned they should be spread out to dry in the sun. They should be replanted in a new location. Since the bacteria that cause soft rot are highly susceptible to drying as well as to sunlight, shallow planting with the upper half of the rhizome above the surface of the soil will aid considerably in preventing further trouble. A well-drained soil is desirable. Control of the iris borer is especially important.

Iris leaves often die back from the tips on plants affected by soft rot of the rhizomes.

TOPPLE

Symptoms. The topple disease of Dutch iris is first characterized by a water-soaking of tissues in the last internode of the flower stem. This is sometimes followed by the formation of small droplets of a viscous liquid. Shortly thereafter, the affected tissue shrinks and the flower topples. Following the initial symptoms, affected stems never produce a normal, fully expanded flower. Occasionally the floral parts are partially expanded, but floral expansion is usually halted in the bud stage. The elapsed time for symptom sequence is a matter of only a few hours.

Control. This disease is nonparasitic but the exact cause is unknown and definite control measures cannot be prescribed. However, a similar disease in gladiolus and tulips has been minimized by treating the soil with calcium nitrate.

KALANCHOE

Kalanchoe is relatively free of serious diseases but powdery mildew and crown rot occasionally become troublesome.

POWDERY MILDEW

Symptoms. A grayish-white, powdery growth of the causal fungus, *Sphaerotheca humuli* var. *fuliginea,* appears on the leaves. Badly infected areas dry out and leaves may die.

Control. Spray with wettable sulfur, benomyl, or Karathane.

CROWN ROT

Symptoms. The fungus *Phytophthora cactorum* attacks the base of the stems, causing black lesions. The rot progresses upward, causing the leaves, flower stalks, and flowers to wilt.

Control. Plant in a light, porous soil which should be steam sterilized before it is used. Avoid overwatering. Do not reuse old pots unless they have been sterilized.

LILAC

Lilacs (*Syringa vulgaris* and *S. persica*) are susceptible to a few diseases, the most common being powdery mildew and the most destructive being bacterial blight and Phytophthora blight.

BACTERIAL BLIGHT

Symptoms. The bacterial blight organism, *Pseudomonas syringae,* attacks young lilac shoots as they develop in early spring, causing brown spots on leaves and internodes. These spots become black and enlarge rapidly, especially in rainy weather. On somewhat mature stems the spots usually elongate and kill the leaves. The rest of the twig remains alive and upright. When the spots occur on very immature internodes, the infection spreads around the twig, girdling it for a considerable distance. The stem bends over at this lesion and the part above it withers and dies. Infected areas are typically black, as contrasted to the brown cankers caused by Phytophthora blight.

Control. Prune out and burn blighted twigs as soon as they appear. Spraying with bordeaux mixture 2-2-50 as soon as the disease appears will help check it.

COLD INJURY

Symptoms. Cold injury in lilacs is sometimes mistaken for a parasitic disease. Near-freezing temperatures in late spring sometimes cause the leaves to become brown and torn around the edges and along the veins. The leaves may be somewhat puckered.

Control. There is no control for this condition.

GRAFT BLIGHT

Symptoms. In graft blight the leaves are smaller and fewer than normal. They become yellow between the veins and at the margins. They are curled and brittle, and either fall prematurely or abnormally late. The plants are stunted.

Control. Graft blight occurs on lilacs grafted or budded on privet understock. The growth of the privet root does not keep pace with the growth of the lilac top. Consequently the root cannot supply sufficient moisture for the tops, and manufactured foods are prevented from moving into the roots. Graft blight can be avoided by propagating lilacs on their own roots, either by using the layering technique, or by means of cuttings.

LEAF BLIGHT

Symptoms. Large, brown, irregular, zoned spots caused by the fungus *Cladosporium herbarum* are formed on lilac leaves. The spots are gray-brown at first but a secondary fungus, *Heterosporium syringae,* may give the spots a velvety olive-colored bloom. Diseased areas may crack and fall away.

Control. Spraying with bordeaux mixture 2-2-50 will control leaf blight. Several applications, beginning the middle of June, are usually necessary.

PHYTOPHTHORA BLIGHT

Symptoms. Phytophthora blight on lilacs is quite similar in some respects to bacterial blight. Lesions caused by the fungus *Phytophthora cactorum* are dark brown instead of black, and infection may advance much farther than is common with bacterial blight. Phytophthora blight often kills all the young sucker shoots that arise from the roots of old lilac bushes. Affected blooms become light brown. The disease is most severe when spring weather is wet and when the bushes are crowded or improperly pruned.

Control. Prune lilacs each year so the branches will not become too crowded. If bushes have been infected, prune out all dead twigs. Spray the bushes with bordeaux mixture when the leaves are opening and again when they are fully opened.

POWDERY MILDEW

Symptoms. Grayish-white blotches of the fungus *Microsphaera alni* appear on the leaves in midsummer or later. Tiny,

Lilac leaf covered with powdery mildew. Such leaves are common in late summer.

black, spherical fruiting bodies of the causal fungus are abundant in the feltlike patches of mycelium late in the summer.

Control. Mildew is common but comes so late in the season that it does little harm. Control measures are seldom necessary but if control is desirable, dust the leaves with dusting sulfur or spray with wettable sulfur, Karathane, or benomyl.

VERTICILLIUM WILT

Symptoms. When lilacs are attacked by the fungus *Verticillium albo-atrum* the leaves wilt, become pale, and lose their glossiness. They fall early, leaving the branches bare. Branches of infected plants die during the winter.

Control. The wilt fungus is soilborne and persists for many years. Dig up and burn infected plants. Do not replant lilacs in the same location.

WITCHES'-BROOM

Symptoms. Typical witches'-brooms are formed in the top part of the plant when lateral buds produce 2 to 6 slender shoots that branch freely and bear leaves one-fourth the size of normal ones. Most of the small leaves are normal in shape but some of them may be twisted or rolled. A few nearly normal leaves may be scattered along the broomed shoots. Some of these normal leaves have lighter green, chlorotic flecks and some distortion of the leaf surface. The disease is caused by a virus.

Control. Destroy affected plants.

LILY

Lilies (*Lilium* spp.), whether grown in the greenhouse or out-of-doors, are subject to a number of serious diseases. Virus infections constitute a major hazard, and other troublesome diseases are Botrytis blight and the root-rot complex.

ANTHRACNOSE

Symptoms. Anthracnose on Easter lily blossoms is caused by the black scale fun-

gus, *Colletotrichum lilii*. In most respects the plants appear normal — satisfactory in height and vigor, with good foliage color, and with only a few brown and withered leaves at the base of the stem. Many of the unopened buds, however, are aborted and turn brown or black. Large, brown, irregular lesions appear on the trumpet tissues of many of the open blooms. The pedicels of some of the affected blooms are blackened; in some cases the discoloration affects all the pedicel tissues, in other cases only the surface layer of cells. The petal lesions are light brown and the affected tissues are collapsed and paper thin. Close inspection will reveal the presence of many small, circular, water-soaked lesions. Larger irregular lesions arise by coalescence of numerous small lesions. Lesions occur on top, bottom, and sides of horizontally oriented blooms.

Control. Control is dependent primarily upon detection and elimination of black scale infected bulbs. Spread of infection from diseased plants to plants grown from noninfected bulbs is unlikely in a properly managed greenhouse. Spread from diseased to healthy plants, however, might occur in an operation in which soil is not sterilized or in which overhead sprinkling or splashing of water is permitted.

BLACK SCALE

Symptoms. Bulbs affected by black scale, caused by the fungus *Colletotrichum lilii*, vary in color from brown to nearly black, in contrast to the white or lemon yellow of healthy bulbs. The injury extends to several layers of the scales but the outermost layer is most severely affected. Young lesions appear as more or less irregular, light-brown areas on the scales. Older lesions are darker brown and somewhat sunken. Still older lesions are nearly black, and the affected tissues are shriveled and dry. The lesions are more numerous on the apex half of the scales and usually occur on the outer surface, but they may be found on the inner surface also. The cores of severely diseased bulbs appear perfectly normal, and when diseased bulbs are planted they grow almost normally and produce flowers. However, because of their unsightly appearance, diseased bulbs are unsalable.

Control. Sort out and destroy all infected bulbs. Dust the healthy-appearing bulbs with Arasan to protect against reinfection from the soil.

BLUE-MOLD BULB ROT

Symptoms. Blue-mold bulb rot, caused by *Penicillium* sp., is primarily a storage rot and is dry and punky rather than soft and wet. Lesions on the scales are commonly sunken and dark brown. Blue-green spore masses of the causal fungus develop on the outer scales, and between the inner scales in advanced stages of decay. The rot develops slowly, 2 or 3 months sometimes being required to completely destroy a bulb.

Control. Mixing 5½ ounces of calcium hypochlorite (20 to 27 percent available chlorine) in 50 pounds of packing soil will effectively control this rot without injuring the bulbs.

BOTRYTIS BLIGHT

Symptoms. The most common symptom of Botrytis blight, caused by the fungus *Botrytis elliptica,* is a spotting of the leaves. The spots are circular or oval, varied in size, and usually orange or reddish brown. In some varieties the spots are light brown, surrounded by a definite reddish-purple margin. Under damp conditions the spots soon become covered with a grayish mold. The spots, when dried out, are thin, brittle, translucent, and commonly ash gray. Heavily infected leaves may be completely destroyed, and typical leaf blight, advancing from the base of the plant upward, becomes evident. Lesions may also occur on the stems, buds, and flowers. Spots on the flowers usually are brown, and in cool, moist weather the flowers are converted rapidly into wet, slimy masses covered with powdery layers of spores. In some cases bulb rotting also occurs.

Control. In the fall, clean up and burn all tops of old plants growing out-of-doors. If the plants are growing in the greenhouse, remove primary infections on the foliage. Keep the humidity down, and water when the foliage will dry rapidly. Spray with bordeaux mixture, or dust the plants with copper-lime dust.

There is some evidence that benomyl at the rate of 2 pounds in 100 gallons of water sprayed on the plants 4 times at 2-week intervals becomes systemic in the lily plants and will protect the foliage throughout the remainder of the season.

DIEBACK AND BUNCHY TOP

Symptoms. In dieback, caused by bud and leaf nematodes, leaves on any part of the plant may turn yellow and droop, or they may turn blackish brown. Nematodes may congregate in the flower buds and cause blindness (failure to produce flowers).

In bunchy top, also caused by bud and leaf nematodes, the plants always emerge with thick, pointed leaves. Further development is irregular, and branching of the stems is common. Typical bunchy-top plants frequently show dieback symptoms during the later stages of their growth.

Control. Dieback and bunchy top are effectively controlled by rigid roguing of affected plants from the field, and by hot-water treatment of planting stock. Bulbs should be held for 1 hour in water at 111°F to which commercial formaldehyde has been added at the rate of 1 pint to 25 gallons of water.

The hot-water-formalin treatment may cause injury to Croft lily bulbs intended for forcing in the greenhouse and is not recommended for this variety. All stunted or distorted plants and plants that tend to develop branched shoots should be removed and destroyed as soon as they are noticed. Destroy all plants suspected of dieback infection as soon as detected. Isolate every pot of lilies that was exposed to the affected plants; if symptoms are not apparent in 14 days these plants can be safely returned to their original location.

FLECK

Symptoms. Necrotic flecks in lily leaves are produced by two viruses, a symptomless lily virus and the cucumber-mosaic virus, neither of which alone causes symptoms in lilies. Characteristic flecks are variable in size, usually elongated parallel to the veins, chlorotic at first, but becoming gray to brown and necrotic. When fully developed the dead areas are depressed, but the surface remains intact. Severely flecked plants are dwarfed and the foliage is curled. Flowers are subnormal in size, fail to open fully, and are variously distorted by thin streaks that become brown and necrotic by the time the flower fully develops. After flowering, and sometimes before, plants begin to lose leaves from the base upward. Such leaves first turn pale yellow with irregular green blotches, then wither away. Affected plants mature early and yield small bulbs. Such bulbs, when planted, produce plants that show the necrotic fleck symptoms.

Control. Remove and destroy diseased plants. Keep aphids under control at all times.

FUSARIUM OR BASAL ROT

Symptoms. Yellowing or purpling and premature dying of the basal leaves occurs in plants affected by basal rot, caused by *Fusarium oxysporum* f. *lilii.* Flowering stems, when produced at all, are stunted and inferior. Brown decay first appears at the base of the scales next to the basal plate and progresses until the scales fall away completely. The bulbs of growing plants may be in an advanced stage of decay before the tops show any sign of disease, especially if stem roots are developed freely. Scales from diseased bulbs often will develop bulblets, but these usually are infected and succumb to the disease.

Control. The source of Fusarium infection may be either diseased bulbs or contaminated soil. Bulbs showing Fusarium rot should never be used for planting stock. Unblemished bulbs from a contaminated or suspected lot should be treated 30 minutes in a solution of 1 part commercial formaldehyde in 50 parts of water.

When scales are removed from bulbs for propagation purposes their exposed bases are vulnerable to attack by the basal rot organism. The formaldehyde treatment is injurious to such scales and should not be used on them. Scales have been effectively protected by dusting with Arasan or Spergon. Arasan is used at the rate of 2 ounces to 60 pounds of scales, and Spergon is used at the rate of 2 ounces to 100 pounds of scales. These materials can be

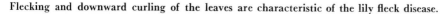

Flecking and downward curling of the leaves are characteristic of the lily fleck disease.

applied by shaking small amounts of weighed scales in a paper bag containing the required amount of fungicide. The scales should be dusted in this manner as soon as they are removed from the bulbs; then they should be planted at once.

MOSAIC (MOTTLE)

Symptoms. Several virus strains cause mosaic in various species of lilies. The general symptom is a mottling of the leaves with definite light- and dark-green areas, but the pattern of the mottling varies with the virus and with the species of lily affected. Affected plants may be stunted, and affected leaves may be twisted, distorted, and curled. In some

Lily leaves affected by mosaic are mottled with light- and dark-green areas.

cases few flower buds are produced on diseased plants, or flower buds may be split or distorted in shape, or may fail to open. Flowers of colored varieties may be blotched or broken.

Control. Several factors must be considered in attempting to control mosaic disease in lilies. Mosaic is spread from plant to plant by aphids, and infection that occurs in the field is transmitted to the bulbs. The virus is carried from one season to the next in diseased bulbs. Aphids can transmit viruses during storage of the bulbs as well as in the field and greenhouse. Thus, the control of aphids at all times is extremely important.

Mosaic-affected plants resulting from infected bulbs show symptoms early in the season, usually before the aphid appears. Removing and destroying diseased plants as soon as they appear will do much toward eliminating the source of the causal virus.

Easter lilies are essentially unharmed by the mottle viruses but they may be a source of infection for some of the common garden lilies. These viruses also cause color breaking in tulips. Easter lilies should therefore never be planted with *Lilium formosanum, L. tigrinum,* or the Elegans group of garden lilies, or next to tulips.

RHIZOPUS BULB ROT

Symptoms. The fungus *Rhizopus* sp. sometimes causes a rot of bulbs in transit and storage, especially when temperatures are high. Bulbs become soft and mushy and have a slightly sour odor. Infected areas on the scales have a water-soaked appearance and are somewhat darker than the healthy portion. Because of their soft, wet condition, completely rotted bulbs adhere to the soil or to any other material used as a packing medium.

Control. Handle bulbs carefully to avoid wounding or bruising. Avoid high temperatures in transit and in storage.

ROOT AND BULB ROT

Root and bulb rot has become one of the most serious diseases of Croft lilies, but not all of the factors involved in this disease are completely understood. A complex of organisms has been found associated with the disease. The fungi *Rhizoctonia solani, Fusarium* spp., *Pythium* spp., *Phytophthora* spp., and *Cylindrocarpon radicicola* have been found in rotted root tissues. Bacteria, nematodes, mites, and symphilids frequently are found also.

Symptoms. Basal roots are rotted and diseased bulbs become rotted and fall apart, or become yellow and blemished. Associated with the root and bulb disorders are varying degrees of plant wilting and stunting, yellowing of basal leaves, leaf scorch, blasted buds, and reduced bud production.

Control. Because the lily root and bulb rot problem is a disease complex rather than a single disease, the problem of control has been approached by attempting to get healthy planting stock rather than by attempting to cure the disease components singly. The most feasible way of doing this is to maintain a mother block of plants descended from a single bulb. The mother-block material is maintained true to type and kept healthy by regular selection and pesticidal treatment of the best bulbs for the next year's mother block. They are planted in soil that has not previously grown lilies and has been fumigated against nematodes.

Eliminating root and bulb disease organisms from planting stocks does not ensure the elimination of the disease complex from field-grown lilies. Healthy planting stocks need protection from reinfection. The most effective single method of giving protection has been to dip scales, bulblets, and bulbs in PCNB-ferbam before planting. Use 2 pounds of the regular formulation for each material in 100 gallons of water. Soak the planting stocks for 15 minutes. Stirring is necessary to keep the fungicides in suspension.

ROSETTE OR YELLOW FLAT

Symptoms. Symptoms of this disease vary with lily species and variety but, in general, diseased plants have a flat rosette or cylindrical appearance, rather than the pyramidal shape of healthy plants. The upper leaves curl downward, are yellow or reddish, and may be twisted or distorted. The internodes are shortened, giving the plants a dwarfed appearance. Flowers are much smaller than normal and the number of flowers is reduced, and many plants do not bloom at all.

Lily rosette is one of the most difficult lily diseases to diagnose because the symptoms may be confused with those of other diseases and injuries. Not all symptoms of rosette are evident in a given plant at a given time. Feeding injuries by the foxglove aphid (*Myzus convolvuli*) cause symptoms that resemble those of rosette and of mottle or mosaic, although this aphid does not transmit either disease.

Control. Remove and destroy diseased plants as soon as they are noticed.

RUST

Symptoms. Small, circular or elliptical rust pustules are formed on the lower surface of the leaves or along the stems when they are attacked by the fungus *Uromyces holwayi*.

Tip burn on lily leaves, caused by fumigation injury. Similar symptoms result from other causes, including unbalanced nutrition.

Control. Remove and destroy infected leaves.

SCALE TIP ROT

Symptoms. In this disease, caused by a bacterium, *Pseudomonas* sp., the outer scales of lily bulbs and the tips of the inner scales are darkened and shriveled. The decaying areas appear black in freshly dug bulbs and brown in cured bulbs. The disease is chiefly damaging when soft rots follow the initial lesions, especially at high temperatures.

Control. No chemical treatments have proved effective. Planting stock should be selected carefully.

SCORCH, LEAF BURN, TIP BURN

Symptoms. Brown, dead areas develop on the leaves either as dying back of the leaf tips, or as semicircular areas along the edges of the leaves. In some cases spots ordinarily occur on the margins of the leaves, usually an inch or more from the tip. The spots are often crescent-shaped at first, but may increase in size until the entire leaf tip is brown and dry. In severe cases nearly all of the leaves on a plant may be affected, although more frequently only a few of those on the upper half of the plant show the symptoms.

Control. There are several causes of burns on lily leaves and a knowledge of these causes will help the grower prevent the troubles. Nicotine fumigation is sometimes responsible for tip burn. Leaf burn commonly occurs on plants affected by root rot. Scorch is often associated with unbalanced nutrition, being most severe in highly acid soils where it can largely be prevented by heavy applications of calcium and nitrogen fertilizers. In moderately acid soils, nitrogen fertilizers alone have prevented scorch.

STEM ROT

Symptoms. In stem rot, caused by the fungus *Phytophthora cactorum*, the plants suddenly fall over, wilt, and die. The lower stem shrinks considerably.

Control. Plant only healthy, vigorous bulbs obtained from a reliable source. Sterilize the soil used in the greenhouse. Avoid planting lilies in a location where the disease occurred the previous year.

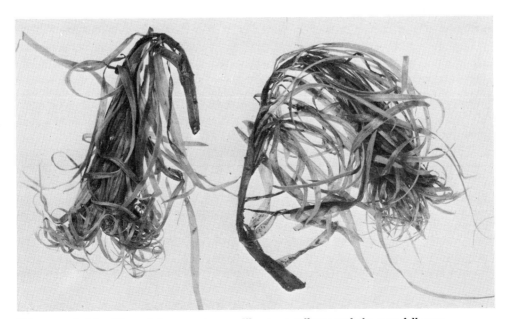

When attacked by ***Phytophthora cactorum***, lily stems collapse and the tops fall over.

LOBELIA

The most serious disease of lobelia (*Lobelia* spp.) is stem rot. This plant is also subject to attacks by leaf-spotting fungi.

STEM ROT

Symptoms. The lower leaves turn yellow, and necrotic lesions form at the base of the stem. The affected organs rot, and the upper parts of the plant wilt and die. The mycelium of the causal fungus, *Rhizoctonia solani,* sometimes grows all over the rotting plant. Sometimes aerial roots are formed just above the lesions at the base of the stems. After the tops die, new shoots may develop from the crowns. In some cases the plants become stunted and exhibit abnormally dark foliage. Sometimes the plants may be killed throughout large areas of a planting.

Control. Treat the soil with Terraclor before planting lobelias.

LEAF SPOT

Symptoms. Small, dead spots appear on the leaves as the result of attacks by the fungi *Cercospora lobeliae, Phyllosticta bridgesii,* and *Septoria lobeliae.*

Control. Control measures usually are not necessary. A good foliage fungicide may be used if desired.

MARIGOLD

Marigolds (*Tagetes* spp.) are more nearly disease-free than most other annuals but a few diseases may occasionally become troublesome.

WILT AND STEM ROT

Symptoms. When plants are attacked by the fungus *Phytophthora cryptogea* the foliage is conspicuously wilted. Blackened and sunken areas on the stems extend from the crown to several inches above the soil surface. Under moist conditions this discoloration may extend into the pith of the stems. Roots and seeds also may be rotted. Plants are usually completely killed in 1 to 3 weeks after infection occurs.

Control. Keep the plants well spaced and avoid overwatering. Remove and burn all infected plants. Applications of copper-containing fungicides to the soil provide some degree of control against wilt and stem rot.

LEAF SPOT

Symptoms. Flecks appear on leaflets that are attacked by the fungus *Septoria tageticola.* Under favorable conditions these flecks enlarge rapidly. At first a darker green than the surrounding tissue, they become smoky gray to nearly black, oval to irregular in shape, and speckled with minute black pycnidia. As the disease develops, the leaflets become curled and twisted but remain attached to the leaf rachis. Lesions on the petioles, stems, and peduncles, less conspicuous than on the leaflets, form elongate, narrow, discolored areas in which black pycnidia usually appear. Seeds that develop in heads enclosed by diseased bracts also become infected.

Control. Spraying with a good foliage fungicide should prevent serious outbreaks of the disease. Do not plant seed from infected plants.

NARCISSUS

Narcissus, or daffodils (*Narcissus* spp.), are subject to a number of diseases, the most common being basal rot and yellow stripe. Diseases generally are more troublesome in large commercial plantings than in home gardens.

BASAL ROT

Symptoms. Basal rot, caused by the fungus *Fusarium oxysporum* f. *narcissi,* usually begins in the root plate at the base of the scales and spreads through the inside of the bulb, generally attacking the central portions first. After infection has started at the base of a scale, the rot extends more rapidly within this scale than across the faces of successive scales, but the basal-rot fungus is capable of spreading in all directions and does so in highly susceptible varieties. In partly resistant va-

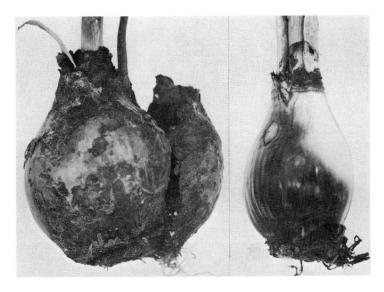

Basal rot of narcissus. At left, external appearance of bulb showing rotted root plate. At right, bulb with outer scales removed showing advanced stage of the rot, which has progressed upward from the base of the bulb.

rieties, the rot tends to advance in streaks and layers, with layers of healthy tissue intervening.

The rotted tissue is a characteristic chocolate brown or purplish brown, and the mycelium of the fungus appears as a weft of delicate white or pinkish-white threads between the scales. The rotted tissue remains somewhat dry and spongy. Usually there is no slimy or mushy breakdown. The outer membranous scale becomes slightly darker and duller in appearance. In a moderately humid en-vironment, the mycelium may break through to the surface, producing a small patch of white mold at the juncture of scales and root plate, but often there is little external evidence of the disease until it has advanced sufficiently to be recognized by the softened texture of the bulb.

Although basal rot primarily affects narcissus bulbs during storage or transit, it may develop during the later stages of growth in the field and destroy the bulbs to some extent before they are dug. When this occurs the tops turn yellow and die

Basal rot of narcissus. At left, longitudinal section of an infected bulb, showing how the rot progresses up the scales from the base. At right, an infected bulb, showing patches of mold at the juncture of scales and root plate.

down in advance of normal maturity. Sometimes slightly infected bulbs survive storage and are planted again, but the fungus eventually resumes activity. Plants from such bulbs are generally stunted, the leaves are short and a pale yellow green, and there is little or no root development.

Control. After bulbs are dug, dry them rapidly but protect them against sunburning. Avoid cutting or bruising the bulbs when digging, cleaning, and grading. Carefully sort out and discard all infected bulbs. Treat the bulbs with benomyl or thiabendazole as soon as possible, preferably not more than one day after digging. The bulbs should be soaked 10 to 30 minutes in a suspension containing 1,000 to 2,000 parts per million of the chemicals, or the dry chemicals may be dusted on the bulbs. Keep storage quarters dry, cool, and well ventilated.

DECLINE

Symptoms. The decline of narcissus is a complex disease caused by the presence of one, two, or more viruses in the same plant. Names that have been associated with this disease are white streak, silver streak, zilverblad, paper tip, chocolate spot, and purple streak. Decline is a late-season disease; symptoms do not appear until after the plants have bloomed. The principal virus in this complex produces white-streak symptoms, with the first symptoms appearing as narrow, dark-green streaks of varying length, which are closely associated and parallel with the main veins of the leaf blade. Flower stems are also affected. Later these streaks become white, gray, or yellowish white. During the late stage, two or more streaks may coalesce. The leaf tips may die, independently of or coincidentally with the white-streak symptoms.

The foliage wilts suddenly and falls down prematurely. Bulbs from affected plants do not attain the size of healthy bulbs. The virus survives in bulbs from infected plants and the stock continues to decline if replanted.

Chocolate-colored spots or purple streaks

are produced by another virus that frequently is present in plants showing white streak.

Control. Rogue out diseased plants. Plant only the largest bulbs. Start foundation stocks from healthy plants. Bulbs from affected plants can be used for forcing since the disease does not affect the flowers. Spray with malathion to control the aphids that spread the disease.

FIRE

Symptoms. The fungus *Sclerotinia polyblastis* produces small, watery, light-brown spots on the flowers. Under humid conditions, flowers may be completely destroyed in a short time. Large, ashen-gray, watery spots develop on the stems below the flowers. Bright-yellow, elongated spots with reddish-brown centers appear on the leaves, usually appearing first near the tips of the leaves. In moist, warm weather the disease spreads rapidly, and leaves may be completely killed within a few days. Bulbs are not attacked.

Control. Remove flowers before they mature. Spray the plants with bordeaux mixture, ferbam, or zineb to protect newly developing leaves and flowers. Pick off and burn infected leaves. Rake up and burn all old foliage. Plant in a new location where the disease has not occurred.

LEAF SCORCH

Symptoms. The first symptom of leaf scorch, caused by the fungus *Stagonospora curtisii,* is a blighted appearance resembling frost injury, evident on the leaf tips when they emerge. The blighted area may extend down one-third or more the length of the leaf. It is separated from the healthy basal portions by a definite margin. Minute, round or oval, reddish-brown reproductive bodies of the causal fungus form within the dead tissue and erupt through the surface on either side of the leaf. During wet weather, spores released from these pustules are splashed by rain to adjacent plants and there cause secondary infections. These infections are elliptical, round, or irregular, distinctly reddish-brown raised spots. Considerable areas of leaf tissue may be killed when such spots coalesce. In severe infections the foliage may die down several weeks in advance of normal maturity.

Control. Treat the bulbs to kill the fungus that may survive in the husks. Formaldehyde may be used. Dusting wet foliage with copper-lime dust or spraying with bordeaux mixture will largely prevent secondary infection. Change the annual planting site and remove mature foliage before it disintegrates in the ground.

MOSAIC

Symptoms. The virus disease commonly known as mild mosaic does not express symptoms until about the time the plants are ready to bloom. At that time mild, blue-green mottles appear in the leaves. Flowers are not affected.

Control. The disease does not seriously damage the plants and control measures are not necessary unless disease-free foundation plantings are being established. In this case all affected plants should be rogued out, and mother blocks should be started from healthy plants.

RAMULARIA BLIGHT OR WHITE MOLD

Symptoms. Advanced stages of Ramularia blight are distinguished by the presence of conspicuous masses of fluffy, white spores covering the upper portions of affected leaves. When plants come up through soil that harbors the causal fungus, *Ramularia vallisumbrosae,* the leaf tips are browned in a way that resembles the leaf scorch disease. Later the browned leaf tips and green tissues below become covered with white spores. Close examination of such leaves will show the presence of small, round, black bodies embedded in the leaf surface beneath the white spore masses. These bodies are another stage of the fungus and, when present with the white spore masses, offer conclusive evidence of the disease.

Control. This disease occurs only under conditions of extreme moisture. If the disease arises, disinfect the bulbs as outlined for the control of basal rot. Before treating, clean the bulbs thoroughly and remove all debris about the neck portion. After treating the bulbs, plant them in soil where the disease has never occurred. Spray the plants with bordeaux mixture or zineb during the growing season. Apply the first spray as soon as possible after emergence.

SMOULDER

Symptoms. The developing shoots are sometimes blighted or deformed when they emerge from the ground. The leaves are crumpled as if unable to expand and separate, and brown streaks, on which black, crustlike structures (sclerotia) develop, appear on the tips or along the margins. A feltlike growth of filaments and spores of the causal fungus (the *Botrytis* stage of *Sclerotinia narcissicola*) may be present on those bodies during wet weather. Flower stems may be rotted, and brown spots may develop on the flowers.

Control. Carefully sort to exclude infected bulbs from the planting stock. Do not plant narcissus bulbs in low, wet sites with heavy soil and poor drainage. Remove and destroy diseased plants as soon as they appear. During wet weather, spray every two weeks with 4-6-50 bordeaux mixture. Do not replant narcissus in an area where the disease occurred the previous year.

SOFT ROT

Symptoms. Soft rot is a mushy form of bulb breakdown associated with high temperature, dense packing, and lack of ventilation. These factors permit the development of the ordinary black mold, *Rhizopus stolonifer,* which also causes decay of some kinds of vegetables under similar conditions. Affected tissues have a soggy, dull appearance and readily disintegrate under pressure.

Control. Prevention of soft rot is entirely a matter of avoiding the conditions favorable to its development. The presence of the causal mold is definite evidence that the bulbs have been exposed to overheating in some form. Except under very moist conditions, the mold does not develop to any appreciable extent at temperatures lower than 85°F, and it only attacks bulbs that were previously weakened by over-heating or mechanical injury. Excessive sunning of freshly dug bulbs, producing sunburn or scald, is one of the primary factors leading to soft rot, and should be avoided.

WET SCALE ROT

Symptoms. Wet scale rot, or crown rot, is caused by the fungus *Sclerotium rolfsii.* The surface of infected bulbs is covered by a conspicuous, coarse, white mold. Several layers of the scales may be rotted through and the color of the decayed tissue is light reddish brown with white streaks. The texture is moist or slimy at first, becoming tough and woody upon drying. Small, round or oval, reddish-brown sclerotia may be found embedded in the rotted scales, lying between them, or borne on the superficial white mold.

Control. Once this fungus is introduced into the soil it is likely to persist indefinitely unless measures to eliminate it are taken promptly. Complete removal of infected plants, including all underground parts, and treatment of the soil with a fungicide are necessary to get rid of the causal fungus. Terraclor is an effective material for treating the soil. It may be applied broadcast to the entire field, or dusted over the bulbs in the open furrow, or it may be used as a spot soil treatment after removal of the diseased plants.

YELLOW STRIPE

Symptoms. Yellow stripe is the most common virus disease on narcissus. Prominent, yellow mottling and streaking occur on the leaves. Diseased leaves are conspicuously roughened and may develop gall-like, raised, elongated areas associated with the veins. The flowers are noticeably smaller, poorer in texture, and thinner tissued than healthy flowers. Dis-

eased flowers, especially the strong yellow ones, develop prominent hyaline streaks or translucent, cleared areas in the tubes and perianth segments. White-flowered forms are also streaked but the effect is much less noticeable.

Control. Rogue out diseased plants as soon as symptoms become evident. Make final roguing during the blooming period. Selection of disease-free plants from partly diseased stock is a desirable method of starting foundation planting stocks in varieties that show a high occurrence of disease. Spray with malathion to control the several species of aphids that transmit the disease.

NASTURTIUM

The most common disease of nasturtium (*Tropaeolum majus*), as well as the most destructive, is bacterial wilt. The Heterosporium disease sometimes causes serious losses in seed-producing areas.

BACTERIAL WILT

Symptoms. When plants are affected by bacterial wilt, caused by *Pseudomonas solanacearum,* the leaves wilt, turn yellow, and die. The stems appear translucent or water-soaked, and the vascular bundles appear as dark streaks beneath the unbroken epidermis. A grayish-white, viscid slime, containing the causal bacteria, oozes out when the stem is cut across. Rotted roots are black. The plants die without blooming.

Control. Remove and destroy diseased plants. Do not plant nasturtiums in areas where the disease has occurred unless the soil has been sterilized. This disease also occurs on tomatoes, eggplants, peppers, potatoes, peanuts, and tobacco; consequently, nasturtiums should not be planted in soil where any of these plants have shown wilt symptoms.

HETEROSPORIUM DISEASE

Symptoms. The Heterosporium disease of nasturtium, caused by the fungus *Heterosporium tropaeoli,* occurs on leaves, stems, and seed, but the most characteristic symptom is a leaf spot. Leaf spots appear first as tiny red flecks that enlarge to round or angular spots up to 1 inch in diameter. The spots occur on both sides of a leaf and frequently coalesce. The lesions on yellow-flowered varieties are tan without a dark margin, whereas those on red varieties have brown centers and dark borders. Under moist conditions, copious dark, greenish-brown conidiophores and spores appear mainly on the lower surface but to some extent on the upper surface also. Yellowing develops around the spots and may involve the whole leaf blade, causing it to wither. Centers of old spots become dry and sometimes crack.

Stem cankers occur commonly on plants grown from infected seed under moist conditions in the greenhouse. These lesions start underground at the point of attachment of seed and stem. The stem develops a reddish-brown rot, which may progress downward into the roots and, under moist conditions, upward to a point 1 inch above soil level. Seedlings may be girdled and die in the first- or second-leaf stage, or death may not occur until the plant is 5 to 6 inches high. Infected seedlings turn yellow, die, fall over, and, under moist conditions, develop profuse, dark spore masses. If the fungus develops slowly, roots may form on the stem above the lesion.

Control. Heterosporium disease can be prevented by a hot-water seed treatment as follows: presoak for 1 hour in cool water; treat in water at 125°F for 30 minutes; cool at once; dry within 12 to 20 hours.

If the disease occurs in gardens, nasturtiums should be eliminated for 1 year.

PANSY, VIOLET

Members of the genus *Viola* are subject to a number of diseases, most of which are leaf spots and root rots.

ANTHRACNOSE

Symptoms. Dead spots, at first small with distinct black margins but soon be-

Anthracnose lesions on violet leaves begin as small water-soaked spots with dark centers and margins. The spots soon enlarge, become tan, sometimes zoned, and have a dark margin.

coming larger, appear on the leaves affected by anthracnose, caused by the fungus *Colletotrichum violae-tricoloris.* Lesions often coalesce, and concentric zones may occur on the spots. Small, dark-brown, elongated lesions surrounded by a light halo appear on the sepals. On the petals the lesions are dark brown in the center, with lighter shades of brown progressing out to the lesion margin. Sunken, elongated, tan to dark-brown, water-soaked areas are characteristic of stem, petiole, and flower-stalk lesions. Pinching of the petioles and flower stalks at the point of the first lesion is common, and progressive dying of tissue down the petiole and stalk often follows. In severe cases the entire plant may be killed.

Control. In small plantings, infected leaves may be collected and burned. Large plantings may be sprayed with maneb or zineb at the rate of 2 pounds to 100 gallons of water. Rake up all old leaves and burn them in the fall.

APHANOMYCES WILT AND ROOT ROT

Symptoms. Plants attacked by the fungus *Aphanomyces cladogamus* show symptoms of wilt, which become increasingly severe. In the early stages of the disease, a deep-red or orange-red discoloration may be found in the vascular cylinder of the roots and stems. Later a general decay involves the base of the stems and the roots some distance downward. The above-ground parts then collapse, dry up completely, and die.

Control. Control measures are the same as for Fusarium wilt.

BLACK ROOT ROT

Symptoms. In black root rot, caused by the fungus *Thielaviopsis basicola,* the plants are dwarfed, the leaves turn yellow, and a brown to black rot of the roots occurs.

Control. Remove and destroy diseased plants. Plant in new or sterilized soil.

COLOR BREAKING

Symptoms. Color breaking in pansies is caused by viruses of the cucumber-mosaic group. The first symptom on the youngest leaves is a clearing of the veins and veinlets, followed by dwarfing and malformation. In some plants some of the older leaves are amber yellow except for small green areas enclosed by yellow veins and veinlets. In the later stages of the disease such plants turn completely yellow. Young infected plants are stunted, with shortened internodes, and die before reaching maturity.

The color changes in the breaking of flower petals vary according to the normal color of the pansies. Red varieties develop red streaks, which later become yellow and then white. Purple varieties show purple streaks and later white streaks. Dark-blue and pale-blue varieties develop dark-blue and pale-blue streaks followed by white streaks. So-called black varieties show black streaks, which turn purple and then white. All of the petals may show breaking, or all but the lowest, or only the two upper petals.

Pansies infected in the seed flats develop malformed and dwarfed flowers when transplanted in home gardens. Pansies infected when older may continue to blossom, and develop ruffled flowers, or flowers with the margins rolled inward. Color breaking may occur on one or more branches while on other stems of the same plant the flowers are normal.

Control. This disease is spread by aphids. Destroy the diseased plants and spray the remaining ones with malathion or nicotine sulfate to control the aphids.

CROWN AND STEM ROT

Symptoms. When plants are attacked by the fungus *Myrothecium roridum,* the leaves wilt. Initial attacks usually occur near the soil level on the stems. The diseased tissue first appears water-soaked, then becomes sunken, dry, and brittle, and is covered with thin, white mycelium and numerous black spore masses of the causal fungus. Infected leaves turn purplish black in spots or streaks.

Control. Excessive moisture favors the spread and destructiveness of the disease. Control of the disease is largely a matter of sanitation and proper culture. Water should not be used in excess, and overhead sprinkling should be avoided. Infected plants should be removed and burned.

CURLY TOP

Symptoms. The curly-top virus causes dwarfing and rosetting of shoots, and reduced flower size. Diseased plants prematurely cease blooming, and gradually deteriorate. Many die before the end of the season.

Control. This disease is spread by the beet leafhopper. Plants should be dusted or sprayed with an insecticide to control the leafhopper.

FUSARIUM WILT

Symptoms. Plants attacked by the fungus *Fusarium oxysporum* wilt and die suddenly. When one is pulled, a dark, slightly sunken area may be seen on the stem near the ground line. The root system is destroyed to the extent that only stubs of the main roots are left.

Control. Diseased plants should be removed and destroyed. Sterilize the soil before planting. There is evidence that the causal fungus may be carried to the soil in barnyard manure.

LEAF SPOT

Symptoms. During cold, wet, windy weather, leaves, petioles, and inflorescences of pansy plants become infected by the fungus *Centrospora acerina* in less than 12 hours. At first all lesions are small, ranging in size from mere flecks to 1 or 2 millimeters in diameter. They appear blue-black on the upper surface of the leaf and have a wet, greasy appearance on the lower surface. Distribution of the lesions is more or less irregular and at random. They occur between, adjacent to, or on the veins and veinlets. Sometimes more lesions develop on one side of the midrib than on the other. They also appear on the petioles. A day or two after infection, lesions may enlarge to 5 or more millimeters in diameter and develop a light-tan center surrounded by a blue-black ring. The lesions tend to retain their individual identities, although some coalescence occurs with age. On older leaves, the tissues surrounding the lesions may become chlorotic and form a light-green halo. Lesions are roughly round to elliptical. Severe infection causes pansy plants to die within a few days.

In addition to pansy and viola, the following ornamental bedding plants have been found to be highly susceptible to natural infection by *C. acerina*: Canterbury bells, columbine, *Delphinium cul-torum, Petunia hybrida, Ranunculus asiaticus, Scabiosa atropurpurea, Lobelia hybrida,* Chinese forget-me-not, *Pentstemon barbatus,* bachelor button or cornflower.

Control. Copper oleate sprays at a concentration of 1 to 800 applied to the foliage of the plants immediately after a rain, or between rains, have given excellent control of this disease.

SCAB

Symptoms. The first symptoms of scab, caused by the fungus *Sphaceloma violae,* may be seen on the leaf blade as minute, green, water-logged dots occurring between the veins. At first they are visible on only one side of the leaf, often the lower, but they are soon seen on the opposite side as well. These areas enlarge into more or less scabby, circular spots. They may be white, ashen, or buff in color. In some cases they are surrounded by a deep-green border. The adjacent normal-green tissue may be noticeably bulged on one surface and depressed on the other.

Lesions frequently extend for a half-inch or more along a vein, either as several more or less distinct lesions or as one continuous lesion. These lesions may cause the vein to become bowed or otherwise malformed. Leaves may become perforated by the falling out of affected tissue. Where the infection is severe, the tissue be-

Violet scab lesions on petioles and leaf blades. The dead tissue has fallen away in many of the older lesions, giving the leaves a perforated appearance.

tween the lesions may become brown and dead. Wilting of the entire blade may result from severe petiole infection. Lesions on runners, petioles, and peduncles are generally linear to elliptical in shape. They may begin as minute points or roughenings, becoming distinctly raised, and finally rupturing lengthwise. Occasionally the affected part is noticeably swollen. Lesions on the capsules and the sepals are small and circular to irregular in shape, often being raised on the capsules.

Control. Spray with maneb or zineb at intervals of 10 to 14 days.

PEONY

The peony (*Paeonia* spp.) is not only one of the most popular and satisfactory garden perennials but it is used extensively by the florist's trade in the spring of the year. Peonies are subject to a number of destructive diseases that must be controlled if peony-growing is to be a success.

ANTHRACNOSE

Symptoms. Anthracnose is caused by the fungus *Gloeosporium* sp. The disease affects stems, leaves, bud scales, and flower petals. Most infections occur when the shoots are still young and the leaf and stem tissues are quite succulent.

Lesions on stems range from small, elongated, reddish spots, which enlarge into lesions with somewhat grayish centers and reddish borders, to extensive, zoned cankers. Cankered stems are commonly twisted, bent, or curled. When very young stems are infected they may be rapidly blighted and completely killed.

On the leaves, spots occur along the veins as well as in the tissue between the veins, and on the petioles. These spots vary from small, elongated, reddish lesions — some of which, as they enlarge, become circular in outline with grayish centers and reddish borders — to irregular, brownish lesions at the edges of the leaf blades. Infected leaves are often curled and puckered, when spots develop at the edges of leaflets before the leaves are mature.

Buds are blasted when bud scales and outer petals become infected. Development of spots and cankers on the upper portions of stems disfigures and distorts the flower pedicel, and can indirectly cause bud blast and otherwise interfere with flower development.

Control. The control measures suggested for leaf blotch and stem spot (page 131) may be used to combat anthracnose. In addition, plants should be sprayed with maneb several times, early in the season.

Peony leaves showing distortion as a result of early infection by the anthracnose fungus.

Stem cankers and stem distortion typical of peony anthracnose.

Peony leaf affected by anthracnose.

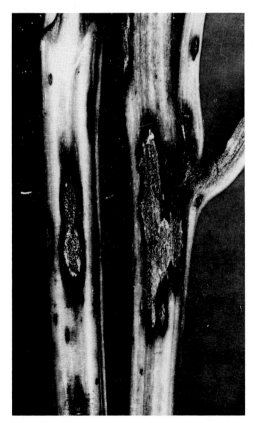

Peony anthracnose stem lesions are characterized by ash-gray centers and dark-red borders.

Peony buds affected by anthracnose are blasted when the bud scales and outer petals become infected. Infection of the flower stem caused this bud to bend to one side.

BOTRYTIS BLIGHT

Symptoms. The fungus *Botrytis cinerea* attacks stems, buds, and leaves. Young stalks in early spring suddenly wilt and fall over. Young buds turn black and dry up. Larger buds, which become infected later, turn brown and become covered with a brown mass of fungus spores. Even the opening flowers may be destroyed. Usually the stalks below infected buds and flowers are rotted for short distances below the necks. Large, irregular, dark-brown areas may also occur on the leaves. Crown and root rots may occur in severe cases. In wet weather the diseased parts soon become covered with a brown, felty coat of fungus spores. Small, black sclerotia are formed on the bases of infected stalks and sometimes in other invaded portions of the plants that have fallen on the ground. The causal fungus will overwinter in this sclerotial stage.

Control. Sanitary measures are the most effective means of control. Remove and destroy all infected parts as soon as they appear. In the fall, cut all stalks just below the surface of the ground, removing as much of the stalk as possible without injuring the bud. Spraying with ferbam, 1 ounce in 4 gallons of water, or with Botran, Bravo, benomyl or bordeaux mix-

Botrytis blight on peony buds. The browned bud is covered with a mass of fungus spores, and the stalk is rotted for some distance below the bud.

ture several times in the spring, beginning when the young tips first break through the ground, is helpful. It is well to soak the soil around the plants with the spray.

BUD BLAST

Symptoms. Although bud blast of peony is associated with some of the diseases described above, buds are frequently blasted from unknown causes. The young buds turn brown or black and dry up while still quite small. Some cases of bud blast have been attributed to potassium deficiency in the soil.

Control. Control measures are unknown.

CROWN ELONGATION

Symptoms. The most striking symptom of this disease, of unknown cause, is a marked elongation of the crowns, with small, weak buds at the tips. These elongated crowns are more numerous than the crowns on healthy plants. Besides growing longer, the crowns also branch from numerous adventitious buds along their sides. The buds from these elongated crowns send up slender, weak shoots that seldom grow to more than 6 inches. The shoots have small, dwarfed foliage and no flower buds. The roots apparently live for years, but never produce vigorous, blooming shoots.

Control. Remove and destroy affected plants.

LEAF BLOTCH AND STEM SPOT (MEASLES)

Symptoms. The fungus *Cladosporium paeoniae* produces spots that are glossy and dark purple on the upper surfaces of the leaves, appearing dull chestnut below. Unless abnormal drought conditions prevail, the leaf cells are not killed. Infection is most pronounced at the margins, especially near the leaf tips, and slight distortion may occur as growth continues. Outer leaves usually are attacked first.

On young stems, infection is first apparent as elongated, reddish-brown streaks with slightly diffuse margins. The lesions present a flat surface, but as growth con-

Cladosporium leaf blotch on lower surface of peony leaf.

raised rather than pitted. Infection spots are abundant at branch and petiole bases where debris of old, infected parts may have lodged.

Control. Remove old tops in the fall, or early in the spring before new growth appears. Cut the stems at the ground level, rake from the plants, and burn. In the spring, just before the new shoots start to break through the ground, spray the soil around the plants with a 1-percent Elgetol solution at the rate of 1 gallon to 200 square feet. Take care to cover uniformly all stem stubs and all scattered bits of old leaves and stems on the ground, as well as the soil surface within the area, as a precaution against measles.

LE MOINES DISEASE

Symptoms. Irregularly swollen, short, stubby roots are formed on plants affected by Le Moines disease, the cause of which is unknown. There is abnormally rapid growth of crown buds that show swollen rings of tissue at their bases. The shoots

tinues those near the crown of the plant tend to coalesce, darken, and become somewhat depressed. Lesions on the upper stems are similar in shape and color, but are fewer in number. They tend to retain their individuality and may become slightly

Typical lesions of peony measles on stems and underside of leaves.

are dwarfed and spindly and the plants fail to bloom.

Control. Remove and destroy affected plants.

MOSAIC OR RING SPOT

Symptoms. This virus disease of peony is characterized by circular areas consisting of concentric bands of alternating dark and light green that develop on the leaves. The spots vary in size. The plants are not dwarfed, and apparently suffer no other injury.

Control. Usually control measures are unnecessary. If plants become so unsightly as to be objectionable, they should be removed and destroyed.

PHYTOPHTHORA BLIGHT

Symptoms. The symptoms of the blight caused by the fungus *Phytophthora cactorum* are easily confused with those of Botrytis blight, described above. The stems, leaves, and buds are affected by both diseases. In Phytophthora blight, the affected parts are dark brown or black and somewhat leathery. When the lower part of the stem is attacked, black lesions several inches long are formed, and the shoot droops over. The central portion of the lesion is black but is lighter toward the edge so that the color of the infected portion gradually merges with the reddish color of the healthy stem. When young stalks are attacked near the ground line, entire shoots turn black. The fungus that causes this disease may also cause a destructive crown rot.

Control. The control measures suggested for Botrytis blight may be used to combat Phytophthora blight also. Where severe infection has occurred, it is well to remove 2 inches of topsoil around the plants and replace with fresh soil. A top-dressing of sand will prevent excessive moisture around the stalks and aid the circulation of air around the young shoots.

STEM ROT

Symptoms. The symptoms of stem rot, caused by the fungus *Sclerotinia sclerotiorum,* are similar to those of Botrytis and

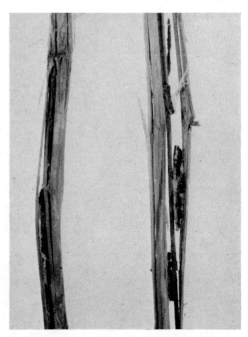

Mottling and ring-spot patterns of peony mosaic.

Sclerotia of the stem-rot fungus form in the center of affected stems.

Phytophthora blights, except that *Sclerotinia* usually does not attack the upper portions of the plants. The stems rot off near the ground line and wilt suddenly. Stem rot can be distinguished by the large, black sclerotia that are formed in the centers of the diseased stems.

Control. The removal and destruction of all plant debris will do much to reduce the number of sclerotia, in which form the causal fungus overwinters. If infections are severe, dig up and burn the affected plants. In less severe cases, the diseased portions may be cut away and the plants reset in a new location. It is advisable to keep manure away from the crowns of plants in locations where stem rot has been a problem, since manure often carries the causal organism.

VERTICILLIUM WILT

Symptoms. Plants that have been attacked by the fungus *Verticillium albo-atrum* gradually wilt and die at blooming time or shortly before. Characteristic brown discoloration of the water-conducting tissues may be seen in cross or longitudinal sections of the roots or stems.

Control. Since the causal fungus is perennial in the roots, diseased plants should be removed and destroyed by burning. Change or sterilize the soil before replanting with healthy peonies. Never use diseased plants for dividing.

PEPEROMIA

Peperomia (*Peperomia obtusifolia*), the popular foliage plant, is subject to a few diseases that are rather easily controlled, yet can become quite destructive.

CUTTING ROT

Symptoms. Cutting rot may be caused by the fungi *Rhizoctonia solani, Pythium* spp., and *Phytophthora* spp. Cuttings attacked by *Rhizoctonia,* the most frequent cause of this trouble, have brown, water-soaked areas in the petioles that sometimes extend into the leaf blades. Roots are frequently rotted.

Control. The control measures suggested for Phytophthora rot will control this disease also.

OEDEMA

Symptoms. Oedema is recognized by the presence of small, raised areas on the leaf, giving it a pimply appearance. The protrusions initially are darker green than surrounding areas, later becoming brown and corky, and often necrotic and sunken. The protrusions occur on both sides of the leaf, but are most pronounced on the under surface. The leaf blades may be distorted and smaller than healthy leaves. The exact cause of oedema in peperomias is unknown but there is some evidence that the cause may be a virus.

Control. Satisfactory control is obtained by carefully roguing infected plants, and by selecting clean cuttings from healthy stock for propagation.

PHYTOPHTHORA ROT

Symptoms. Phytophthora rot, caused by the fungi *Phytophthora palmivora* and *P. nicotianae,* occurs on all parts of the plant. On large plants the first symptom is a pronounced darkening at the ground line. This darkening may either be one-sided or encircle the stem. Soon the lower leaves droop and eventually the whole plant wilts. On very small plants infection seems to start where the blade of the leaf touches the soil, and progresses into the stem where it girdles the plant and causes death. In the cutting box the disease affects the base of the plant, and if the cuttings are rooted the roots can be involved first.

Control. Use cuttings from known healthy plants. Steam sterilize propagation boxes, pots, sand, and soil mixtures before putting cuttings or plants into them.

RING SPOT

Symptoms. Ring spot, caused by a virus, can be recognized by the concentric zonal markings that disfigure the leaves. Sometimes the leaves are distorted and the entire plant is stunted. Each ring spot begins

Depressed, necrotic areas or zones are characteristic of ring-spot disease on peperomia leaves (left). Above, blackened peperomia stem, petioles, and base of leaf blades affected by Phytophthora rot.

as a small, translucent spot that grows larger by the addition outwardly of a number of narrow bands or lines. Some of these lines are light in color, and translucent, while others are brown and opaque. On the upper surface of the leaf, the tissue over the brown lines quite often is sunken and forms narrow furrows or grooves. The area covered by the ring spot is lighter-colored than the healthy portion of the leaf. When only one or a few ring spots occur on a leaf the outlines of the spots and ring patterns are quite regular, but when many spots occur close together, they coalesce and their outlines and rings form irregular patterns.

Control. Select for propagating purposes plants that are vigorous and free of ring-spot symptoms. Discard all diseased plants as soon as they are discovered. Keep plants as free of insects as possible. Insects may carry the causal virus.

PETUNIA

Petunias (*Petunia hybrida*) are relatively free of disease. Of the few diseases

that do affect them, mosaic is the most common.

ALTERNARIA BLIGHT

Symptoms. Small, round, dark-brown spots with faint concentric markings on the upper surface appear on petunia leaves attacked by the fungus *Alternaria tenuis*. Spots that are close together may coalesce, and entire leaves may become involved. The dead leaves remain attached to the plant, and in the most serious cases the disease spreads to the petiole and finally into the stem. If stems are girdled the part above the girdle dies. In most severe cases complete plants are killed.

Control. Spray with ferbam or zineb.

CROWN ROT

Symptoms. When petunias are affected by crown rot, caused by *Phytophthora* sp., there is a black discoloration and dry rot of the crown and lateral branches near the soil line. This is accompanied by wilting and eventual death.

Control. In the greenhouse, plant petunias in steamed soil and keep them on raised benches. In the home garden the soil may be fumigated with Mylone before petunias are planted. When transplanting, eliminate all plants with blackened lesions on stems or crown. Do not cover the crown of the plant with soil. If necessary apply a weekly drench of Dexon.

FASCIATION

Symptoms. Clusters of short branches bearing small leaves develop near the soil line on the main stem. *Corynebacterium fascians,* the bacterium that causes this condition, produces a similar condition in several other kinds of plants.

Control. Plant petunia seedlings in soil that has been steam sterilized.

FUSARIUM WILT

Symptoms. Wilt, stem rot, or root rot of petunia is caused by *Fusarium* sp. Under favorable conditions a gradual wilt is followed by severe stunting. In advanced stages of the disease the plant dies. The disease inoculum builds up in the soil if continuous petunia culture is practiced on the same ground.

Control. Petunia wilt can be controlled by fumigating the soil with Dowfume MC-2, Picfume, or Vapam before planting. Following fumigation, wait 7 days before planting. This allows sufficient time for the chemicals to dissipate, thus avoiding injury to new plantings.

MOSAIC

Symptoms. Although mosaic in petunias may be caused by more than one virus, the symptoms are essentially the same in all cases. Leaves of affected plants are mottled with yellowish-green and dark-green areas, and are usually crinkled and deformed. Blossoms also are deformed and usually show mottling. Diseased plants are stunted.

Control. Remove and destroy diseased plants. Keep aphids under control, because they transmit the mosaic virus. Mosaic

Clusters of short, leafy branches near the soil line on petunia plant are characteristic of fasciation, a condition caused by a bacterium.

can also be transmitted by persons who handle petunias while using chewing or smoking tobacco that is infected with tobacco-mosaic virus.

Petunia leaves affected by mosaic are mottled and crinkled.

PHLOX

The common diseases of phlox (*Phlox* spp.) are powdery mildew, leaf spot, and nonparasitic leaf blight.

ASTER YELLOWS

Symptoms. The aster yellows organism causes breaking in petal color in phlox. The breaking usually consists of white veinbanding. Sometimes one or more petals show breaking and the remainder are white with a few streaks of the normal flower color. Frequently, greening of the petals occurs without breaking. In the advanced stage of the disease, proliferation and greening of the flowers are common on infected plants, the petals being reduced to green, leafy structures resembling sepals. Sometimes there is a dwarfed flower, with one or more petals absent, at the tip of the cluster. Frequently, clusters of green flowers develop with no proliferation of flowers.

Control. Destroy diseased plants. Use insecticides to control leafhoppers, which transmit this disease.

CERCOSPORA LEAF SPOT

Symptoms. The leaf spot caused by the fungus *Cercospora omphakodes* usually appears first on the lower, older leaves and gradually progresses up the plant producing 1 to 3 large, yellow lesions with tan centers on each leaf. Under ideal conditions, however, the fungus may rapidly infect the entire plant, producing 10 to 20 small lesions per leaf. Many of these small lesions do not develop tan centers. Heavily infected leaves yellow rapidly but adhere to the plant.

Control. This disease can be controlled by spraying once every 7 days with Benlate 50W or thiabendazole at the rate of 8 ounces in 100 gallons of water.

LEAF BLIGHT

Symptoms. The lower leaves die, followed by progressive death of leaves up the stem, and sometimes death of the en-

Leaf blight on phlox. The leaves die progressively from the base upward.

tire shoot. The disease is most severe on old clumps, and never affects seedlings or newly rooted cuttings.

Control. Leaf blight of phlox occurs because the old stems from which the new shoots arise in the spring are unable to supply sufficient water to the leaves. Additional irrigation may be helpful, but usually the condition cannot be corrected.

LEAF SPOT

Symptoms. Several fungi are known to cause leaf spots on phlox but the disease caused by *Septoria divaricata* is the most common and the most destructive. Circular, brown spots with light-gray centers develop on the leaves, and the diseased foliage eventually withers and dies. The disease is usually most serious on the lower leaves.

Control. Rake up and burn all tops and fallen leaves in autumn. In severe cases, dust the plants with sulfur or copper-lime dust. Spraying with bordeaux mixture will help control the disease.

POWDERY MILDEW

Symptoms. Grayish-white, powdery growths of the fungus *Erysiphe cichoracearum* appear on the leaf surfaces. This disease usually does not appear until August. Tiny, black fruiting bodies, the over-wintering stage of the causal fungus, develop on the mildew growth late in the season.

Control. Remove and burn all tops in the fall. When the disease first appears, dust the plants with dusting sulfur, or spray with wettable sulfur, Karathane, or Acti-dione PM. Several mildew-resistant strains of phlox have been developed.

Phlox leaves affected by powdery mildew.

ROOT AND CROWN ROT

Symptoms. The leaves turn yellow, wither, and die from the base of the plant upward. These symptoms are most severe in young plants. Usually the plants do not die rapidly but decline slowly. Large, brown lesions develop on the stem below ground near the plant crown. Stems with these lesions often wither and die. The new roots of young, recently divided plants may be brown or black. Chlamydospores of the causal fungus, *Thielaviopsis basicola*, develop on the rotted roots and in the lesions.

Control. The soil and containers must be treated to exclude the causal fungus. This may be done by mixing benomyl or thiabendazole in the soil at the rate of 50 parts per million. Any containers used in propagating should be sterilized before they are reused.

STEMPHYLIUM LEAF SPOT

Symptoms. The leaf spot disease caused by the fungus *Stemphylium botryosum* is most prevalent in plants grown under crowded conditions. Small, circular, tan lesions with darker borders appear on infected leaves. In severe infections the lesions coalesce. The causal fungus may sporulate in brown rings near the margins of old lesions.

Control. Since periods of high humidity are a major factor in development of this disease, and crowding of plants reduces air circulation and raises humidity around the leaves, procedures must be taken to avoid these conditions, or a suitable fungicide must be used to prevent infection.

POINSETTIA

Root and stem rot are the most serious diseases of poinsettias (*Euphorbia pulcherrima*) and have become increasingly important in poinsettia production. In recent years growers in all sections of the United States have lost entire crops, with the result that some growers have given up poinsettia production.

BACTERIAL CANKER

Symptoms. The symptoms of bacterial canker, caused by *Corynebacterium poinsettiae,* appear on all above-ground plant parts. Longitudinal, water-soaked streaks, usually on one side of green stems, are the most characteristic symptoms. Such streaks may continue upward through the leaf petioles, resulting in spotting or blotching of the leaves and even complete defoliation.

The streaking may continue downward into the woody stem, but this can be seen only by cutting into the bark. A yellowing of the cortex and browning of the vascular system are revealed when the epidermis is removed above the water-soaked lesions on green stems. In advanced stages of the disease these stems crack open in an unsightly manner, and then bend sharply downward toward the unaffected sides. Glistening, golden-brown masses of bacteria occasionally ooze from ruptured stems and from leaf lesions.

Control. Take cuttings from healthy plants. Rooted cuttings and young plants obtained from questionable sources should be kept separate from those known to have come from healthy stock. Avoid overhead watering and syringing to prevent spread of bacteria that ooze from infected stems and leaves. Strict sanitary measures — such as burning all diseased plants, sterilization of soil, and disinfection of benches, pots, and other greenhouse equipment — should be practiced diligently if a serious outbreak of bacterial canker occurs.

BACTERIAL STEM ROT

Symptoms. A soft, watery rot may develop in cuttings that have come in contact with the soft-rot bacterium *Erwinia carotovora* var. *chrysanthemi.* The rot develops rapidly and results in complete disintegration of the affected portions of the stem, especially during the late part of the propagation season when poinsettias are forced at higher temperatures. A second phase, stem rot, occurs mostly during the last 2 weeks of the growing season when late plantings under high rates of fertilization are forced at temperatures of 75° to 87°F. Affected plants first lose their normal turgidity, stems become darker and leaves appear water-soaked. Necrotic streaks can be seen in the vascular tissue at the crown after the white, milky exudate is washed off. Within 48 hours after the first symptoms appear, entire stems and petioles become macerated, leaving only the woody crown and the xylem bundles of stems and petioles intact. Roots of collapsed plants often are rotted also. Sometimes a new, apparently healthy, shoot grows from the crown of macerated plants.

Control. Use careful sanitation measures during propagation. Steam sterilize cutting benches and rooting media.

The cultured-cutting technique used in the control of Fusarium and bacterial wilts of carnations is useful in the control of bacterial stem rot of poinsettias but it is not as reliable on poinsettias as it is on carnations. The pathogen does not occur as a continuous mass of cells in the vascular tissues of poinsettias so a stock plant could possibly pass several cultured-cutting procedures and still be infected.

LEAF ROT

Symptoms. A leaf-rot disease of unrooted and rooted poinsettia cuttings, grown under excessively wet conditions, is caused by the fungus *Rhizoctonia solani.* Small, irregularly shaped, dark-brown, water-soaked lesions are distributed at random on the lower leaves of cuttings that are in contact with or near the surface of the soil mixture or sand. The adjoining healthy tissues are chlorotic, and the edges of the leaves curl upward. As the discolored areas enlarge, some spots may coalesce to form larger lesions, and the tissues become soft and flaccid. Within 2 or 3 days the leaves usually are completely blackened and may fall off. Occasionally the petioles are infected but the main stem and roots are not involved. The disease spreads rapidly from the lower to the upper leaves. As a result of severe leaf infection, cuttings may die in less than a week.

Stem rot caused by *Rhizoctonia solani* on an unrooted poinsettia cutting.

Control. Reducing the amount of water used in propagation will control this disease. If cuttings are rooted under mist, the misting should be reduced to the minimum that will keep the cuttings from wilting. If syringing is used in propagation, it too should be reduced to a minimum.

ROOT ROT AND STEM ROT

Symptoms. There are two periods in poinsettia culture when rots are most prevalent — soon after cuttings are potted, and just before the plants mature for Christmas sale. Occasionally the rots occur on cuttings in the propagating benches also.

The first phase of stem and root rot appears just before, or soon after, the cuttings are rooted and is caused chiefly by the fungi *Rhizoctonia solani* and *Pythium* spp. The second phase appears as a late-season rot just before the plants mature. In older plants, *Thielaviopsis basicola* is the primary pathogen, but if *Rhizoctonia* and *Pythium* also are present the root injury is more extensive.

Cuttings placed in moist sand in propagating benches may become infected by *R. solani* or *Pythium* spp. before roots have formed. Dark-brown, water-soaked lesions appear on the stems, extending above and below the soil line for some distance. The lesions may completely encircle the stem, causing it to become weak and constricted. The foliage may become chlorotic if the disease progresses slowly. The lower, yel-

Stems from young poinsettia plants showing Rhizoctonia stem-rot lesions, and roots rotted off by *Thielaviopsis*.

lowed leaves fall off first, followed by those higher on the stem. Yellowed leaves may remain flat before or after dropping, or the edges may curve upward along the midrib. If the disease progresses rapidly, the foliage wilts suddenly and the stem lesions cause the plants to fall over. New roots may form on cuttings before infection occurs on the stem. It is common to find fibrous roots and stems simultaneously showing discoloration, accompanied by yellowing, or sudden wilting without yellowing, of the foliage. When the roots and stems become severely infected, the plants die suddenly.

Infection by *T. basicola* results in stunted plants, excessive leaf drop, and badly rotted roots. Occasionally, leaves and flower bracts are distorted. Symptoms are influenced by the time of infection. Cuttings that are infected soon after potting may suffer almost complete loss of roots and leaves, whereas those infected near maturity may have only mild symptoms. One of the most characteristic symptoms is an inward rolling of the leaves before they turn yellow and fall off.

Infection usually is confined to the roots and the below-ground portion of the stem but occasionally the lower leaves may be infected also. Elongate, black lesions, up to 1 centimeter in length, appear mainly on the larger veins and petioles of the leaves and occasionally on the smaller veins and main stem. Infected roots turn brown-black and decay. Stems may become excessively reddened; black, rough, longitudinal cracks frequently occur on the swollen below-ground part of the stems. These cracks are filled with black resting spores of the fungus.

Plants attacked by *Pythium* alone are dwarfed and have rotted roots. Leaf drop is usually not conspicuous.

Chalaropsis thielavioides is a weak pathogen on poinsettias and sometimes occurs as a minor component of the poinsettia root rot complex.

Control. Successful control of root and stem rots in poinsettias depends on a knowledge of the causal organisms and sources of contamination. *T. basicola* is the principal pathogen in this disease complex, and is the most difficult to control. This fungus is widespread in nature and difficult to eliminate once it has become established in the greenhouse. It may be present on cuttings, and in propagating beds if old sand or vermiculite was used without sterilizing. It may be present in the boards of benches in which diseased plants were grown, on old, dirty pots, dirty potting tables, and especially in the gravel, cinders, or soil where the pots were set.

Poinsettia plants affected by root rot in various degrees of severity. The plant at right is severely stunted and will not bloom.

If a control program is to be effective against *Thielaviopsis,* all of the following steps must be carried out carefully. Steam sterilize the propagating benches and the sand or vermiculite in them. Make certain that a temperature of 180°F is maintained for at least 1 hour in order to sterilize the bottoms and sides of the benches, as well as the rooting medium itself. If sterilization is impossible, empty the bench, scrub the sides and bottom thoroughly, spray or paint with ferbam suspension containing 2 or more tablespoonfuls per gallon of water, plus about ½ teaspoonful of a good wetting agent, and fill the bench with new sand or vermiculite.

Dust the bases of the cuttings with ferbam just before sticking them in the sand. Use new pots for the rooted cuttings if possible. If old pots are used they should be cleaned thoroughly, soaked for 10 minutes or more in a 1:50 formaldehyde solution, and dried before use. Before every potting session, thoroughly scrub the surface of the potting bench and swab with either a ferbam suspension or a 1:50 formaldehyde solution before loading the bench with soil.

Steam sterilize all potting soil. Sterilize the sand, cinders, or soil on which the potted plants are to be placed. This is one of the most important steps in the control program. If steam is not available, the gravel or cinders may be drenched with 1:50 formaldehyde solution or a ferbam suspension containing 1½ to 2 pounds per 100 gallons of water. Since it is possible that the roots of stock plants may carry *Thielaviopsis,* the soil in which the stock plants were grown should be sterilized before reuse, and, if plants were pot-grown, the gravel or cinders on which they were placed should be sterilized before placing other potted plants upon it.

Root rot is favored by high soil moisture and by temperatures below 60°F. A temperature of 70°F delays but does not prevent disease development. Soil pH levels of 6.2 to 7.2 are more favorable for disease development than are more acid soil conditions. Adjusting the cultural conditions accordingly will aid in delaying development of root and stem rot, but greater emphasis must be placed on elimination of the causal fungi if successful control is to be achieved.

Benomyl and thiabendazole in the planting mix at concentrations of 50 parts per million have given excellent control of Thielaviopsis root rot of poinsettia. Mixtures of benomyl and Dexon or benomyl and Terrazole have given excellent control of the entire poinsettia root rot complex. Mixing the fungicides in the soil prior to

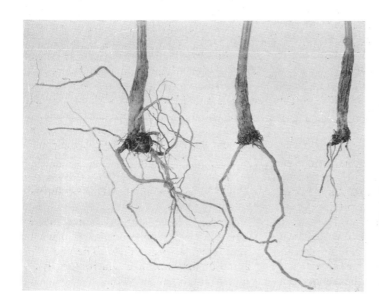

Poinsettia stems with swollen and cracked bark caused by Thielaviopsis infection. Severe root reduction is shown in plants in center and at right.

planting is usually more effective than applying the fungicides as a drench. However, soil drenches applied to newly-potted rooted cuttings and established plants with root-rot symptoms have been effective in reducing poinsettia root rot.

SCAB

Symptoms. Scab, caused by the fungus *Sphaceloma* sp., is evidenced by numerous conspicuous, raised lesions or cankers on diseased stems. The cankers are circular to elongate, with the longer diameter running lengthwise of the stem, and range from about 1 millimeter to ½ inch or more in length. Frequently they unite to cover irregular areas, sometimes completely encircling the stem. When this occurs the stems lose their foliage above the girdled area and die back from the tip. Eventually the centers of individual cankers become somewhat depressed and covered with a grayish to grayish-brown, velvety layer of the fungus.

Control. This disease is uncommon and specific control measures have not been worked out. However, spraying with bordeaux mixture or some other good fungicide should keep the disease in check.

SOFT ROT

Symptoms. A soft, watery rot may develop in cuttings that have come in contact with the soft-rot bacterium, *Erwinia carotovora*. The rot develops rapidly and results in complete disintegration of the affected portions of the stem.

Control. Use careful sanitation measures during propagation. Steam sterilize cutting benches and rooting media.

STUNT

Symptoms. A stunt disease sometimes occurs in container-grown poinsettia stock plants. The first visible symptoms appear several weeks after the container-grown stock plants have been placed on greenhouse benches for forcing. New leaves are extremely small, slightly chlorotic, and somewhat drooping in comparison with normal growth, and are borne on thin, undersized stems arising from the main trunk. They fail to gain in size and become more chlorotic and less turgid with age. Eventually, and usually suddenly, all the leaves wilt and hang vertically.

A marked shortening of the internodes gives a stunted appearance to diseased plants. A soft, watery, odorless rot involves the root system, with the smaller roots disintegrating before the larger ones. When the foliage wilts only three to five stubs of the larger main roots remain. In the final stages of the disease the entire top turns brown and the plant dies. An occasional diseased plant may live for some months in the stunted condition, although there is no recovery from the disease.

Control. Stunt is caused by water-logged soils. There are no parasitic organisms involved. Predisposing factors are heavy, poorly drained soils, no drainage outlets in the containers, excessive watering, and lack of soil aeration. The disease can be controlled by correcting these unfavorable growing conditions.

WILT

Symptoms. The earliest symptoms consist of sudden wilting, yellowing, and upward curling along the edges of one or several of the lowest leaves. Abscission follows. Then the next lower leaves become affected. Soon the remaining leaves and bracts become involved, leaving only a bare main stem surmounted by a cluster of true flowers. There is no visible external discoloration of the main stem, crown, or roots. Internally, the main stems of diseased plants always show a slight vascular discoloration. Usually, but not always, affected plants die within 1 week after the first symptoms appear. Although the condition may be found on a few plants in pots and pans early in the season, the principal damage occurs when the bracts commence to change color.

Control. This condition occurs only in poinsettia plants grown in soil mixes to which lime has been added. The wilting is caused by lime toxicity. Control merely involves using lime-free soils.

POPPY

Poppies (*Papaver orientale* and *P. rhoeas*) are relatively free of serious diseases, but bacterial blight and anthracnose occasionally become quite destructive.

ANTHRACNOSE

Symptoms. Anthracnose on oriental poppy, caused by the fungus *Gloeosporium* sp., is characterized by gray, necrotic lesions with brownish-black borders on the diseased flower stems. The fungus sporulates in the gray areas of older lesions. Infected stems may be bent or curled, giving them a crookneck appearance. Stems are characteristically bent toward the lesion side and it is not uncommon to have more than one bend in a stem, depending upon the number and location of the lesions. Similar lesions occur on petioles and midveins of leaves, and with severe infection a malformation and curling of leaves results.

Control. A protective spray with maneb before the disease appears will give effective control.

BACTERIAL BLIGHT

Symptoms. Intensely black lesions are formed on the leaves, stems, flower parts, and pods of plants affected by bacterial blight, caused by *Xanthomonas papavericola*. Infections are first evident as minute, water-soaked areas that soon darken into definite spots bounded by a hyaline or water-soaked ring. This ring is seldom evident in older spots. The distribution of the primary lesions on the leaf affects the size and shape of the mature spots. When scattered, the lesions are distinctly circular, clearly defined, and often zoned. Eventually the tissues between the spots turn yellow and then brown, but the individual spots remain distinguishable by their darker color and zonate markings. When the infections occur close together the spots are small, but they may coalesce to form large, black or sepia-black areas. A slimy, bacterial exudate is noticeable at times on the lesions. Leaf infections weaken the leaves to such an extent that defoliation results.

The lesions on the stems are similar to those on the leaves, but, unlike those on the leaves, the stem lesions tend to elongate longitudinally. When close together they may coalesce and girdle the stems.

All floral parts are susceptible but the young sepals are especially so; these may be partially or entirely blackened. The causal bacteria are able to pass through the sepals and attack the young petals beneath, stopping further development of the flower.

The spots on the pods are black and conspicuous, and the margins are prominently water-soaked. The slimy bacterial exudate is more noticeable on the pods than on any other part of the plant. In severe cases the plants are killed.

Control. Remove and destroy infected plants. Poppies should not be planted in locations where the disease has occurred recently, and seed should not be collected from diseased plants.

ROSE

Roses (*Rosa* spp.) are perhaps the most widely grown flowers, both in greenhouses and in gardens. They are susceptible to a number of diseases that can become very serious if they are not controlled. The control of rose diseases is not difficult if the grower understands the nature of the troubles and applies the control measures systematically. When rose diseases become serious it is usually because control measures were used spasmodically or not at all.

ANTHRACNOSE

Symptoms. Anthracnose, caused by the fungus *Sphaceloma rosarum*, produces lesions on leaves and stems. Circular dark spots, seldom more than one-fourth inch across, are formed on the leaflets. Infected areas first lose their dark-green color and change through dark brown or purple to almost black. Finally the spots turn white or ash color at the centers. Tissues in the lesions may fall away underneath, leaving only a thin, papery membrane; or they may fall out entirely, producing a shot-hole effect. Affected leaves may become distorted and ragged at the margins, and may change in color, from normal green to yellow, red and yellow, or red shading to brown. Lesions may occur on any part of the leaf, including the midrib and veins.

Stem lesions are considerably smaller than leaf spots. They are usually raised and sometimes depressed at the center. The spots are a dull, livid brown, becoming white or ashen at the centers. Lesions may occur on the thorns also.

The anthracnose fungus occasionally may attack the flowers. On a given petal the often numerous spots differ in size but may reach a maximum diameter of about 2 millimeters. The spots are scattered over much of the upper surface; below they may be indistinct or scarcely noticeable. When well developed, the spots are distinctly pale at the center, surrounded by a pink to purplish zone.

Lesions on flower hips and pedicels resemble the stem lesions, and those on the calyx lobes resemble the leaf spots.

Control. Remove and destroy the affected parts. Spray with lime-sulfur before leaf buds open, and follow with bordeaux mixture or some other copper-containing fungicide after the leaves develop.

BLACK MOLD

Symptoms. The fungus *Chalaropsis thielavioides* causes graft failure in propagating frames. Newly infected rose grafts show a white or grayish-white to black fungus growth over the cut surfaces of both stock and scion. Scions affected by the black-mold fungus show discoloration above the union that may later spread upward. Some discoloration may be found in the stocks. The disease prevents the formation of a callus and "taking" of the grafts, and results in death of the scions involved. The fungus also causes failure of bud unions in nurseries. The black fungus crust develops under the bud shield and causes it to die.

Control. Florists can avoid black mold by using budded plants. Use resistant or immune rootstocks when possible, and disease-free budwood or scions. Ragged Robin rootstocks are immune and *Rosa multiflora* is resistant whereas *R. manetti* and *R. odorata* are highly susceptible. Practice rigid sanitation in the grafting cases; steam the pots, soil, and cases before using them. Before planting, soak stocks 2 hours in a solution of formaldehyde, 1 part to 320 parts of water, or potassium permanganate, 1 pound to 25 gallons of water.

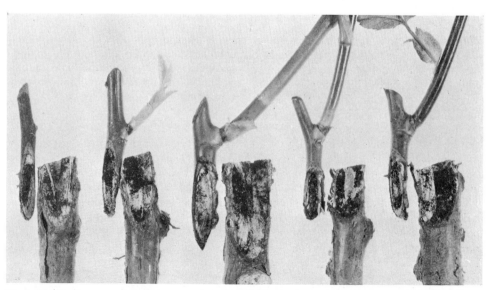

Black mold of rose grafts. Growth of the fungus on the cut surfaces prevented the stock and scion from forming a union.

BLACK SPECK

Symptoms. Black speck is not a disease but is frequently mistaken for one. Leaves on greenhouse roses become covered with numerous black specks about half the size of a pinhead. The spots resemble fly specks or particles of soot, but are actually spore-containing sacs of the fungus *Pilobolus,* which occurs in manures. Animals eat grass carrying the spores, which pass unaltered through the alimentary canal and are introduced into the greenhouse when the manure is used as fertilizer. In the greenhouse the fungus develops rapidly in the moist manure, sending out short stalks that bear the spore sacs. These stalks are sensitive to light and therefore point upward from the bench. When sufficient water pressure is developed within the stalks, the sacs pop off and are projected for a considerable distance into the air. The sacs are sticky and adhere to whatever they strike. *Pilobolus* is not a parasite, however, and is not harmful to the roses aside from the appearance.

Control. Usually no control is necessary. If fresh-manure mulches are avoided the condition is not likely to occur.

BLACK SPOT

Symptoms. Black spot, caused by the fungus *Diplocarpon rosae,* produces nearly circular, black lesions on the leaves, and is distinguished from the other leaf spots by the generally fringed margins and also by the darker and consistently black color. The spots vary in size from less than $\frac{1}{16}$ inch to $\frac{1}{2}$ inch or more in diameter. Spots may coalesce to produce large, irregular lesions. Yellowing often occurs over the entire leaf or it may develop only around the lesions. When the plants are badly infected the leaves are shed prematurely, and the canes may become almost completely defoliated.

Control. Black spot ceased to be a problem on greenhouse roses when the practice of syringing for control of red spider was replaced by aerosol fumigation. The water used for syringing served to spread the spores from plant to plant, and the film of water left on the leaves allowed the spores to germinate and initiate new infections.

On roses grown out-of-doors, control measures should start at the time the bushes are pruned back during the dormant season. The black-spot fungus is known to overwinter in the canes as well as in the infected leaves. Canes of diseased plants should be cut back as severely as possible without cutting too close to the graft. All old leaves should be raked up and burned before spring.

Black-spot lesions on rose leaves. The spots are round, uniformly black, with a fringed margin.

Defoliation commonly occurs on rose plants severely affected by black spot.

Several fungicides have been found to give good control of black spot. One of the best materials is a sulfur-copper dust containing about 90 percent of unconditioned 325-mesh dusting sulfur and about 10 percent of an insoluble copper fungicide such as basic copper sulfate or copper oxychloride sulfate. Other fungicides that are effective against black spot are captan, ferbam, phaltan, maneb, zineb, benomyl, Polyram, Fore, and Bravo.

The sulfur-copper mixture has the advantage of controlling mildew also. The roses should be dusted or sprayed at the first appearance of black spot on the foliage. Repeat the applications at weekly intervals until hot, dry weather begins. Thereafter, apply the dust within 24 hours after each rain, but not more than once a week, until growth of the plants is checked by cool weather. Apply enough dust to cover the foliage lightly.

BLAST

Symptoms. Blast, caused by the bacterium *Pseudomonas syringae,* involves receptacles, calyx lobes, flower stalks, and leaf petioles of rose, but the infections are most abundant on receptacles and rarest on leaf petioles. Blackish-brown, dead spots and streaks appear on the affected portions. These spots and streaks appear depressed or sunken as compared with adjoining healthy tissue. A narrow red border often delimits diseased areas. Affected buds usually fail to open.

Control. Cut and burn affected parts.

BORON DEFICIENCY

Symptoms. Symptoms of boron deficiency in roses resemble those caused by a hormone-type weed killer. Leaves become variously distorted and elongated, with irregular serration. A lack of apical dominance results in multiple branching of flowering stems, with stems curved and distorted. Flowers are truncate and darker in color than those not affected. The petals have a serrate margin and are irregularly pigmented. Necrosis of stem tips, flowering shoots, and leaf tips may occur.

Control. An application of a 21 percent boron material (Solubor) at the rate of 1 ounce per 500 square feet has been reported as correcting the condition. Do not apply too much boron because excess boron also will cause severe injury.

BOTRYTIS BLIGHT

Symptoms. Botrytis blight, caused by the fungus *Botrytis cinerea,* causes the flower buds to droop and fail to open. The interior of the bud is usually filled with a cobwebby mold. Just below the flower head there is sometimes a smooth, slightly sunken, grayish-black lesion extending down the stem. The buds appear blasted, and frequently lop over at or near the lesion. The fungus may also attack the stub ends of stems from which flowers have been cut. Black lesions usually develop several inches down the stem from the point of infection. Under warm, humid conditions a gray fungus growth may completely cover the affected parts.

Control. Cut, and destroy by burning, all infected blossoms as soon as they droop or appear blasted. In order to destroy the lesions and to prevent further infection by the spores of the causal fungus, the stems adjoining the affected buds should be cut back several inches below the bud. The remainder of the plant should be sprayed with captan, zineb, benomyl, daconil, or Botran.

Blighted terminals of rose plants caused by infection with *Botrytis cinerea.*

BRAND CANKER

Symptoms. Brand canker, caused by the fungus *Coniothyrium wernsdorffiae,* is most common on the rambler roses. The cankers, which are confined to the canes, vary greatly in size and somewhat in appearance, according to age. The first symptom is a small, reddish spot on the cane. This increases in size and becomes darker, the margin becomes somewhat more definite, and the center of the spot turns light brown. Around this spot the reddish-brown or purple margin contrasts strikingly with the green of the cane. This dark and rather definite zone is usually surrounded by a more indeterminate, reddish area. Pycnidia of the causal fungus are first seen as minute elevations just before the center of the lesion turns brown. As the pycnidia increase in size, small longitudinal slits appear in the bark above them, exposing a black mass of spores. These small slits are particularly characteristic of brand canker.

Botrytis growing on rose flowers and stems that were exposed to a humid atmosphere for several days after infection occurred.

Mature brand cankers on rose stems. (Reproduced from Cornell University Agricultural Experiment Station Memoir 153.)

Control. Brand canker may be almost entirely controlled by leaving the roses uncovered during the winter. Pruning out infected canes helps to eradicate the disease. Use of fungicides during the growing season is of no value.

BROWN CANKER

Symptoms. In most varieties the first signs of brown canker infection, caused by the fungus *Cryptosporella umbrina,* are purple to white spots on the canes and small, dark-gray, circular spots on the leaves. The small cane lesions are usually slightly raised, circular, purple in color, and quite superficial. Later they become grayish-white. When large numbers of these tiny spots are massed together a whitish patch is produced. Sometimes little damage occurs the first year but eventually the white lesions become surrounded by a purple margin that continues to enlarge, leaving a brown, dead area. In time the cane is girdled and killed. Cankers may extend for several inches down the canes and, upon reaching the crown, may destroy other canes or the entire plant.

Leaves and flowers also are attacked. Leaf infections vary in appearance, depending on the type of rose. On some kinds of roses the leaf spots are much like those on the canes — purple, with or without white centers. Reddish spotting is typical on some varieties, and on others dark-gray, circular spots are produced on the upper surface of the leaves. Usually only the outer petals of blossoms are infected. Diseased petals become tan or brown and are dotted with fruiting bodies of the causal fungus. Buds infected early in their development fail to bloom.

Control. Care in selection of disease-free planting stock is essential to prevent the introduction of brown canker in new rose plantings. Prune out and burn infected parts of diseased plants. In removing dead or diseased wood, make cuts well below the diseased areas. Dip the pruning shears in a sterilizing solution of formaldehyde before each cut is made. Bordeaux mixture 4-4-50 is efficient in controlling infection but has the disadvantage of discoloring the foliage. Dusting sulfur is an efficient dust form of fungicide. Time between applications may vary with conditions, but applications made at 10- to 14-day intervals usually are sufficient. A dormant spray of lime-sulfur, one part to nine parts water, applied in the fall, and again before the buds open in the spring, is also helpful in combatting brown canker.

CROWN CANKER

Symptoms. Crown canker, caused by the fungus *Cylindrocladium scoparium,* usually is confined to greenhouse roses but has been reported on field-grown multiflora roses. Since infection usually occurs as a result of the growth of the fungus in the soil, the portion of the stem near the ground is most commonly affected. Any part of the stem is susceptible, however, especially if wounds are present.

The first indication of the disease is a slight discoloration of the bark. As the disease advances the color rapidly deepens to black and the tissue appears water-soaked. The lesions frequently encircle the stem. Soon cracks appear in the bark, extending into the wood. In old lesions the

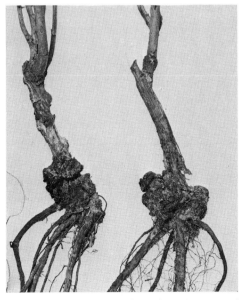

Crown galls at the junction of rose stems and roots.

black, water-soaked appearance is lost. One outstanding characteristic of crown canker is the punky consistency of the diseased tissue, especially those below ground. Foliage of affected plants often is a lighter green than that of healthy plants. Suckers developing from the roots of diseased plants are usually spindling and yellow. Affected plants fail to respond to forcing treatments and produce poor and few blossoms, but do not die quickly.

Control. Soil in which diseased plants have grown should be replaced or sterilized. Benches, pots, and tools should be thoroughly cleaned and sterilized. Take special care to avoid bringing infested soil into houses that are free of the disease.

CROWN GALL

Symptoms. Crown gall of rose, caused by the bacterium *Agrobacterium tumefaciens,* is characterized by gall-like growths that occur at or near the ground level, but may be found also on the upper portion of the stem or on the roots. Beginning as small swellings, the galls enlarge slowly and may attain great size before any effect on plant growth is noticeable. Infected plants become stunted, lack vitality, and fail to produce blossoms and foliage of good quality.

Control. Remove and burn all infected plants. Roses should not be replanted in the same soil unless it has been sterilized. Because the disease is commonly spread by infected nursery stock, the grower should take particular care to secure disease-free stock, especially if the plants are grafted. Infection takes place only through wounds. For this reason, carefully wrap grafts and protect them from injury until the union of stock and scion has healed perfectly, leaving no wound where infection might occur.

Bacticin, a new horticultural bactericide, has been effective in eradicating crown gall on several woody hosts. Bacticin selectively kills galled tissue but does not harm healthy tissue. The emulsion is painted on the entire gall surface. Galls are killed in about 2 weeks.

DOWNY MILDEW

Symptoms. Downy mildew, caused by the fungus *Peronospora sparsa,* is not to be confused with powdery mildew. Downy mildew is chiefly a disease of cuttings under glass, but it sometimes occurs on outdoor roses. Red to brown spots appear on the leaves, with downy fungus growth on the undersides. Leaves rapidly turn yellow and drop; under continuously moist, cool conditions plants are defoliated except for the tip leaves. If the weather turns dry, leaf spots may appear as brown, burned areas. Reddish stem spots also may appear.

Control. Keeping the relative humidity below 85 percent will prevent the disease in greenhouses. Spraying with Parzate, 2 pounds in 100 gallons of water, is helpful on outdoor plants.

LEAF SPOT

Symptoms. The first symptoms of leaf spot, caused by the fungus *Mycosphaerella rosicola,* are small, yellowish-green dots on the leaves. These spots increase in size, become brown, and usually develop a purplish border. In some cases the diseased tissue falls out, giving the leaves a shot-hole appearance.

Control. Collect all affected leaves and destroy by burning. The sulfur-copper dust recommended for black spot should be

Mycosphaerella leaf spot on rose. The spots are brown and usually have a purplish border.

used during the growing season. Spraying with ferbam is also effective.

MERCURY INJURY

Symptoms. Many varieties of roses are susceptible to injury from mercury vapors that may be formed by the volatilization of mercury-containing paints or fungicides. Flowers may be off-color, the petals ranging from bluish through pink to white or brown instead of the normal color. Young buds often fail to open and the bud scales turn brown. In such cases all the bud scales and petals can easily be lifted off the receptacle. An abnormally large number of old leaves may fall, and many of those remaining on the plants are brown in places. Chronic exposure of roses to mercury results in slow growth and reduced flower production.

Control. The use of mercury-containing fungicides, paints, or other mercury compounds should be avoided in the greenhouse and near garden roses.

MOSAICS

Symptoms. Roses are affected by two types of mosaic, known as typical mosaic and yellow mosaic, caused by two different viruses carried in buds, scions, and root stocks.

Typical mosaic is characterized by small chlorotic spots, somewhat angular or fringed in appearance because of the clearing of small veins adjacent to the spot proper. The chlorotic areas are more numerous at or near the midvein, and often appear in greater numbers near the base of the leaflet. The leaf blade around the spot often is more or less distorted. Other symptoms consist of more or less clearly defined rings, erratic wavy or "water-marked" lines, and oakleaf patterns. There may be no reduction in vigor, or the plant may be slightly to severely dwarfed.

The symptoms of yellow mosaic differ from those of typical mosaic chiefly in color. The chlorotic areas are generally a brighter and lighter yellow than in typical mosaic, and are often extensively developed and conspicuous. In most varieties there is less tendency toward puckering of the leaves in yellow-mosaic infections.

Control. As far as is known, the rose mosaics are spread only in budding and grafting operations. Therefore, control of these diseases rests primarily with the nurseryman in providing disease-free understocks, and with the commercial rose grower in providing disease-free budding and grafting material. Practical control in propagation on manetti understocks can be accomplished by establishing a disease-free mother block. A mosaic-free mother block may be expanded and renewed as desired by means of cuttings. With such an established source of healthy cuttings available, mosaic will occur only if infected buds are used. The disease will not spread naturally to other varieties, or to other plants of the same variety.

Wood for cuttings, scions, or bud sticks should be taken only from healthy plants. A good plan is to tag all mosaic-infected plants as soon as they are seen and avoid these plants when collecting wood for propagation purposes. Regular checking and tagging should be done throughout the year because symptoms appear sporadically and are not always visible. If this plan is followed carefully the cuttings, scions, or bud sticks should be mosaic-free.

Roses with mosaic have been cured by

Rose leaf showing angular, fringed, chlorotic spots and veinclearing symptoms typical of mosaic.

keeping the affected plants at a constant temperature of 94°F for 4 weeks, and an additional 2 weeks at 97°. Such a procedure is hardly practical, however.

In yellow mosaic of rose the chlorotic spots are a brighter yellow and are often more extensively developed than are the spots of typical mosaic.

POWDERY MILDEW

Symptoms. Powdery mildew of roses is caused by the fungus *Sphaerotheca pannosa* var. *rosae*. The disease starts on the young leaves as raised, blisterlike areas that soon become covered with a grayish-white, powdery fungus growth. Older leaves may be affected, usually with little distortion, but growing leaves become twisted and misshapen. Young growing tips may be completely covered with the mildew, resulting in dwarfing and curling of leaves, stems, and buds. In serious infections the tips of canes may be killed. Frequently the unopened buds are white with mildew before the leaves are affected to any great extent. Often infected buds do not open. Petals, sepals, and receptacles of the flower buds are liable to attack. The petals may become discolored, dwarfed, and eventually dried.

Control. Powdery mildew is probably the easiest of all plant diseases to control if the nature of the mildew fungus is understood, and if control measures are applied in a systematic manner. It is entirely unnecessary for greenhouse roses to have mildew. The problem is somewhat more difficult when roses are grown out-of-doors. The secret of control lies in beginning early to guard against the initial infections, and in applying a fungicide

often enough to provide protection throughout the growing season.

If rose mildew is to be combatted successfully, several facts must be kept in mind. (1) The life cycle of the mildew fungus is short. Under favorable conditions it takes only about 72 hours for the mildew fungus to go through a complete cycle from one spore generation to the next. (2) Spores are produced by the hundreds of thousands, and each spore is a potential source of new infection. (3)

A severe case of powdery mildew on rose leaf (at right) and flowers. The outer petals have been crippled by the mildew fungus, therefore the flowers will not open normally.

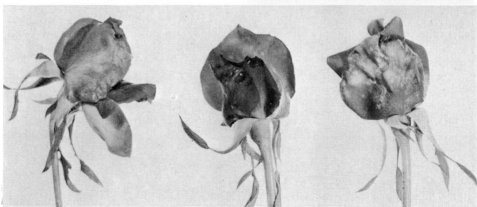

Homemade sulfur vaporizer used to control powdery mildew on greenhouse roses. A hole was cut through the side, near the bottom of a tin can, and a 60-watt lightbulb inserted in the can and screwed into a suitable socket. Flowers of sulfur, placed in the bottom of the can, will be vaporized by heat from the lightbulb.

Rose plants grow rapidly. New growth not protected by a fungicide is readily attacked by any mildew spores that settle there.

Several fungicides are known to be toxic to the mildew fungus, but sulfur is the most satisfactory from the standpoint of effectiveness, convenience, and economy. Sulfur may be used as a spray, as a dust, or as a vapor. Vaporized sulfur will give perfect control of mildew in greenhouses if the directions given below are carefully followed.

Make a slurry consisting of 1 pint of water and 1 pound of wettable sulfur (not flowers of sulfur) for each 90,000 cubic feet of greenhouse to be treated. Apply this slurry with a paintbrush to two steam pipes in each house. It is not necessary to paint the entire length of pipe; paint sections about 3 feet long and leave approximately equal intervals unpainted. Make applications regularly, twice a week. Do not relax this schedule, even though mildew is not present. If the schedule must be broken in order to apply insecticides, resume it within 3 or 4 days.

When steam is unavailable in the greenhouse the sulfur may be vaporized in small vaporizers that use lightbulbs or small heating elements as a source of heat. Such vaporizers may be homemade, or

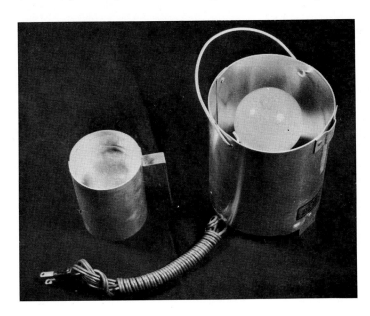

A commercially made sulfur vaporizer. The sulfur container, shown at side, fits over the lightbulb and is secured by inserting the bracket into the clamp on the outer container.

they may be purchased readymade. One vaporizer should be used for each 1,000 to 1,500 square feet of greenhouse space. Flowers of sulfur (not wettable sulfur) should be used in the vaporizers. The vaporizers should be kept in operation day and night. The greenhouse vents should not be opened more than necessary for proper ventilation. Care must be taken to prevent ignition of the sulfur from too much heat in the vaporizer, because fumes of burning sulfur seriously injure the foliage. A 60-watt bulb should be used in homemade vaporizers. Weaker bulbs will not melt the sulfur, and stronger ones will cause the sulfur to ignite. Commercial vaporizers come equipped with bulbs of the proper size, and burnt-out bulbs should be replaced by the same size.

It is practically impossible to control temperature and relative humidity in the greenhouse to such an extent that conditions will always be unfavorable for mildew, but it is possible to control these factors sufficiently to help the situation. Guard against sudden drops in temperature such as usually occur in the evening as the sun sets. Careful regulation of the ventilation is important. Keep moist air moving up and out of the greenhouse, and avoid cold drafts as much as possible.

On outdoor roses the best practice for control of powdery mildew is to protect against infection by using effective sprays and dusts. Various fungicides have been recommended for this purpose. Because mildew is prevalent both early and late in the season when temperatures are comparatively low, the grower who begins early to protect against mildew before it starts will find few instances where sulfur is unsafe or ineffective.

Wettable sulfur should be used at the rate of 1 pound in 25 gallons of water. Sufficient wetting agent should be added to the spray mixture to make sure the spray will adhere to the waxy surface of the leaf and also to the oily patches of mildew. An ordinary household detergent may be used as the wetting agent. The minimum amount necessary for good wetting should be used; about one-third teaspoon-ful per gallon of water is usually adequate. It is important to use a nozzle with a small orifice, and to use sufficient pressure to break the spray into a fine mist.

In dusting with sulfur, a dust of at least 325-mesh fineness should be used; ordinary sulfur is too coarse. Mixtures of sulfur, arsenate of lead, ferbam, and other materials are satisfactory if sulfur comprises about 50 percent of the mixture. Sulfur dust is used principally for protection; it is not effective as an eradicant. Wettable sulfur sprays should be used to eradicate mildew infections that are already established. Other materials that have been used successfully are Acti-dione PM, Mildex, benomyl, Parnon, and Karathane.

For both spraying and dusting, thorough coverage of the canes and both upper and under surfaces of the leaves, especially the growing tips, is essential. Under most conditions, weekly applications will be adequate. However, rapid development of new growth, temperature fluctuations, and frequent rains that dissipate the fungicide may make it advisable to treat more often in the spring and autumn. Absence of these conditions may make fewer treatments necessary during the middle of the summer.

RUST

Symptoms. Rust is a fungus disease caused by species of *Phragmidium*. Small, orange or yellow pustules appear on any green portions of the plant. In early spring these masses may be so inconspicuous as to be unnoticed. Later, larger and more conspicuous spots occur and this condition exists throughout the summer. In late summer or early fall the spots change and black pustules appear, frequently in the same affected areas. These pustules overwinter within the leaf and stem tissues after the leaves fall, and later produce the spores that cause the spring infection. Young stems and the green parts of the flower also may be infected. Distortion of these diseased portions sometimes results.

Control. Rake up and burn the fallen

In the summer stage, rust pustules on rose stems and leaves are orange-colored.

leaves. Severe spring pruning, the use of a dormant spray of lime-sulfur, one part to nine parts water, or bordeaux mixture 4-4-50, and weekly applications of dusting sulfur during the growing season will control the disease. Nabam is also effective.

SPRING DWARF

Symptoms. The most conspicuous symptoms of rose spring dwarf occur in early spring on plants maintained outdoors; these consist of delayed or dwarf shoots with downward-curved or rolled leaves and leaflets (epinasty). Such leaves generally also have a conspicuous yellow vein-banding (netting) and often are readily detached when brushed with the hand. As the season advances, subsequent new growth is normal in appearance and the early occurring symptoms become less conspicuous. In the summer, infected plants are difficult or impossible to recognize. In the late fall, new shoot growth may develop mild leaf epinasty similar to the spring leaf symptoms. Infected plants removed from the field and maintained in a greenhouse at temperatures conducive to active growth have failed to develop symptoms of the disease.

Black overwintering stage of rose rust; infected branches on left; close-up of pustules on right.

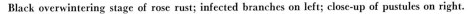

Control. Rogue all plants showing symptoms. Nurserymen should be especially careful in the selection of plants used as sources for scion wood and root stocks to avoid propagating roses infected with this graft-transmissible disease.

STEM AND GRAFT CANKER

Symptoms. Stem and graft canker is caused by the fungus *Leptosphaeria coniothyrium*. Nearly all varieties of outdoor roses are susceptible to this disease but it is more prevalent on hybrid tea roses than on any other. The first symptoms are small, pale-yellow or reddish spots on the bark. These gradually increase in size and several spots may grow together, resulting in a large infected area; sometimes the entire stem is girdled and the part above wilts and dies. Small, black fruiting bodies of the causal fungus may be found on the cankered area.

A canker sometimes appears at or near the point of union of stock and scion on grafted plants while they are in the frames for callusing. The canker may completely encircle the stem and cause death of the entire plant. Frequently, however, the canker does not encircle the stem but only spreads up one side. In this case the bark of the affected portion becomes brown and cracked but the plant does not

Graft cankers on Better Times scions on *Rosa manetti* stocks. The root stocks are disease-free. Such cankers are caused by the fungus *Leptosphaeria coniothyrium*. First symptoms are small, yellow or reddish spots on the bark.

die immediately. The plant may live in a weak, one-sided condition for several years after being transplanted to the garden. Eventually the stems are girdled and the plant dies.

Infection of healthy plants or of new wood may take place through the cut ends left in pruning or in cutting blooms. On some varieties these cankers may progress down the canes to the base, ultimately killing the entire plant, but on other varieties the cankers are checked at the base of the branch.

Control. Prune out and burn all infected canes. Make cuts well back of the cankered areas. Since spores of the fungus may be carried from one bush to another on the pruning shears, it is advisable to disinfect the shears each time after they are used on a diseased plant. This may be done by dipping the shears in a solution of 1 ounce of commercial formalin to 2 gallons of water. The use of a dormant spray of lime-sulfur, one part of concentrated lime-

Rose stem canker at left, brown canker, center and at right. At center, a stem with initial infection lesions of brown canker; at right a later stage of the same disease. (Reproduced from New Jersey Agricultural Experiment Station Circular 385.)

sulfur in nine parts of water, in the fall and again before the buds open in the spring may be beneficial.

In making grafts, select scion wood from disease-free plants. *Rosa manetti* is highly resistant to this disease and should be used for root stocks when possible.

STREAK

Symptoms. Streak, like mosaic, is a virus disease that affects roses, but the symptoms are distinct from those of mosaic. Three types of symptoms have been associated with streak: (1) brownish rings and brown veinbanding in fully expanded leaves, usually accompanied by brownish or greenish, often water-soaked, ring patterns in canes; (2) green senescence designs (resembling those usually associated with

Five-year-old rose plant showing dieback symptoms associated with Verticillium wilt.

aging) similar to the brown patterns, which are often expressed in leaves that later drop prematurely; (3) a yellowish-green banding, usually accompanied by greenish, water-soaked rings or dull, brownish rings in the canes.

Control. The control measures recommended for mosaic will control streak also.

VERTICILLIUM WILT

Symptoms. In Verticillium wilt of roses, one or more shoots of a plant shed the leaves and die back from the tip. The disease usually progresses rather slowly.

Control. The causal soilborne fungus, *Verticillium albo-atrum*, is spread when buds from infected stems are placed in the highly resistant *Rosa manetti* root stock. Less resistant root stocks may be infected through the roots. Plants should be propagated from stock known to be free of *Verticillium*. If Verticillium wilt is suspected the bud sticks should be cultured and all infected ones discarded. Plants should be set in steam-sterilized soil in the greenhouse.

SANSEVIERIA

Only two diseases are of importance on sansevieria (*Sansevieria thyrsiflora* and *S. zeylanica*). These are Fusarium leaf spot and bacterial soft rot.

BACTERIAL SOFT ROT

Symptoms. When sansevieria plants are affected by bacterial soft rot the leaves become yellowish green to pale yellow, develop soft, water-soaked spots at or above the soil line, rot off at the base, and topple over. The root stocks become water-soaked, soft, and straw-colored. The roots die and dry up.

Control. Use steamed soil for growing sansevierias. Avoid over-watering. Propagate only from healthy plants.

LEAF SPOT

Symptoms. The fungus *Fusarium moniliforme* produces roundish, somewhat

Fusarium leaf spot of sansevieria. The spots are reddish brown with yellowish borders, and may extend through the leaf. (Photograph courtesy of Washington State University.)

sunken, reddish-brown lesions with yellowish borders. The spots may be limited to one side of the leaf and develop a raised, corky surface. In many cases the spots extend through the leaf and the center dries and falls out. Lesions may sometimes coalesce, encircle the leaf, and cause death of the portion above the lesion.

Control. Cutting out and destroying diseased leaves, and care in watering so that spores of the causal fungus are not washed about on wet leaves, should aid in reducing infection. Spraying with a copper-containing fungicide may be helpful.

SNAPDRAGON

Snapdragons (*Antirrhinum majus*) are subject to several diseases, some of which completely destroy the plants while others make the plants unsightly and reduce flower production.

ANTHRACNOSE

Symptoms. Numerous elliptical, sunken spots are produced on the stems, and circular, dead spots appear on the leaves of plants affected by anthracnose. At first the spots on the stems are dirty white with a narrow, brown or reddish-brown border. Later, minute black pimples appear in the center of the spots. The causal fungus, *Colletotrichum antirrhini,* may attack stems of all ages. If several large spots coalesce they may girdle the plant at the base. A single large spot may cause the death of a succulent terminal portion or the causal fungus may kill the lateral shoots while the main stem remains green. On the older, woody stems the spots are considerably sunken, but on succulent shoots this characteristic is scarcely noticeable.

The leaf spots, which are circular and slightly sunken, begin as yellowish-green spots with indefinite outlines. Very soon they become dirty white and are sometimes greenish and definitely outlined, and they often have narrow brown borders.

In the greenhouse, anthracnose is more destructive in the fall and spring than during the winter. Out-of-doors it is most conspicuous in August and September.

Control. Propagate new snapdragon plants from seed, or take cuttings from healthy plants. Give the plants good ventilation, and keep the foliage as dry as possible. Spraying with bordeaux mixture will aid in controlling this disease.

BOTRYTIS BLIGHT

Symptoms. When plants are attacked by the fungus *Botrytis cinerea* the flower spikes wilt. Tan-colored areas occur on the stems in the region of the lowest flowers and enlarge rapidly, girdling the stem and killing the entire spike. Infection usually starts in the blossoms and extends downward, but rarely extends below the first lateral branches. Entire plants are never killed. Brownish spore masses of the causal fungus appear on old infected parts under conditions of high humidity.

Control. Remove and burn infected parts and cut flower spikes as early as possible. Avoid excessive humidities by controlling the heat and ventilation, avoid splashing water, and provide air circulation. Keep all plant debris cleaned up. Frequent dusting with zineb or spraying with benomyl or Bravo is helpful.

CERCOSPORA BLIGHT

Symptoms. The fungus *Cercospora antirrhini* produces subcircular lesions, 0.5 to 7.0 millimeters in diameter, on the leaves. These lesions are discrete to confluent, with dull-white or gray centers surrounded by light-brown, slightly raised margins. The central portions of the lesions are ½ to ⅝ of the total diameter. Under humid conditions, lesions may expand rapidly, leading to the development of irregular, poorly defined, gray or tan necrotic areas

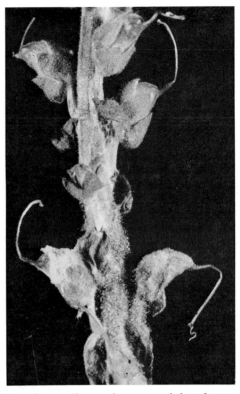

Botrytis mycelium and spores on infected snapdragon spike.

Stem lesion and withered leaves on a snapdragon affected by anthracnose.

that extend to 15 millimeters in diameter and occasionally exhibit faint concentric zonation. Sporulation may be abundant on the central portions of lesions, and heavily infected leaves may become chlorotic and eventually drop off.

Stem lesions, which occur predominantly on the basal portions near the soil, are depressed, dull white to gray, with brown margins, at first discrete, subcircular, oval or elliptical 1 to 10 by 1 to 5 millimeters, becoming confluent and up to 4 centimeters long. The cortical tissue of one-fourth to three-fourths of the stem circumference becomes necrotic and develops minute longitudinal cracks. Sporulation is sparse on lesion surfaces. Plants with stem and leaf infections are stunted and chlorotic.

Control. Spray the plants with bordeaux mixture or some other good foliage fungicide.

CROWN AND STEM CANKER

Symptoms. The most conspicuous symptom of crown and stem canker, caused by the fungus *Myrothecium roridum,* is a wilting of leaves and flowering stems. The crowns at first have water-soaked lesions, which later become sunken, dry, cracked cankers, covered with thin, white mycelium and numerous sporodochia (spore-producing structures of the causal fungus). These sporodochia are black, about 1 millimeter in diameter, with a margin of white mycelium; they frequently coalesce to form larger patches. Sporodochia are quite characteristic and are formed abundantly on infected stems grown under moist conditions. Cankers may extend several inches up the stem.

Control. Excessive moisture favors the spread and destructiveness of the disease. Control is largely a matter of sanitation and proper culture. Water should not be used in excess, and overhead syringing or sprinkling should be avoided. Sterilized soil should be used consistently in seed flats as well as in benches or ground beds. Infected plants should be removed and burned.

DOWNY MILDEW

Symptoms. Downy mildew, caused by the fungus *Peronospora antirrhini,* is most common on snapdragon seedlings. It causes a downward curling of the leaves and reduced size of leaves and plants. The infected leaves are paler than normal and the lower surface is covered by a white to bluish-purple downy fungus growth. Often the seedlings are killed from the top of the plant down to the soil surface. On older plants the terminal shoot growth is checked and the leaves become pallid. On plants about to flower, a rosetting of the growth point occurs.

Control. This disease is favored by low temperature and high humidity. Heat and ventilation of greenhouses should be regulated to prevent condensation on the plants. Spraying with zineb at 7-day intervals will give good control if care is taken to cover the lower surfaces of the leaves with the fungicide. Plant seeds and seedlings in sterilized soil.

PHYLLOSTICTA BLIGHT

Symptoms. The fungus *Phyllosticta antirrhini* produces large, circular, dark-brown or black spots on snapdragon leaves. These spots usually show a series of concentric ridges. They may be located on any part of the infected leaf but are most common near the tips and edges. These spots are visible on both sides of the leaf and soon become cream colored and slightly sunken in the center. As the lesions spread, the cream color changes to pale brown, and the advancing margins remain dark.

The older lesions are distinctly zoned, with fine, raised ridges limiting the zones. The upper surfaces are thickly dotted, especially toward the center, with small, black fruiting bodies of the causal fungus. Leaves attacked when young become distorted and curled, and if the attack is severe the entire leaf shrivels and dies but remains clinging to the stem. Lesions become dry, hard, and brittle, readily breaking to pieces when handled.

Brown, elongated lesions occur on the

petioles. The petiole is quickly girdled and the leaf droops and dies. Petiole lesions usually spread downward and result in stem infections at the axils of the leaves.

Two types of symptoms occur on the stems. A water-soaked area suddenly appears on the young shoots several inches back of the tip, and spreads rapidly around and lengthwise of the stem. In a few days the affected tissue shows a rather firm, dark-brown rot, then soon collapses and dries. Sometimes the whole shoot is affected and becomes very brittle. The leaves also turn brown and shrivel. In other instances the spread of the water-soaked area is checked for some reason and the terminal portion of the shoot remains green. In this case the collapsing and drying of the rotted area soon cuts off the water supply to the green tip so that the shoot tip gradually wilts, often falling over at the affected point.

In addition to the blight or rot of the branches, a form of the disease occurs in which more definite lesions are produced on the stems. These lesions are first visible as dark-green, water-soaked and slightly sunken spots. In a few days the spots develop dark-brown or purplish margins and ashy-white centers. Often the spots split or crack. The spots are covered with the small, dark pycnidia of the blight fungus.

In other cases, usually in succulent stems, the spots enlarge rapidly so that the stem is completely girdled in a few days. These lesions do not become white, cracked, or sunken, but are yellowish to dark brown and smooth, with numerous pycnidia arranged over the surface in close concentric circles. The dead epidermis adheres closely to the stem in these brown lesions, but in the white spots on woody stems it is loose and brittle, and flakes off easily.

On young seedlings the stem lesions may completely girdle the plant near the base and cause rapid wilting and death, similar to damping-off symptoms.

Control. All forms of Phyllosticta blight, with the exception of damping-off, can be controlled by spraying with bordeaux mixture 4-4-50. Sterilization of the seedbed is effective in controlling damping-off. Other practices that will help to control the disease are removing and burning dead or dying plants as soon as they are noticed, cleaning up and burning all plant debris in the fall, and surface watering to avoid wetting the leaves. Maintaining a temperature below 60°F will aid in checking the disease on greenhouse snapdragons.

PHYTOPHTHORA STEM ROT AND WILT

Symptoms. The first symptom of stem rot and wilt, caused by the fungus *Phytophthora cactorum,* is the appearance of slightly yellow, water-soaked areas on the healthy, white stem tissues. As these spots increase in size the older portions of the lesions become yellow, then brown, and finally almost black. The lesions usually enlarge until they girdle the plant and extend up and down the stem for several inches. The plants wilt, and in the final stages of the disease the outer portion of the stem sloughs off.

Control. Sterilize the soil before planting snapdragons. To check the spread of the disease in areas where it is already established, remove the diseased plants and flood the soil with ferbam, zineb, or thiram. Any of these materials should be used at the rate of 1 pound in 50 gallons of water.

POWDERY MILDEW

Symptoms. In powdery mildew of snapdragons a white, powdery growth of the fungus *Oidium* sp. appears on upper and lower leaf surfaces but predominantly on the upper surface. Stem and flower infections also occur. Some of the older leaves wilt and die.

Control. Powdery mildew on greenhouse snapdragons has been controlled by spraying benomyl on the foliage, applying it as a soil drench at 3-week intervals, or mixing in the soil prior to planting. Spraying with wettable sulfur or using sulfur vaporizers in the greenhouse is effective also.

RUST

Symptoms. Rust, caused by the fungus *Puccinia antirrhini,* is characterized by reddish-brown, powdery pustules on the leaves, stems, and seed pods. The pustules are most abundant on the lower surfaces of the leaves, although they may occur on the upper surfaces also. The number of pustules may increase rapidly, causing severe injury or outright killing of the plants.

Control. Start seedlings in a house that is free of rust-infected snapdragons. If cuttings are used, select them from disease-free stock. In greenhouses, avoid excessive syringing and high humidities. Space the plants far enough apart to allow free air circulation. Watering should be done in the morning rather than in the evening, and surface watering is better than sprinkling.

To prevent infections spray young plants with zineb at the rate of 1 ounce to 4 gallons of water. The plants should be sprayed every 10 to 14 days until they are 15 to 16 inches high.

Rust-resistant snapdragons are available in most colors and should be used in preference to the susceptible varieties.

SCLEROTINIA WILT

Symptoms. In snapdragons, early infections of Sclerotinia wilt, caused by the fungus *Sclerotinia sclerotiorum,* appear as water-soaked lesions. Individual branches, especially those near the ground, soon wilt. As large portions of the stems and branches become involved, entire plants wilt and fall to the ground. The shrunken stems become covered with a copious, white mycelial growth of the wilt fungus, and numerous large sclerotia are formed on the outside and inside of the infected roots and stems.

Control. Soil in which this disease has occurred should be sterilized by heat or replaced with new soil. Destroy and burn all dead and dying plants.

A severe case of rust on snapdragon. The pustules on the leaves are reddish brown.

SEEDLING BLIGHT

Symptoms. The bacterium *Pseudomonas antirrhini* causes a leaf-spot condition in snapdragons which, when severe, is perhaps better termed a seedling blight. The leaf lesions when first visible are small, pale green and less than 0.5 millimeter in diameter, enlarging slightly to 1 millimeter and becoming brown with a narrow, green halo. The fully developed lesions are discrete, almost circular, 4 to 5 millimeters in diameter, sunken and papery brown with a well-defined dark-brown margin but sometimes with a water-soaked dark-green zone around the lesion. When the disease becomes aggressive the lesions coalesce to form irregular blotches and this is often followed by the complete collapse of infected leaves. On dark-leaved cultivars lesions are usually less discrete and the tissue surrounding the lesion becomes chlorotic.

The disease usually appears after the seedlings have been pricked out but it may occur earlier. Lesions occur on all but the very youngest leaves and the disease continues to develop until the plant reaches a height of 6 to 7 inches. After this stage of growth the disease fails to establish itself on subsequently exposed foliage. Although most seedlings in a bedding box, unless severely blighted, will survive to maturity, the unsightliness of the plants during the early stages renders the box unsalable.

Spread of the disease is often rapid as soon as the bedding boxes are placed in the open and exposed to rain splashes. Seedling blight also can be a problem to producers of snapdragon seed who raise plants under mist propagation. However, once plants have passed through the susceptible phase, highly humid conditions do not promote re-establishment of the disease.

Control. Streptomycin sprays applied at weekly or 10-day intervals starting before the disease becomes established have given good control of this disease. Streptomycin sprays, however, may check plant growth somewhat and may cause some chlorosis.

TIP BLIGHT

Symptoms. The leaves show a gradual wilting that starts at the tips and eventually involves the petioles and stems. Sunken, water-soaked lesions form on the

Dead leaf tips and stem lesion on snapdragon affected by nonparasitic tip blight. The branch at the left has been girdled, causing the tip to die as shown in photo at right. Wilting usually begins on the center leaves of the plant.

stem, sometimes completely girdling it, causing the tip to wilt and die. The wilting usually begins on the center leaves of the plant.

Control. The cause of this nonparasitic condition has not been determined. The symptoms usually occur during the cloudy winter months and disappear with the return of brighter weather in the spring. Some varieties are much more susceptible than others.

VERTICILLIUM WILT

Symptoms. When snapdragons are affected by Verticillium wilt, caused by the fungus *Verticillium albo-atrum,* the leaves become flaccid more or less simultaneously, and wilting of the shoots follows quickly. Rapid death follows.

Control. Soil in greenhouses should be steamed before snapdragons are planted. If snapdragons are to be grown out-of-doors the soil may be treated with chloropicrin or Vapam before planting. The fumigants must be allowed to escape completely before the plants are set in the soil.

SNOWBERRY

The most troublesome diseases on snowberry (*Symphoricarpus racemosus*) are anthracnose and alternariosis. These diseases may occur simultaneously on the same plant.

ALTERNARIOSIS

Symptoms. Alternariosis, caused by the fungus *Alternaria solani* f. *symphoricarpi,* is often associated with anthracnose but the two diseases may be distinguished as follows: snowberries affected with alternariosis are yellow or brown, while those affected with anthracnose are red or black. A soft, watery rot generally accompanies alternariosis while a dry rot, wrinkling, and mummifying of the snowberries accompany anthracnose. Bark of the young twigs and bud scales are also parasitized by *A. solani* f. *symphoricarpi.*

Control. Alternariosis is controlled by the same procedures used in controlling anthracnose.

ANTHRACNOSE

Symptoms. The first symptoms of anthracnose, caused by the fungus *Glomerella rufomaculans,* appear in late summer as minute hazel-colored areas which continue to enlarge until the whole snowberry is a cinnamon-rufous color. Later the infected berries turn shades of hazel and finally black. Most of the infected berries shrivel and fall to the ground. Leaves that are attacked become discolored and drop. The bark of infected twigs has a water-soaked dark appearance and twigs are killed back about 2 or 3 nodes from the infected inflorescence. Flesh-colored spore masses or acervuli rupture the epidermis and appear on the diseased berries, leaves, and twigs.

Control. Observe sanitation by destroying diseased plant parts and cultivate the soil around the shrubs. Prune out the diseased twigs and stems during the dormant season. Apply a dormant spray of limesulfur in the spring before growth starts. Then spray the plants regularly with phaltan to keep the leaves and berries protected as they develop. The spray applications should be continued until freezing weather.

Snowberry anthracnose, showing infected leaves and berries.

STEPHANOTIS

Stephanotis floribunda is a tropical vine frequently grown in greenhouses for its clusters of white, waxy flowers, which are commonly used in bridal bouquets. Although usually free from serious diseases, it may occasionally be troubled by flower blights.

BOTRYTIS BLIGHT

Symptoms. The disease caused by the fungus *Botrytis elliptica* is first observed on the white buds and open flowers in the form of numerous, irregular-shaped, pink to dark purplish-red spots, ranging in size from mere flecks to small lesions 1 to 5 millimeters in diameter. Later, some lesions may coalesce, frequently involving, in the aggregate, one-half or more of the entire surface of the bud or open flower. The disease causes marked distortion.

Control. Keep the greenhouse ventilators closed during the stephanotis flowering season. Air temperatures above 75°F are unfavorable for Botrytis infections.

SCLEROTINIA BLIGHT

Symptoms. The fungus *Sclerotinia sclerotiorum* produces tan-to-brown spots, several millimeters to a centimeter in diameter, on stephanotis flowers. Occasionally the spots are numerous and coalesced so that nearly whole flowers are affected. The tissues in the small spots tend to be firm, but become soft in the larger spots. Other parts of the plant are not affected.

Control. Remove and destroy diseased flowers as soon as they appear. Keep the greenhouse ventilators closed during the stephanotis flowering season.

STOCK

Stock (*Matthiola incana*) is subject to relatively few diseases, the most destructive being bacterial blight and the foot rots.

ALTERNARIA LEAF SPOT

Symptoms. The fungus *Alternaria raphani* produces round or elongated spots on leaves, flowers, and stems of stock, starting at the base of the plant and progressing upward. The spots, which vary in size from pinpoints to three-fourths inch in diameter, are at first gray-green with water-soaked margins. Later they become brown, with concentric bands covered with black powdery spores.

Control. Spray with dilute fixed coppers such as Copper A Compound or Tribasic copper sulfate, 2 pounds to 100 gallons of water.

BACTERIAL BLIGHT

Symptoms. Bacterial blight, caused by *Xanthomonas incanae,* affects plants grown in the field and in the greenhouse. Under field conditions the first evidence of bacterial blight is a sudden wilting and collapsing of the young plants when they are 2 to 4 inches high. The main stem is soft and water-soaked from the ground upward, sometimes into the growing tip. The stem tissues are yellowish, soft, and mushy. If the seedlings are close together the disease may spread rapidly from plant to plant. The small collapsed plants soon dry up and disappear.

Under greenhouse conditions the seedlings are attacked soon after they emerge from the soil. One or both cotyledons may wilt and collapse, and the bases of the cotyledon petioles appear water-soaked. The growing tip is quickly invaded, often causing collapse and death of the young plants as described for field conditions.

The disease progresses less rapidly in older plants. Primary infection then usually occurs at old leaf scars near the ground line, appearing as a dark, water-soaked area around the leaf scar. Often all the leaf scars, for 2 to 3 inches up the stem from the ground, may show infection and the entire stem soon becomes girdled. There is a noticeable yellowing and dropping of the lower leaves. Severely diseased plants wilt and die or may continue to grow feebly. Older and more woody plants often are encircled by a somewhat sunken and darkened infected area with irregular cracking of the cortex.

Control. The bacteria that cause this disease are seedborne. To treat seed, enclose a small amount in a loose cheesecloth bag, immerse in water at 127.5° to 131°F for 10 minutes, cool rapidly after treatment, and spread in a thin layer on the cheesecloth to dry.

There is evidence that the causal bacteria persist in the soil. For this reason a 2- to 3-year rotation should be practiced for field-grown stocks. Infested garden or greenhouse soil should be sterilized with steam or formaldehyde.

BOTRYTIS BLIGHT

Symptoms. When the fungus *Botrytis cinerea* infects the flowers of stock, a soft, brown rot is produced. Abundant gray mold may appear on the surface during periods of high humidity. The disease may start in dead leaves at stem tips, and rot the growing point and young flower buds.

Control. Avoid high humidity if possible. Spray with captan or benomyl.

FOOT ROT OR WIRE STEM

Symptoms. Stocks in all stages of development may be affected by foot rot or wire stem caused by the fungus *Rhizoctonia solani*. Symptoms vary considerably with the size of the plant involved. Small seedlings usually damp-off within 2 or 3 days after being set in infested soil. Slightly larger plants, up to 3 or 4 inches tall, may wilt completely but remain green and erect though entirely girdled at the soil line.

When older plants become affected the first symptom is a yellowing of the lower leaves followed by complete wilting of the foliage. The small leaves and the unfolding buds of both small and large plants usually become bluish and remain turgid long after the older foliage has wilted. Girdling lesions are formed at or just below the soil line on the stems. The affected tissues turn black and become markedly constricted. Although infection almost invariably occurs at the soil line, the entire root system may be involved eventually. Quite often lesions are at first restricted to one side of the stem, causing one-sided development of the plant.

Control. Steam sterilize or treat the soil with chloropicrin at the rate of 10 cubic milliliters per cubic foot of soil before planting to stocks. Treating the soil with Terraclor may be beneficial.

Girdling lesions formed near the soil line on stock plants affected by Rhizoctonia foot rot.

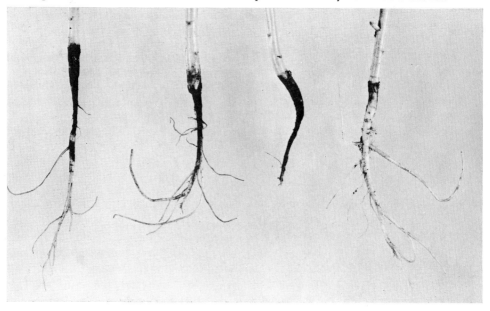

Foot rot or wire stem of annual stocks. Two diseased plants with black basal lesions at left; healthy plant showing white stem and abundant roots at right. All plants are the same age and from the same flat of greenhouse soil. (Photograph courtesy of Cornell University.)

FUSARIUM WILT

Symptoms. Wilt, caused by the fungus *Fusarium oxysporum* f. *mathioli,* usually does not affect stocks unless soil temperatures remain above 70°F. The leaves first have a characteristic yellowing of the veins, then turn yellow, wither, and drop. This condition progresses from the base of the plant upward. Symptoms may appear on only one side of the plant. Plants are stunted and sometimes die suddenly. Seed pods become a light, tawny color, are flat, and contain undeveloped seeds. There is commonly a brown discoloration of the vascular tissues in roots and stems of affected plants.

Control. Since the disease is trouble-some only in parts of the country where stocks are grown into the warm summer months for seed production, control measures are generally not necessary.

MOSAIC

Symptoms. Several aphidborne viruses attack stocks and produce variegation of the flowers. In mild mosaic, flower breaking consists of a marked change in, or disarrangement of the normal pigmentation. The ground color of individual petals from infected plants may be modified to show many white, irregular-shaped islands, or less frequently, circular lesions, or sometimes both. Sometimes infected plants show marked distortion, curling, and puckering of the leaves, with pronounced shortening of the internodes. A rarer symptom is veinclearing, which changes into a diffuse, somewhat coarse, mottling consisting of irregular, nonraised, light- and dark-green areas.

The symptoms of severe mosaic are more prominent and striking. Flower breaking is of a coarser type. Leaf symptoms consist of a conspicuous, coarse mottling.

Control. Rogue out and destroy diseased plants as soon as they are detected. Keep aphids under control.

PHYTOPHTHORA FOOT ROT

Symptoms. Stock plants of any age may be affected by foot rot, caused by the fungus *Phytophthora cryptogea,* but heaviest infection occurs prior to or during the flowering period. The symptoms are sudden wilting and drooping of all but the youngest tuft of leaves, infection and rotting of the roots and lower part of the stem, and ultimate breakage of the stem at or near the soil level. The invaded tissues are blackish brown, water-soaked, soft, and odorless. Infected plants are easily pulled from the soil.

Control. The incidence of this disease can be greatly reduced by growing the plants on well-drained sites, and by supplying only enough moisture to satisfy growth requirements.

VERTICILLIUM WILT

Symptoms. The symptoms of Verticillium wilt of stocks, caused by the fungus *Verticillium albo-atrum,* appear as a progressive yellowing and wilting of the leaves, beginning at the base of the plant. The yellowing on individual leaves begins at the margins and progresses inward, sometimes following the veins so that the interveinal tissues are the last to lose their color. Plants infected early in their development may be stunted severely. The vascular tissues of infected plants often are discolored, the discoloration extending up through the petioles into the leaves.

Control. Steam sterilize or treat the soil with chloropicrin before planting stocks.

WHITE BLIGHT AND COTTONY ROT

Symptoms. The fungus *Sclerotinia sclerotiorum* causes two types of disease when it attacks stocks. These are commonly known as white blight and cottony rot. White blight is characterized by a chalky-white, girdling canker on above-ground stems. The parts above this canker die and turn brown. Cottony rot appears as white, cottony fungus masses at the bases of rotted stems. It spreads rapidly in wet soil. With either type of the disease, hard, black sclerotia form inside affected stems in advanced cases.

Control. Avoid excessively wet planting locations and excessive watering. Steam sterilize greenhouse soil.

STRAWFLOWER

Strawflower (*Helichrysum bracteatum*) is relatively free from disease, but Verticillium wilt sometimes causes serious losses.

VERTICILLIUM WILT

Symptoms. The first visible sign of Verticillium wilt, caused by *Verticillium albo-atrum,* usually appears at the beginning of the flowering period. The lower leaves of infected plants may wilt suddenly without noticeable change in color. As the disease progresses the upper whorls of leaves also wilt. Soon the wilted leaves become chlorotic; subsequently, brown necrotic areas, which later coalesce, develop along the margins. Still later, affected leaves become entirely dry and brown, remaining attached to the main stem of the plant but hanging downwards.

Internally the stem shows a blackish-brown discoloration of the vascular tissues

Black stem bases on stock plants affected by Phytophthora foot rot. The roots had rotted off and remained in the soil when the plants were pulled.

Verticillium wilt of straw-flower. The two short, wilted plants are shown 5 weeks after artificial infection in the greenhouse. The tall plant is healthy. (Photograph courtesy of Division of Plant Pathology, University of California, Berkeley.)

which may extend for a considerable distance above the soil level. Early infection reduces the length of the stem internodes, with consequent stunting of the plants. Sections of infected roots show a discoloration of the vascular tissues similar to that in the stem.

Occasionally, infected plants die just before flowering, or die without producing flower buds. Generally, however, they develop flowers and may live for a considerable time after infection.

Control. The causal fungus is a soil inhabitant that may persist in the soil for many years. Strawflowers therefore should not be planted in areas where wilt has occurred. Infested soil may be treated with chloropicrin or Vapam.

SWEET ALYSSUM

Stem rot is sometimes a serious disease of sweet alyssum (*Lobularia maritima*).

STEM ROT

Symptoms. The lower leaves of plants attacked by the fungus *Rhizoctonia solani* become water-soaked, rotted, and shriveled. Definite lesions appear on the stems and usually the portion of the plant above the lesion is killed. During wet weather a cobwebby growth of the causal fungus appears on infected plants.

Control. Treat the soil with Terraclor before planting sweet alyssum.

SWEET PEA

Sweet peas (*Lathyrus odoratus*) are susceptible to a number of diseases but most of them can be reduced to a minimum by proper control measures.

ANTHRACNOSE

Symptoms. Anthracnose, caused by the fungus *Glomerella cingulata*, usually appears at about flowering time on outdoor-grown sweet peas. The disease occurs on stems, leaves, flowers, and pods. There is a general wilting of the affected parts, followed by dying that begins at the tips of the younger shoots and works downward. White areas appear on the leaves, sometimes involving the entire leaf and causing it to wither and fall. Flower stalks may wither and dry up before the blossoms develop. Infected seed pods lose their green color and shrivel. Salmon-colored, spore-producing areas may appear on the affected spots.

The fungus that causes sweet pea anthracnose also causes bitter rot of apples.

For this reason the disease is likely to be more destructive on sweet peas planted near infected orchards. The fungus overwinters in cankered apple limbs and mummified apples, on sweet pea refuse, and in sweet pea seed from infected pods.

Control. Select seed from disease-free pods. Only plump, sound-appearing seed should be planted. All plant parts should be raked up and burned in the fall, to destroy spores of *Glomerella* that might overwinter in such refuse.

BACTERIAL STREAK

Symptoms. In bacterial streak of sweet peas, light reddish-brown to dark-brown spots and streaks originate near the ground and extend upward on the stem on mature plants as they near the blooming stage. The disease spreads, with similar symptoms, from the stems to the petioles, flowers, and seed pods. On the leaves, the disease appears as small, roundish spots that gradually coalesce and eventually involve the entire leaf, which appears dark brown when killed. Finally the entire plant dies prematurely.

The symptoms of this disease are similar to those of spotted wilt, and there is some question whether streak and spotted wilt are distinct diseases, or a complex involving the bacterium *Erwinia lathyri* and a virus.

Control. The agents that cause streak are seedborne. Avoid planting infected seed. Seed may be treated by soaking for 5 minutes in a solution of 5 parts of commercial formaldehyde and 95 parts of water. Rogue out infected plants to prevent the spread of the disease to healthy plants.

BUD DROP

Symptoms. In bud drop of sweet peas, young flower buds turn yellow and drop off at an early age. This condition is not caused by a parasitic organism but rather by improper cultural conditions, such as deficiencies of phosphorus and potassium and an excess of nitrogen in the soil, together with low light intensity in the greenhouse. An excess of nitrogen in the soil as sometimes occurs following steam sterilization may cause bud drop.

Control. To control bud drop, grow sweet peas in soil that is low in moisture and high in air content. Test the soil at regular intervals to make sure the soil nutrients maintain a proper balance. Water the soil only after some wilting of the plants occurs. Apply water sparingly during cloudy weather. Maintain temperature below 50°F, and relative humidity below 50 percent if possible. In sand culture a relatively high concentration of soil nutrients has been found beneficial.

FASCIATION

Symptoms. The disease known as fasciation is caused by the bacterium *Corynebacterium fascians.* In sweet peas, many short, fleshy, thick, and aborted stems with misshapen leaves develop at or below the soil line. These fasciated or abnormally developed shoots originate at either the first or the second node of the stem. The mass of fasciated growth on old plants resembles a witches'-broom and may reach a diameter of 3 inches, but usually does not extend over 1 or 2 inches above the ground. A normal green color develops in the portion exposed to light. The main stem of an affected plant apparently grows normally, except that it is dwarfed, and flower production is reduced. Plants are not killed.

Control. Sterilize infested soil to destroy the causal organism.

MOSAIC

Symptoms. Mosaic of sweet peas is a virus disease that may be recognized by a yellowing, dotting, or mottling of the leaves. Another symptom is curling of the leaves. Infected plants usually are dwarfed, flower stalks are shorter than normal, and the color of the blossoms is broken. Frequently the affected plants appear to outgrow the disease entirely and the newer growth above the diseased portions appears normal. The color of blossoms on

Fasciation at base of sweet pea stems. The plant at the right has developed a witches'-broom.

such plants usually is broken, however. At other times, infected plants continue to grow, and even flower, with the disease keeping pace.

Control. Mosaic is spread from plant to plant by aphids; consequently, greenhouse fumigation should be practiced to control these insects. Spray outdoor plants with a contact insecticide. Remove and destroy diseased plants as soon as they are noticed.

POWDERY MILDEW

Symptoms. A white, powdery growth of the causal fungus, *Microsphaera alni*, develops on the upper leaf surfaces, causing malformation and falling of the leaves in severe attacks. Mildew is common in greenhouses in the spring, when temperature and humidity are difficult to control.

Control. Dusting the plants with sulfur or spraying with a sulfur-containing fungicide usually will check this trouble. Painting the steam pipes with sulfur is effective as long as the heat is kept on. Sulfur fumigators also may be used.

RAMULARIA LEAF SPOT (WHITE BLIGHT)

Symptoms. In white blight of sweet peas, circular or irregular, tan- to buff-colored, dead areas are formed on the

Powdery mildew on sweet pea leaves: scattered infections on lower leaf; almost completely covered leaf, center; healthy leaf at top.

leaves and merge readily into healthy tissue. These spots are angular at first, then increase in size and become more or less circular, and sometimes coalesce to involve entire leaves. The margins of the spots are indefinite and tend to appear water-soaked. Spores are produced in white tufts, visible with a hand lens, on both sides of the leaf but most abundantly on the under surface. A high percentage of leaves may drop in severe cases. Lesions may occur on the wings of stems. The cause of this disease was thought to be *Cladosporium album,* but Baker, Snyder, and Davis (1950) have shown it to be *Ramularia deusta.*

Control. Dust the plants with sulfur at frequent intervals.

ROOT ROT

Symptoms. Root rots are caused by several different soil-inhabiting fungi, the most common being *Thielaviopsis basicola, Rhizoctonia solani,* and *Fusarium solani* f. *pisi.* Symptoms produced by these organisms are varied enough to facilitate accurate diagnosis and treatment.

The disease caused by *T. basicola* is commonly known as black rot. The plants appear dwarfed, yellow, and sickly. Severely infected plants have little or no root system left, and what root system remains is stubby and blackened. The fungus sometimes works upward along the stem to a distance of 2 or 3 inches above the ground, but never to the extent of invading the entire stem. Diseased plants are seldom killed but their growth is retarded and they fail to bloom.

In the very early stages of infection caused by *R. solani* the seedlings have a wilted appearance. As the disease progresses, the infected seedlings collapse and fall over. Severely infected plants have practically no root system. The causal fungus produces a browning effect on the roots before total destruction sets in. Older plants that become infected are dwarfed and yellow, and often wilt. They produce no blossoms and die prematurely. A brown, shrunken area on the stem at or above the soil line may result from the upward spread of the infection.

The first symptom of Fusarium root rot is a sudden flagging of the leaves, accompanied by general wilting and collapse of the plant. The plants are usually killed when they reach a height of about 8 to

Black root rot of sweet peas, caused by **Thielaviopsis basicola.** The root system is almost completely destroyed in the plant at far right. In the plant farthest left in the photo, the infection has spread up the stem.

10 inches. Stems are attacked below ground, and a short distance above.

Control. The root rot diseases may be controlled in greenhouses by planting sweet peas in steam-sterilized soil. Garden soil may be treated with chloropicrin or Vapam, several weeks before planting.

SPOTTED WILT

Symptoms. A characteristic symptom of virus-caused spotted wilt is a necrotic streaking of stems and petioles. The streaks are reddish brown to dull purple and are conspicuous in the advanced stage. They may extend the entire length of the stem. Leaves and shoots may turn yellow and die. Early symptoms on the foliage are circular or oval spots with diffuse margins. The spots are yellowish at first, becoming somewhat brownish. One or more yellowish sections or zones develop from these spots. The spotting of the foliage is fairly definite, although not striking, in the early stages, but the general yellowing that may follow becomes a conspicuous symptom. Plants infected early may yellow and die without showing other symptoms. Blossoms on infected plants may develop a circular pattern in the pigment, or blighting of the whole shoot may occur prior to blossom formation.

Control. Control measures consist of isolating sweet peas from other plants that are susceptible to spotted wilt. Among these are: tomato, cauliflower, celery, amaryllis, begonia, browallia, campanula, delphinium, gloxinia, godetia, gaillardia, poppy, pentstemon, primula, salvia, and verbena. Remove and destroy all diseased plants as soon as they are noticed.

SWEET WILLIAM

Sweet william (*Dianthus barbatus*) is subject to some of the same diseases that affect carnation. Fusarium wilt is the only one that is seriously destructive.

FUSARIUM WILT

Symptoms. The first symptoms of Fusarium wilt, caused by *Fusarium oxysporum* f. *barbati*, is yellowing of the new growth. The yellowing may involve the entire leaf or may occur only on parts of it, as large, indefinite blotches, or streaks. Growth becomes greatly retarded, finally resulting in conspicuous stunting, especially when infection occurs early. As the disease progresses the leaves point downward instead of upward as in a healthy plant, and the edges tend to curl slightly toward the under surface. Usually the leaves do not

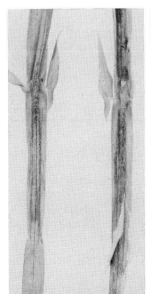

Streaks on sweet pea stems, and spotted leaves, caused by the spotted wilt virus. (Photographs courtesy of Division of Plant Pathology, University of California, Berkeley.)

The sweet william plant at right shows advanced symptoms of Fusarium wilt. A healthy plant is at left. (Photograph courtesy of Division of Plant Pathology, University of California.)

wither or wrinkle, but tend to become leathery. They gradually turn yellow and become tinged with tan as they die. A brown discoloration of the vascular system of the roots and lower stem accompanies the foliage symptoms. Infection may occur in plants of any age.

Control. Plant sweet william in new soil or in sterilized soil. Treating infested soil with Vapam may be beneficial.

TULIP

The best known diseases on tulips (*Tulipa gesneriana*) are fire and breaking. Several other diseases occasionally become troublesome.

ANTHRACNOSE

Symptoms. Anthracnose, caused by the fungus *Gloeosporium thuemenii* f. *tulipae,* produces small to large, elliptical lesions on the peduncles and leaf blades. In general, the lesions run lengthwise along the peduncles and leaf blades. At first the lesions are water-soaked; later they become dry and black around the margins. Numer-ous small, black acervuli — fruiting bodies of the anthracnose fungus — develop in the centers of the lesions.

Control. Infected parts should be removed and destroyed as soon as detected. Spraying with bordeaux mixture affords protection against infection. Spraying with ferbam also should be effective.

BASAL ROT

Symptoms. Bulbs affected by basal rot, caused by the fungus *Fusarium oxysporum,* are dull white and the rotted area is firm, shrunken, and may be zoned. A white or pink mold with powdery masses of spores may develop on or under the husk, usually at the base of the bulb. The rotted tissue eventually turns chalky unless organisms that produce soft rot are present also. Leaves that develop from diseased bulbs wilt, turn red, and usually die. Diseased bulbs develop a few or no roots.

Control. Discard all affected bulbs and treat the healthy-appearing bulbs with Arasan or benomyl before planting. Avoid planting in locations where the disease has occurred.

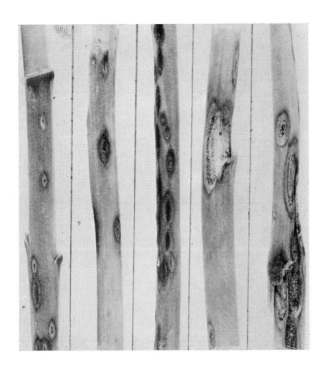

Tulip anthracnose lesions. Acervuli of the causal fungus are clearly visible in the larger lesions. (Photograph courtesy of Division of Plant Pathology, University of California, Berkeley.)

BLOSSOM BLIGHT

Symptoms. The first indication of blossom blight of tulips, caused by the fungus *Phytophthora cactorum,* is a shriveling of the flower stalk just below the flower, followed by falling over of the blossom. The blossom withers and dries up, or, under humid conditions, the petals become covered with the mycelium of the causal fungus and a soft decay follows rapidly.

Double varieties planted in wet, shaded locations are most seriously affected.

Control. Avoid wet, shaded locations when planting tulips.

FIRE OR BOTRYTIS BLIGHT

Symptoms. Botrytis blight or fire, caused by the fungus *Botrytis tulipae,* causes lesions on the leaves which first show as minute, yellowish spots, some-

Botrytis blight lesions on tulip bulbs occur mostly on the sides but may appear at the nose or base of the bulb. The outer scales have been removed from the bulbs shown here.

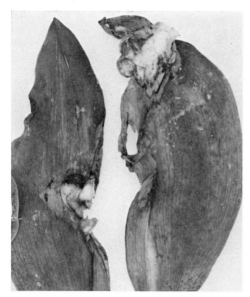

Botrytis blight of tulip. Infections on one side of a leaf will cause the leaf to curl to that side. The leaves may be completely destroyed as the disease progresses.

blighted. Blighting may take place when the flower is still in the bud, preventing it from opening.

Lesions on the stalks resemble those on the leaves but are more elongate and more depressed. A lesion may extend through the stem, causing it to weaken and break over at the point of attack.

Small black bodies the size of a pinhead often are found on the brown outer bulb scales. These are the sclerotia or resting bodies of the fungus. If the outer scales are removed, deep-yellow or brown, usually circular, lesions may be seen. These lesions are usually on the sides of the bulbs but may occur at the nose or at the base of the bulb. The lesions rarely penetrate to the inner white scales.

Control. Effective control of blight or fire may be achieved by certain cultural practices. Once an area becomes infested, the disease becomes more serious with each succeeding tulip crop. An area should

what elongated in the direction of the leaf veins and surrounded by a darker, water-soaked area. The lesions are slightly sunken and give the leaf a speckled appearance. As they enlarge the areas become more depressed, the color changes to a whitish gray with a brownish tinge, and a translucent or water-soaked area appears about the margin. At this stage the margins of the lesions are quite definite. The lesions may enlarge and coalesce, frequently involving the entire leaf. When an infection occurs on the margin of the leaf near the tip, there is a characteristic wrinkling and bending of the leaf to one side. A gray growth of the causal fungus develops on the dead areas during humid weather.

Lesions on the flower begin as minute spots that are whitish to light brown. The color is bleached from the flower. After the lesions enlarge they turn a deeper brown and may involve an entire segment of the perianth which then becomes dry and wrinkled. At this time abundant conidiophores, or spore-forming branches, of the fungus may appear on the dead areas. The entire flower may be affected and appear

Lesions caused by Botrytis blight on tulip flowers begin as small, white to light-brown spots.

be planted to tulips no oftener than every third year. It is best to dig the bulbs not later than 3 weeks after the petals fall. To prevent the fungus from spreading to the scales, remove stems from the bulbs as soon as they are dug. After the bulbs are dried and cleaned, store them for the summer in a cool, dry place. Examine the bulbs carefully before planting, and discard the diseased ones. Careful handling of the bulbs is important since infection occurs more easily on injured bulbs than on sound ones.

When the tulips come up in the spring, remove and destroy all infected plant parts as soon as they are noticed. Clean up and destroy all plant debris as soon as blooming ceases. If the bulbs are not to be taken up, as soon as the plants become yellow and mature the entire tops should be cut below the ground, removed, and burned.

Spraying the plants with ferbam, 2 pounds per 100 gallons of water (2 tablespoonfuls per gallon in small quantities), has given effective control in some cases. Apply the spray at 7- to 10-day intervals, beginning when the plants are about 4 inches high. At least four applications should be made.

Terraclor, applied to the soil in autumn when tulips are planted, will aid in controlling the disease.

BREAKING

Symptoms. Tulip breaking is the oldest known virus disease of plants. Flowers of affected plants become variegated and the leaves become striped with lighter green or even with white. The variegation in the flowers consists of bars, stripes, flames, streaks, or feathering of a darker color overlaid on a lighter shade of some color or on pure white or yellow. Often the broken color is limited to a pencilling of the edges and tops of the petals and sepals; or it may be in the form of heavy streaks of color in this region. At other times it will have, in addition to the pencilling, narrow or broad streaks or flames of color up to the middle portion of the individual petals or sepals; other flames may break out toward the edges. Reduced size and vigor of the plant, and the production of fewer offsets or bulbils are also symptoms of tulip breaking.

Control. Diseased plants should be removed and destroyed as soon as they appear. The virus is transmitted from diseased to healthy plants by several species of aphids. A spray or dust program to con-

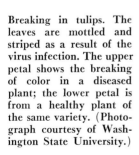

Breaking in tulips. The leaves are mottled and striped as a result of the virus infection. The upper petal shows the breaking of color in a diseased plant; the lower petal is from a healthy plant of the same variety. (Photograph courtesy of Washington State University.)

trol aphids should be practiced. Malathion and nicotine sulfate are effective for this purpose. Tulips and lilies should not be planted in adjoining areas because some of the same viruses affect both kinds of plants, and each can infect the other.

GRAY BULB ROT

Symptoms. The first evidences of gray bulb rot, caused by the fungus *Rhizoctonia tuliparum,* are the bare spots in the tulip beds where the plants fail to come up. When affected bulbs do send up leaves their growth is greatly retarded. The leaves soon die and wither away, usually before they can expand, because the causal fungus gradually rots them off below ground. When diseased bulbs are dug they are found to be more or less rotted, with the infection usually beginning at the tip of the bulb. In most cases the roots are abundant and healthy. The leaves and flower shoots, if they have started, are rotted, and the adjacent bulb scales are more or less involved. The normally white tissue turns gray or reddish gray, a particularly distinctive symptom of this disease. The rot is dry and the tissue remains rather firm for a time.

The soil clings to the exterior of the rotted parts. Imbedded in the soil about the bulb are numerous, more or less globular, dark-brown bodies, the sclerotia of the fungus. These become almost black when dry. These sclerotia are loosely attached to the surface of the diseased tissues, and come away easily with the removal of the soil. There is an abundance of grayish-white mycelium on the outer bulb scales covering the diseased parts. Within the bulbs the mycelium frequently forms a felty layer between the diseased scales.

Control. Selection of clean bulbs, sterilization of soil, and removal and burning of infected plants are effective control measures. It is helpful to dust the bulbs with Terraclor dust, or dip them in a Terraclor suspension, just before planting.

Treating infested soil with Terraclor is also recommended.

VINCA

Stem blight is the most serious disease of *Vinca minor* and is also one of the most difficult diseases to control.

STEM BLIGHT

Symptoms. The fungus *Phoma exigua* var. *exigua* causes a dieback of *Vinca minor* which begins soon after new growth appears. Dark-brown to black lesions first appear on the old overwintered runners, causing them to die back to the base. These old runners are usually well hidden under the new shoots, and may serve as a source of inoculum for later infections. Girdling lesions appear at the base of new shoots and cause conspicuous wilting and drying. Symptom development continues for several weeks, often resulting in wilting and death of entire clumps of vincas.

Dark spots that may develop on the leaves may be followed by browning and death of affected leaves, but diseased leaves usually fall off and are not associated with stem infections. However, the fungus often spreads from stem lesions into the leaf petiole and the base of the leaf. The stem lesions expand rapidly and cause wilting and dieback of the stem. Some lesions may extend the entire length of the stem within a few days after initial appearance. Pycnidia of the causal fungus appear in new lesions within a few days.

Control. Apply a drench of 1 pound benomyl 50 percent wettable powder or thiabendazole 60 percent wettable powder per 1,000 square feet of planted area 2 or 3 times at monthly intervals, beginning about April 1. In newly planted vinca beds, soil drenches may be combined with suitable mulches until plantings become established. After vinca beds are well established, the number of annual soil drenches may be reduced or eliminated entirely, but may be resumed if stem blight again becomes a serious problem.

ZINNIA

Only two diseases are commonly trouble-some on zinnias (*Zinnia elegans*). These are powdery mildew and Alternaria blight.

ALTERNARIA BLIGHT

Symptoms. The most common and con-spicuous symptom of zinnia blight, caused by the fungus *Alternaria zinniae,* is the spotting of the foliage. Individual spots are at first circular in outline but rapidly be-come irregular. The spots vary from 2 to 10 millimeters in diameter, are reddish brown, and may have grayish-white cen-ters on the upper leaf surfaces. Differen-tiation of margin and center is lacking on the lower surface. As the spots increase in size and number, the affected leaves be-come brown and dry.

Blossoms may be severely affected. Brown spots, 1 or 2 millimeters in di-ameter, and sometimes with grayish-white centers, appear on the petal tissues of the conspicuous ray flowers. Affected plants soon darken and wither, causing the blos-soms to become unsightly.

Numerous small, reddish spots, some-times with grayish-white centers, may be seen on stem internodes of affected plants. Such spots are usually superficial. Some-times large areas may become involved through coalescence of smaller spots. Large lesions, frequently girdling the stems, often form at the nodes, caused either by growth of the fungus inward from affected leaves, or by direct infection of the leaf axils. The lesions at the nodes ordinarily do not re-main superficial, and the upper portions of the affected stems may be killed by girdling at the nodes. Dark-brown to black cankers with sunken centers are common at the base of the stems of diseased plants. Affected plants often wilt completely, even when the basal cankers do not completely encircle the stems.

The outer tissues of affected roots may become dark gray, and may rot com-

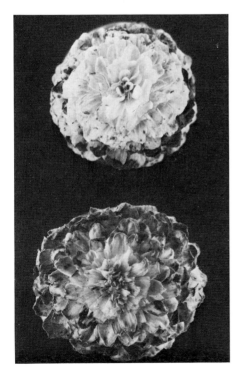

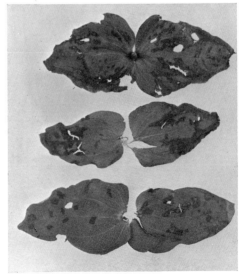

Zinnia affected by Alternaria blight, a fungus disease that results in spotting of the leaves and flowers.

pletely and slough off, resulting in wilting and death of the plants. Damping-off of seedlings also may occur.

Control. Treat seed with a fungicide to kill any fungus on the surface of the seed. Practice thorough sanitation of fields and gardens, and employ long rotations of planting sites if possible. Spray young plants frequently with a good protective fungicide such as maneb or zineb, making sure to cover lower surfaces of the leaves.

BACTERIAL LEAF SPOT

Symptoms. The bacterium *Xanthomonas nigromaculans* f. sp. *zinniae* produces angular to irregularly circular, reddish-brown to dark-brown spots 1 to 4 millimeters in diameter, and surrounded by a prominent yellow halo on the leaves. These lesions are readily distinguished from those of Alternaria blight, which are larger, reddish brown to purple, often with gray centers, and lacking a yellow halo.

Control. Spray the plants with one of the streptomycin formulations developed for control of bacterial diseases of plants.

There is evidence that *X. nigromaculans* f. sp. *zinniae* is disseminated on seed of zinnia. Therefore, to inhibit spread of the pathogen, seedsmen should rogue and destroy infected plants.

Seed suspected of being infected may be soaked for 2 minutes in 0.52 percent sodium hypochlorite (10 percent Clorox solution) immediately before planting.

POWDERY MILDEW

Symptoms. A white, powdery growth of the causal fungus, *Erysiphe cichoracearum,* appears on the leaves. The disease usually appears in late summer and is most severe on plants in partly shaded locations.

Control. Dust the plants with dusting sulfur, or spray with wettable sulfur, Karathane, or Acti-dione PM at the first signs of mildew. Repeat as often as necessary to hold the disease in check.

Two zinnia leaves affected by powdery mildew, top and center; healthy leaf below. The center leaf is severely infected; individual infections can be distinguished on the top leaf.

BIBLIOGRAPHY

Alexander, P. 1955. Results of poinsettia disease studies in Ohio. Ohio Florists' Assoc. Bul. 310:2–3.

Alexander, P. 1956. Poinsettias profit or problems — penthouse or poorhouse? Ohio Florists' Assoc. Bul. 321:2–3.

Allard, H. A. 1916. The mosaic disease of tomatoes and petunias. Phytopathology 6:328–335.

Anderson, C. G., R. A. Young, and E. T. Palm. 1952. *Curvularia* on gladiolus in Oregon. Plant Dis. Reptr. 36:474.

Anderson, C. W. 1958. Tobacco ringspot virus on florists' hydrangea. Plant Dis. Reptr. 42:932–933.

Anderson, P. J. 1918. Rose canker and its control. Mass. Agr. Exp. Sta. Bul. 183:11–46.

Anzalone, L., Jr., and L. W. Baxter. 1956. Protecting camellia grafts with fungicides. (Abstr.) Phytopathology 46:6–7.

Anzalone, L., Jr., and A. G. Plakidas. 1956. Fungicides for control of dieback of camellias. (Abstr.) Phytopathology 46:7.

Anzalone, L., Jr., and A. G. Plakidas. 1958. Control of flower blight of camellias in Louisiana with fungicides. Plant Dis. Reptr. 42:804–806.

Ark, P. A., and J. T. Barrett. 1946. A new bacterial leaf spot of greenhouse-grown gardenias. Phytopathology 36:865–868.

Ark, P. A., and T. A. DeWolfe. 1951. Phytophthora rot of peperomia. Plant Dis. Reptr. 35:46–47.

Ark, P. A., and W. S. Sibray. 1954. Use of Panogen drench to control damping-off in nursery flats. Plant Dis. Reptr. 38:204–206.

Ark, P. A., and C. M. Tompkins. 1939. Bacteriosis of tuberous begonia. Phytopathology 29:633–637.

Ark, P. A., and C. M. Tompkins. 1941. The boron-deficiency disease of gloxinia and its control. Phytopathology 31:467–469.

Ark, P. A., and C. M. Tompkins. 1946. Bacterial leaf blight of bird's-nest fern. Phytopathology 36:758–761.

Ark, P. A., C. M. Tompkins, and R. E. Smith. 1938. A bacterial bud- and stem-rot of rocket larkspur. Phytopathology 28:281–283.

Armstrong, G. M., and J. K. Armstrong. 1965. Wilt of chrysanthemum caused by race 1 of the cowpea Fusarium. Plant Dis. Reptr. 49:673–675.

Arthur, J. C. 1900. Chrysanthemum rust. Ind. Agr. Exp. Sta. Bul. 85:143–150.

Aycock, R. 1959. Relation of fungicidal and nematocidal bulb treatments to phytotoxicity and control of basal rot in narcissus. Phytopathology 49:12–16.

Aycock, R. 1959. Soil treatments for control of *Sclerotium rolfsii* in Dutch iris. Plant Dis. Reptr. 43:283–286.

Aycock, R., and F. A. Haasis. 1963. Corm treatments for control of Fusarium disease of gladiolus. N.C. Agr. Exp. Sta. Tech. Bul. 154. 24 p.

Bain, D. C. 1946. Die-back and stem canker of camellia. Plant Dis. Reptr. 30:206–208.

Baker, K. F. 1947. Heterosporium disease of nasturtium and its control. (Abstr.) Phytopathology 37:359.

Baker, K. F. 1948. Diseases of delphinium in California. Amer. Delphinium Soc. Yearb., 1947:15–30.

Baker, K. F. 1948. Fusarium wilt of garden stock (*Mathiola incana*). Phytopathology 38:399–403.

Baker, K. F. 1948. The history, distribution, and nomenclature of the rose black-spot fungus. Plant Dis. Reptr. 32:260–274.

Baker, K. F. 1948. History and distribution of rose black spot: a correction. Plant Dis. Reptr. 32:397.

Baker, K. F. 1951. Moisture and diseases; control of humidity important factor in reducing crop losses. Florists' Rev. 108 (2798):15–16, 46–51.

Baker, K. F. 1953. Fusarium wilt of China aster. Plant Diseases. U.S. Dept. Agr. Yearb. 1953:572–577.

Baker, K. F. 1953. Recent epidemics of downy mildew of rose. Plant Dis. Reptr. 37:331–339.

Baker, K. F., and L. H. Clark. 1947. Stemphylium leaf spot of China aster. (Abstr.) Phytopathology 37:842–843.

Baker, K. F., and L. H. Davis. 1950. Heterosporium disease of nasturtium and its control. Phytopathology 40:553–566.

Baker, K. F., and L. H. Davis. 1950. Stemphylium leaf spot of China aster. Mycologia 42:477–486.

Baker, K. F., and L. H. Davis. 1953. Greasy blotch of carnation. (Abstr.) Phytopathology 43:585.

Baker, K. F., A. W. Dimock, and L. H. Davis. 1949. Life history and control of the Ascochyta ray blight of chrysanthemum. Phytopathology 39:789–805.

Baker, K. F., A. W. Dimock, and L. H. Davis. 1950. *Ramularia cyclaminicola* Trel., the cause of cyclamen stunt disease. Phytopathology 40:1027–1034.

Baker, K. F., A. W. Dimock, and L. H. Davis. 1961. Cause and prevention of the rapid spread of the Ascochyta disease of chrysanthemum. Phytopathology 51:96–101.

Baker, K. F., and N. A. MacLean. 1950. Powdery mildew of snapdragon on the Pacific coast. Plant Dis. Reptr. 34:183–185.

Baker, K. F., O. A. Matkin, and L. H. Davis. 1954. Interaction of salinity injury, leaf age, fungicide application, climate, and *Botrytis cinerea* in a disease complex of column stock. Phytopathology 44:39–42.

Baker, K. F., and R. H. Sciaroni. 1952. Diseases of major floricultural crops in California. Calif. State Florists' Assoc., Los Angeles, 57 p.

Baker, K. F., W. C. Snyder, and L. H. Davis. 1950. Ramularia leaf spots of *Lathyrus odoratus* and *L. latifolius*. Mycologia 42:403–422.

Baker, K. F., and H. E. Thomas. 1942. The effect of temperature on symptom expression of a rose mosaic. Phytopathology 32:321–326.

Baker, K. F., and H. E. Thomas. 1946. Failure of bud and graft unions induced by *Chalaropsis thielavioides*. Phytopathology 36:281–291.

Baker, R. 1956. Control of Fusarium stem rot with cutting dips. Colo. Flower Growers' Assoc. Bul. 76:1–3.

Baker, R. 1957. Detection of *Fusarium roseum* in nucleus blocks. Colo. Flower Growers' Assoc. Bul. 88:1–3.

Baker, R. 1959. The influence of depth of planting and soil drainage on the development of lily root rot. Colo. Flower Growers' Assoc. Bul. 112:1–3.

Baker, R. 1967. Systemic fungicides control carnation rust. Colo. Flower Growers' Assoc. Bul. 211:5–6.

Baker, R. 1968. Control of rust using Plantvax in fertilizing systems. Colo. Flower Growers' Assoc. Bul. 220:1.

Baker, R., and J. Tammen. 1954. Fusarium stem rot of carnations. Colo. Flower Growers' Assoc. Bul. 58:1–3.

Bald, J. G. 1953. Control of disease by heat-curing and dipping gladiolus corms. I. Wound periderm and the extension of lesions. II. Incidence of lesions. III. Dipping trials. Phytopathology 43:141–155.

Bald, J. G. 1953. Life history of *Pleospora* sp. found on gladioli. (Abstr.) Phytopathology 43:585.

Bald, J. G. 1953. Neck rot phase of the Botrytis disease of gladiolus. Phytopathology 43:167–171.

Bald, J. G. 1956. Development and production of pathogen-free gladiolus cormels. Plant Dis. Reptr. Suppl. 238:81–84.

Bald, J. G. 1971. Scorch disease of rhizomatous iris. Calif. Agr. 25(2):6–7.

Bald, J. G., and P. A. Chandler. 1957. Reduction of the root rot complex on Croft lilies by fungicidal treatment and propagation from bulb scales. Phytopathology 47:285–291.

Bald, J. G., P. A. Chandler, J. V. Lenz, R. H. Sciaroni, and A. O. Paulus. 1958. Root rot of Easter lilies. Calif. Agr. 12(4):3, 14.

Bald, J. G., J. Ferguson, and B. B. Markley. 1956. Treatment of gladiolus cormels. Calif. Agr. 10(6):15–16.

Bald, J. G., A. M. Kofranek, and O. R. Lunt. 1955. Leaf scorch and *Rhizoctonia* on Croft lilies. Phytopathology 45:156–162.

Bald, J. G., and B. B. Markley. 1955. Application of hot-water treatment to growers' lots of gladiolus cormels. (Abstr.) Phytopathology 45:693.

Bald, J. G., A. O. Paulus, J. V. Lenz, P. A. Chandler, and T. Suzuki. 1969. Disease control with pathogen-free bulb stocks for Easter lily improvement. Calif. Agr. 23(11):6–8.

Bateman, D. F. 1959. The influence of soil moisture on the poinsettia root rots. (Abstr.) Phytopathology 49:533.

Bateman, D. F., and A. W. Dimock. 1959. The influence of temperature on root rots of poinsettia caused by *Thielaviopsis basicola, Rhizoctonia solani,* and *Pythium ultimum.* Phytopathology 49:641–647.

Baxter, L. W., and A. G. Plakidas. 1953. Dieback and canker of camellias. (Abstr.) Phytopathology 43:466.

Baxter, L. W., and A. G. Plakidas. 1954. Dieback and canker of camellias caused by *Glomerella cingulata.* Phytopathology 44:129–133.

Beaumont, A., J. P. Cleary, and J. H. Bant. 1958. Control of damping-off of zinnias caused by *Alternaria zinniae.* Plant Pathol. 7:52–53.

Beaumont, A., W. A. R. Dillon Weston, and E. R. Wallace. 1936. Tulip fire. Ann. Appl. Biol. 23:57–88.

Beck, G. E., and J. R. Vaughn. 1949. Botrytis leaf and blossom blight of saintpaulia. Phytopathology 39:1054–1056.

Berkeley, G. H. 1953. Some viruses affecting gladiolus. Phytopathology 43:111–115.

Bertus, A. L. 1970. Controlling azalea petal blight. Agr. Gaz. New So. Wales 81:286–287.

Bertus, A. L. 1971. Control of azalea petal blight. Agr. Gaz. New So. Wales 82:287.

Besemer, S. T., A. H. McCain, and A. O. Paulus. 1969. Control of Verticillium and Sclerotinia of chrysanthemums with systemic fungicides. Calif. Agr. 23(11):12–13.

Beute, M. K. 1970. Effect of virus infection on susceptibility to certain fungus diseases and yield of gladiolus. Phytopathology 60:1809–1813.

Beute, M. K. 1971. Factors affecting Stromatinia root rot of gladiolus. Phytopathology 61:1329–1331.

Bickerton, J. M. 1942. Fusarium wilt of carnations caused by *Fusarium dianthi* Prill. et Del. Cornell Univ. Agr. Exp. Sta. Bul. 788. 31 p.

Bickerton, J. M. 1943. Alternaria blight of carnations caused by *Alternaria dianthi* Stev. and Hall. Cornell Univ. Agr. Exp. Sta. Bul. 790. 29 p.

Bivins, J. L., and A. H. McCain. 1971. Control of geranium rust with oxycarboxin. Ill. State Florists' Assoc. Bul. 325:5–6.

Blanton, F. S., and F. A. Haasis. 1942. Insect transmission of the virus causing narcissus mosaic. Jour. Agr. Res. 65:413–419.

Bode, F. A. 1972. Zonal geranium rust. Florists' Rev. 150(3875):30–31, 46.

Bosher, J. E., and W. Newton. 1948. The control of *Penicillium* spp. on tulip and iris bulbs in storage by fungicidal dusts. Sci. Agr. 28:47–48.

Bozarth, R. F., and M. K. Corbett. 1958. Tomato ringspot virus associated with stunt or stub head disease of gladiolus in Florida. Plant Dis. Reptr. 42:217–221.

Braun, H. 1924. Geranium stemrot caused by *Pythium complectens* n. sp. Jour. Agr. Res. 29:399–419.

Bridgmon, G. H., and J. C. Walker. 1952. Gladiolus as a virus reservior. Phytopathology 42:65–70.

Brierley, P. 1933. Studies on mosaic and related diseases of dahlia. Contrib. Boyce Thompson Inst. 5:235–288.

Brierley, P. 1933. Virus diseases of dahlia. (Abstr.) Pytopathology 23:6.

Brierley, P. 1939. Two distinct viruses from the mosaic complex in *Lilium longiflorum.* (Abstr.) Phytopathology 29:3.

Brierley, P. 1940. Prevalence of cucumber and the tulip viruses in lilies. Phytopathology 30:250–257.

Brierley, P. 1941. Current-season development of virus symptoms in tulips. Phytopathology 31:838–843.

Brierley, P. 1947. Status of rose mosaic and its effect on production today. Florists' Rev. 101(2610):55.

Brierley, P. 1950. Eradicant fungicides of possible value against the azalea petal blight fungus, *Ovulina azaleae*. Phytopathology 40:153–155.

Brierley, P. 1951. Value of index plants for detecting dahlia viruses. Plant Dis. Reptr. 35:405–407.

Brierley, P. 1951. A witches'-broom of lilac. Plant Dis. Reptr. 35:556.

Brierley, P. 1952. Evidence on the significance of cucumber mosaic and tobacco ringspot viruses in gladiolus. Gladiolus Mag. 16(2):28–29, 36–37.

Brierley, P. 1952. Indexing the Beltsville mums, a practical method of selecting virus-free plants. Florists' Rev. 110 (2843):19–20, 108–111.

Brierley, P. 1953. Virus diseases of the chrysanthemum. Plant Diseases. U. S. Dept. Agr. Yearb. 1953: 596–601.

Brierley, P. 1954. Symptoms in the florist's hydrangea caused by tomato ring-spot and an unidentified sap-transmissible virus. Phytopathology 44:696–699.

Brierley, P. 1955. Dodder transmission of lilac witches'-broom virus. Plant Dis. Reptr. 39:719–721.

Brierley, P. 1955. Symptoms induced in chrysanthemums on inoculation with the viruses of mosaics, aspermy, and flower distortion. Phytopathology 45:2–7.

Brierley, P. 1962. Transmission of some gladiolus viruses on tools in harvesting flowers and corms. Plant Dis. Reptr. 46:505.

Brierley, P. 1963. Gladiolus cormels free from cucumber mosaic virus from infected parent corms. Plant Dis. Reptr. 47:863.

Brierley, P. 1964. Effects of four viruses on yield and quality of King Cardinal carnations. Plant Dis. Reptr. 48:5–7.

Brierley, P. 1964. Heat cure of carnation viruses. Plant Dis. Reptr. 48:143.

Brierley, P., and S. P. Doolittle. 1940. Some effects of strains of cucumber virus 1 in lily and tulip. Phytopathology 30:171–174.

Brierley, P., and P. Lorentz. 1956. Detection and transmission of hydrangea ringspot virus. (Abstr.) Phytopathology 46:466.

Brierley, P., and P. Lorentz. 1957. Hydrangea ringspot virus, the probable cause of "running-out" of the florist's hydrangea. Phytopathology 47:39–43.

Brierley, P., and P. Lorentz. 1958. A dieback of Belmont gardenias. Plant Dis. Reptr. 42:986–987.

Brierley, P., and M. B. McKay. 1938. Experiments with aphids as vectors of tulip breaking. Phytopathology 28:123–129.

Brierley, P., and F. P. McWhorter. 1936. A mosaic disease of iris. Jour. Agr. Res. 53:621–635.

Brierley, P., and C. J. Olson. 1956. Development and production of virus-free chrysanthemum propagating material. Plant Dis. Reptr. Suppl. 238:63–67.

Brierley, P., and F. F. Smith. 1940. Mosaic and streak diseases of rose. Jour. Agr. Res. 61:625–660.

Brierley, P., and F. F. Smith. 1944. Studies on lily virus diseases: the mottle group. Phytopathology 34:718–746.

Brierley, P., and F. F. Smith. 1944. Studies on lily virus diseases: the necrotic-fleck complex in *Lilium longiflorum*. Phytopathology 34:529–555.

Brierley, P., and F. F. Smith. 1945. Additional species of *Lilium* susceptible to lily-rosette virus. Phytopathology 35:129–131.

Brierley, P., and F. F. Smith. 1945. Spread of fleck disease. Florists' Rev. 96(2491):31.

Brierley, P., and F. F. Smith. 1947. Virus diseases of gladiolus. Gladiolus Mag. 11(1):16–18.

Brierley, P., and F. F. Smith. 1948. Canna mosaic in the United States. Phytopathology 38:230–234.

Brierley, P., and F. F. Smith. 1948. Gladiolus virus disease. Florists' Rev. 102 (2650):90–94.

Brierley, P., and F. F. Smith. 1948. Two additional mosaic diseases of iris. (Abstr.) Phytopathology 38:574–575.

Brierley, P., and F. F. Smith. 1950. Some vectors, hosts, and properties of dahlia mosaic virus. Plant Dis. Reptr. 34:363–370.

Brierley, P., and F. F. Smith. 1951. Chrysanthemum stunt. Florists' Rev. 107 (2778):27–30.

Brierley, P., and F. F. Smith. 1951. Survey

of virus diseases of chrysanthemums. Plant Dis. Reptr. 35:524–526.

Brierley, P., and F. F. Smith. 1953. Tomato ringspot virus in the florist's hydrangea. (Abstr.) Phytopathology 43:404.

Brierley, P., and F. F. Smith. 1957. Carnation viruses in the United States. Phytopathology 47:714–721.

Brierley, P., and F. F. Smith. 1957. Symptoms of chrysanthemum flower distortion, dodder transmission of the virus, and heat cure of infected plants. Phytopathology 47:448–450.

Brierley, P., and F. F. Smith. 1958. Carnation viruses. Florists' Rev. 122(3168): 21–22, 93–94.

Brierley, P., and F. F. Smith. 1960. Transmission of tobacco ringspot virus on tools during harvesting flowers and corms of gladiolus. Plant Dis. Reptr. 44:463–464.

Brierley, P., F. F. Smith, and F. P. McWhorter. 1947. Symptoms and controls for diseases of Easter lilies. Florists' Rev. 100(2597):41–45.

Brierley, P., F. F. Smith, and F. P. McWhorter. 1953. Virus enemies of gladiolus. Plant Diseases. U. S. Dept. Agr. Yearb. 1953:608–611.

Brown, J. G., and A. M. Boyle. 1944. Bacterial soft rot of sansevieria. Phytopathology 34:350–351.

Brown, N. A. 1923. Bacterial leaf spot of geranium in the eastern United States. Jour. Agr. Res. 23:361–372.

Brown, N. A. 1927. Sweet pea fasciation, a form of crown gall. Phytopathology 17: 29–30.

Brown, S. U., and L. W. Baxter, Jr. 1969. Phomopsis dieback of azaleas. (Abstr.) Phytopathology 59:112.

Bryan, M. K. 1915. A nasturtium wilt caused by *Bacterium solanacearum*. Jour. Agr. Res. 4:451–458.

Bryan, M. K. 1924. Bacterial leafspot of delphinium. Jour. Agr. Res. 28:261–270.

Bryan, M. K. 1928. Lilac blight in the United States. Jour. Agr. Res. 36:225–235.

Bryan, M. K., and F. P. McWhorter. 1930. Bacterial blight of poppy caused by *Bacterium papavericola* sp. nov. Jour. Agr. Res. 40:1–9.

Bugbee, W. M. 1962. Whitefly transmission of *Xanthomonas pelargonii*. (Abstr.) Phytopathology 52:5.

Burkholder, W. H. 1937. A bacterial blight of iris. Phytopathology 27:613–621.

Burkholder, W. H. 1937. A bacterial leaf spot of geranium. Phytopathology 27: 554–560.

Burkholder, W. H. 1938. A bacterial blight of stocks caused by *Phytomonas syringae*. Phytopathology 28:935–936.

Burkholder, W. H. 1959. The causal agents of the black stem disease of annual larkspur. Plant Dis. Reptr. 43:934–935.

Burkholder, W. H., and C. E. F. Guterman. 1932. Synergism in a bacterial disease of *Hedera helix*. Phytopathology 22:781–784.

Burkholder, W. H., and C. E. F. Guterman. 1935. Bacterial leaf spot of carnations. Phytopathology 25:114–120.

Burkholder, W. H., L. A. McFadden, and A. W. Dimock. 1953. A bacterial blight of chrysanthemums. Phytopathology 43: 522–526.

Burkholder, W. H., and P. P. Pirone. 1941. Bacterial leaf spot of gardenia. Phytopathology 31:192–194.

Burnett, G. 1934. Stunt — a virosis of delphinium. Phytopathology 24:467–481.

Butler, O. 1923. Experiments on the field control of snapdragon rust together with a description of a method for the control of the disease in greenhouses. N. H. Agr. Exp. Sta. Tech. Bul. 22. 14 p.

Buxton, E. W. 1955. Chalky dry rot of freesia corms. Plant Pathol. 4:69–70.

Buxton, E. W. 1955. Fusarium diseases of gladiolus. Trans. Brit. Mycol. Soc. 38: 193–201.

Buxton, E. W., and N. F. Robertson. 1953. The Fusarium yellows disease of gladiolus. Plant Pathol. 2:61–64.

Castillo, B. S., C. E. Yarwood, and A. H. Gold. 1956. Canna-mosaic virus. Plant Dis. Reptr. 40:169–172.

Cayley, D. M. 1928. "Breaking" in tulips. Ann. Appl. Biol. 15:529–539.

Cayley, D. M. 1932. "Breaking" in tulips. II. Ann. Appl. Biol. 19:153–172.

Chadwick, L. C. 1933. Blight of rhododendrons. Florists' Rev. 72(1867):44.

Changsri, W., and G. F. Weber. 1958. Leaf-spot of marigold, *Tagetes erecta*, caused by *Septoria tageticola* n. sp. Phytopathology 48:561–565.

Chester, F. D. 1937. A bacterial disease of delphinium. Phytopathology 27:855–858.

Chester, F. D. 1938. A bacteriosis of dahlia, *Erwinia cytolytica*. Phytopathology 28:427–432.

Chester, K. S. 1931. Graft-blight: a disease of lilac related to the employment of certain understocks in propagation. Jour. Arnold Arboretum 12:79–146.

Clark, L. H. 1948. *Botrytis polyblastis* found in California. Plant Dis. Reptr. 32:445–446.

Cochrane, V. W. 1945. The common leaf rust of cultivated roses, caused by *Phragmidium mucronatum* (Fr.) Schlecht. Cornell Univ. Agr. Exp. Sta. Mem. 268. 39 p.

Cole, J. R. 1944. Low-lime bordeaux mixture controls leaf gall on azaleas. Phytopathology 34:354–355.

Cook, M. T. 1923. A disease of dahlias. Phytopathology 13:285.

Cook, M. T. 1924. A bacterial wilt of cosmos. Jour. Dept. Agr. Puerto Rico 8(4): 14.

Cook, M. T., and C. A. Schwarze. 1913. A Botrytis disease of dahlias. Phytopathology 3:171–174.

Coons, G. H. 1918. The soft rot of hyacinth. Mich. Acad. of Sci., 20th Rep., 353–354.

Coons, G. H. 1937. Progress in plant pathology: Control of disease by resistant varieties. Phytopathology 27: 622–632.

Cooper, D. C., and C. L. Porter. 1928. Phytophthora blight of peony. Phytopathology 18:881–899.

Cooper, K. W. 1940. Relations of *Pediculopsis graminum* and *Fusarium poae* to central bud rot of carnations. Phytopathology 30:853–859.

Courtney, W. D., and C. J. Gould. 1951. Tolerance of Wedgewood iris bulbs to a hot-water-formalin treatment. Phytopathology 41:40–45.

Cox, E. A., W. J. Manning, and F. J. Campbell. 1969. *Cylindrocarpon radicicola* found associated with wilt of azalea. Plant Dis. Reptr. 53:620.

Cox, R. S. 1953. Crown canker on a field planting of multiflora rose cuttings. Plant Dis. Reptr. 37:447.

Cox, R. S. 1969. Control of Pythium wilt of chrysanthemum in South Florida. Plant Dis. Reptr. 53:912–913.

Cox, R. S. 1970. Control of *Rhizoctonia solani* on chrysanthemum. Plant Dis. Reptr. 54:679.

Creager, D. B. 1933. Fusarium basal rot of bulbous iris. (Abstr.) Phytopathology 23:7.

Creager, D. B. 1933. Leaf scorch of narcissus. Phytopathology 23:770–786.

Creager, D. B. 1941. Control black mold of rose grafts by chemical treatments. Florists' Rev. 89(2290):21–22.

Creager, D. B. 1941. Control program for peony measles. Florists' Rev. 89(2296): 22–23.

Creager, D. B. 1941. Ring spot of popular peperomias caused by virus. Florists' Rev. 87(2256):15–16.

Creager, D. B. 1942. Carnations attacked by bacterial wilt on coast and in midwest. Florists' Rev. 91(2348):13–15.

Creager, D. B. 1943. Carnation mosaic. Phytopathology 33:823–827.

Creager, D. B. 1943. Successful culture of callas requires prevention of diseases. Florists' Rev. 92 (2382):11–12.

Creager, D. B. 1944. How to recognize and control mosaic on carnation plants. Florists' Rev. 93(2409):27–29.

Creager, D. B. 1945. Mosaic of the common coleus. Phytopathology 35:223–229.

Creager, D. B. 1945. Rhizoctonia neck rot of gladiolus. Phytopathology 35:230–232.

Creager, D. B., and G. H. Boewe. 1942. Peony anthracnose found in Illinois. Plant Dis. Reptr. 26:280–281.

Cremer, M. C., and P. K. Schenk. 1967. Notched leaf in *Gladiolus* spp., caused by viruses of the tobacco rattle virus group. Neth. Jour. Plant Pathol. 73(2): 33–48.

Cropsey, M. G., and R. A. Young. 1954. Drying and curing gladiolus corms. Oreg. Agr. Exp. Sta. Circ. 542. 7 p.

Cummings, M. B. 1935. Rust on hollyhocks and how to control it. Florists' Exch. and Hort. Trade World 85(11):19.

Dana, B. F., and F. P. McWhorter. 1935. An outbreak of curly top on pansy. (Abstr.) Phytopathology 25:894.

Davis, B. H. 1938. The Cercospora leaf spot of rose caused by *Mycosphaerella rosicola*. Mycologia 30:282–298.

Davis, B. H., and P. P. Pirone. 1941. Anthracnose of camellia. (Abstr.) Phytopathology 31:6.

Davis, L. H., R. H. Sciaroni, and F. Pritchard. 1949. Alternaria leafspot of garden stock in California. Plant Dis. Reptr. 33:432–433.

Davis, S. H., Jr. 1954. Control of Phomopsis canker of gardenia in the cutting-bench and on mature plants. (Abstr.) Phytopathology 44:109–110.

Davis, S. H., Jr., and C. C. Hamilton. 1955. Diseases and insect pests of rhododendron and azalea. N. J. Agr. Exp. Sta. Circ. 571. 30 p.

Davis, W. H. 1931. Anthracnose, alternariose, and Botrytis rot of the snowberry. Mycologia 23:159–190.

Davis, W. H. 1939. A bud and twig blight of azaleas caused by *Sporocybe azaleae*. Phytopathology 29:517–529.

de Bruyn, H. L. G. 1924. The Phytophthora disease of lilac. Phytopathology 14:503–517.

Deep, I. W., and A. Bartlett. 1961. Comparison of standard fungicides recommended for control of powdery mildew of roses. Plant Dis. Reptr. 45:628–631.

Dickens, L. E., and W. D. Thomas, Jr. 1952. Results of spray tests for the control of carnation rust. Colo. Flower Growers' Assoc. Bul. 31:3.

Dimock, A. W. 1940. Epiphytotic of Botrytis blight on gladiolus in Florida. Plant Dis. Reptr. 24:159–161.

Dimock, A. W. 1941. The Rhizoctonia foot-rot of annual stocks (*Matthiola incana*). Phytopathology 31:87–91.

Dimock, A. W. 1945. Disease-free mum cuttings. Florists' Rev. 96(2495):32.

Dimock, A. W. 1945. Fermate and poinsettia cutting rot. N. Y. State Flower Growers' Bul. 3:5.

Dimock, A. W. 1947. Calla root rot control. Florists' Rev. 100(2595):34.

Dimock, A. W. 1947. Chrysanthemum stunt. N. Y. State Flower Growers' Bul. 26:2.

Dimock, A. W. 1951. Bud transmission of *Verticillium* in roses. Phytopathology 41:781–784.

Dimock, A. W. 1951. Poinsettia trouble a result of root rot. N. Y. State Flower Growers' Bul. 69:4–8.

Dimock, A. W. 1954. Chloropicrin fumigation and the new plastic covers. N. Y. State Flower Growers' Bul. 107:4.

Dimock, A. W. 1956. Production of chrysanthemum propagating material free from certain major pathogens. Plant Dis. Reptr. Suppl. 238:59–62.

Dimock, A. W., and H. Allyn. 1944. Dipping rooted chrysanthemum cuttings in Fermate for Septoria leaf spot control. Chrysanthemum Soc. of Amer. Bul. 12:8–11.

Dimock, A. W., and K. F. Baker. 1944. Hot-water treatment for control of Phytophthora root rot of calla. Phytopathology 34:979–981.

Dimock, A. W., and K. F. Baker. 1948. Aspects of fungicidal control of snapdragon rust. (Abstr.) Phytopathology 38:7.

Dimock, A. W., and K. F. Baker. 1951. Effect of climate on disease development, injuriousness, and fungicidal control, as exemplified by snapdragon rust. Phytopathology 41:536–552.

Dimock, A. W., and T. G. Byrne. 1966. Anthracnose on Easter lily blossoms caused by the black-scale *Colletotrichum*. Plant Dis. Reptr. 50:751–752.

Dimock, A. W., and C. Geissinger. 1969. A newly recognized disease by a graft-transmissible agent. (Abstr.) Phytopathology 59:1024.

Dimock, A. W., C. M. Geissinger, and R. K. Horst. 1971. Chlorotic mottle: a newly recognized disease of chrysanthemum. Phytopathology 61:415–419.

Dimock, A. W., and L. A. McFadden. 1954. New bacterial disease affects chrysanthemums. N. Y. State Flower Growers' Bul. 104:2–4.

Dimock, A. W., and J. H. Osborn. 1943. An Alternaria disease of zinnia. Phytopathology 33:372–381.

Dimock, A. W., and K. Post. 1944. An efficient, labor-saving method of steaming soil. Cornell Univ. Agr. Exp. Sta. Bul. 635. 7 p.

Dimond, A. E., and E. M. Stoddard. 1955. Toxicity to greenhouse roses from paints containing mercury fungicides. Conn. Agr. Exp. Sta. Bul. 595. 19 p.

Dodge, B. O. 1934. Controlling the hollyhock rust. Jour. N. Y. Botan. Gard. 35:186–189.

Dodge, B. O. 1936. Marigold wilt. Jour. N. Y. Botan. Gard. 37:211–214.

Doran, W. L. 1921. Rust of *Antirrhinum*. Mass. Agr. Exp. Sta. Bul. 202:39–66.

Dorworth, C., and J. Tammen. 1969. Influence of nutrition, soil moisture, and soil temperature on the proneness of *Dianthus caryophyllus* to attack by *Fusarium roseum*. Phytopathology 59:1703–1705.

Dosdall, L. T. 1928. A mosaic disease of gladiolus. Phytopathology 18:215–217.

Dosdall, L. T. 1944. Rhizome treatments for controlling Botrytis crown rot in iris. Phytopathology 34:772–789.

Dosdall, L. T. 1955. Calla rhizome treatments. Plant Dis. Reptr. 39:779–780.

Doucette, C. F. 1953. *Botrytis polyblastis* on narcissus in the Pacific Northwest. Plant Dis. Reptr. 37:556–557.

Dowson, W. J. 1924. A new disease of sweet peas. Jour. Roy. Hort. Soc. 49:211–221.

Drayton, F. L. 1926. The dry rot disease of gladioli. Sci. Agr. 6:199–209.

Drayton, F. L. 1934. The gladiolus dry rot caused by *Sclerotinia gladioli* (Massey) n. comb. Phytopathology 24:397–404.

Drechsler, C. 1926. Foot-rot of *Lilium candidum* and *Lilium pyrenaicum* caused by *Phytophthora cactorum*. Phytopathology 16:51–53.

Drechsler, C. 1934. Vascular wilt and root rot of pansies due to *Aphanomyces* sp. (Abstr.) Phytopathology 24:7–8.

Drechsler, C. 1954. Association of *Aphanomyces cladogamus* with severe root rot of pansies. Sydowia Ann. Mycol. 8:334–342.

Dunlap, A. A. 1950. Control of anthracnose canker of camellia. (Abstr.) Phytopathology 40:7.

Elmer, O. H. 1928. Penicillium corm rot of gladioli. (Abstr.) Phytopathology 18:151.

Emsweller, S. L., and H. A. Jones. 1934. The inheritance of resistance to rust in the snapdragon. Hilgardia 8:197–211.

Engelhard, A. W. 1969. Bulb mites associated with diseases of gladioli and other crops in Florida. (Abstr.) Phytopathology 59:1025.

Engelhard, A. W. 1969. Fungicidal efficiency of three benzimidazole compounds and Dithane M-45 against *Diplocarpon rosae* on two rose cultivars. (Abstr.) Phytopathology 59:113.

Engelhard, A. W. 1971. Efficacy of benzimidazole dips, drenches and sprays for the control of *Cylindrocladium* on azalea. Plant Dis. Reptr. 55:679–682.

Engelhard, A. W. 1972. Chemical control of Alternaria and Botrytis on carnations under epiphytotic conditions. (Abstr.) Phytopathology 62:11.

Engelhard, A. W., H. N. Miller, and R. T. DeNeve. 1971. Etiology and chemotherapy of Pythium root rot on chrysanthemums. Plant Dis. Reptr. 55:851–855.

Engelhard, A. W., and S. S. Woltz. 1971. Fusarium wilt of chrysanthemum: Symptomatology and cultivar reactions. Proc. Fla. State Hort. Soc. 84:351–354.

Engelhard, A. W., and S. S. Woltz. 1972. Complete control of Fusarium wilt of chrysanthemum with chemotherapeutants combined with a high lime and nitrate-nitrogen culture regime. (Abstr.) Phytopathology 62:756.

Engelhard, A. W., and S. S. Woltz. 1972. The Fusarium wilt disease of chrysanthemum. Fla. Flower Grower 9(7):1–6.

Engelhard, A. W., and S. S. Woltz. 1973. Pathogenesis and dissemination of the Fusarium wilt pathogens of chrysanthemum. (Abstr.) Phytopathology 63:441.

Faris, J. A. 1923. Anthracnose of the Boston fern. Mycologia 15:89–95.

Farnham, R. B. 1936. Factors associated with bud-drop of sweet peas and method of control. Proc. Amer. Soc. Hort. Sci. 33:655–662.

Ferguson, J. 1951. Powdery mildew of begonia. Begonian 18:245.

Forsberg, J. L. 1946. Diseases of ornamental plants. Colo. Agr. and Mech. Col. 172 p.

Forsberg, J. L. 1949. Greenhouse management in relation to disease control. Ill. State Florists' Assoc. Bull. 114:15–18.

Forsberg, J. L. 1950. Healthy carnations from cultured cuttings. Ill. State Florists' Assoc. Bul. 119:5–8.

Forsberg, J. L. 1950. So you have rose mildew. Ill. State Florists' Assoc. Bul. 129:1–3.

Forsberg, J. L. 1952. Drying gladiolus corms. Florists' Rev. 111(2862):33–34, 45.

Forsberg, J. L. 1952. Rose mildew control in summer. Ill. State Florists' Assoc. Bul. 143:5–6.

Forsberg, J. L. 1955. Fusarium disease of gladiolus: its causal agent. Ill. Nat. Hist. Survey Bul. 26:447–503.

Forsberg, J. L. 1955. The use of insecticides as corm and soil treatments for control of bacterial scab of gladiolus. Plant Dis. Reptr. 39:106–114.

Forsberg, J. L. 1957. A vascular form of the Curvularia disease of gladiolus. (Abstr.) Phytopathology 47:12.

Forsberg, J. L. 1959. Relationship of the bulb mite Rhizoglyphus echinopus to bacterial scab of gladiolus. (Abstr.) Phytopathology 49:538.

Forsberg, J. L. 1961. Hot-water and chemical treatment of Illinois-grown gladiolus cormels. Ill. Nat. Hist. Survey Biol. Notes 43. 12 p.

Forsberg, J. L. 1965. The relationship of Pseudomonas marginata, Stromatinia gladioli, bulb mites, and chemical soil treatments to the occurrence and control of scab and Stromatinia rot of gladiolus. (Abstr.) Phytopathology 55:1058.

Forsberg, J. L. 1969. An unexpected effect of benomyl on two gladiolus varieties. Plant Dis. Reptr. 53:318–319.

Forsberg, J. L. 1970. A comparison of the effects of thiram and benomyl used as gladiolus corm treatments. Plant Dis. Reptr. 54:289–290.

Forsberg, J. L., and W. Hartstirn. 1969. A transmissible disorder of gladiolus flowers. Plant Dis. Reptr. 53:818–819.

Fosler, G. M. 1962. Soil sterilization methods for the indoor gardener. Univ. Ill. Ext. Circ. 793. 8 p.

Frazier, N. W., and H. H. P. Severin. 1945. Weed-host range of California aster yellows. Hilgardia 16:621–650.

Frietag, J. H., and C. M. Tompkins. 1963. Corkscrew symptoms caused by western aster yellows virus on gladiolus. Plant Dis. Reptr. 47:617–621.

Fulton, R. W. 1970. A disease of rose caused by tobacco streak virus. Plant Dis. Reptr. 54:949–951.

Gardner, M. W., C. M. Tompkins, and O. C. Whipple. 1935. Spotted wilt of truck crops and ornamental plants. (Abstr.) Phytopathology 25:17.

Garman, P. 1920. The relation of certain greenhouse pests to the transmission of a geranium leaf spot. Md. Agr. Exp. Sta. Bul. 239:57–80.

Garrard, E. H. 1948. Fasciation of sweet peas. Canad. Jour. Res., Sec. C. 26:158–163.

Garren, K. H. 1946. A disease of English ivy in Georgia. Plant Dis. Reptr. 30:209–210.

Gasiorkiewicz, E. C., and C. J. Olson. 1956. Progress in the development and production of virus-free carnation varieties. Plant Dis. Reptr. Suppl. 238:77–80.

Gill, D. L. 1948. Information on azalea petal blight and its control. Florists' Rev. 103(2660):38–39, 102–103.

Gill, D. L. 1950. Effectiveness of fungicidal sprays and dusts in azalea petal blight control. Phytopathology 40:333–340.

Gill, D. L. 1953. Petal blight of azalea. Plant Diseases. U. S. Dept. Agr. Yearb. 1953: 578–582.

Gill, D. L. 1959. Effects of soaking Easter lily bulbs in Puratized Agricultural Spray or demeton, or in combined soaks, on aphids, black scale, and yield. Plant Dis. Reptr. 43:1274–1276.

Gill, D. L. 1959. Reducing Amaryllis leaf spot by spraying. Plant Dis. Reptr. 43: 1272–1273.

Gill, D. L., F. F. Smith, and P. Brierley. 1955. Necrotic fleck on Easter lilies. Florists' Rev. 117(3026):31–32.

Glenn, W. K., Jr., L. W. Baxter, Jr., and W. Witcher. 1972. Studies on fungicidal control of black spot on roses after severe disease development. (Abstr.) Phytopathology 62:803.

Gloyer, W. O. 1915. *Ascochyta clematidina,* the cause of stem-rot and leaf-spot of clematis. Jour. Agr. Res. 4:331–342.

Gloyer, W. O. 1931. China aster seed treatment and storage. N. Y. (Geneva) Agr. Exp. Sta. Tech. Bul. 177. 41 p.

Godfrey, G. H. 1936. Control of soil fungi by soil fumigation with chloropicrin. Phytopathology 26:246–256.

Golden, A. M. 1953. A root-knot nematode attacking the crown, petiole, and leaf of African violet. (Abstr.) Phytopathology 43:406.

Good, H. M. 1947. Studies on the Cladosporium blight of sweet pea. Canad. Jour. Res., Sect. C. 25:137–154.

Gottlieb, D. 1946. *Phyllosticta hederae* on English ivy. Plant Dis. Reptr. 30:124.

Gould, C. J. 1944. Tulip blight controlled by organic sulphurs. Phytopathology 34: 703–704.

Gould, C. J. 1946. Narcissus diseases in Washington. Wash. Agr. Exp. Sta. Bul. 480. 27 p.

Gould, C. J. 1947. The comparative value of certain organic and inorganic sulphur compounds in the control of Botrytis blight of tulips. (Abstr.) Phytopathology 37:361–362.

Gould, C. J. 1949. Narcissus diseases in Washington. Wash. Agr. Exp. Sta. Pop. Bul. 194. 27 p.

Gould, C. J. 1950. Diseases of bulbous iris. Wash. Agr. Ext. Bul. 424. 32 p.

Gould, C. J. 1953. Blights of lilies and tulips. Plant Diseases. U. S. Dept. Agr. Yearb. 1953:611–617.

Gould, C. J. 1954. Bacterial streak, a new disease of narcissus. (Abstr.) Phytopathology 44:489.

Gould, C. J. 1954. Botrytis diseases of gladiolus. Plant Dis. Reptr. Suppl. 224:1–33.

Gould, C. J. 1954. Control of *Sclerotium rolfsii* Sacc. in iris bulbs. Phytopathology 44:711–713.

Gould, C. J. 1954. Soil treatment tests for the control of *Sclerotium rolfsii* in bulbous iris. (Abstr.) Phytopathology 44: 489–490.

Gould, C. J. 1958. The dry rot disease of gladiolus. Plant Dis. Reptr. 42:1011–1024.

Gould, C. J. 1959. Zineb shows promise for the control of leaf spot of bulbous iris. Plant Dis. Reptr. 43:491–493.

Gould, C. J., M. Eglitis, and N. A. MacLean. 1958. *Botrytis hyacinthi* in the United States. Plant Dis. Reptr. 42:534–535.

Gould, C. J., W. D. McClellan, and V. L. Miller. 1949. Phytotoxicity of certain fungicide treatments to narcissus bulbs. (Abstr.) Phytopathology 39:8.

Gould, C. J., and V. L. Miller. 1949. A cheaper and safer treatment for controlling basal rot of narcissus bulbs. Wash. Agr. Exp. Sta. Mimeo. Circ. 147. 3 p.

Gould, C. J., and V. L. Miller. 1970. Effectiveness of benzimidazole fungicides in controlling Fusarium basal rot of bulbous iris. Plant Dis. Reptr. 54:235–239.

Gould, C. J., and V. L. Miller. 1970. Effectiveness of benzimidazole fungicides in controlling Fusarium basal rot of narcissus. Plant Dis. Reptr. 54:377–380.

Gould, C. J., and V. L. Miller. 1971. Effective methods of controlling Fusarium basal rot of narcissus with benomyl and thiabendazole. Plant Dis. Reptr. 55: 428–430.

Gould, C. J., and V. L. Miller. 1971. Improved control of Fusarium basal rot of iris with benomyl and thiabendazole. Plant Dis. Reptr. 55:425–427.

Gould, C. J., and T. S. Russell. 1965. Efficiency of various methods of applying PCNB for preventing soil-borne infestation of bulbous iris by *Sclerotium rolfsii.* Plant Dis. Reptr. 49:149–153.

Gould, C. J., and T. S. Russell. 1965. Soil-borne infection of bulbous iris by *Sclero-*

tinia bulborum controlled by bulb and soil treatments with PCNB. Plant Dis. Reptr. 49:443–446.

Gould, N. K. 1935. Stripe disease of daffodils. Jour. Royal Hort. Soc. 60:492–500.

Graves, C. H., Jr., and T. E. Ashley. 1960. Thiram for azalea petal blight control. (Abstr.) Phytopathology 50:576.

Green, D. E. 1936. The ink disease (or bulb scab) of *Iris reticulata* caused by *Mystrosporium adustum* Massee. Jour. Royal Hort. Soc. 61:167–175.

Green, D. E., and A. V. Brooks. 1958. A note on the effect of P.C.N.B. in controlling tulip fire disease in the soil. Jour. Royal Hort. Soc. 83:517–518.

Gregory, P. H. 1932. The Fusarium bulb rot of narcissus. Ann. Appl. Biol. 19:475–514.

Gregory, P. H. 1938. *Sclerotinia polyblastis* n. sp. on narcissus the perfect stage of *Botrytis polyblastis* Dowson. Trans. Brit. Mycol. Soc. 22:201–203.

Gregory, P. H. 1939. The life history of *Ramularia vallisumbrosae* Cav. on narcissus. Trans. Brit. Mycol. Soc. 23:24–54.

Gregory, P. H. 1940. The control of narcissus leaf diseases. I. White mould and fire on "Golden Spur." Ann. Appl. Biol. 27:338–347.

Gregory, P. H., and G. W. Gibson. 1946. The control of narcissus leaf diseases. III. *Sclerotinia polyblastis* Greg. on *Narcissus tazetta* var. Soleil d'Or. Ann. Appl. Biol. 33:40–45.

Guba, E. F. 1945. Carnation wilt diseases and their control. Mass. Agr. Exp. Sta. Bul. 427. 64 p.

Guba, E. F. 1947. Carnation wilt disease identification guide. Florists' Rev. 101 (2613):31.

Guba, E. F. 1948. Action of chemicals on fungous pathogens causing carnation diseases. Carnation Craft. 7:4, 7–8.

Guba, E. F. 1949. Anther smut disease of carnations. Carnation Craft 9:5.

Guba, E. F. 1949. Fungicidal soil treatments for controlling carnation stem rot and wilt diseases. Carnation Craft 10:7–8.

Guba, E. F. 1952. Culturing carnation cuttings. Carnation Craft 21:4–5.

Guba, E. F., and R. W. Ames. 1950. Topsoil application of chemicals for control of carnation wilt diseases. Carnation Craft 15:3–7.

Guba, E. F., and R. W. Ames. 1953. Infectious diseases of carnation. Plant Diseases. U. S. Dept. Agr. Yearb. 1953:583–592.

Guba, E. F., and P. J. Anderson. 1919. Phyllosticta leaf spot and damping off of snapdragons. Phytopathology 9:315–325.

Gunesch, W. 1944. Steam sterilization. Florists' Rev. 94(2430):21.

Guterman, C. E. F. 1935. Control of aster leaf rust. (Abstr.) Phytopathology 25:17–18.

Guterman, C. E. F. 1935. Diseases of iris. Cornell Univ. Agr. Exp. Sta. Ext. Bul. 324:26–33.

Guterman, C. E. F. 1935. Peony diseases. Cornell Univ. Agr. Exp. Sta. Ext. Bul. 321:32–43.

Guterman, C. E. F. 1935. Use of wilt-resistant strains of asters in effective disease control. Florists' Rev. 76(1951):9–10.

Haas, J. H., and J. Tammen. 1962. Control of rose black spot with fungicides. (Abstr.) Phytopathology 52:923–924.

Haasis, F. A. 1934. Control of the narcissus leaf-scorch under Long Island conditions. (Abstr.) Phytopathology 24:9–10.

Haasis, F. A. 1939. Studies on narcissus mosaic. Cornell Univ. Agr. Exp. Sta. Mem. 224. 22 p.

Haasis, F. A. 1939. White streak, a virus disease of narcissus. Phytopathology 29:890–895.

Haasis, F. A. 1952. Soil fumigation with chlorobromopropene for control of *Sclerotium rolfsii* in Dutch iris. Plant Dis. Reptr. 36:475–478.

Haasis, F. A. 1953. Topple disease of Dutch iris. Plant Dis. Reptr. 37:558–559.

Haasis, F. A. 1954. Control of dry rot of gladiolus corms in storage with fungicides applied after harvest. Plant Dis. Reptr. 38:518–520.

Hansen, H. N., and J. T. Barrett. 1938. Gardenia canker. Mycologia 30:15–19.

Hansen, H. N., and C. E. Scott. 1934. A canker and gall disease of gardenia. Science 79:18.

Hansen, H. N., and H. E. Thomas. 1940. Flower blight of camellias. Phytopathology 30:166–170.

Harris, M. R. 1934. A Phytophthora disease of snapdragons. Phytopathology 24:412–417.

Harrison, A. L. 1935. The perfect stage of *Phomopsis stewartii* on cosmos. Mycologia 27:521–526.

Harrison, D. J. 1958. A Fusarium rot of bulbous iris. Plant Pathol. 7:16–18.

Harvey, J. M., and H. N. Hansen. 1950. Camellia flower blight and its control. Phytopathology 40:965–966.

Hawker, L. E. 1935. Further experiments on the Fusarium bulb rot of narcissus. Ann. Appl. Biol. 22:684–708.

Hawker, L. E. 1940. Experiments on the control of basal rot of narcissus bulbs caused by *Fusarium bulbigenum* Cke. and Mass. with notes on *Botrytis narcissicola* Kleb. Ann. Appl. Biol. 27:205–217.

Hawker, L. E. 1943. Notes on basal rot of narcissus. I. A comparison of various methods of using formalin in connection with the hot-water treatment against eelworm. II. Infection of bulbs through dying roots in summer. Ann. Appl. Biol. 30:323–326.

Hawker, L. E. 1944. Diseases of the gladiolus. I. Control of hard rot, due to *Septoria gladioli* Passer., by fungicidal treatment of the corms. Ann. Appl. Biol. 31:204–210.

Hawker, L. E. 1944. Notes on basal rot of narcissus. III. Eradication of the disease from narcissus stocks by repeated use of formalin in the hot-water bath. Ann. Appl. Biol. 31:31–33.

Hawker, L. E. 1946. Diseases of the gladiolus. III. Botrytis rot of corms and its control. Ann. Appl. Biol. 33:200–208.

Hawker, L. E. 1946. Diseases of the gladiolus. IV. Note on the incidence and control of scab disease (*Bacterium marginatum* McCull.) Ann. Appl. Biol. 33:209–210.

Hawker, L. E., R. J. Bray, and T. W. Burrows. 1944. Diseases of the gladiolus. II. Experiments on dry rot disease caused by *Sclerotinia gladioli* Drayt. Ann. Appl. Biol. 31:211–218.

Heinis, J. L. 1954. Gladiolus virus survey in Oregon in 1954. Plant Dis. Reptr. 38:733–735.

Henneberry, T. J., and R. V. Travis. 1958. New fungicides for the control of blackspot on roses. Plant Dis. Reptr. 42:1297–1298.

Herr, L. J. 1966. Thermal dusting with tetrachloroisophthalonitrile for control of Botrytis on geranium. Plant Dis. Reptr. 50:777–779.

Hildebrandt, A. C., G. E. Beck, and R. Reinert. 1957. Bulb treatments on lilies. Florists' Rev. 121(3123):63–64, 127–129.

Hobbs, E. L. 1963. Stemphylium petal blight of carnations. Plant Dis. Reptr. 47:917–919.

Hobbs, E. L., and W. E. Waters. 1964. Influence of nitrogen and potassium on susceptibility of *Chrysanthemum morifolium* to *Botrytis cinerea*. Phytopathology 54:674–676.

Hoitink, H. A. J., and G. C. Daft. 1972. Bacterial stem rot of poinsettia, a new disease caused by *Erwinia carotovora* var. *chrysanthemi*. Plant Dis. Reptr. 56:480–484.

Hoitink, H. A. J., and A. F. Schmitthenner. 1969. Rhododendron wilt caused by *Phytophthora citricola*. Phytopathology 59:708–709.

Hoitink, H. A. J., and A. F. Schmitthenner. 1972. Control of Phytophthora root rot of rhododendron. Trees Mag. 32(2):7–8.

Holcomb, G. E., and R. E. Motsinger. 1969. Fusarium flower and bud rot of chrysanthemum found in Louisiana. Plant Dis. Reptr. 53:356.

Holley, W. D. 1954. Care of carnation mother blocks. Colo. Flower Growers' Assoc. Bul. 56:1–2.

Hollings, M. 1955. Physiological ring pattern in some Gesneraceae. Plant Pathol. 4:123–128.

Hollings, M., and O. M. Stone. 1946. Investigation of carnation viruses. I. Carnation mottle. Ann. Appl. Biol. 53:103–118.

Holloman, A., Jr., and R. A. Young. 1951. Evaluation of fungicides for control of the leaf-spot disease of gladiolus caused by *Botrytis gladiolorum* Timmermans. Plant Dis. Reptr. 35:456–458.

Holmes, F. O. 1948. Elimination of spotted wilt from a stock of dahlia. (Abstr.) Phytopathology 38:314.

Holmes, F. O. 1955. Elimination of spotted wilt from dahlias by propagation of tip cuttings. Phytopathology 45:224–226.

Holmes, F. O. 1960. Rose mosaic cured by heat treatments. Plant Dis. Reptr. 44:46–47.

Hopkins, E. F. 1921. The Botrytis blight of tulips. Cornell Univ. Agr. Exp. Sta. Mem. 45:315–361.

Horst, R. K., and H. A. J. Hoitink. 1968. Occurrence of Cylindrocladium blights on nursery crops and control with Fungicide 1991 on azalea. Plant Dis. Reptr. 52:615–617.

Horst, R. K., and P. E. Nelson. 1968. Losses from Fusarium stem rot caused by *Fusarium roseum*, in commercial production of cuttings of carnation, *Dianthus caryophyllus*. Plant Dis. Reptr. 52:840–843.

Huber, G. A., and L. K. Jones. 1934. The Verticillium disease of chrysanthemum. Wash. Agr. Exp. Sta. Bul. 290. 14 p.

Imle, E. P. 1940. A bulb disease of lilies caused by *Fusarium* spp. (Abstr.) Phytopathology 30:11.

Isaac, I. 1956. Some soil factors affecting Verticillium wilt of *Antirrhinum*. Ann. Appl. Biol. 44:105–112.

Jackson, A. B. 1927. The Fusarium wilt of China asters. Sci. Agr. 7:233–247.

Jackson, C. R. 1960. Cercospora blight of snapdragon. Phytopathology 50:190–192.

Jackson, C. R. 1962. Penicillium core rot of gladiolus. Phytopathology 52:794–797.

Jeffers, W. F. 1952. Downy mildew of snapdragon found in Maryland. Plant Dis. Reptr. 36:211.

Jenkins, A. E. 1918. Brown canker of roses, caused by *Diaporthe umbrina*. Jour. Agr. Res. 15:593–599.

Jenkins, A. E. 1931. Development of brown canker of roses. Jour. Agr. Res. 42:293–299.

Jenkins, A. E. 1932. Rose anthracnose caused by *Sphaceloma*. Jour. Agr. Res. 45:321–337.

Jenkins, A. E. 1944. Oedema of cultivated violet identified as scab. (Abstr.) Phytopathology 34:992.

Jenkins, J. E. E., and R. H. Hawken. 1969. The control of narcissus white mould. Plant Pathol. 18:122–129.

Jones, B. M., and H. G. Swartwout. 1961. Systemic control of powdery mildew of roses (*Sphaerotheca pannosa*) with the semicarbazone derivative of Acti-dione. Plant Dis. Reptr. 45:366–367.

Jones, L. H. 1938. Relation of soil temperature to chlorosis of gardenia. Jour. Agr. Res. 57:611–621.

Jones, L. K. 1940. Fusarium leaf spot of sansevieria. Phytopathology 30:527–530.

Jones, L. K. 1940. Leaf curl and mosaic of geranium. Wash. Agr. Exp. Sta. Bul. 390. 19 p.

Jones, L. K. 1941. Bacterial wilt of carnation. Phytopathology 31:199.

Jones, L. K. 1944. Streak and mosaic of cineraria. Phytopathology 34:941–953.

Jones, L. K. 1945. Mosaic, streak, and yellows of carnations. Phytopathology 35:37–46.

Jones, L. R., and R. S. Riker. 1928. Studies upon the Fusarium wilt of China aster. (Abstr.) Phytopathology 18:150.

Jones, L. R., and R. S. Riker. 1929. Progress with the control of aster wilt and yellows. (Abstr.) Phytopathology 19:101.

Jones, L. R., and R. S. Riker. 1931 Wisconsin studies on aster diseases and their control. Wis. Agr. Exp. Sta. Res. Bul. 111. 39 p.

Judd, R. W., Jr., and J. L. Peterson. 1971. Development and control of *Cercospora omphakodes* on *Phlox divaricata*. Plant Dis. Reptr. 55:1120–1121.

Judd, R. W., Jr., and J. L. Peterson. 1971. Leaf spot of garden and sultan balsam caused by *Stemphylium*. Plant Dis. Reptr. 55:374–375.

Judd, R. W., Jr., and G. S. Walton. 1973. Benomyl dip for the control of Ascochyta decay of chrysanthemum cuttings. Plant Dis. Reptr. 57:624.

Keller, J. R. 1954. Conditions influencing Thielaviopsis root rot of poinsettias. (Abstr.) Phytopathology 44:389.

Keller, J. R., and J. B. Shanks. 1955. Poinsettia root rot. Phytopathology 45:552–558.

Kendrick, J. B. 1938. A seed-borne bacterial disease of garden stocks, *Matthiola incana*. (Abstr.) Phytopathology 28:12.

Kendrick, J. B., and K. F. Baker. 1942. Bacterial blight of garden stocks and its control by hot-water seed treatment. Calif. Agr. Exp. Sta. Bul. 665. 23 p.

Kiplinger, D. C. 1973. Oedema on geraniums — a review. Florists' Rev. 152 (3934):23, 64–66.

Kivilaan, A., and R. P. Scheffer. 1958. Factors affecting development of bacterial stem rot of *Pelargonium*. Phytopathology 48:185–191.

Knauss, J. F. 1973. Common diseases of tropical foliage plants. Florists' Rev. 152 (3937):26–27, 55–58.

Knauss, J. F., and J. Tammen. 1967. Resistance of *Pelargonium* to *Xanthomonas pelargonii*. Phytopathology 57:1178–1181.

Kryczynski, S. P., R. K. Horst, and A. W. Dimock. 1971. Some properties of chrysanthemum chlorotic mottle virus. (Abstr.) Phytopathology 61:899.

Kunkel, L. O. 1926. Studies on aster yellows. Amer. Jour. Bot. 13:646–705.

Kunkel, L. O. 1928. Further studies on the host range of aster yellows. (Abstr.) Phytopathology 18:156.

Kunkel, L. O. 1929. Wilt-resistant asters. (Abstr.) Phytopathology 19:100–101.

Kunkel, L. O. 1929. Wire-screen fences for the control of aster yellows. (Abstr.) Phytopathology 19:100.

Kunkel, L. O. 1931. Studies on aster yellows in some new host plants. Contrib. Boyce Thompson Inst. 3:85–123.

Laskaris, T. 1940. A new Phoma disease of perennial delphinium. (Abstr.) Phytopathology 30:15.

Laskaris, T. 1949. Fusarium stem canker and wilt of delphinium. Phytopathology 39:913–919.

Laskaris, T. 1950. The Diplodina disease of delphinium. Phytopathology 40:615–626.

Laskaris, T., and B. O. Dodge. 1941. Red-blotch of *Hippeastrum*. Torrey Bot. Club Bul. 68:463–466.

Lauritzen, J. I., and R. C. Wright. 1934. Factors affecting gladiolus in storage. Jour. Agr. Res. 48:265–282.

LeBeau, F. J. 1946. The eradicant action of a fungicide on *Colletotrichum lilii* in lily bulbs. Phytopathology 36:391–393.

LeBeau, F. J. 1947. A fungicide for protecting lily bulbs from infection by *Colletotrichum lilii*. Phytopathology 37:194–196.

LeBeau, F. J., and F. J. Reynolds. 1947. Treatment of lily bulbs for black scale control. Phytopathology 37:801–808.

LeClerg, E. L. 1929. Some common diseases of ornamental plants. Colo. Agr. Exp. Sta. Bul. 351. 31 p.

Lelliott, R. A. 1956. Slow wilt of carnations caused by a species of *Erwinia*. Plant Pathol. 5:19–23.

Lenz, J., A. O. Paulus, and J. G. Bald. 1969. Control of Botrytis blight of Easter lilies with systemic fungicides. Calif. Agr. 23(2):18–19.

Lenz, J., A. O. Paulus, and J. G. Bald. 1971. Systemic fungicides for control of some diseases of Easter lilies. Calif. Agr. 25(3):4–5.

Limber, D. P. 1949. Notes on *Curvularia* sp. on gladiolus, with five new distribution records. Plant Dis. Reptr. 33:66–68.

Linn, M. B. 1942. Cephalosporium leaf spot of dieffenbachia. Phytopathology 32:172–175.

Littrell, R. H. 1965. A Myrothecium rot of gloxinias. Plant Dis. Reptr. 49:78–80.

Littrell, R. H. 1966. Effects of nitrogen nutrition on susceptibility of chrysanthemum to an apparently new biotype of *Fusarium oxysporum*. Plant Dis. Reptr. 50:882–884.

Littrell, R. H., and C. M. Heald. 1967. Effect of *Meloidogyne hapla* and *Fusarium oxysporum* on severity of Fusarium wilt of chrysanthemum. Plant Dis. Reptr. 51:736–738.

Lloyd, P. J., and D. F. Crossan. 1958. Anthracnose of pansy and violet caused by *Colletotrichum violae-tricoloris.* Plant Dis. Reptr. 42:86–90.

Longley, L. E. 1936. Flower color in "broken" or mosaic tulips. Proc. Amer. Soc. Hort. Sci. 33:674–677.

Longree, K. 1939. The effect of temperature and relative humidity on the powdery mildew of roses. Cornell Univ. Agr. Exp. Sta. Mem. 223. 43 p.

Longree, K. 1940. *Chalaropsis thielavioides,* cause of "black mold" of rose grafts. Phytopathology 30:793–807.

Lorentz, P., and P. Brierley. 1953. Graft transmission of lilac witches'-broom virus. Plant Dis. Reptr. 37:555.

Lumsden, R. D., and F. A. Haasis. 1964. Pythium root and stem diseases of chrysanthemum in North Carolina. N. C. Agr. Exp. Sta. Tech. Bul. 158. 27 p.

Lyle, E. W. 1938. The black-spot disease of roses, and its control under greenhouse conditions. Cornell Univ. Agr. Exp. Sta. Bul. 690. 31 p.

Lyle, E. W. 1940. Rose diseases. Tex. Agr. Exp. Sta. Circ. 87. 16 p.

Lyle, E. W. 1944. Control of blackspot of roses with sulphur-copper dust. Tex. Agr. Exp. Sta. Bul. 648. 27 p.

Lyle, E. W. 1956. Development of rose propagative material free from black spot. Plant Dis. Reptr. Suppl. 238:91–92.

Lyle, E. W. 1959. New sprays cut threat of black spot on roses. Amer. Nurseryman 109(10):8, 73–75.

MacLean, N. A. 1951. Botrytis on lilies. (Abstr.) Phytopathology 41:941.

MacLean, N. A., and K. F. Baker. 1951. Downy mildew of roses. Roses Inc. Bul. 160:5–6.

MacLean, N. A., and R. H. Sciaroni. 1951. Greenhouse roses — control of powdery mildew and rust on certain varieties in bay area. Calif. Agr. 5(4):9.

MacMillan, H. G., and O. A. Plunkett. 1938. An occurrence of soft rot of hyacinth. Plant Dis. Reptr. 22:31–34.

Magie, R. O. 1948. Abnormal florets, result from Fusarium bulb rot. Gladiolus Mag. 12(2):28–29.

Magie, R. O. 1948. The Curvularia and other important leaf and flower diseases of gladiolus in Florida. Florists' Rev. 101(2616):35–36.

Magie, R. O. 1948. Curvularia spot, a new disease of gladiolus. Plant Dis. Reptr. 32:11–13.

Magie, R. O. 1948. Stemphylium leaf spot of gladiolus in Florida. Plant Dis. Reptr. 32:344–345.

Magie, R. O. 1950. New approach to control of gladiolus Fusarium. Florists' Rev. 107(2759):92–94.

Magie, R. O. 1951. Botrytis and Curvularia diseases of gladiolus. N. Amer. Gladiolus Counc. Bul. 27:85–90.

Magie, R. O. 1953. Some fungi that attack gladioli. Plant Diseases. U.S. Dept. Agr. Yearb. 1953:601–607.

Magie, R. O. 1956. Gladiolus Botrytis control. Proc. Fla. State Hort. Soc. 69:337–343.

Magie, R. O. 1956. Gladiolus Stromatinia disease controlled by soil treatments and cultural methods. (Abstr.) Phytopathology 46:19.

Magie, R. O. 1956. Hot water treatment for controlling gladiolus corm-borne pathogens. (Abstr.) Phytopathology 46:19.

Magie, R. O. 1971. Effectiveness of treatments with hot water plus benzimidazoles and ethephon in controlling Fusarium disease of gladiolus. Plant Dis. Reptr. 55:82–85.

Magie, R. O. 1971. Gladiolus corm disease spread in storage: cause and control. N. Amer. Gladiolus Counc. Bul. 106:37–38.

Magie, R. O. 1971. Spraying gladiolus and treating corms with fungicides. N. Amer. Gladiolus Counc. Bul. 106:35–36.

Magie, R. O., and W. G. Cowperthwaite. 1954. Commercial gladiolus production in Florida. Fla. Agr. Exp. Sta. Bul. 535. 67 p.

Magie, R. O., F. F. Smith, and P. Brierley. 1952. Occurrence of western aster yellows virus infection in gladiolus in eastern United States. Plant Dis. Reptr. 36:468–470.

Mains, E. B. 1934. Host specialization in the rust of iris, *Puccinia iridis*. Amer. Jour. Bot. 21:23–33.

Mains, E. B. 1935. Rust resistance in *Antirrhinum*. Phytopathology 25:977–991.

Mains, E. B. 1938. Additional studies concerning the rust of iris, *Puccinia iridis*. Phytopathology 28:67–71.

Mains, E. B. 1942. Phlox resistant to powdery mildew. Phytopathology 32:414–418.

Manning, W. J., F. J. Campbell, P. M. Papia, and P. A. Hughes. 1970. Effectiveness of benomyl soil drenches for control of Thielaviopsis root rot of poinsettia. Plant Dis. Reptr. 54:328–330.

Manning, W. J., and M. Glickman. 1969. Effectiveness of several systemic and nonsystemic fungicides in the prevention of Botrytis blight of geranium cuttings and stock plants. Plant Dis. Reptr. 53:412–415.

Manning, W. J., and P. M. Papia. 1972. Benomyl soil treatments and natural occurrence of Alternaria leaf spot on carnation. Plant Dis. Reptr. 56:9–11.

Manning, W. J., P. M. Vardaro, and M. D. Connor. 1972. Effectiveness of several fungicides for control of powdery mildew of Kalanchoe. Plant Dis. Reptr. 56:405.

Manns, T. F., and J. J. Taubenhaus. 1913. Streak: A bacterial disease of sweet peas and clover. Gardeners' Chron. 53:215–216.

Marlatt, R. B. 1966. Brown leaf spot of Dieffenbachia. Plant Dis. Reptr. 50:687–689.

Massey, L. M. 1916. The hard rot disease of gladiolus. Cornell Univ. Agr. Exp. Sta. Bul. 380:151–181.

Massey, L. M. 1917. The crown canker disease of rose. Phytopathology 7:408–417.

Massey, L. M. 1918. Experiments for the control of blackspot and powdery mildew of roses. Phytopathology 8:20–23.

Massey, L. M. 1926. Fusarium rot of gladiolus corms. Phytopathology 16:509–523.

Massey, L. M. 1928. Dry rot of gladiolus corms. Phytopathology 18:519–529.

Massey, L. M. 1948. Understanding powdery mildew. Amer. Rose Ann. 33:136–145.

Massey, L. M., and A. E. Jenkins. 1935. Scab of violet caused by *Sphaceloma*. Cornell Univ. Agr. Exp. Sta. Mem 176. 9 p.

Massey, L. M., and P. E. Tilford. 1932. Cyclamen stunt. (Abstr.) Phytopathology 22:19.

Massey, L. M., R. P. White, and A. E. Jenkins. 1933. Disease of cultivated sweet violet caused by *Sphaceloma*. (Abstr.) Phytopathology 23:22–23.

McCain, A. H. 1971. Chemical immunization of chrysanthemums. Plant. Dis. Reptr. 55:347–348.

McCain, A. H., and T. G. Byrne. 1968. Crown gall control in greenhouse roses. Florists' Rev. 142(3670):25, 78.

McCain, A. H., and D. S. Farnham. 1971. Control of Fusarium stem rot of carnations by the use of fungicides in rooting powders. Ill. State Florists' Assoc. Bul. 329:7–8.

McCain, A. H., and R. H. Sciaroni. 1968. Grey mold (Botrytis) control with fungicides. Florists' Rev. 141(3666):15, 39–40.

McCallan, S. E. A. 1946. Dithiocarbamate fungicides. Agr. Chem. 17:15–18, 55.

McCallan, S. E. A., L. P. Miller, and M. A. Magill. 1955. Chemical names for active ingredients of fungicides. Phytopathology 45:295–302.

McClellan, W. D. 1942. Control of powdery mildew of roses in the greenhouse. Cornell Univ. Agr. Exp. Sta. Bul. 785. 39 p.

McClellan, W. D. 1947. Black scale disease on bulbs of *Lilium umbellatum erectum*. Plant Dis. Reptr. 31:31.

McClellan, W. D. 1947. Efficacy of certain soil fumigants and fertilizers against crown rot in annual larkspur caused by *Sclerotium rolfsii*. Phytopathology 37:198–200.

McClellan, W. D. 1947. Insecticides and their relationship to mildew on roses. Florists' Rev. 101(2604):39.

McClellan, W. D. 1947. Symptoms of the Fusarium disease of gladiolus. Gladiolus Mag. 11(1):26–32.

McClellan, W. D. 1948. New fungicides for control of narcissus basal rot. (Abstr.) Phytopathology 38:17.

McClellan, W. D. 1949. *Botrytis* on greenhouse roses. Plant Dis. Reptr. 33:137–138.

McClellan, W. D. 1952. Effect of temperature on the severity of Fusarium basal rot in narcissus. Phytopathology 42:407–412.

McClellan, W. D. 1953. Narcissus basal rot. Plant Diseases. U.S. Dept. Agr. Yearb. 1953:617–620.

McClellan, W. D. 1966. Common names for pesticides. Plant Dis. Reptr. 50:725–729.

McClellan, W. D., K. F. Baker, and C. J. Gould. 1948. The Botrytis disease of gladiolus in the United States. Florists' Rev. 102(2633):38–39.

McClellan, W. D., and F. F. Smith. 1950. Karathane looks promising for mildew and spider control. Florists' Rev. 106 (2753):24–26.

McClellan, W. D., and F. F. Smith. 1951. Karathane for controlling two-spotted spider mites and powdery mildew on roses. (Abstr.) Phytopathology 41:563.

McClellan, W. D., F. F. Smith, and E. A. Taylor. 1955. Control of blackspot of roses with dust combinations containing fungicides, insecticides, and miticides. (Abstr.) Phytopathology 45:465.

McClellan, W. D., A. W. Specht, B. H. Marshall, Jr., J. W. Resnicky, and C. J. Gould. 1950. Mercury content of narcissus in relation to plant injury. (Abstr.) Phytopathology 40:872.

McClellan, W. D., and N. W. Stuart. 1944. The use of fungicides and growth substances in the control of Fusarium scale rot of lilies. Phytopathology 34:966–975.

McClellan, W. D., and N. W. Stuart. 1945. Prevention of scale rot in propagation of Easter lily bulbs. Florists' Rev. 95 (2467):19–20.

McClellan, W. D., and N. W. Stuart. 1947. The influence of nutrition on Fusarium basal rot of narcissus and on Fusarium yellows of gladiolus. Amer. Jour. Bot. 34:88–93.

McClellan, W. D., E. A. Taylor, and F. F. Smith. 1956. Effect of fungicides in miticide-fungicide dust combinations on winter carry-over of the fungus causing blackspot of roses. (Abstr.) Phytopathology 46:20.

McClellan, W. D., E. A. Taylor, and F. F. Smith. 1957. Relation of fungicide and miticide treatments to winter injury and spring blackspot development on roses. Phytopathology 47:357–360.

McClellan, W. D., E. A. Taylor, and F. F. Smith. 1957. Synergism between copper and sulfur in dust mixtures for the control of rose blackspot. Phytopathology 47:240–241.

McClellan, W. D., E. A. Taylor, and F. F. Smith. 1958. Winter treatments of dormant roses and their relation to blackspot and spider mite control. Phytopathology 48:408–410.

McCulloch, L. 1924. A bacterial blight of gladioli. Jour. Agr. Res. 27:225–230.

McCulloch, L. 1924. A leaf and corm disease of gladioli caused by *Bacterium marginatum*. Jour. Agr. Res. 29:159–177.

McCulloch, L. 1937. Bacterial leaf spot of begonia. Jour. Agr. Res. 54:583–590.

McCulloch, L. 1938. Leaf blight of iris caused by *Bacterium tardicrescens*. Phytopathology 28:642–649.

McCulloch, L. 1944. A vascular disease of gladiolus caused by *Fusarium*. Phytopathology 34:263–287.

McCulloch, L., and P. P. Pirone. 1939. Bacterial leaf spot of *Dieffenbachia*. Phytopathology 29:956–962.

McCulloch, L., and C. Thom. 1928. A rot of gladiolus corms caused by *Penicillium gladioli* L. McC. and Thom. Jour. Agr. Res. 36:217–224.

McCulloch, L., and C. A. Weigel. 1941. Gladiolus diseases and insects. U.S. Dept. Agr. Farmers' Bul. 1860. 18 p.

McDonough, E. S. 1948. Etiology and control of begonia bacteriosis. (Abstr.) Phytopathology 38:17.

McDonough, E. S. 1948. Tenacious begonia leaf spot disease brought under control. Florists' Rev. 101(2623):44–45.

McDonough, E. S., and R. J. McGray. 1957. Botrytis on saintpaulia and its relation to mite control. Phytopathology 47:109–110.

McFadden, L. A. 1961. A bacterial leaf spot of florists' chrysanthemums, *Chrysanthemum morifolium*. Plant Dis. Reptr. 45:16–19.

McFadden, L. A. 1961. Bacterial stem and leaf rot of dieffenbachia in Florida. Phytopathology 51:663–668.

McKenny Hughes, A. W. 1930. Aphis as a possible vector of "breaking" in tulip species. Ann. Appl. Biol. 17:36–42.

McKenny Hughes, A. W. 1931. Aphides as vectors of "breaking" in tulips. Ann. Appl. Biol. 18:16–29.

McKenny Hughes, A. W. 1934. Aphides as vectors of "breaking" in tulips. II. Ann. Appl. Biol. 21:112–119.

McKenzie, M. A., L. H. Jones, and C. J. Gilgut. 1940. *Phomopsis gardeniae* in relation to gardenia culture. Plant Dis. Reptr. 24:58–62.

McWhorter, F. P. 1931. Ramularia blight of narcissus. Plant Dis. Reptr. 15:3–4.

McWhorter, F. P. 1932. A preliminary analysis of tulip breaking. (Abstr.) Phytopathology 22:998.

McWhorter, F. P. 1939. The white streak or white stripe disease of narcissus. (Abstr.) Phytopathology 29:826.

McWhorter, F. P. 1947. Scale tip rot of *Lilium longiflorum* in the Pacific Northwest. Plant Dis. Reptr. 31:159–161.

McWhorter, F. P. 1948. Identifying and controlling nematodes in forcing lilies. Florists' Rev. 101(2617):40–41.

McWhorter, F. P. 1948. The story of a gladiolus virus. N. Amer. Gladiolus Counc. Bul. 13:22, 66.

McWhorter, F. P. 1954. Investigation on presence of viruses in glads. N. Amer. Gladiolus Counc. Bul. 38:84–85.

McWhorter, F. P. 1957. Association between *Rhizoctonia* and yellow coloration of Easter lily bulbs. Phytopathology 47:447–448.

McWhorter, F. P. 1957. A localized occurrence of cucumber mosaic virus in gladiolus. Plant Dis. Reptr. 41:141–142.

McWhorter, F. P. 1957. Terraclor for control of lily root rot. Oreg. Ornamental and Nursery Dig. 1(4):1, 4.

McWhorter, F. P. 1957. Virus diseases of geranium in the Pacific Northwest. Plant Dis. Reptr. 41:83–88.

McWhorter, F. P., L. Boyle, and B. F. Dana. 1947. Production of yellow bean mosaic in beans by virus from mottled gladiolus. Science 105:177–178.

McWhorter, F. P., and H. J. Reynolds. 1934. New narcissus Botrytis disease in the Pacific Northwest. Plant Dis. Reptr. 18:51–53.

McWhorter, F. P., and F. Weiss. 1932. Diseases of narcissus. Oreg. Agr. Exp. Sta. Bul. 304. 41 p.

Melchers, L. E. 1926. Botrytis blossom blight and leaf spot of geranium, and its relation to the gray mold of head lettuce. Jour. Agr. Res. 32:883–894.

Melching, J. S. 1966. Effects of environment and of selected chemicals upon the development of black spot of rose and of the pathogen, *Diplocarpon rosae* Wolf. Cornell Univ. Agr. Exp. Sta. Mem. 397. 40 p.

Mendiola-Ela, V. 1952. The Curvularia disease of gladiolus in the Philippines. Phil. Agriculturist 35:517–538.

Meuli, L. J. 1937. Cladosporium leaf blotch of peony. Phytopathology 27:172–182.

Meyers, J. A. 1971. Biological control of Fusarium stem rot. Colo. Flower Growers' Assoc. Bul. 252:1–2.

Middleton, J. T., and C. M. Tucker. 1939. A disease of gloxinia caused by *Phytophthora cryptogea*. (Abstr.) Phytopathology 29:17–18.

Middleton, J. T., C. M. Tucker, and C. M. Tompkins. 1938. Pythium disease of fibrous-rooted begonia. (Abstr.) Phytopathology 28:672.

Middleton, J. T., C. M. Tucker, and C. M. Tompkins. 1942. Pythium disease of fibrous-rooted begonia and its control. Jour. Agr. Res. 65:89–95.

Middleton, J. T., C. M. Tucker, and C. M. Tompkins. 1944. A disease of gloxinia caused by *Phytophthora cryptogea*. Jour. Agr. Res. 68:405–413.

Mikkelsen, J. 1950. Stunt control program. Florists' Rev. 105(2725):26.

Mildner, R. A., and R. P. Scheffer. 1959. Mechanical transmission and host ranges of dahlia ringspot viruses. (Abstr.) Phytopathology 49:546.

Miles, L. E. 1932. Control of basal-rot of narcissus. Miss. Agr. Exp. Sta. Tech. Bul. 19. 12 p.

Milholland, R. D. 1969. Effect of soil fumigation on disease control and yield of gladiolus in southeastern North Carolina. Plant Dis. Reptr. 53:132–136.

Milholland, R. D., and R. Aycock. 1965. Propagation of disease-free gladiolus from hot-water treated cormels in Southeastern North Carolina. N. C. Agr. Exp. Sta. Tech Bul. 168. 15 p.

Miller, H. N., and R. O. Magie. 1950. Control of Fusarium storage rot of gladiolus corms. Phytopathology 40:209–212.

Miller, H. N., and R. T. DeNeve. 1971. Disease control on bedding plants with the use of 5-ethoxy-3-(trichloromethyl)-1,2,4-thiadiazole. Plant Dis. Reptr. 55:587–590.

Miller, H. N., and K. A. Noegel. 1970. Comparisons of methods of application, rates and formulations of nematicides for control of root-knot nematodes, *Meloidogyne incognita,* on gardenia plants. Plant Dis. Reptr. 54:966–969.

Miller, S. B., and L. W. Baxter, Jr. 1970. Dieback in azaleas caused by *Phomopsis* species. Phytopathology 60:387–388.

Mulford, F. L., and F. Weiss. 1939. Culture and diseases of delphiniums. U.S. Dept. Agr. Farmers' Bul. 1827. 11 p.

Muncie, J. H., and M. K. Patel. 1930. Fasciation of sweet peas. Amer. Jour. Bot. 17:218–230.

Munnecke, D. E. 1954. Bacterial stem rot and leaf spot of *Pelargonium.* Phytopathology 44:627–632.

Munnecke, D. E. 1956. Alternaria leaf spot of geranium. Plant Dis. Reptr. 40:452–454.

Munnecke, D. E. 1956. Development and production of pathogen-free geranium propagative material. Plant Dis. Reptr. Suppl. 238:93–95.

Munnecke, D. E. 1956. Survival of *Xanthomonas pelargonii* in soil. Phytopathology 46:297–298.

Munnecke, D. E. 1960. Bacterial stem rot of dieffenbachia. Phytopathology 50:696–700.

Munnecke, D. E., and P. A. Chandler. 1953. Some diseases of variegated peperomia. Plant Dis. Reptr. 37:434–435.

Munnecke, D. E., and P. A. Chandler. 1955. Disease-free geranium stock. Calif. Agr. 9(5):8, 14.

Nelson, P. E. 1964. Carnation as a symptomless carrier of *Fusarium oxysporum* f. *dianthi.* Phytopathology 54:323–329.

Nelson, P. E., and R. S. Dickey. 1968. Symptom expression and varietal susceptibility in carnation, *Dianthus caryophyllus,* inoculated with the carnation strain of *Erwinia chrysanthemi.* Phytopathology 58:142–146.

Nelson, P. E., J. Tammen, and R. Baker. 1960. Control of vascular wilt diseases of carnation by culture-indexing. Phytopathology 50:356–360.

Nelson, P. E., C. E. Williamson, and W. D. McClellan. 1956. Ovulinia flower spot of azalea found on Long Island. Plant Dis. Reptr. 40:1115.

Nelson, R. 1925. Chrysanthemum yellows. A new disease in the greenhouse. Mich. Agr. Exp. Sta. Quart. Bul. 7(4):157–160.

Nelson, R. 1935. Dahlia diseases. Mich. Agr. Exp. Sta. Spec. Bul. 226:70–83.

Nelson, R. 1937. Basal dry rot of gladiolus corms. (Abstr.) Phytopathology 27:137.

Nelson, R. 1938. Fusarium yellows of gladiolus. (Abstr.) Phytopathology 28:17.

Nelson, R. 1938. Fusarium yellows of gladiolus. The Gladiolus (New Eng. Gladiolus Soc., Boston) 1938:124–131.

Nelson, R. 1948. Diseases of gladiolus. Mich. Agr. Exp. Sta. Spec. Bul. 350. 63 p.

Nelson, R., and M. Mooar. 1952. Life history of the *Stemphylium* that causes red leaf spot of gladiolus. Phytopathology 42:363–366.

Newhall, A. G., and W. T. Schroeder. 1951. New flash-flame soil pasteurizer. Cornell Univ. Agr. Exp. Sta. Bul. 875. 19 p.

Obee, D. J. 1937. A note on the canker disease of gardenias. Trans. Kans. Acad. Sci. 39:103–104.

Ogilvie, L., and C. E. F. Guterman. 1929. A mosaic disease of the Easter lily. Phytopathology 19:311–315.

O'Leary, K., and C. E. F. Guterman. 1937. Penicillium rot of lily bulbs and its control by calcium hypochlorite. Contrib. Boyce Thompson Inst. 8:361–374.

Olsen, C. M., and M. M. Afanasiev. 1956. Root rot of sweet peas. Proc. Mont. Acad. Sci. 16:37–38.

Olson, C. J. 1949. Intensive program conducted to whip chrysanthemum stunt. Florists' Rev. 105(2711):33–34.

Palmer, J. G., T. J. Henneberry, and E. A. Taylor. 1959. Sprays for control of powdery mildew of roses. Plant Dis. Reptr. 43:494–495.

Parmelee, J. A. 1954. *Curvularia* on gladiolus in Canada. Plant Dis. Reptr. 38:515–517.

Parmelee, J. A. 1956. The identification of the Curvularia parasite of gladiolus. Mycologia 48:558–567.

Parris, G. K. 1958. Soil fumigants and their use: a summary. Plant Dis. Reptr. 42:273–278.

Paulson, G. A., and D. F. Schoeneweiss. 1971. Epidemiology of stem blight of *Vinca minor* incited by *Phoma exigua* var. *exigua*. Phytopathology 61:959–963.

Peiris, J. W. L. 1949. The Botrytis disease of gladiolus with special reference to the causal organism. Trans. Brit. Mycol. Soc. 32:291–304.

Peltier, G. L. 1919. Carnation stem rot and its control. Ill. Agr. Exp. Sta. Bul. 223:579–607.

Peltier, G. L. 1919. Snapdragon rust. Ill. Agr. Exp. Sta. Bul. 221:533–548.

Perry, R. S. 1970. *Chalaropsis thielavioides,* a new pathogen on poinsettias. Plant Dis. Reptr. 54:451–452.

Perry, R. S., and J. L. Forsberg. 1972. Incidence of the Curvularia disease of gladiolus in Illinois. Plant Dis. Reptr. 56:995–997.

Petersen, L. J. 1956. Control of Fusarium stem rot of carnations with fungicidal cutting dips. Colo. Flower Growers' Assoc. Bul. 84:1–3.

Petersen, L. J. 1957. A look at some of the new spray materials for carnation mother blocks. Colo. Flower Growers' Assoc. Bul. 92:3–5.

Petersen, L. J. 1958. Control of Fusarium stem rot of carnations with cutting dips and drenches. Colo. Flower Growers' Assoc. Bul. 99:1–4.

Petersen, L. J., and R. Baker. 1959. Control of Fusarium stem rot of carnations: II. The use of dips and drenches. Plant Dis. Reptr. 43:1209–1212.

Petersen, L. J., R. Baker, and R. E. Skiver. 1959. Control of Fusarium stem rot of carnations: I. Application of fungicides to mother blocks. Plant Dis. Reptr. 43:1204–1208.

Peterson, J. L. 1967. Leaf spot of annual phlox caused by *Stemphylium botryosum*. Plant Dis. Reptr. 51:741–742.

Peterson, J. L. 1967. Root and crown rot of perennial phlox caused by *Thielaviopsis basicola*. Plant Dis. Reptr. 51:436–437.

Peterson, J. L., and S. H. Davis, Jr. 1963. Chrysanthemum flower rot caused by *Fusarium tricinctum* f. *poae* (Pk.) Synd. and Hans. Plant Dis. Reptr. 47:722–723.

Peterson, J. L., and S. H. Davis, Jr. 1970. Anthracnose of poppy caused by *Gloeosporium*. Plant Dis. Reptr. 54:1037–1039.

Peterson, J. L., and S. H. Davis, Jr. 1970. Suppression of *Erysiphe polygoni* and *Botrytis cinerea* on hydrangea with benomyl. Plant Dis. Reptr. 54:606–607.

Peterson, J. L., and S. H. Davis, Jr. 1971. Varietal susceptibility of chrysanthemums to Verticillium wilt. Chrysanthemum Bul. 27(5):184–187.

Phillips, D. J. 1963. Control of carnation streak virus by shoot-tip culture. Colo. Flower Growers' Assoc. Bul. 155:1–3.

Phillips, D. J. 1965. *Fusarium roseum* and the carnation shoot tip. Colo. Flower Growers' Assoc. Bul. 182:1–3.

Phillips, D. J. 1965. Home garden control of Phytophthora crown rot of petunia. Colo. Flower Growers' Assoc. Bul. 183: 1–2.

Phillips, D. J., and R. Baker. 1962. Phytophthora crown rot of petunia. Plant Dis. Reptr. 46:506–508.

Phillips, D. J., and J. L. Green. 1964. Report on Phytophthora crown rot of petunia. Colo. Flower Growers' Assoc. Bul. 166:3–5.

Pirone, P. P. 1938. Where are gardenia cankers initiated? Phytopathology 28: 597–598.

Pirone, P. P. 1939. Bacterial leaf spot of dieffenbachia. (Abstr.) Phytopathology 29:19.

Pirone, P. P. 1939. Diseases of ornamental plants. N. J. Agr. Exp. Sta. Circ. 385. 80 p.

Pirone, P. P. 1940. Diseases of the gardenia. N. J. Agr. Exp. Sta. Bul. 679. 10 p.

Plakidas, A. G. 1944. Black scale: a disease of Easter lily bulbs. Phytopathology 34: 556–571.

Plakidas, A. G. 1949. Effect of sclerotial development on incidence of azalea flower blight. Plant Dis. Reptr. 33:272–273.

Preston, N. C. 1936. The parasitism of *Myrothecium roridum* Tode. Trans. Brit. Mycol. Soc. 20:242–251.

Price, D. 1970. The seasonal carry-over of *Botrytis tulipae* (Lib.) Lind., the cause of tulip fire. Ann. Appl. Biol. 65:49–58.

Price, T. V. 1970. Epidemiology and control of powdery mildew (*Sphaerotheca pannosa*) on roses. Ann. Appl. Biol. 65: 231–248.

Raabe, R. D. 1969. *Thielaviopsis basicola* leaf spot of poinsettia. (Abstr.) Phytopathology 59:14–15.

Raabe, R. D. 1971. Sclerotinia blight of Stephanotis flowers. Phytopathology 61: 1524–1525.

Raabe, R. D., and J. H. Hurlimann. 1970. Fungicide mixes for poinsettia root rot control. Calif. Agr. 24(1):9–10.

Raabe, R. D., and J. H. Hurlimann. 1970. Fungicides for control of Easter lily root rots. Calif. Agr. 24(11):14–15.

Raabe, R. D., and J. H. Hurlimann. 1970. Outdoor experiments for controlling rose powdery mildew. Calif. Agr. 24(8):8.

Raabe, R. D., and J. H. Hurlimann. 1971. Control of *Thielaviopsis basicola* root rot of poinsettia with benomyl and thiabendazole. Plant Dis. Reptr. 55:238–240.

Raabe, R. D., and J. H. Hurlimann. 1971. Effectiveness of soil fungicide mixtures added prior to planting as compared with those added as drenches. (Abstr.) Phytopathology 61:1323.

Raabe, R. D., J. H. Hurlimann, and R. H. Sciaroni. 1969. Powdery mildew control on greenhouse-grown snapdragons with benomyl. Florists' Rev. 145(3754):73, 116–117.

Raabe, R. D., J. H. Hurlimann, and R. H. Sciaroni. 1970. Powdery mildew control with benomyl for greenhouse-grown snapdragons. Calif. Agr. 24(1):8.

Raabe, R. D., and J. V. Lenz. 1958. Septoria leaf scorch of azalea. Calif. Agr. 12(10):11.

Raabe, R. D., and R. H. Sciaroni. 1955. Petal blight disease of azaleas. Calif. Agr. 9(5):7, 14.

Raabe, R. D., and S. Wilhelm. 1958. Verticillium wilt of garden stock (*Matthiola incana*). Phytopathology 48:610–613.

Reinert, R. A., A. C. Hilderbrandt, and G. E. Beck. 1961. Geranium viruses. Florists' Rev. 128(3323):17–19; 75–78.

Riker, R. S., and L. R. Jones. 1935. Fusarium strains in relation to wilt of China aster. Phytopathology 25:733–747.

Robison, R. S., R. L. Starkey, and O. W. Davidson. 1954. Control of bacterial wilt of chrysanthemums with streptomycin. Phytopathology 44:646–650.

Rogers, M. N. 1959. Decay of poinsettia cuttings by the soft rot bacterium, *Erwinia carotovora* (Jones) Holland. Plant Dis. Reptr. 43:1236–1238.

Roistacher, C. N., and K. F. Baker. 1956. An inexpensive multipurpose soil steamer. Phytopathology 46:329–333.

Roistacher, C. N., K. F. Baker, and J. G. Bald. 1957. Hot-water treatment of gladiolus cormels for the eradication of *Fusarium oxysporum* f. *gladioli*. Hilgardia 26:659–684.

Rosen, H. R. 1935. Rose blast induced by *Phytomonas syringae*. Jour. Agr. Res. 51:235–243.

Rosenau, W. A., and J. J. McRitchie. 1964. An observation of boron deficiency symptoms on roses. Plant Dis. Reptr. 48:948–949.

Ruehle, G. D. 1941. Poinsettia scab caused by *Sphaceloma*. Phytopathology 31:947–948.

Saaltink, G. J. 1969. Root rot of hyacinths caused by species of *Pythium*. Neth. Jour. Plant Pathol. 75:343–354.

Schmitz, H. 1920. Observations on some common and important diseases of the rhododendron. Phytopathology 10:273–278.

Schneider, B. A. 1966. Petals of a hybrid tea rose attacked by spotted anthracnose (*Sphaceloma rosarum*). Plant Dis. Reptr. 50:934.

Schoeneweiss, D. F. 1972. Control of stem blight of *Vinca minor*. Plant Dis. Reptr. 56:238–241.

Schreiber, L. R. 1964. Stem canker and dieback of rhododendron caused by *Botryosphaeria ribis* Gross and Dug. Plant Dis. Reptr. 48:207–210.

Seeley, J. G. 1949. Leaf burn on Croft lilies as affected by varying nutrients. Florists' Rev. 105(2717):17–18.

Seeley, J. G. 1950. Mineral nutrient deficiencies and leaf burn of Croft Easter lilies. Proc. Amer. Soc. Hort. Sci. 56:439–445.

Seeley, J. G. 1951. Leaf burn of lilies reduced by nitrogen fertilizer. Pa. Flower Growers' Bul. 2:1–2, 6–7.

Seeley, J. G., and D. de C. Velazquez. 1952. The effect of fertilizer applications on leaf burn and growth of Croft lilies. Proc. Amer. Soc. Hort. Sci. 60:459–472.

Senner, A. H. 1934. Application of steam in the sterilization of soil. U.S. Dept. Agr. Tech. Bul. 443. 19 p.

Severin, H. H. P. 1942. Infection of perennial delphiniums by California-aster-yellows virus. Hilgardia 14:411–440.

Severin, H. H. P. 1943. Breaking in color of flowers of annual phlox caused by the aster-yellows virus. Phytopathology 33:741–743.

Severin, H. H. P. 1947. Viruses that induce breaking in color of flower petals in pansies and violas. Hilgardia 17:577–594.

Severin, H. H. P., and S. J. Oliver. 1939. Delphinium aster yellows. (Abstr.) Phytopathology 29:826.

Severin, H. H. P., and C. M. Tompkins. 1948. Aphid transmission of mild mosaic virus of annual stock. Hilgardia 18:539–552.

Severin, H. H. P., and C. M. Tompkins. 1950. Aphid transmission of a mosaic virus and symptoms of other virus diseases of *Primula obconica*. Hilgardia 20:279–298.

Severin, H. H. P., and C. M. Tompkins. 1950. Aphid transmission of severe-mosaic virus of annual stock. Hilgardia 20:93–108.

Shanks, J. B., and J. R. Keller. 1954. Low pH joins sanitation measures in fight on poinsettia root rot. Florists Exch. and Hort. Trade World 122(17):14, 56.

Shurtleff, M. C., and C. H. Sherwood. 1956. A simplified method for culturing carnation cuttings for Fusarium wilt. (Abstr.) Phytopathology 46:26.

Simmons, S. A. 1949. Research on Botrytis corm rot. N. Amer. Gladiolus Counc. Bul. 17:93–94.

Simmons, S. A. 1951. Alternaria leaf spot of gladiolus. Plant Dis. Reptr. 35:333–334.

Simpson, C. J., G. E. Jones, and J. D. Taylor. 1971. A seedling blight of *Antirrhinum* caused by *Pseudomonas antirrhini*. Plant Pathol. 20:127–130.

Siradhana, B. S., C. W. Ellett, and A. F. Schmitthenner. 1968. Crown rot of peperomia. Plant Dis. Reptr. 52:244.

Sleesman, J., D. G. White, and C. W. Ellett. 1973. Bacterial leaf spot of zinnia: a new disease in North America. Plant Dis. Reptr. 57:555–557.

Smiley, E. M. 1920. The Phyllosticta blight of snapdragons. Phytopathology 10:232–248.

Smith, F. F., and P. Brierley. 1948. Aphid transmission of lily viruses during storage of the bulbs. Phytopathology 38:841–844.

Smith, F. F., and P. Brierley. 1948. Aster yellows in shallot and gladiolus. Phytopathology 38:581–583.

Smith, F. F., and P. Brierley. 1948. Simulation of lily rosette symptoms by feeding injury of the foxglove aphid. Phytopathology 38:849–851.

Smith, F. F., and P. Brierley. 1951. Aster yellows in canna. Phytopathology 41:190–191.

Smith, F. F., and P. Brierley. 1953. Grassy-top symptoms in gladiolus reproduced by experimental inoculation with western aster yellows virus. Plant Dis. Reptr. 37:547–551.

Smith, F. F., and P. Brierley. 1955. Aphid transmission of tobacco ringspot virus in gladiolus. Plant Dis. Reptr. 39:35.

Smith, R. E. 1899. A new Colletotrichum disease of the pansy. Bot. Gaz. 27:203–204.

Smith, R. E. 1940. Diseases of flowers and other ornamentals. Calif. Agr. Ext. Circ. 118. 108 p.

Snow, G. F. 1955. A virus from gladiolus similar to common bean mosaic. (Abstr.) Phytopathology 45:696.

Snyder, W. C. 1941. A Fusarium wilt of sweet william (*Dianthus barbatus*). Phytopathology 31:1054–1056.

Snyder, W. C., and H. R. Thomas. 1936. Spotted wilt of the sweet pea. Hilgardia 10:257–262.

Sonderman, C. H., and N. A. MacLean. 1949. Rhizoctonia neck and bulb rot of iris in the Pacific Northwest. Phytopathology 39:174–175.

Spencer, J. L., and H. E. White. 1950. Anther smut disease of carnations. Carnation Craft 14:4–5.

Starr, M. P., and P. P. Pirone. 1942. *Phytomonas poinsettiae* n. sp. the cause of a bacterial disease of poinsettia. Phytopathology 32:1076–1081.

Stathis, P. D., and A. G. Plakidas. 1958. Anthracnose of azaleas. Phytopathology 48:256–260.

Stevens, F. L. 1907. The chrysanthemum ray blight. Bot. Gaz. 44:241–258.

Stevens, F. L., and O. A. Plunkett. 1925. Tulip blossom blight. Ill. Agr. Exp. Sta. Bul. 265:297–307.

Stewart, F. C. 1900. An anthracnose and a stem rot of the cultivated snapdragon *Antirrhinum majus* L. N. Y. (Geneva) Agr. Exp. Sta. Bul. 179:105–114.

Stoddard, E. M. 1952. Chemotherapeutic control of *Rhizoctonia* on greenhouse stock. (Abstr.) Phytopathology 42:476.

Stone, O. M. 1958. Some observations on *Septoria gladioli* Pass. Trans. Brit. Mycol. Soc. 41:505–518.

Stone, O. M. 1968. The elimination of four viruses from carnation and sweet william by meristem-tip culture. Ann. Appl. Biol. 62:119–122.

Strider, D. L. 1973. Bacterial leaf and flower spot of zinnia in North Carolina. Plant Dis. Reptr. 57:1020.

Stuart, N. W. 1947. The effects of Ceresan dips and fertilizer applications on growth, flower production, and basal rot development in narcissus. Proc. Amer. Soc. Hort. Sci. 50:411–415.

Stuart, N. W. 1949. Leaf burning of Croft Easter lilies linked to nutrients. Florists' Rev. 104(2693):23–24.

Stuart, N. W., and W. D. McClellan. 1943. Severity of narcissus basal rot increased by the use of synthetic hormones and nitrogen bases. Science 97:15.

Stuart, N. W., W. Skou, and D. C. Kiplinger. 1952. Further studies on causes and control of leaf scorch of Croft Easter lily. Proc. Amer. Soc. Hort. Sci. 60:434–438.

Swift, M. E. 1932. Pythium crown- and stem-rot of begonia. Jour. N. Y. Bot. Gard. 33:141–143.

Takahashi, T. 1927. A Sclerotium disease of larkspur. Phytopathology 17:239–245.

Tammen, J. 1953. Fusarium stem rot of carnation. (Abstr.) Phytopathology 43:485.

Tammen, J. 1960. The production of pathogen-free geraniums from cultured cuttings. Florists' Rev. 127(3286):69–70, 140–141.

Tammen, J., R. R. Baker, and W. D. Holley. 1956. Control of carnation diseases through the cultured-cutting technique. Plant Dis. Reptr. Suppl. 238:72–76.

Tammen, J., and D. F. Muse. 1961. Control of Pythium root and basal stem rot of *Chrysanthemum morifolium* with Dexon. Plant Dis. Reptr. 45:863–865.

Taubenhaus, J. J. 1914. The diseases of the sweet pea. Del. Coll. Agr. Exp. Sta. Bul. 106. 93 p.

Taubenhaus, J. J. 1916. A wilt disease of the columbine. Phytopathology 6:254–257.

Taubenhaus, J. J. 1935. On a black crown rot of greenhouse snapdragons caused by *Myrothecium roridum* Tode. (Abstr.) Phytopathology 25:969–970.

Taubenhaus, J. J., and W. N. Ezekiel. 1932. Sclerotinia wilt of greenhouse snapdragons. Amer. Jour. Bot. 19:808–811.

Taubenhaus, J. J., and W. N. Ezekiel. 1933. Fusarium wilt and corm rot of freesias. Bot. Gaz. 95:128–142.

Taubenhaus, J. J., and W. N. Ezekiel. 1933. A new hollyhock rust. Mycologia 25:509–512.

Teng, S. C. 1929. Rhizoctonosis of lobelia. Phytopathology 19:585–588.

Thomas, H. E., and H. N. Hansen. 1946. Camellia flower blight. Phytopathology 36:380–381.

Thomas, H. E., and L. M. Massey. 1939. Mosaic diseases of the rose in California. Hilgardia 12:647–663.

Thomas, W. D., Jr., R. R. Baker, J. G. Zoril, and O. V. Holtzmann. 1952. The effect of mosaic on the yield and quality of carnations. Colo. Flower Growers' Assoc. Bul. 28:2–4.

Thomas, W. D., Jr., and L. E. Dickens. 1953. Carnation pimple. Plant Dis. Reptr. 37:634–635.

Thompson, H. S. 1958. Pythium rot of saintpaulia, the African violet. Canad. Jour. Bot. 36:843–863.

Thurston, H. W., Jr., and C. R. Orton. 1921. A *Phytophthora* parasitic on peony. Science 54:170–171.

Tilford, P. E. 1930. Carnation rust. Ohio Agr. Exp. Sta. Bimonth. Bul. 15(147): 191–195.

Tilford, P. E. 1930. Dahlia stunt disease. Ohio Agr. Exp. Sta. Bul. 446:64–65.

Tilford, P. E. 1930. A Rhizoctonia disease of sweet alyssum. Phytopathology 20: 587–590.

Tilford, P. E. 1932. Calla lily root rot and its control. Ohio Agr. Exp. Sta. Bimonth. Bul. 17(157):138–140.

Tilford, P. E. 1932. Diseases of ornamental plants. Ohio Agr. Exp. Sta. Bul. 511. 82 p.

Tilford, P. E. 1934. Stem canker disease of gardenia. Ohio Agr. Exp. Sta. Bimonth. Bul. 19(168):116–117.

Tilford, P. E. 1935. Fasciation of sweet peas: a bacterial disease. (Abstr.) Phytopathology 25:36.

Tilford, P. E. 1936. Fasciation of sweet peas caused by *Phytomonas fascians* n. sp. Jour. Agr. Res. 53:383–394.

Tilford, P. E. 1936. Sterilization recommended to control fasciation of sweet peas. Florists' Rev. 78(2021):9–10.

Tilford, P. E. 1941. Leaf curl of poinsettia. Ohio Florists' Assoc. Bul. 145:7–8.

Tilford, P. E., and H. A. Runnels. 1942. Verticillium wilt of chrysanthemums and its control. Ohio Agr. Exp. Sta. Bul. 603. 23 p.

Timonin, M. I., and R. L. Self. 1955. *Cylindrocladium scoparium* Morgan on azaleas and other ornamentals. Plant Dis. Reptr. 39:860–863.

Tisdale, W. B. 1920. Iris leaf spot caused by *Didymellina iridis*. Phytopathology 10:148–163.

Tisdale, W. B., and G. D. Ruehle. 1949. Pythium root rot of aroids and Easter lilies. Phytopathology 39:167–170.

Tompkins, C. M. 1934. Breaking in stock (*Matthiola incana*), a virosis. (Abstr.) Phytopathology 24:1137.

Tompkins, C. M. 1939. Two mosaic diseases of annual stock. Jour. Agr. Res. 58:63–77.

Tompkins, C. M. 1950. Botrytis stem rot of tuberous-rooted begonia. Hilgardia 19:401–410.

Tompkins, C. M. 1950. Pythium rot of pink and yellow calla corms and its control. Hilgardia 20:183–190.

Tompkins, C. M. 1959. A disease of poinsettia stock plants caused by waterlogged soil and its control. Plant Dis. Reptr. 43:1034–1035.

Tompkins, C. M. 1959. Leaf rot of poinsettia cuttings caused by *Rhizoctonia solani* and its control. Plant Dis. Reptr. 43:1036–1037.

Tompkins, C. M. 1959. Wilting of poinsettia, a disease of unknown etiology. Plant Dis. Reptr. 43:1067–1069.

Tompkins, C. M. 1972. Poinsettia wilt — its cause and control. Plant Dis. Reptr. 56:415.

Tompkins, C. M., and P. A. Ark. 1941. Verticillium wilt of strawflower. Phytopathology 31:1130–1134.

Tompkins, C. M., and H. N. Hansen. 1941. Tulip anthracnose. Jour. Agr. Res. 62:61–64.

Tompkins, C. M., and H. N. Hansen. 1948. Cyclamen petal spot, caused by *Botrytis cinerea*, and its control. Phytopathology 38:114–117.

Tompkins, C. M., and H. N. Hansen. 1950. Flower blight of *Stephanotis floribunda*, caused by *Botrytis elliptica*, and its control. Phytopathology 40:780–781.

Tompkins, C. M., and H. N. Hansen. 1950. Pansy leafspot, caused by *Centrospora acerina*, host range, and control. Hilgardia 19:383–398.

Tompkins, C. M., and J. T. Middleton. 1942. Root rot of *Ranunculus asiaticus* caused by *Pythium debaryanum*. Jour. Agr. Res. 64:179–183.

Tompkins, C. M., and J. T. Middleton. 1950. Etiology and control of poinsettia root and stem rot caused by *Pythium* spp. and *Rhizoctonia solani*. Hilgardia 20:171–182.

Tompkins, C. M., and H. H. P. Severin. 1950. Spotted wilt of white, yellow, and pink callas. Hilgardia 20:207–232.

Tompkins, C. M., and W. C. Snyder. 1972. Cyclamen wilt in California and its control. Plant Dis. Reptr. 56:493–497.

Tompkins, C. M., and C. M. Tucker. 1937. Foot rot of China-aster, annual stock, and Transvaal daisy caused by *Phytophthora cryptogea*. Jour. Agr. Res. 55:563–574.

Tompkins, C. M., and C. M. Tucker. 1947. Leaf blight of pink calla caused by *Phytophthora erythroseptica*. Phytopathology 37:382–389.

Tompkins, C. M., and C. M. Tucker. 1947. Stem rot of *Dieffenbachia picta* caused by *Phytophthora palmivora* and its control. Phytopathology 37:868–874.

Tompkins, C. M., and C. M. Tucker. 1950. Rhizome rot of white calla caused by *Phytophthora erythroseptica*. Phytopathology 40:712–714.

Tompkins, C. M., C. M. Tucker, and A. E. Clarke. 1935. Root rot of aster caused by *Phytophthora cryptogea*. (Abstr.) Phytopathology 25:895.

Torgeson, D. C. 1952. Observations on Verticillium wilt of geranium in Oregon. Plant Dis. Reptr. 36:51.

Travis, R. V. 1957. Virus diseases of iris. (Abstr.) Phytopathology 47:454.

Travis, R. V., and T. J. Henneberry. 1960. Fungicide-acaricide combinations for the control of *Diplocarpon rosae*. Phytopathology 50:573.

Traylor, J. A., H. K. Wagnon, and H. E. Williams. 1971. Rose spring dwarf, a graft-transmissible disease. Plant Dis. Reptr. 55:294.

Trelease, W. 1916. Two leaf-fungi of cyclamen. Trans. Ill. State Acad. Sci. 9:143–146.

Turner, N. J., and D. Lamont. 1965. Control of fungal diseases in the greenhouse with thermally induced dusts of tetrachloroisophthalonitrile. Contrib. Boyce Thompson Inst. 23:51–54.

Ullstrup, A. J. 1936. Leaf blight of China aster caused by *Rhizoctonia solani*. Phytopathology 26:981–990.

Ward, H. M. 1888. A lily-disease. Ann. Bot. 2:319–382.

Waterman, A. M. 1928. Rose diseases: their causes and control. U.S. Dept. Agr. Farmers' Bul. 1547. 19 p.

Waterman, A. M. 1930. Diseases of rose caused by species of *Coniothyrium* in the United States. Jour. Agr. Res. 40:805–827.

Weber, G. F., and W. Changsri. 1957. Septoria leafspot of marigold, *Tagetes erecta*. (Abstr.) Phytopathology 47:537.

Weber, G. F., and L. van Weerdt. 1956. A gladiolus disease caused by *Curvularia* sp. (Abstr.) Phytopathology 46:30.

Wehlburg, C. 1970. Pelargonium rust (*Puccinia pelargonii-zonalis*) in Florida. Plant Dis. Reptr. 54:827–828.

Wehlburg, C., and R. S. Cox. 1966. Rhizoctonia leaf blight of azalea. Plant Dis. Reptr. 50:354–355.

Wehlburg, C., and A. P. Martinez. 1967. Leaf spot of *Dracaena marginata* Lam. caused by *Fusarium moniliforme* Sheld. and its control. Proc. Fla. State Hort. Soc. 80:454–456.

Weihing, J. L., M. L. Schuster, J. H. Riesselman, and J. A. Cook. 1971. Control of Fusarium wilt of petunia with three soil fumigants. Plant Dis. Reptr. 55:580–582.

Weihing, J. L., M. L. Schuster, and J. H. Riesselman. 1972. Control of petunia wilt. Univ. Nebr. Coll. Agr. Quar. 19(1):11–13.

Weinard, F. F. 1942. "Black speck" of roses. Ill. State Florists' Assoc. Bul. 56:251.

Weiss, F. 1929. The basal rot of narcissus bulbs caused by *Fusarium* sp. (Abstr.) Phytopathology 19:99–100.

Weiss, F. 1929. The relation of the hotwater treatment of narcissus bulbs to basal rot. (Abstr.) Phytopathology 19:100.

Weiss, F. 1934. The red leaf spot or "rust" of amaryllis. Amer. Amaryllis Soc. Yearb. 1:92–94.

Weiss, F. 1940. Anthracnose and Cladosporium stem spot of peony. Phytopathology 30:409–417.

Weiss, F., F. A. Haasis, and C. E. Williamson. 1942. Prestorage disinfection of narcissus bulbs. Phytopathology 32:199–205.

Weiss, F., and F. F. Smith. 1941. A flowerspot disease of cultivated azaleas. U.S. Dept. Agr. Circ. 556. 26 p.

Wellman, F. L. 1949. Successful spray control of Alternaria blight of petunias grown for seed in Costa Rica. Plant Dis. Reptr. 33:69–72.

Westcott, C. 1934. Brand canker of rose, caused by *Coniothyrium wernsdorffiae* Laubert. Cornell Univ. Agr. Exp. Sta. Mem. 153. 39 p.

Westcott, C. 1946. Another conquest for chemistry: azalea petal blight. Home Garden 7(2):61–63.

Whetzel, H. H. 1928. The crown elongation disease of the peony. Phytopathology 18:243–244.

Whetzel, H. H. 1944. The scab disease of violets. Plant Dis. Reptr. 28:769–770.

Whetzel, H. H., and J. M. Arthur. 1925. The gray bulb-rot of tulips caused by *Rhizoctonia tuliparum* (Klebh.) n. comb. Cornell Univ. Agr. Exp. Sta. Mem. 89. 18 p.

White, H. E. 1954. Response of roses and gardenias to treatment with chelated iron and a chelating agent. Proc. Amer. Soc. Hort. Sci. 64:423–430.

White, R. P. 1930. Pathogenicity of *Pestalotia* spp. on rhododendron. Phytopathology 20:85–91.

White, R. P. 1930. Two Phytophthora diseases of rhododendron. (Abstr.) Phytopathology 20:131.

White, R. P. 1931. Diseases of hollyhocks. N. J. Agr. Exp. Sta. Circ. 236. 2 p.

White, R. P. 1931. Diseases of ornamental plants. N. J. Agr. Exp. Sta. Circ. 226. 98 p.

White, R. P. 1931. Diseases of perennial and annual phlox. N. J. Agr. Exp. Sta. Circ. 240. 3 p.

White, R. P. 1935. Dahlia diseases. N. J. Agr. Exp. Sta. Circ. 361. 4 p.

White, R. P. 1937. Rhododendron wilt and root rot. N. J. Agr. Exp. Sta. Bul. 615. 32 p.

White, R. P., and C. C. Hamilton. 1935. Diseases and insect pests of rhododendron and azalea. N. J. Agr. Exp. Sta. Circ. 350. 23 p.

Wickens, G. M. 1935. Wilt, stem rot, and dieback of the perpetual flowering carnation. Ann. Appl. Biol. 22:630–683.

Wilhelm, S. 1943. Observations on the bacterial crown, stem, and bud rot of delphinium. Phytopathology 33:806–811.

Wilhelm, S., and J. Ferguson. 1953. Soil fumigation against *Verticillium albo-atrum*. Phytopathology 43:593–596.

Wilhelm, S., W. Gunesch, and K. F. Baker. 1945. Myrothecium crown and stem canker of greenhouse snapdragons in Colorado. Plant Dis. Reptr. 29:700–702.

Wilhelm, S., and R. D. Raabe. 1956. Culture-indexing of budwood to provide *Verticillium*-free greenhouse roses. Plant Dis. Reptr. Suppl. 238:85–87.

Wilhelm, S., and R. H. Sciaroni. 1953. Control of *Verticillium* in outdoor mums. Chrysanthemum Soc. of Amer. Bul. 21(1):26–27.

Williamson, C. E. 1954. Is your soil steaming adequate? N. Y. State Flower Growers' Bul. 107:2–3.

Willis, W. W., C. T. Rogerson, and W. J. Carpenter. 1959. An evaluation of several fungicides for control of root rot of Croft lilies. Plant Dis. Reptr. 43:745–749.

Wilson, A. 1927. Preliminary report on the gardenia bud drop. Phytopathology 17:671–672.

Wilson, J. D. 1943. Influence of soil type and temperature on rate of escape of chloropicrin. Ohio Agr. Exp. Sta. Bimonth. Bul. 28(220):38–41.

Winstead, N. N., and F. A. Haasis. 1954. A flower blight of camellias in North Carolina incited by *Sclerotinia sclerotiorum*. Phytopathology 44:717–718.

Winstead, N. N., J. M. Jenkins, Jr., and F. A. Haasis. 1956. Reaction of Dutch iris varieties to *Puccinia iridis* in North Carolina. Plant Dis. Reptr. 40:1112–1114.

Wolf, F. A. 1910. A Fusarium disease of the pansy. Mycologia 2:19–22.

Wolf, F. A. 1931. Diaporthe blight of larkspur. Phytopathology 21:77–81.

Woltz, S. S., and A. W. Engelhard. 1973. Fusarium wilt of chrysanthemum: Effect of nitrogen source and lime on disease development. Phytopathology 63:155–157.

Yarwood, C. E. 1947. Snapdragon downy mildew. Hilgardia 17:241–250.

Young, P. A. 1934. Stem canker of hollyhock caused by *Sclerotinia sclerotiorum*. Phytopathology 24:538–543.

Young, R. A. 1954. Fungicide-insecticide mixtures in pre-planting corm treatments for control of bacterial scab of gladiolus. Plant Dis. Reptr. 38:55–56.

Zentmyer, G. A. 1955. Coined names for fungicides. Phytopathology 45:109.

Zimmerman, P. W., and W. Crocker. 1934. Plant injury caused by vapors of mercury and compounds of mercury. Contrib. Boyce Thompson Inst. 6:167–187.

GLOSSARY

Abscission — A natural process involving the formation of a separation layer causing leaves, fruits, and other parts to fall.

Acervulus (plural, acervuli) — A saucer-shaped spore-producing body of a fungus.

Adventitious roots — Roots that appear in an unusual place or position.

Annual — A plant that completes its life cycle from seed in one year.

Axil — Angle between the upper side of a leaf or stem and the supporting stem or branch.

Bactericide — A substance that kills bacteria.

Bacterium — A microscopic, one-celled plant that lacks chlorophyll and reproduces by fission.

Bacticin — A bactericide used for eradication of crown gall tumors.

Blight — Any disease that causes plants to wither and decay.

Bract — A small leaf at the base of a flower or flower stalk.

Breaking — Discolored streaks or blotches in a normal, solid color of a flower; usually caused by a virus.

Bulblets — Small bulbs produced on the stem or at the base of an older bulb.

Calyx — The sepals, collectively, of a flower.

Canker — A localized lesion on a stem which usually results in the corrosion and sloughing away of tissue with the final production of an open wound.

Capsule — A dry fruit of the pod type developed from a compound pistil that consists of two or more united carpels.

Carpel — A simple pistil, or one member of a compound pistil.

Chlorophyll — The green coloring matter in plants.

Chlorosis — A yellowish, pale-green to white discoloration of normally green plant parts due to the destruction of the chlorophyll.

Chlorotic — Exhibiting chlorosis.

Coalesce — To grow together or unite.

Conidium (plural, conidia) — An asexual type of fungus spore.

Convolute — Rolled up longitudinally.

Corm — The enlarged fleshy base of a stem, bulblike but solid.

Cormel — A small or secondary, usually hard-shelled, corm.

Corolla — The petals, collectively, of a flower.

Cortex — The tissues between the epidermis and the vascular tissues of a stem or root.

Cortical tissue — The cortex.

Crustose — Forming a thin, brittle crust.

Desiccation — Drying up.

Dieback — Death of twigs, progressing from tips toward the base.

Discrete — Separate; distinct.

Epiphytotic — The rapid spreading of a plant disease.

Etiolated — Blanched or yellowed as a result of insufficient light.

Fasciated — Formed by abnormal growth of several buds that fuse laterally in their formative stage.

Fibrillose — Furnished or abounding with fine fibers.

Flaccid — Flabby; lacking firmness.

Fleck — Translucent lesion visible through leaf.

Follicle — A dry, dehiscent, many-seeded pod originating from a single, simple pistil and opening along a single suture.

Frond — The divided leaf of a fern.

Fungicide — A chemical that kills fungi.

Girdled — Completely encircled.

Glaucous — Covered with whitish powder.

Host — The plant on which or in which the parasite is living and obtaining its food.

Hyphae — The threadlike elements of fungus mycelium.

Infested — Containing undesirable agents such as parasites.

Inflorescence — A more or less compact flower cluster.

Inoculum — A quantity of bacteria or fungus spores capable of causing disease on coming in contact with a susceptible host.

Insecticide — A chemical that will kill insects.

Internode — The region between two nodes of a stem.

Lamina — The flat, wide part of a leaf.

Lesion — A diseased or injured region.

Lodging — Falling over or lying down, as in plants beaten down by wind or rain.

Mosaic — A mottled pattern consisting of light- and dark-green areas in a leaf; a type of virus disease.

Mycelial — Referring to mycelium.

Mycelium — The mass of interwoven threads that constitute the vegetative portion of a fungus.

Mycoplasmas — Highly pleomorphic, plastic organisms without cell walls. Some cause diseases formerly thought to be caused by viruses. (Yellows diseases are caused by mycoplasmalike organisms.)

Necrosis — A localized or general death of plant tissues.

Necrotic — Pertaining to localized or general death of plant tissues.

Node — The place upon a stem that normally bears a leaf or whorl of leaves.

Parasite — An organism living in or on another living organism, called the host, from which it obtains its food.

Pathogen — An organism or virus capable of causing a disease.

Pedicel — The support of a single flower.

Peduncle — A primary flower stalk, supporting either a solitary flower or a cluster.

Perennial — A plant that lives for many years.

Perianth — The external envelope of a flower, consisting of sepals and petals.

Periderm — A layer of protective tissue in a stem or root.

pH — Measure of acidity and alkalinity.

Phloem — The outer portion of a vascular bundle, primarily devoted to food-carrying.

Phytotoxic — Poisonous to plants.

Pinna (plural, pinnae) — One of the primary divisions of a pinnate leaf or frond.

Pinnate leaf — A leaf with leaflets arranged on each side of a common petiole.

Pistil — The seed-bearing organ of the flower.

Primordial roots — The nodules from which the roots develop on the bottom of a corm.

Proliferation — The continued production of new growths by an organ after it has reached the form or stage that would normally end its development.

Pustule — Any small pimplelike elevation, or spot, resembling a blister.

Pycnidium (plural, pycnidia) — A closed, asexual type of spore-producing body of a fungus.

Receptacle — The more or less expanded portion of the stem upon which the flower parts are borne.

Rhizome — A horizontal underground stem.

Roguing — Removal of undesirable plants from a planting.

Saprophyte — An organism that feeds on dead plant or animal matter.

Scape — A peduncle, rising from the ground, naked or without leaves.

Sclerotium (plural, sclerotia) — A compact mass of hardened mycelium stored with reserve food material.

Sepal — A division of the outer floral envelope or calyx.

Spore — A reproductive body of lower plants that corresponds in function to a seed but possesses no embryo.

Sporodochium (plural, sporodochia) — A cushion-shaped, spore-producing body of a fungus.

Stroma (plural, stromata) — A cushion-like body on or in which fungus reproductive bodies are produced.

Symptomless virus — A virus that is present in a plant but produces no visible effects on the plant.

Translucent — So clear as to permit the passage of light rays.

Transpiration — The giving off of water vapor from the internal tissues of living plants.

Tuber — A thickened, short, underground stem having numerous buds or eyes.

Unilateral — Of, on, or affecting one side only.

Vascular bundle — A distinct group of

conducting cells in a root, stem, or leaf, consisting of xylem for water conduction and phloem for food conduction.

Vascular element — A cell of the vascular tissue.

Variegation — The presence of two or more colors in leaves, flowers, or stems.

Veinbanding — A broad band of chlorotic tissue along the veins or bands of normally green tissue, set off by chlorosis or necrosis in the interveinal tissue.

Veinclearing — A clearing or chlorosis of the tissue in or immediately adjacent to the veins.

Virescent — Greenish.

Viruliferous — Containing a virus.

Virus — A submicroscopic entity capable of causing disease and able to reproduce only in the plants or animals it infects.

Xylem — The inner or water-conducting portion of a vascular bundle.

Zonate — Marked with zones.

INDEX

Acervulus: structure of, 4

Actidione, 8

African violet: diseases of, 17–18; Botrytis blight, 17; *Botrytis cinerea* on, 17; petiole rot, 17; powdery mildew, 17; *Pythium ultimum* on, 17; ring spot, 17; root and crown rot, 17; root-knot nematodes on, 18

Agrimycin, 8

Agrobacterium tumefaciens: rose, 149

Alternaria: spores of, 3

Alternaria blight: carnation, 36, 37; petunia, 134; zinnia, 179

Alternaria dianthi: carnation, 36

Alternaria leaf spot: geranium, 77; stock, 165

Alternaria raphani: stock, 165

Alternaria solani f. *symphoricarpi*: snowberry, 164

Alternaria tenuis: geranium, 77; petunia, 134

Alternaria zinniae: zinnia, 179

Alternariosis: snowberry, 164

Althaea rosea, 104

Amaryllis: diseases of, 18–19; *Botrytis cinerea* on, 19; bulb rots, 19; red blotch, 18; *Rhizopus stolonifera* on, 19; *Sclerotium rolfsii* on, 19; *Stagonospora curtisii* on, 19

Amerosporium trichellum: English ivy, 73

Anther smut: carnation, 38

Anthracnose: azalea, 23; Boston fern, 74; hollyhock, 104; lily, 114; peony, 128, 129; poppy, 143; rose, 143; snapdragon, 158; snowberry, 164; sweet pea, 169; tulip, 174, 175; violet, 125

Antirrhinum majus, 158

Aphanomyces cladogamus: pansy, 125

Aphanomyces root rot: pansy, 125

Aphanomyces wilt: pansy, 125

Aphid injury: carnation, 45; lily, 118

Aquilegia spp., 58

Arasan, 8

Ascochyta asteris: aster, 21

Ascochyta chrysanthemi: chrysanthemum, 46

Ascochyta clematidina: clematis, 57

Ascochyta disease: chrysanthemum, 46

Asplenium nidus, 74

Aster: diseases of: 20–23; foot rot, 20; Fusarium wilt, 20, 21; leaf blight, 21; leaf spots, 21; root rot, 21; rust, 21; stem rot, 21; yellows, 22

Aster yellows: aster, 22; canna, 36; chrysanthemum, 54; delphinium, 66; gladiolus, 101; phlox, 136

Azalea: diseases of, 23–28; anthracnose, 23; bud blast, 23; chlorosis, 23; crown rot, 23; Cylindrocarpon wilt and blight, 24; Cylindrocladium blight and wilt, 24; dieback, 24, 27; flower spot, 24; galls, 25, 26; leaf spots, 25; petal blight, 24; Rhizoctonia leaf blight, 26; root rot, 27; stem canker, 27; wilt, 27; witches'-broom, 28

Bacillus subtilis: in control of carnation stem rot, 42

Bacteria, 2; definition of, 2; reproduction of, 2

Bacterial blight: chrysanthemum, 47; geranium, 78; lilac, 112; poppy, 143; stock, 165

Bacterial canker: English ivy, 73; poinsettia, 138

Bacterial leaf blight: bird's-nest fern, 74; gladiolus, 86

Bacterial leaf rot: dieffenbachia, 71

Bacterial leaf spot: begonia, 28; carnation, 38; chrysanthemum, 48; delphinium, 67; dieffenbachia, 71; English ivy, 73; gardenia, 75; geranium, 78, 79; iris, 107, 110; zinnia, 180

Bacterial slow wilt: carnation, 38

Bacterial soft rot: sansevieria, 157

Bacterial stem rot: dahlia, 63; dieffenbachia, 71; geranium, 78, 79

Bacterial wilt: carnation, 39; cosmos, 59; dahlia, 63; nasturtium, 124

Bactericide, 8

Bacticin, 8

Balsam: diseases of, 28; leaf spots, 28

Basal rot: lily, 116; narcissus, 120, 121; tulip, 174

Beet curly-top virus: geranium, 83

Begonia: diseases of, 28–29; bacterial leaf spot, 28; Botrytis blight, 29; powdery mildew, 29; Pythium crown and stem rot, 29; stem rot, 29

Benlate, 8

Benomyl, 8

Bird's-nest fern: bacterial leaf blight on, 74

Black mold: rose grafts, 144

Black rot: geranium, 78

Black root rot: pansy, 126

Black scale: lily, 114

Black slime disease: iris, 107

Black speck: rose, 145

Black spot: rose, 145

Black tip: iris, 108

Blackleg: geraniums, 80

Blanche mosaic: chrysanthemum, 54

Blast: rose, 146

Blight: azalea, 24, 26

Blindness: lily, 115

Blossom blight: tulip, 175

Blue mold: iris, 108

Blue-mold bulb rot: lily, 115

Bordeaux mixture: composition of, 6, 7; home-made, 6; preparation of, 6, 7; ready-prepared, 7

Boron-deficiency disease: gloxinia, 102, 103; roses, 146

Boston ivy: diseases of, 30; leaf spots, 30

Botran, 8

Botryosphaeria ribis: rhododendron, 27

Botryotinia convoluta: iris, 109

Botrytis: structure of conidiophore, 4; on narcissus, 123

Botrytis blight: African violet, 17; begonia, 29; chrysanthemum, 48; cyclamen, 59; dahlia, 63; geranium, 80, 81; hyacinth, 105; hydrangea, 105; lily, 115; peony, 130; rose, 146, 147; snapdragon, 158; stock, 166; tulip, 175, 176

Botrytis cinerea: African violet, 17; amaryllis, 19; begonia, 29; carnation, 40; chrysanthemum, 48; cyclamen, 59; dahlia, 63; geranium, 80; peony, 130; rose, 146, 147; snapdragon, 158; stock, 166

Botrytis corm rot: gladiolus, 86, 87

Botrytis elliptica: lily, 115; stephanotis, 165

Botrytis gladiolorum: gladiolus, 86

Botrytis hyacinthi: hyacinth, 105

Botrytis leaf spot: gladiolus, 86, 87

Botrytis stem rot: begonia, 29; gladiolus, 86

Botrytis tulipae: tulip, 175

Brand canker: rose, 147, 148

Bravo, 8

Breaking: of tulips, 177

Briosia azaleae: azalea, 23

Brown canker: rose, 148

Brown leaf spot: dieffenbachia, 72

Bud blast: azalea, 23; peony, 130

Bud drop: gardenia, 75; sweet pea, 170

Bud rot: canna, 35; carnation, 40; chrysanthemum, 49; delphinium, 66

Buds: axillary and terminal, 14

Bulb: structure of, 15

Bunchy top: lily, 115

Burgundy mixture: composition of, 7; preparation of, 7

Buttercup: root rot of, 30

Calla lily: diseases of, 30–33; leaf blight, 30; leaf spot, 31; Pythium rot, 31; rhizome rot, 31; root rot, 32; soft rot, 32; spotted wilt, 33

Callistephus chinensis, 20

Camellia: diseases of, 33–35; canker, 33, 34; dieback, 33; flower blight, 34, 35

Camellia japonica, 33

Camellia sasanqua, 33

Canker: camellia, 33–35; English ivy, 73; gardenia, 76; rhododendron, 27

Canna: diseases of, 35–36; aster yellows, 36; bud rot, 35; mosaic, 36

Capsule: structure of, 15

Captan, 8

Carnation: diseases of, 36–46; Alternaria blight, 36, 37; anther smut, 38; bacterial leaf spot, 38; bacterial slow wilt, 38; bacterial wilt, 39; Botrytis blight, 40; central bud rot, 40; fairy ring spot, 41; fasciation, 41; Fusarium stem rot, 41; Fusarium wilt, 42; greasy blotch, 43; mosaic, 45, 46; mottle, 45; petal blight, 43; pimple, 44; Rhizoctonia stem rot, 44; ringspot, 45; rust, 44; Septoria leaf spot, 45; streak, 45, 46; stunt, 38; virus diseases, 45

Causes of plant diseases: bacteria, 2; fungi, 1, 3–4; mycoplasmas, 2; nematodes, 2; nonparasitic, 1; parasitic, 1; viruses, 2

Central bud rot: of carnation, 40

Centrospora acerina: bachelor button, 127; canterbury bells, 127; Chinese forget-me-not, 127; columbine, 127; cornflower, 127; *Delphinium cultorum*, 127; *Lobelia hybrida*, 127; pansy, 127; *Penstemon barbatus*, 127; *Petunia hybrida*, 127; *Ranunculus asiaticus*, 127; *Scabiosa atropurpurea*, 127

Cephalosporium dieffenbachiae: dieffenbachia, 72

Cephalosporium leaf spot: dieffenbachia, 72

Cercospora althaeina: hollyhock, 104

Cercospora ampelopsidis: Boston ivy, 30

Cercospora antirrhini: snapdragon, 159

Cercospora blight: snapdragon, 159

Cercospora brunkii: geranium, 81

Cercospora fukushiana: balsam, 28

Cercospora leaf spot: geranium, 81; phlox, 136

Cercospora lobeliae: lobelia, 120

Cercospora omphakodes: phlox, 136

Cercospora rhododendri: azalea, 25

Cercospora sp.: cosmos, 59; dahlia, 64; spores of, 3

Chalaropsis thielavioides: poinsettia, 140; rose, 144

China-aster: *See* Aster

Chloranil, 8

Chloropicrin: methods of use, 12; precautions in use, 13

Chlorosis: azalea, 23; gardenia, 76; hydrangea, 106

Chlorothalonil, 8

Chlorotic mottle virus: chrysanthemum, 55

Chrysanthemum: diseases of, 46–55; Ascochyta disease, 46; aster yellows, 54; bacterial blight, 47; bacterial leaf spot, 48; Blanche mosaic, 54; Botrytis blight, 48; chlorotic mottle, 55; flower distortion virus, 55; flower spots, 49; Fusarium flower and bud rot, 49; Fusarium wilt and stem rot, 49; Good News mosaic, 54; Ivory Sea Gull mosaic, 55; leaf spots, 50; powdery mildew, 51; Pythium root rot and stem rot, 50; ray blight, 46; rust, 51; stem rot, 49, 52; stunt, 52; tomato aspermy virus, 55; tomato spotted-wilt virus, 54; Verticillium wilt, 53; virus diseases, 54; yellows, 54

Chrysanthemum morifolium, 46

Cineraria: diseases of, 55–57; mosaic, 55, 56; streak, 55, 56

Cladosporium album: sweet pea, 172

Cladosporium herbarum: lilac, 113

Cladosporium paeoniae: peony, 130

Clematis: leaf spot and stem rot, 57

Cold injury: lilac, 113

Coleosporium solidaginis: aster, 22

Coleus: mosaic, 57, 58

Coleus blumei, 58

Collectotrichum antirrhini: snapdragon, 158

Collectotrichum lilii: lily, 114

Collectotrichum malvarum: hollyhock, 104

Colletotrichum violae-tricoloris: pansy, violet, 125

Color breaking: carnation, 45; pansy, 126; phlox, 136

Columbine: crown rot or wilt, 59
Conidiophores: types of, 4; structure of, 4
Coniothecium richardiae: calla lily, 31
Coniothyrium wernsdorffiae: rose, 147
Control of plant diseases: by cultural practices, 5; by development of resistance, 5; by eradication, 5; by exclusion, 5; by protection, 5; by sanitation, 5; principles of, 5
Corm: structure of, 15
Corm rot: freesia, 74; gladiolus, 86, 89, 91, 94, 96, 98
Corynebacterium fascians: geranium, 82; petunia, 135; sweet pea, 170
Corynebacterium poinsettiae: poinsettia, 138
Cosmos: diseases of, 59; bacterial wilt, 59; canker, 59; leaf spots, 59; powdery mildew, 59; stem blight, 59
Cosmos bipinnatus, 59
Cottony rot: stock, 168
Crinkle: geranium, 81, 82
Crown and stem rot: pansy, 126
Crown and stem rot, Pythium: begonia, 29
Crown canker: rose, 149; snapdragon, 160
Crown elongation: peony, 130
Crown gall: rose, 149
Crown rot: azalea, 23; columbine, 59; delphinium, 69, 70; iris, 108; kalanchoe, 112; petunia, 134; phlox, 137
Cryptosporella umbrina: rose, 148
Cultural practices: in disease control, 5
Cultured cuttings: source of disease-free plants, 43, 53
Curly top: pansy, 126
Curvularia: spores of, 3
Curvularia corm rot: gladiolus, 89, 90
Curvularia leaf spot: gladiolus, 89
Curvularia trifolii f. *gladioli*: gladiolus, 89
Cutting rot: peperomia, 133
Cyclamen: diseases of, 59–63; Botrytis blight, 59; Fusarium wilt, 60; gray-mold disease, 59; leaf spots, 60; petal spot, 61; soft rot, 61, 62; stunt, 62, 63; wilt, 60
Cyclamen persicum, 59
Cylindrocarpon radicicola: lily, 118
Cylindrocarpon wilt and blight: azalea, 24
Cylindrocladium blight and wilt: azalea, 24
Cylindrocladium scoparium: azalea, 24; rose, 149
Cylindrosporium chrysanthemi: chrysanthemum, 50
Cyme: structure of, 15

Daconil 2787, 8
Daffodils: *See* Narcissus, 65
Dahlia: diseases of, 63–66; bacterial stem rot, 63; bacterial wilt, 63; Botrytis blight, 63; dwarf, 64; Fusarium wilt, 65; hopperburn, 63; leaf spots, 64; mildew, 64; mosaic, 64; powdery mildew, 64; ring spot, 65; spotted wilt, 65; stem rot, 65; storage rots, 65; stunt, 64; Verticillium wilt, 65
Decline: narcissus, 122

Delphinium: diseases of, 66–70; aster yellows, 66; bacterial bud rot, 66; bacterial leaf spot, 67; crown rot, 66; Diaporthe blight, 68; Diplodina disease, 68; Fusarium canker and wilt, 68; Phoma crown rot, 69; powdery mildew, 69; Sclerotinia wilt and stem rot, 70; Sclerotium root and crown rot, 70; stem rot, 66, 70
Dexon, 8
Dianthus barbatus, 173
Dianthus caryophyllus, 36
Diaporthe arctii: delphinium, 68
Diaporthe blight: delphinium, 68
Diaporthe stewartii: cosmos, 59
Dichlone, 8
Didymellina macrospora: iris, 110
Didymellina poecilospora: iris, 108
Dieback: azalea, 24, 27; camellia, 33; gardenia, 77; lily, 115
Dieffenbachia: diseases of, 71–72; bacterial leaf spot, 71; bacterial stem and leaf rot, 71; brown leaf spot, 72; Cephalosporium leaf spot, 72; stem rot, 72
Dieffenbachia picta, 71
Diplocarpon rosae: rose, 145
Diplodina delphinii: delphinium, 68
Diplodina disease: delphinium, 68
Diseases, causes of: bacteria, 2; fungi, 1, 3–4; mycoplasmas, 2; nematodes, 2; nonparasitic, 1; parasitic, 1; viruses, 2
Dithane Z-78, 8
Downy mildew: rose, 150; snapdragon, 160
Dry fruits: types of, 15
Dusting: *vs.* spraying, 6
Dusts: copper lime, 7; sulfur, 7
Dwarf: dahlia, 64
Dyrene, 8

Empoasca fabae: dahlia, 63
English ivy: diseases of, 73; bacterial leaf spot and canker, 73; fungus leaf spots, 73
Eradication: in disease control, 5
Erwinia aroideae: calla lily, 32
Erwinia atroseptica: delphinium, 66
Erwinia carotovora: cyclamen 62; hyacinth, 105; iris, 111; poinsettia, 142
Erwinia carotovora var. *chrysanthemi*: poinsettia, 138
Erwinia chrysanthemi: carnation, 38; chrysanthemum, 47; delphinium, 66
Erwinia cytolytica: dahlia, 63
Erwinia dieffenbachia: dieffenbachia, 71
Erwinia lathyri: sweet pea, 170
Erysiphe cichoracearum: chrysanthemum, 51; cosmos, 59; dahlia, 64; phlox, 137; zinnia, 180
Erysiphe polygoni: delphinium, 69; hydrangea, 106
Euphorbia pulcherrima, 137
Exobasidium burti: azalea, 26
Exobasidium vaccinii: azalea, 25, 26
Exobasidium vaccinii-uliginosae: azalea, 28

Exclusion: in disease control, 5; use of mother blocks, 5, 43

Fairy ring spot: carnation, 41
Fasciation: carnation, 41; geranium, 82; petunia, 135; sweet pea, 170, 171
Ferbam, 8
Fermate, 8
Ferns: anthracnose on, 74; bacterial leaf blight on, 74
Fire: narcissus, 122; tulip, 175
Fleck: lily, 116
Florets: disc and ray, 14
Flower blight: camellia, 35
Flower, complete: arrangement of component parts, 14
Flower composite: structure of, 14
Flower distortion virus: chrysanthemum, 55
Flower rot: chrysanthemum, 49
Flower spot: azalea, 24
Follicle: structure of, 15
Folpet, 8
Foot rot: aster, 20; gerbera, 85; stock, 166, 167, 168
Fore, 8
Formalin: for treating soil, 13
Freesia: wilt and corm rot of, 74
Freesia refracta, 74
Fruits, dry: types of, 15
Fumigants: chloropicrin, 12, 13; directions for use, 12; kinds, 12, 13; tear gas, 12, 13; temperatures necessary, 12; Vapam, 13
Fungi: definition of, 1; reproduction of, 1, 3–4; spores of, 1, 3–4; structure of, 1, 3–4
Fungicides: application of, 6; composition of, 6; copper-containing, 6; definition of, 6; directions for mixing spray materials, 9; names of, 8–9; organic, 7; purpose of, 6; systemic, 6; timing of applications, 6; undesirable, 6; uses of, 6; when to use, 6
Fusarium: spores of, 3
Fusarium basal rot: gladiolus, 91, 92; iris, 109; lily, 116
Fusarium canker and wilt: delphinium, 68
Fusarium flower and bud rot: carnation, 40; chrysanthemum, 49
Fusarium moniliforme: sansevieria, 157
Fusarium oxysporum: chrysanthemum, 49; freesia, 74; iris, 109; pansy, 126; tulip, 174
Fusarium oxysporum f. *barbati*: sweet william, 173
Fusarium oxysporum f. *callistephi*: aster, 20
Fusarium oxysporum f. *cyclaminis*: cyclamen, 60
Fusarium oxysporum f. *delphinii*: delphinium, 68
Fusarium oxysporum f. *dianthi*: carnation, 42
Fusarium oxysporum f. *gladioli*: gladiolus, 91
Fusarium oxysporum f. *lilii*: lily, 116
Fusarium oxysporum f. *mathioli*: stock, 167
Fusarium oxysporum f. *narcissi*: narcissus, 120
Fusarium roseum f. *cerealis*: carnation, 41
Fusarium rot: gladiolus, 91, 92; lily, 116
Fusarium solani f. *pisi*: sweet pea, 172

Fusarium sp.: dahlia, 65; lily, 118; petunia, 135
Fusarium stem rot: carnation, 41; chrysanthemum, 49
Fusarium tricinctum f. *poae*: carnation, 40; chrysanthemum, 49
Fusarium wilt: aster, 20, 21; carnation, 42; chrysanthemum, 49; cyclamen, 60; dahlia, 65; delphinium, 68; pansy, 126; petunia, 135; stock, 167; sweet william, 173, 174

Galls: azalea, 25, 26
Gardenia: diseases of, 75–77; bacterial leaf spot, 75; bud drop, 75; canker, 76; chlorosis, 76; dieback, 77; Rhizoctonia leaf spot, 77; root knot, 77
Gardenia jasminoides, 75
Geranium: diseases of, 77–85; Alternaria leaf spot, 77; bacterial blight, 78; bacterial leaf spot, 78, 79; backleg, 80; Botrytis blight, 80, 81; Cercospora leaf spot, 81; crinkle, 81, 82; fasciation, 82; leaf breaking, 82, 83; leaf cupping, 83; leaf curl, 81; oedema, 83, 84; rust, 84; spotted wilt, 85; stem rot, 79
Gerbera: foot rot of, 85
Gerbera jamesonii, 85
Gladiolus: diseases of, 86–102; aster yellows, 101; bacterial leaf blight, 86; Botrytis leaf spot, stem rot and corm rot, 86, 87; control of corm rots, 88, 89, 93, 94, 99; curing of corms, 88, 93, 99; Curvularia leaf spot and corm rot, 89; Fusarium rot, 91; ink spot, 93; mild mosaic, 100; notched leaf, 102; Penicillium core rot, 94; Penicillium rot, 94; protrusions, 94, 95; Rhizoctonia neck rot, 94, 95; ring spot, 102; scab, 96; Septoria leaf spot and corm rot, 96; Stemphylium leaf blight, 97; storage breakdown, 98; Stromatinia dry rot, 98, 99; stunt, 102; virus diseases, 100; white break mosaic, 100
Gladiolus hortulanus, 86
Gloeosporium sp.: peony, 128; poppy, 143
Gloeosporium thuemenii f. *tulipae*: tulip, 174
Glomerella cingulata: azalea, 23; camellia, 33; cyclamen, 60; English ivy, 73; sweet pea, 169
Glomerella nephrolepsis: Boston fern, 74
Glomerella rufomaculans: snowberry, 164
Gloxinia: diseases of, 102–104; boron deficiency disease, 102; leaf and stem rot, 103; Myrothecium rot, 103
Good News mosaic: chrysanthemum, 54
Graft blight: lilac, 113
Graft canker: rose, 156
Gray bulb rot: tulip, 178
Gray-mold disease: cyclamen, 59
Gray-mold rot: iris, 109
Greasy blotch: carnation, 43
Greens: delphinium, 66
Guignardia bidwellii: Boston ivy, 30; Virginia creeper, 30
Guignardia rhodorae: azalea, 25

Helichrysum bracteatum, 168
Heterosporium disease: nasturtium, 124
Heterosporium echinulatum: carnation, 41
Heterosporium syringae: lilac, 113
Heterosporium tropaeoli: nasturtium, 124
Hollyhock: diseases of, 104–105; anthracnose, 104; leaf spots, 104; rust, 104; stem canker, 104
Hopperburn: dahlia, 63
Hot water: treatment of gladiolus cormels, 93
Hyacinth: diseases of, 105; Botrytis blight, 105; mosaic, 105; root rot, 105; soft rot, 105; yellow rot, 105
Hyacinthus orientalis, 105
Hydrangea: diseases of, 105–107; Botrytis blight, 105; chlorosis, 106; powdery mildew, 106; ring spot, 106
Hydrangea macrophylla, 105

Impatiens balsamina, 28
Inflorescence: types of, 15
Ink spot: iris, 109
Ink spot disease: gladiolus, 93
Iris: diseases of, 107–112; bacterial leaf spot, 107, 110; black slime disease, 107; black tip, 108; blue mold, 108; crown rot, 108; Didymellina leaf spot, 110; Fusarium basal rot, 109; gray-mold rot, 109; ink spot, 109; mosaic, 110; Rhizoctonia neck and bulb rot, 111; rust, 111; scorch, 111; soft rot, 111, 112; topple, 112
Iris borer: relation to soft rot, 111
Ivory Sea Gull mosaic: chrysanthemum, 55
Ivy: Boston, 30; English, 73

Kalanchoe: diseases of, 112; crown rot, 112; powdery mildew, 112
Karathane, 8

Larkspur: *See* Delphinium
Lathyrus odoratus, 169
Leaf and stem rot: gloxinia, 103
Leaf blight: aster, 21; azalea, 26; calla lily, 30; lilac, 113; phlox, 136
Leaf blotch: peony, 130, 131
Leaf breaking: geranium, 82, 83
Leaf burn: lily, 119
Leaf cupping: geranium, 83
Leaf curl: geranium, 81
Leaf galls: azalea, 25, 26
Leaf nematodes: lily, 115
Leaf rot: dieffenbachia, 71; poinsettia, 138
Leaf scorch: narcissus, 122
Leaf spot: azalea, 25; bachelor button, 127; begonia, 28; Boston ivy, 30; calla lily, 31; canterbury bells, 127; Chinese forget-me-not, 127; chrysanthemum, 48; clematis, 57; columbine, 127; cornflower, 127; cosmos, 59; cyclamen, 60; dahlia, 64; *Delphinium cultorum,* 127; English ivy, 73; geranium, 77, 79, 81; hollyhock, 104; iris, 107, 110; lobelia, 120; marigold, 120; pansy, 127; petunia, 127; phlox, 136; *Ranunculus asiaticus,* rose, 145,

150; sansevieria, 157; *Scabiosa atropurpurea,* zinnia, 180
Le Moines disease: peony, 131
Leptosphaeria coniothyrium: rose, 156
Leptosphaeria sp.: dieffenbachia, 72
Lilac: diseases of, 112–114; bacterial blight, 112; cold injury, 113; graft blight, 113; leaf blight, 113; Phytophthora blight, 113; powdery mildew, 113; Verticillium wilt, 114; witches'-broom, 114
Lilium spp., 114
Lily: diseases of, 114–119; anthracnose, 114; basal rot, 116; black scale, 114; blue-mold bulb rot, 115; Botrytis blight, 115; bunchy top, 115; dieback, 115; fleck, 116; Fusarium rot, 116; leaf burn, 119; mosaic, 117; mottle, 117; Rhizopus bulb rot, 117; root and bulb rot, 117; rosette, 118; rust, 118; scale tip rot, 119; scorch, 119; stem rot, 119; tip burn, 118, 119; yellow flat, 118
Lime-sulfur: danger of injury from, 7; dormant spray, 7; summer spray, 7
Liquid measure equivalents: use in mixing fungicide sprays, 9
Lobelia: diseases of, 120; leaf spot, 120; stem rot, 120
Lobularia maritima, 169
Lophodermium rhododendri: azalea, 25
Lysol, 8

Macronoctua onusta: relation to soft rot of iris, 111
Mallow: hollyhock rust on, 104
Malva rotundifolia: hollyhock rust on, 104
Maneb, 8
Manzate, 8
Marigold: diseases of, 120; leaf spot, 120; stem rot, 120; wilt, 120
Matthiola incana, 165
Measles: peony, 130, 131
Mercury injury: rose, 150
Microsphaeria alni: lilac, 113; sweet pea, 171
Mild mosaic: gladiolus, 100
Mildex, 8
Mosaic: amaryllis, 19; canna, 36; carnation, 45, 46; cineraria, 55, 56; coleus, 57, 58; dahlia, 64; hyacinth, 105; iris, 110; lily, 117; narcissus, 123; peony, 132; petunia, 135; rose, 150, 151; stock, 167; sweet pea, 170
Mother blocks: use in disease control, 5, 43; source of disease-free cuttings, 43
Mottle: carnation, 45; lily, 117
Mycosphaerella ligulicola: chrysanthemum, 46
Mycosphaerella rosicola: rose, 150
Myrothecium roridum: gloxinia, 103; pansy, 126; snapdragon, 160
Myrothecium rot: gloxinia, 103
Mystrosporium adustum: iris, 109
Myzus convolvuli: lily, 118
Myzus persicae: on dahlia, 64; relation to dahlia mosaic, 64
Myzus polaris: carnation, 45

Nabam, 8

Narcissus: diseases of, 120–124; basal rot, 120, 121; decline, 122; fire, 122; leaf scorch, 122; mosaic, 123; Ramularia blight, 123; smoulder, 123; soft rot, 123; virus diseases, 122, 123, 124; wet scale rot, 124; white mold, 123; yellow stripe, 124

Nasturtium: bacterial wilt, 124; Heterosporium disease, 124

Nematodes: definition of, 2; on African violet, 18; on gardenia, 77; on lily, 115

Nephrolepis exaltata var. *bostoniensis*, 74

Notched leaf: gladiolus, 102

Oedema: geranium, 83; peperomia, 133

Oidium sp.: snapdragon, 161

Ovulinia azaleae: azalea, 24

Paeonia spp., 128

Pansy, violet: diseases of, 125–128; anthracnose, 125; Aphanomyces wilt and root rot, 125; black root rot, 126; color breaking, 126; crown rot, 126; curly top, 126; Fusarium wilt, 126; leaf spot, 127; scab, 127; stem rot, 126

Papaver orientale, 143

Papaver rhoeas, 143

Parthenocissus quinquefolia, 30

Parthenocissus tricuspidata, 30

Parzate, 8

Parzate Liquid, 8

PCNB, 9

Pelargonium hortorum, 77

Penicillium: structure of conidiophore, 4

Penicillium core rot: gladiolus, 94

Penicillium funiculosum: gladiolus, 94

Penicillium gladioli: gladiolus, 94

Penicillium rot: gladiolus, 94

Penicillium sp.: iris, 108; lily, 115

Pentachloronitrobenzene, 9

Peony: diseases of, 128–133; anthracnose, 128, 129; Botrytis blight, 130; bud blast, 130; crown elongation, 130; leaf blotch, 130, 131; Le Moines disease, 131; measles, 130, 131; mosaic, 132; Phytophthora blight, 132; ring spot, 132; stem rot, 132; stem spot, 130; Verticillium wilt, 133

Peperomia: diseases of, 133–134; cutting rot, 133; oedema, 133; Phytophthora rot, 133, 134; ring spot, 133, 134

Peperomia obtusifolia, 133

Peronospora antirrhini: snapdragon, 160

Peronospora sparsa: rose, 150

Pestalotia macrotricha, P. rhododendri: azalea, 25

Petal blight: azalea, 24

Petal spot: cyclamen, 61

Petiole rot: African violet, 17

Petunia: diseases of, 134–135; Alternaria blight, 134; crown rot, 134; fasciation, 135; Fusarium wilt, 135; mosaic, 135

Petunia hybrida, 134

Phaltan, 9

Phlox: diseases of, 136–137; aster yellows, 136; Cercospora leaf spot, 136; leaf blight, 136; leaf spot, 136; powdery mildew, 137; root and crown rot, 137; Stemphylium leaf spot, 137

Phoma crown rot: delphinium, 69

Phoma exigua var. *exigua*: vinca, 178

Phoma sp.: delphinium, 69

Phomopsis gardeniae: gardenia, 76

Phomopsis sp.: azalea, 26

Phragmidium: spores of, 3

Phragmidium sp.: rose, 154

Phygon, 9

Phyllosticta althaeina: hollyhock, 104

Phyllosticta antirrhini: snapdragon, 160

Phyllosticta blight: snapdragon, 160

Phyllosticta bridgesii: lobelia, 120

Phyllosticta concentrica, P. hederae: English ivy, 73

Phyllosticta dahliaecola: dahlia, 64

Phyllosticta sp.: balsam, 28; cyclamen, 60

Phytophthora blight: lilac, 113; peony, 132

Phytophthora cactorum: azalea, 24; kalanchoe, 112; lilac, 113; lily, 119; peony, 132; snapdragon, 161; tulip, 175

Phytophthora cinnamomi: azalea, 27

Phytophthora citricola: azalea, 27

Phytophthora cryptogea: aster, 20; azalea, 23; gerbera, 85; gloxinia, 103; marigold, 120; stock, 167

Phytophthora cryptogea var. *richardiae*: calla lily, 32

Phytophthora drechsleri: gerbera, 85

Phytophthora erythroseptica: calla lily, 30

Phytophthora foot rot: stock, 167

Phytophthora nicotianae: peperomia, 133

Phytophthora palmivora: dieffenbachia, 72; peperomia, 133

Phytophthora rot: peperomia, 133, 134

Phytophthora sp.: petunia, 134

Phytophthora spp.: lily, 118; peperomia, 133

Phytophthora stem rot and wilt: snapdragon, 161

Pilobolus sp.: rose, 145

Pimple: carnation, 44

Plant: parts of, diagram, 14

Plant diseases: control of, 5

Plantvax: for control of carnation rust, 45

Poinsettia: diseases of, 137–142; bacterial canker, 138; bacterial stem rot, 138; leaf rot, 138; root rot, 139; scab, 142; soft rot, 142; stem rot, 139; stunt, 142; wilt, 142

Poppy: diseases of, 143; anthracnose, 143; bacterial blight, 143

Powdery mildew: conidiophores and conidia of, 3; on African violet, 17; begonia, 29; chrysanthemum, 51; cosmos, 59; dahlia, 64; delphinium, 69; hydrangea, 106; kalanchoe, 112; lilac, 113; phlox, 137; rose, 152; snapdragon, 161; sweet pea, 171; zinnia, 180

Protection: for disease control, 5

Protrusions: gladiolus flowers, 94, 95

Pseudomonas antirrhini: snapdragon, 163

Pseudomonas asplenii: bird's-nest fern, 74
Pseudomonas caryophylli: carnation, 39
Pseudomonas cichorii: chrysanthemum, 48
Pseudomonas delphinii: delphinium, 67
Pseudomonas gardeniae: gardenia, 75
Pseudomonas marginata: gladiolus, 96
Pseudomonas solanacearum: cosmos, 59; dahlia, 63; nasturtium, 124
Pseudomonas sp.: iris, 111; lily, 119
Pseudomonas syringae: lilac, 112; rose, 146
Pseudomonas woodsii: carnation, 38
Puccinia: spores of, 3
Puccinia antirrhini: snapdragon, 162
Puccinia chrysanthemi: chrysanthemum, 51
Puccinia iridis: iris, 111
Puccinia malvacearum: hollyhock, 104
Puccinia pelargonii-zonalis: geranium, 84
Pycnidium: structure of, 4
Pythium: geranium, 80
Pythium aphanidermatum: chrysanthemum, 50
Pythium carolinianum: chrysanthemum, 50
Pythium debaryanum: buttercup, 30
Pythium polytylum: chrysanthemum, 50
Pythium root rot: chrysanthemum, 50
Pythium rot: calla lily, 31
Pythium spinosum: chrysanthemum, 50
Pythium spp.: lily, 118; peperomia, 133; poinsettia, 139
Pythium stem rot: chrysanthemum, 50
Pythium ultimum: African violet, 17; calla lily, 31

Ramularia blight: narcissus, 123
Ramularia cyclaminicola: cyclamen, 60
Ramularia deusta: sweet pea, 172
Ramularia hedericola: English ivy, 73
Ramularia leaf spot: sweet pea, 171
Ramularia vallisumbrosae: narcissus, 123
Ranunculus asiaticus, 30
Ray blight: chrysanthemum, 46
Resistance, development of: for disease control, 5
Rhizoctonia leaf spot: gardenia, 77
Rhizoctonia neck and bulb rot: iris, 111
Rhizoctonia neck rot: gladiolus, 94, 95
Rhizoctonia solani: culture of, 1; on aster, 21; azalea, 26; carnation, 44; chrysanthemum, 52; gladiolus, 94; iris, 111; lily, 118; lobelia, 120; peperomia, 133; poinsettia, 138, 139; stock, 166; sweet alyssum, 169; sweet pea, 172
Rhizoctonia sp.: gardenia, 77
Rhizoctonia stem rot: carnation, 44
Rhizoctonia tuliparum: tulip, 178
Rhizoglyphus echinopus: in gladiolus scab, 96
Rhizome: structure of, 15
Rhizome rot: calla lily, 31
Rhizopus bulb rot: lily, 117
Rhizopus sp.: lily, 117
Rhizopus stolonifer: amaryllis, 19; narcissus, 123
Rhododendron: diseases of, 23–28; *See also* Azalaea

Rhododendron ponticum: wilt and root rot, 27
Ring spot: African violet, 17; carnation, 45; dahlia, 65; gladiolus, 102; hydrangea, 106; peony, 132; peperomia, 133, 134
Root and bulb rot: lily, 117
Root and crown rot: African violet, 17; delphinium, 66, 69, 70; phlox, 137
Root knot: African violet, 18; gardenia, 77
Root rot: aster, 21; azalea, 27; buttercup, 30; calla lily, 32; chrysanthemum, 50; hyacinth, 105; lily, 117; phlox, 137; poinsettia, 139; sweet pea, 172
Rosa manetti, 144
Rosa multiflora, 144
Rosa odorata, 144
Rose: diseases of, 143–157; anthracnose, 143; black mold, 144; black speck, 145; black spot, 145; blast, 146; boron deficiency, 146; Botrytis blight, 146, 147; brand canker, 147, 148; brown canker, 148; crown canker, 149; crown gall, 149; downy mildew, 150; graft canker, 156; leaf spot, 150; mercury injury, 150; mosaics, 150, 151; powdery mildew, 152; rust, 154, 155; spring dwarf, 155; stem canker, 156; streak, 157; Verticillium wilt, 157; yellow mosaic, 150–151
Rosette: lily, 118
Rust: aster, 21; carnation, 44; chrysanthemum, 51; geranium, 84; hollyhock, 104; iris, 111; lily, 118; rose, 154, 155; snapdragon, 162

Saintpaulia: *See* African violet, 17
Sanitation: in disease control, 5
Sansevieria: diseases of, 157–158; bacterial soft rot, 157; leaf spot, 157, 158
Sansevieria thyrsiflora, S. zeylanica, 157
Scab: gladiolus, 96; poinsettia, 142; violet, 127
Scale tip rot: lily, 119
Sclerotinia bulbarum: iris, 107
Sclerotinia camelliae: camellia, 35
Sclerotinia narcissicola: narcissus, 123
Sclerotinia polyblastis: narcissus, 122
Sclerotinia sclerotiorum: camellia, 35; columbine, 58; dahlia, 65; delphinium, 70; hollyhock, 104; peony, 132; snapdragon, 162; stephanotis, 165; stock, 168
Sclerotinia wilt: snapdragon, 162
Sclerotinia wilt and stem rot: delphinium, 70
Sclerotium delphinii: delphinium, 70
Sclerotium rolfsii: amaryllis, 19; delphinium, 70; iris, 108; narcissus, 124
Sclerotium root and crown rot: delphinium, 70
Scorch: iris, 111; lily, 119
Seedling blight: snapdragon, 163
Senecio cruentus, 55
Septoria: spores of, 3
Septoria azaleae: azalea, 26
Septoria callistephi: aster, 21
Septoria chrysanthemi: chrysanthemum, 50
Septoria corm rot: gladiolus, 96
Septoria dianthi: carnation, 45

Septoria divaricata: phlox, 136
Septoria leaf spot: carnation, 45; gladiolus, 96, 97
Septoria leucanthemi: chrysanthemum, 50
Septoria lobeliae: lobelia, 120
Septoria noli-tangeris: balsam, 28
Septoria sp.: cosmos, 59
Septoria tageticola: marigold, 120
Sinningia speciosa, 102
Siteroptes graminum: relation to carnation bud rot, 40
Slow wilt: carnation, 38
Smoulder: narcissus, 123
Snapdragon: diseases of, 158–164; anthracnose, 158, 159; Botrytis blight, 158, 159; Cercospora blight, 159; crown and stem canker, 160; downy mildew, 160; Phyllosticta blight, 160; Phytophthora stem rot and wilt, 161; powdery mildew, 161; rust, 162; Sclerotinia wilt, 162; seedling blight, 163; tip blight, 163; Verticillium wilt, 164
Snowberry: diseases of, 164; anthracnose, 164; alternariosis, 164
Soft rot: calla lily, 32; cyclamen, 61, 62; hyacinth, 105; iris, 111, 112; narcissus, 123; poinsettia, 142
Soil fumigants: kinds, 12–13; chloropicrin, 12; directions for use, 12–13; tear gas, 12; temperature necessary, 12; Vapam, 13
Soil sterilization: agents used for, 10–12; in small amounts, 10; purpose of, 10; requirements, 10; with fumigants, 12–13; with hot water, 12; with steam, 10
Soil sterilization, with steam: effects on plants, 12; in benches, 11; in ground beds, 11; inverted pan, 11; methods, 11; temperatures necessary for, 10; Thomas method, 11; time required, 10
Spergon, 9
Sphaceloma rosarum: rose, 143
Sphaceloma sp.: poinsettia, 142
Sphaceloma violae: violet, 127
Sphaerotheca humuli var. *fuliginea*: kalanchoe, 112
Sphaerotheca pannosa var. *rosae*: rose, 152
Spike: structure of, 15
Spores, fungus: kinds, 1, 3–4; methods of spread, 1–2; production of, 1, 3–4
Sporodochium: structure of, 4
Spotted wilt: calla lily, 33; dahlia, 65; geranium, 85; sweet pea, 173
Sprayers: kinds, 6; use of, 6
Spraying: *vs.* dusting, 6
Spray mixtures: how to prepare, 9
Spring dwarf: rose, 155
Stagonospora curtisii: narcissus, 122
Steam: for soil sterilization, 10
Stem blight: vinca, 178
Stem canker: hollyhock, 104; rose, 156; snapdragon, 160
Stemphylium botryosum: aster, 21; balsam, 28; phlox, 137

Stemphylium floridanum: carnation, 43
Stemphylium leaf blight: gladiolus, 97
Stemphylium leaf spot: phlox, 137
Stemphylium sp.: gladiolus, 97
Stem rot: aster, 21; begonia, 29; chrysanthemum, 49; clematus, 57; dahlia, 63, 65; delphinium, 66, 70; dieffenbachia, 71, 72; geranium, 78, 79, 80; lily, 119; lobelia, 120; marigold, 120; peony, 132; petunia, 135; poinsettia, 138, 139; sweet alyssum, 169
Stem rot, bacterial: poinsettia, 138
Stem rot, Fusarium: carnation, 41
Stem rot, Rhizoctonia: carnation, 44
Stems: location of various tissues in, 15
Stems, modified: types of, 15
Stem spot: peony, 130
Stephanotis: diseases of, 165; Botrytis blight, 165; Sclerotinia blight, 165
Stephanotis floribunda, 165
Stock: diseases of, 165–168; Alternatia leaf spot, 165; bacterial blight, 165; Botrytis blight, 166; cottony rot, 168; foot rot, 166, 167; Fusarium wilt, 167; mosaic, 167; Phytophthora foot rot, 167; white blight, 168; wire stem, 166, 167; Verticillium wilt, 168
Storage breakdown: gladiolus corms, 98
Storage rots: dahlia, 65
Strawflower: Verticillium wilt of, 168, 169
Streak: carnation, 45, 46; cineraria, 55, 56; rose, 157
Streptomycin sulfate, 9
Stromatinia dry rot: gladiolus, 98, 99
Stromatinia gladioli: gladiolus, 98
Stunt: carnation, 38; chrysanthemum, 52; cyclamen, 62, 63; dahlia, 64; delphinium, 66; gladiolus, 102; poinsettia, 142
Sulfur: dusting, 7; flowers of, 7; for mildew control, 7; green-colored, 7; vaporized and vaporizers, 7, 153; wettable, 7
Sweet alyssum: stem rot of, 169
Sweet pea: diseases of, 169–173; anthracnose, 169; bacterial streak, 170; bud drop, 170; fasciation, 170, 171; mosaic, 170; powdery mildew, 171; Ramularia leaf spot, 171; root rot, 172; spotted wilt, 173; white blight, 171
Sweet william: Fusarium wilt on, 173, 174
Symphoricarpus racemosus, 164
Syringa persica, *S. vulgaris*, 112

Tagetes spp., 120
Tear gas: *See* Chloropicrin
Termil, 9
Terraclor, 9
Tersan, 9
Thielaviopsis: spores of, 4
Thielaviopsis basicola: pansy, 126; phlox, 137; poinsettia, 139; sweet pea, 172
Thiram, 9
Tip blight: snapdragon, 163
Tip burn: lily, 118, 119
Tobacco rattle virus: gladiolus, 102
Tobacco ring-spot virus: gladiolus, 102

Tomato aspermy virus: chrysanthemum, 55
Tomato spotted-wilt virus: chrysanthemum, 54
Topple disease: iris, 112
Transvaal daisy: *See* Gerbera
Trialeurodes vaporariorum: geranium, 80
Tropaeolum majus, 124
Tubers: illustration of, 15
Tulip: diseases of, 174–178; anthracnose, 174, 175; basal rot, 174; blossom blight, 175; Botrytis blight, 175, 176; breaking, 177; fire, 175; gray bulb rot, 178
Tulipa gesneriana, 174

Uromyces caryophyllinus: carnation, 44
Uromyces holwayi: lily, 118
Ustilago violaceae: carnation, 38

Vapam: chemical name for, 9; use as a fumigant, 13
Vaporizers: sulfur, 7, 153
Vascular system: diagram of, 14
Verticillium: structure of conidiophore, 4
Verticillium albo-atrum: chrysanthemum, 53; dahlia, 65; lilac, 114; peony, 133; rose, 157; snapdragon, 164; stock, 168; strawflower, 168, 169
Verticillium wilt: chrysanthemum, 53; dahlia, 65; lilac, 114; peony, 133; rose, 157; snapdragon, 164; stock, 168; strawflower, 168, 169
Vinca: stem blight of, 178
Vinca minor, 178
Viola, 125
Violet: *See* Pansy
Virginia creeper: leaf spots on, 30
Virus diseases: carnation, 45; chrysanthemum, 52, 54–55; geranium, 81, 82–83, 85; gladiolus, 100–102; narcissus, 122, 123, 124
Viruses: definition of, 2; methods of spread, 2; reproduction of, 2
Vitavax: for control of carnation rust, 45
Vorlex, 9

Wet scale rot: narcissus, 124
Wettable powders: amounts to use in preparing fungicide sprays, 9
White blight: stock, 168; sweet pea, 171
White break mosaic: gladiolus, 100, 101
White fly: geranium, 80
White mold: narcissus, 123
Wilt: azalea, 24, 27; columbine, 59; cyclamen, 60; freesia, 74; marigold, 120; petunia, 135; poinsettia, 142
Wilt and stem rot, Sclerotinia: delphinium, 70
Wire stem: stock, 166, 167
Witches'-broom: azalea, 28; delphinium, 66; lilac, 114

Xanthomonas begoniae: begonia, 28
Xanthomonas cannae: canna, 35
Xanthomonas gummisudans: gladiolus, 86
Xanthomonas hederae: English ivy, 73
Xanthomonas hyacinthi: hyacinth, 105
Xanthomonas incanae: stock, 165
Xanthomonas maculifoliigardeniae: gardenia, 75
Xanthomonas nigromaculans f. sp. *zinniae:* zinnia, 180
Xanthomonas oryzae: carnation, 44
Xanthomonas papavericola: poppy, 143
Xanthomonas perlargonii: geranium, 78
Xanthomonas tardicrescens: iris, 107

Yellow flat: lily, 118
Yellow mosaic: rose, 150, 151
Yellow rot: hyacinth, 105
Yellow stripe: narcissus, 124

Zantedeschia spp., 30
Zineb, 9
Zinnia: diseases of, 179–180; Alternaria blight, 179; bacterial leaf spot, 180; powdery mildew, 180
Zinnia elegans, 179
Ziram, 9
Zygophiala jamaicensis: carnation, 43

METRIC CONVERSIONS

U.S. Liquid Measure Converted to the Metric System

		Fluid ounces (oz.)	Milli- liters (ml.)
1 gallon	= 4 quarts	128.0	3,785.0
1 quart	= 2 pints	32.0	946.0
1 pint	= 2 cups	16.0	473.0
1 cup	= 16 tablespoons	8.0	236.6
1 tablespoon	= 3 teaspoons	.5	14.8
1 teaspoon			5.0

1 liter = 2.11 pints = 1.06 quarts.

U.S. Weights Converted to the Metric System

Pounds (lb.)	Ounces (oz.)	Grams (gm.)
1.0	16.0	453.59
0.06	1.0	28.35

1 kilogram (1,000 grams) = 35.27 ounces = 2.2 pounds.

Temperature Conversion Formula

To convert from Fahrenheit to Centigrade: Subtract 32 from the Fahrenheit reading, multiply by 5, and divide the product by 9.

Example: 131° F. — 32 = 99 × 5 = 495

495 ÷ 9 = 55° C.

Dilution Rates

Dilution	Parts per million	Grams per liter
1:100	10,000	10.0
1:1,000	1,000	1.0
1:10,000	100	.1
1:100,000	10	.01
1:1,000,000	1	.001